LEGAL MOVES

LEGAL MOVES

CHOREOGRAPHIES OF RACE, LAW, AND EMPIRE

ANNA JAYNE KIMMEL

STANFORD UNIVERSITY PRESS
Stanford, California

Stanford University Press
Stanford, California

Library of Congress Cataloging-in-Publication Data
Names: Kimmel, Anna Jayne author
Title: Legal moves : choreographies of race, law, and empire / Anna Jayne Kimmel.
Description: Stanford, California : Stanford University Press, 2026. |
Includes bibliographical references and index.
Identifiers: LCCN 2026012753 (print) | LCCN 2026012754 (ebook) | ISBN 9781503646087 cloth | ISBN 9781503647329 ebook
Subjects: LCSH: Human body—Law and legislation—History | Colonies—Law and legislation—History | Race—Political aspects—History | International law and human rights—History | Social epistemology
Classification: LCC K564.H8 K56 2026 (print) | LCC K564.H8 (ebook)
LC record available at https://lccn.loc.gov/2026012753
LC ebook record available at https://lccn.loc.gov/2026012754

Cover design: Jason Anscomb
Cover art: Pélagie Gbaguidi, *Choreography of Sign* (2025). Courtesy of the artist, Fortes D'Aloia & Gabriel, and Goodman Gallery; photography by Eduardo Ortega
Typeset by Newgen in Garamond Premier Pro, 10.25/13.25 pt

The authorized representative in the EU for product safety and compliance is: Mare Nostrum Group B.V. | Doelen 72 | 4831 GR Breda | The Netherlands | Email address: gpsr@mare-nostrum.co.uk | KVK chamber of commerce number: 96249943

Printed and bound by CPI Group (UK) Ltd, Croydon, CR0 4YY

CONTENTS

Human beings are magical. Bios and Logos. Words made flesh, muscle and bone animated by hope and desire, belief materialized in deeds, deeds which crystallize our actualities. And the maps of spring always have to be redrawn again, in undared forms.

—SYLVIA WYNTER, "The Pope Must Have Been Drunk, The King of Castile a Madman: Culture as Actuality and the Caribbean Rethinking of Modernity" (1995)

"

"

—SYCORAX IN WILLIAM SHAKESPEARE, The Tempest *(1611)*

It has become difficult to write or imagine alternative knowledges, or to act on behalf of alternative projects or ways of being. Within this context, it is necessary to live within but to think beyond this received liberal humanist tradition, and all the while, to imagine a much more complicated set of stories about the emergence of the now, in which what is foreclosed as unknowable is forever saturating the "what-can-be-known."

—LISA LOWE, The Intimacies of Four Continents *(2015)*

FIGURES

ACKNOWLEDGMENTS

A listing of gratitude as a written form of acknowledgment goes against the very nature of this book, whose motivation begins from the belief that something profound exists beyond the capture of words alone. That my acknowledgments can and should exceed the length of this project speaks to the generous community of scholars, artists, and activists in which I have been grateful to partake. As a dancer, I have learned that productions are always an effort of collective labor whose contributions all too often go unseen and unnamed. Against expectations of a monograph, I consider those included here as co-conspirators. *Legal Moves* would not be without your invaluable contributions. To name but a few of those who supported this work:

To my editor, Marcella Maxfield, and the wider team at Stanford University Press: thank you for your trust in a first book and support throughout the process. It is an honor to be included amongst your titles. To Swethaa Ballakrishnen, Sora Han, Amber Musser, Carrie Noland, Tria Blu Wakpa, and Hentyle Yapp: I am humbled to have received your comments on a prior version of this manuscript. You challenged me in the rigor of this work and motivated this final version. Thank you for holding me accountable. Carli Coetzee, my appreciation for your attention at the end. I remain especially grateful to the artists who offered their permissions and personal contributions: Léonore Baulac, Ann Carlson, Pélagie Gbaguidi, Da Ping Luo, Dominik Mentzos, Shamel Pitts, Zoe Scofield, Anna Tenta, Kendall Thomas, and Sander van Bussel. Thank you for trusting me with your work and experience. Pélagie, it is a special privilege to feature your art on the cover.

This research has been generously supported by residency at University of California, Los Angeles, Centre for Performance Studies. It has received additional support from Stanford University's Graduate Research Opportunity fund as well as the Stanford University Center for Comparative Studies in Race and Ethnicity. There I am particularly grateful to librarians Sarah Sussman and Grace Lo, whose due diligence offered invaluable support to the rigor of this research. I have also benefitted from archival support from Forsythe Productions, especially the efforts of the studio director Julian Gabriel Richter, The British Museum, and Les Archives de la Préfecture de Police, Paris.

At George Washington University, this work has benefited from a Humanities Facilitating Fund and wider support extended by my colleagues at the Corcoran School of the Arts and Design. To Holly Dugan and Lauren Onkey in particular, thank you for your steadfast investment in my scholarship. To Manuel Cuellar, your presence and support has meant the world. My gratitude extends to Olivia Earley, whose research assistance here and elsewhere has been invaluable. At Stanford University, my gratitude extends especially deep to my fellow dance studies provocateur, Sariel Golomb. I have appreciated your commitment to our comradery and benefited from your insightful editorial eye. To Janice Ross, Bernadette Meyler, Peggy Phelan, Liisa Malkki, and Jisha Menon: each of you fostered excellence and earnestness in my scholarship as you allowed me permission to think without restriction. Thank you, always.

This book has further benefited from the intellectual community well beyond my home departments and wider campus: the American Institute for Maghreb Studies—including archival workshops but especially the support of Sophia Mo—offered vital space for francophone and North African attentions. Our exchanges offered me historical depth and cultural awareness and led to an emerging friendship. Thank you, truly, for suspending judgment in your reading of early drafts. I am also grateful to the participation in the Law and Humanities Juniors Scholar Workshop (including designated response from David L. Eng, Mark Jerng, and Naomi Mezey, and ongoing dialogue with Zamir Ben-Dan); Stanford Legal Studies Workshop (including feedback from Barbara Fried and Namrata Verghese); l'Atelier Francophone (under the generous direction of Fatoumata Seck and Marie-Pierre Ulloa); the Association for the Study of Law, Culture, and the Humanities Graduate Workshop (with particular gratitude to the follow up of Marianne Constable and Tim Wyman-McCarthy); Dance Studies Association (especially the feedback offered by Linda Tomko and Jim Tuller); and Arts + Justice Humanities Center Workshop (with feedback from Matthew Gilbert, Marina Johnson, and Westley Montgomery).

Chapter 5 in particular has benefited from editorial expertise at *Dance Research Journal,* including careful readings by Thomas DeFrantz, Jasmine Johnson, and Eric Mullis, for which I am most grateful; these pages also received invaluable input from scholars John Inazu and Julie Stone Peters. Thank you both for taking seriously my work before it deserved your attention. Chapter 3 includes material which benefited from the editorial leadership at *Southern California Interdisciplinary Law Journal*; your expertise and attention was appreciated throughout.

To Christine Xiong, thank you for being the constant reminder of my value and my potential as a scholar. To Michelle Yeh, may I forever continue to learn from you. To my students, thank you for keeping me dancing all these years.

And to Kai Yui Samuel Chan, my infinite expression of love and appreciation for your support through it all. My debt, always.

Law is the projection of an imagined future upon reality.
A legal world is built only to the extent that there are commitments
that place bodies on the line.

—*ROBERT M. COVER,*
Violence and the Word,
95 Yale L.J. 1601 (1986)

When politics is treated merely as an idea or ideology, it occurs in stillness, awaiting something that will bring people to action or mobilize them. But this presumed gap between a thinking mind and an acting body makes it impossible to understand how people move from a passive to active state. The presumption of bodies already in motion, what dance takes as its normative condition, could bridge the various splits between mind and body, subject and object, and process and structure.

—*RANDY MARTIN,*
Critical Moves: Dance Studies
in Theory and Politics *(1998)*[1]

LEGAL MOVES

INTRODUCTION

In the familiar traditions of legal theory, the order of knowledge has become particularly calcified. From classical legal thought to legal realism and its humanities turn, logocentrism defines the "conditions of possibility" for many legal thinkers and actors; the black letter of law remains its centripetal force and site of debate.[1] What opens when we expand our disciplinary methods of law—from the lettered to the embodied? From the static and stationary to the mobile and moved? That is, when we invite the vital body and its sensuous sentience to impact ways of knowing in legal theory? How can disciplines such as dance studies, where corporeity is already at the center, advance new insights in the legal humanities? What assumptions, biases, and oversights might be revealed—and potentially remedied? Motivated by the force of these interrogatives, *Legal Moves* engages in a project of epistemological disobedience, suturing the field of dance studies—bodily notation, scripted movements, corporeal awareness, fleshly memory, compulsory gestures, and choreographic activation—to the field of the legal humanities in search of a more complete portrait of the law, its logic, and its impact.

Legal Moves is an attempt to locate the neglected-yet-already-entangled history between the law and the choreographic. This relationship has been lost to legal studies' methods that privilege the literary over the corporeal and obscure the central kinesthetic experience of legal prose. Towards one possible recuperation, *Legal Moves* dwells within the laws and law-making logics of French imperial order and its postcolonial legacy as a foundational site of these intimacies to locate the already-embedded corporeal attentions and choreographic features of legal studies. Chapters move from analysis of French legal codes of conduct that structured race and empire in the seventeenth-century to the interpretative force of police and gendarmes during scenes of anti-colonial protest in the twentieth-century, to anxieties about assembly in postcolonial states of the twenty-first century, to the embodied aesthetics held within human rights discourse more globally.

An attunement toward the body logics, repertoires, and movements of legal texts brings into sharp focus the ways in which laws have disciplined race and reproduced colonial hierarchies in postcolonial contexts, including as disseminated to the Americas and manifold in the contemporary now. It entrenches a deep entanglement wherein law is not merely enacted on bodies, but the law *as rhetoric* and the legal subject *as a body* emerge and shift through and against each other.

In the title of her famed work, "Mama's Baby, Papa's Maybe: An American Grammar Book," Hortense Spillers invites us to think of flesh and law together.[2] The reproductive material logics of anti-black capitalist slavery, in which matrilineal and patrilineal becomings diverge under the legal tradition of chattel slavery, meet in a grammar book. Kevin Quashie summarizes this relationship:

> Right there, in the chiasmic juxtaposition of the black mother's traceable relation to the child—a relation that holds no legal claim—next to the father's wily feasibility, Spillers ideates a linguistic deformation of Western patriarchal lineage. Relatedly, the second half title declares slavery's constitutive gender terror as a "grammar book," securing the intersection between rhetoric (law), pedagogy and epistemology, and materiality (embodiment). *Or words and flesh, flesh and words.*[3]

This is one legal move, engendered by the severance of flesh and body. *A movement away in violent rupture.* Yet the legal moves unevenly, naming for me the multiple, competing ways in which 1) laws conscript the body, choreographing positions and positionalities, 2) bodies press toward alternative positions, deviant yet possible, in response to boundaries of the permissible, and 3) the field of legal studies shifts, ever slightly, toward an otherwise more corporeal, plural, and relational in its ways of knowing. In this book, I sit with historical scenes of the first and second legal moves in order to build toward the third. Held together, these moves outline the tensions between disciplinary ways of understanding the body too often siloed or incomplete.

To attend to these multivalent relationships between body, movement, and law, I suggest a transdisciplinary analytics of *choreo-jurisgenerativity* in which the "creation of legal meaning" is understood to emerge through sites of movement activation and bodily figuration.[4] This analysis attends to the double entendre of "legal moves" as both the process through which law conscripts bodies into disciplined repertories *and also* the ways in which bodies shift and move in response. "These myths," of relationality between the normative and the material, the law and the body, "establish a repertoire of moves—a lexicon of normative action—that may be combined into meaningful patterns culled from the meaningful patterns of the past."[5] Here the familiar drive of *nomos* and narrative, to extend the words of legal scholar Robert Cover, spills readily into kinesthetic space. Mine is a project to keep open the interpretive force of law, to refuse to cede creative and corporeal labor even when other systems fail. Amplifying Fred Moten's jurisgenerative grammars, which center the generative potential of language, allows one to move toward a framework that centers the parallel potential of movement, gesture, and choreography.[6] Choreo-jurisgenerativity, then, accounts for the jurisgenerative helm of flesh and body on the move. It tumbles forth from an attention to movement: errant, oblique, submissive, repetitive, ruptured.

Throughout this book, law takes on an intentionally capacious set of signifiers rather than a reductively singular site. This includes, for example, individual actors, institutional forms, constitutional texts, legislated mandates, court documents, police force, legal verdicts, international agreements, congressional record, and more. It reflects what Greta Olson terms legality, defined in an "inclusive sense to denote all expressions of the legal, such as those in images and sculptures relating to law, as well as in courtrooms and monuments [and] fictional representations of law in movies and television."[7] I focus primarily on derivations of Roman law, especially its outgrowths in France and the United States, with particular emphasis on penal code and civil law. Rather than finding this plurality to be a weakness of definition, I argue that it points to the inevitable requirement that one uses multiple methods within legal studies (though I maintain that even if I were to confine myself to a more restrictive definition of law, as I do elsewhere, an intervention from dance studies would still prove valuable).[8]

I make this proposition on the grounds that the discipline already understands the law to be polysemic—it exists in many forms and in many places. Aharon Barak, for example, when arguing for a purposivism approach to legal interpretation, writes that "the word 'text' is not limited to a written text. For purposes of interpretation, any behavior that creates a legal norm is a 'text'."[9] Adding to this logic, Thomas Grey suggests the potential of an unwritten constitution, one "not to be found in the four corners of our founding document."[10] If law is to be capaciously defined as not only formal texts but also the behaviors which uphold, refuse, and rally around its letter outside the page, then methods of legal interpretation can no longer be limited to textual analysis. They ought to also be inclusive of the fleshly gestures of those who sustain and experience it. A call to dance studies as integral to legal studies, then, emerges not as a whimsical conjuring or experimental idea but as a critical and necessary rider to an already shifting field.

The chapters which follow analyze the risk of excluding corporeal ways of knowing from legal studies. They cross legal histories of slavery, colonialism, and imperialism in which the raced body was subject to legal violence, moving across continents and centuries before concluding in a global turn toward human rights. Dance studies grounds my position given its methods for understanding both the embodied legacy of legal acts and the improvisatory potential of the future as anything but prescripted. Evidence is found in performance pieces, expressive bodies, and scenes in motion captured in film. Precisely by shifting the archival location of law away from the text, I shift toward other ways of being and knowing which nevertheless come to move our understanding of law. Taken together, the chapters cohere toward an understanding of how choreographic features of the law have been mobilized to structure race and empire, and how legal logics have long drawn upon movement politics, if in quiet, unacknowledged, and misunderstood ways.

THE ABSENT FLESH OF LAW

The absent flesh of law is best undestood through a dance studies attunement. It is not just the sign or the image that "represents an invisible presence," as Peter Goodrich argues of sixteenth century humanist legal tradition, but the body and its flesh that affirms the "human presence" in the legal definition of the person.[11] In a section titled "A Semiosis of Flesh Thinking," R. A. Judy explores Hortense Spillers's relationship between fleshiness and persona. For Spillers, the flesh indexes pure matter that exists outside any kinship or state apparatus even as it is enlisted to serve both. By contrast, persona evokes the etymology of mask in Roman law in which persona distinguished those with civil rights from those without.[12] In Western concert dance tradition, however, there is no mask donned to establish the separation between person and (legal) personality. There, the body is presented *through* the flesh, its muscular efforts not its imported rights defining its plane of existence. Dance holds onto the "real person"—the *al-shakhs al-haqiqi* or *personne physique*—as the life which remains even after conditions of social death.[13] The absent flesh of law extends and inverts this attention, holding close to the "outline of the space that body simultaneously took and left."[14]

"Before the body, there is the flesh," writes Spillers with syllables now familiar to many. The simplicity of this sentence cloaks its nuance.[15] The preposition "before" confounds presumptions of relationality and causality. It is not a temporal commentary, as if history summoned flesh into the body.[16] On the contrary, this remark is a metaphysical one, placing the reader in relation to the figure, named or unnamed. In front of the body, there is flesh, an exterior sign and material surface of hieroglyphics. "In order to get to the body," clarifies Spillers, "you have to go through flesh."[17] The flesh thus encases, conceals, masks the body. For the captor and conquistador, it absents the body, evacuated from the scene in the theft of personality. The flesh is left behind, present and hypervisible for the *here and now*. Precisely because it "does not escape concealment under the brush of discourse or the reflexes of iconography," flesh assumes a position of transparency, immediacy.[18] It gives opacity to the body. There is an implicit proximity, a potential vulnerability, a historical presumption of access to this surface for its foregrounded visibility.

These politics of visibility and opacity complicate readymade binaries, shifting the locus of agency and consent across the body and its flesh.

Many scholars have theorized the potential of flesh: as excess, as sentient, as sensational.[19] Separate from the archival propensity of bone, *pace* Rebecca Schneider, but also distinct from skin, as a way to theorize power with soft contours, to analyze differently without reifying position, to slide across a Cartesian duality of mind and body where interiority and exteriority meet. Flesh names the dehumanizing and ungendering of the body as material and anatomical but not constitutive of person/hood. Flesh as "primary narrative" registers wounding, touch, intimacy, and violence.[20] Yet flesh *may* be viewed as shorthand for a derogatory set of signifiers which reduce life to conditions outside of the human. Too often body and flesh elide with the latter limited as inanimate or flattened to the objectified. Might we instead push flesh back into the legal body—to render the abstracted person material, visible, proximate, felt beyond its common abstraction, omnipresent but never quite touched, held?

A dance studies gaze offers one avenue for undoing the body's mythologized naturalization. *The flesh of my abdomen tightens as I prepare to be lifted.* Historical and felt knowledge lives in this visceral form. The divergence is not a contradiction but a nuance. The sentient body is also the fleshed body; both co-mingle: "sentient flesh," confirms Judy, moves as the ontologically discordant being.[21] The exterior imbued with knowledge. Flesh, stripped from its body, presents rupture and exposure. But flesh *folds, tumbles, desires, bounds, mars, braces, and embraces.* It moves in the present and its performance without losing purchase on the choreographic forces at play. Legal apparatuses enforce this perspective in which the distinction between body and flesh is not good or bad but lost and found, then weaponized for the difference.

In contrast to the perceived immediacy of flesh, absence haunts the body. It is the unnamed, misnamed abstraction that allows violences of history to be anonymously inflicted. It emerges in the abstracted, as in when human rights are discussed without attention to the fleshed conditions. "A body with rights," touts visions of a liberal humanity. But whose form? For whom? The captive body denotes an "absence *from* a subject position" that profoundly defines the theft of the body in transatlantic slave trade but continues to appear: the refugee, the migrant, the unhoused minor in which the world happens *to the body*, happens *on the body* even while placing blame, burden, and responsibility onto that figure.[22] Such absence extends from the subject toward epistemological absences whose neglect affirms the reigning choreographic order.

Legal personhood starts at the level of the body and builds out, writing of peoples, rights, and orders, at times without going back through movements of the flesh. On the one hand, scholarship such as Alan Hyde's *Bodies of Law* exemplifies this tendency in which the legal body has been understood as the accumulation of organs, the dissection of the moving body into discrete parts, not sentient flesh: the vagina, penis, bone marrow, and urine as sites of legal claims.[23] The body, then, becomes an object of law, a static form primed to receive legal address. It is overlooked as an affective, moving subject with a unique experience of law, a body in motion, a vessel of its historical application, and a site of its future animation. On the other hand, Althusserian ideologies of interpellation have reinforced a unidirectional force of State power, as the police officer (here the agent and acting subject of law) interpolates the pedestrian (here the mere object of legal address) through the hail. In either instance, of the flesh without a body or a body without its flesh, the totality of the person becomes flattened. Abstracted concepts of biopolitics, freedom, autonomy, consent, and equality have been introduced into legalese as if liberal visions of rights alone could capture a holistic reality without shifting the epistemic foundation.

I do not mean to suggest that the referent of the body is without utility. The body indexes the subject placed within a choreographic frame, located *there and then*. It locates, if it rarely identifies. *The body shudders as collarbones gleam bright with sweat.* Labor and humanity approach in this silhouetted form, the understanding of this dancing body specific and anonymous at once. The body, as I invoke it in the following pages, approximates the person even when I understand the figure to not yet have been fleshed have the liberties of full personhood. It sits liminally, awkwardly, impatiently betwixt the full juris-political construction of the human and the "zero-degree of social conceptualization" of the flesh.[24] Such is the tension held in the absent flesh of law.

I turn to dance studies to clarify this bifocaled attention of presence/absence and flesh/body through the distinction between performance and choreography. Susan Foster establishes performance as the discrete instantiation or execution of an event, gesture, or movement, while choreography situates this event within a framework of conventions, norms, and institutions. Performance might be the articulation of the flesh, but choreography looks beyond at the "structuring of deep and enduring cultural values" of the body.[25] I follow this distinction throughout unless otherwise named. Performance (allegedly) contains a present bias, but choreography is transhistorical even when situated. Twinned analytics of the choreographic and the performance locate the body and its flesh at once. Through both, the legal moves.

To look at law with a choreographic lens moves beyond any immediacy of the performance to understand the wider milieu of production, including the nested forms of social, political, and legal pressures which might compel any one individual to move. Choreography as an "apparatus of capture," suggests André Lepecki in extension of Deleuzian thought, structures across perception and signification, visibility and invisibility, significance and insignificance.[26] It extends to the anachoreographic, what Fahima Ife presents as the "feral spirit of *study, waywardness, tarrying, ritual, practice, rehearsal, shoal, ceremony, series, rematriation, wake, duration, intimacy, pause,* and *refusal.*"[27] This attunement to movement as both choreography and performance provides a method to confront, be in touch with, or otherwise be moved by the law and its imprint on the body. Such a practice is at once fine-grained and contextual, dizzying in the required shifts in perspective.

The partition between performance and choreography summarizes a much wider historical-ontological becoming of dance. As chapter 1 elaborates in fuller detail, dance has been theorized as the intensification of presence. When Raoul-Auger Feuillet published an early tome of Western choreography, *Chorégraphie ou l'Art de Décrire la Danse, par Caractères, Figures et Signes Démonstratif* (1699), he presents a visual schema of the body with the remarkable caption, "De la présence du corps (of the presence of the body)." The repetition "of the" inserts space between the body and its presence. It cleaves "an interval between one and the other that allows choreography to announce and enforce its project of regimentation and inscription of bodily movements," writes Lepecki on the production of the representational body. From this point onward, "the presence of the body is always preceded, always prefaced by, always grounded on, an open field of absence."[28] Dance emerges as the lever between presence and the body to refract the absent flesh of law. This ontological rupture names dance as transgressive, destabilizing, and as such, radical.

At times, the evidence gathered in this book allows the argument to move through close readings of legal performance, sensing the subtle and supple flicks, wrings, convulsions, restorations, and bodily movements at hand. These sensitive moments of the flesh endeavor me to hold the subject as present, seen, valued as a repository of worldly knowledge. In other moments, the discussion attunes toward the wider scale of choreographic structures that stretch into and out of the social, political, historical, institutional, and juridical. This expanded horizon attends to that which is absented, not just the flesh made present, including the onto-epistemological orders which define the terms and condition. Even in scenes, then, in which the body has seemingly been evacuated, we can retrace choreographic threads which rendered the performance possible (and at times, inevitable).

Body slips from flesh, choreography from performance. Absence and presence emerge as conjoined maneuvers. Dance studies, after all, is primed to address that which exists at the vanishing point: capturing the complexities of movement otherwise made to disappear.[29] What would happen if we turned these methods of criticism toward vanishing horizon of the body's own vanishment? If the absented body, not the abject person, was understood as a series of formal dissolutions carefully and strategically written into existence? We arrive, then at the oxymoronic suggestion of the absent flesh of law as a "dynamic confluence," an impossible feat of redress.[30] As Saidiya Hartman lays out, redress emerges as a "re-membering of the social body," a pressing back together of the absented body and its fleshed relief, in a "redemption of the body as human flesh."[31] As she elaborates, "these techniques entail remedying disrupted affiliations, caring for the depleted and broken body, and reconstituting the terms of existence for the socially dead."[32] *Legal Moves* sits with these tense proximities, in which body and flesh, absence and presence, choreography and performance coalesce in redressing a liberal legal humanism that separated person from personhood. There is a symmetry between the leading terms in each coupling—body, absence, choreography—and its antithesis—flesh, presence, performance. Although not quite the same, and not to be collapsed or used interchangeably, these paired concepts point toward separate but related valences in legal humanisms. Dance studies and legal studies crisscross both domains, if variably finessed.

If flesh invokes the hypervisible, the readily available, the body hints at an omni-absence: visible but not accounted for, absent even when there. The omni-absent body of law emerges in indefensible lines of history which shouted, "There are no slaves in France!" and there is "No Human Involved."[33] The paradox carries from the eighteenth century sentiment of French abolitionists to the twentieth century indexes of American police brutality wherein the law evacuated the body of flesh and slogans enforced the absence. Timeless, the repetition of these "no-bodies" points to the originary and inevitably entangled order of law, race, and violence when built upon post-Enlightenment tradition.[34] It is, for Fred Moten, "the outlaw that guarantees the law," the outlined body without fuller portrait, the evacuation central to modern law's Hegelian undercurrent that structures body and law and its interdependent performance.[35] *Legal Moves* extends from these past events to other interrelated and insidious corners of legal history in which entire peoples have been deemed absent and obsolete. Breathless, it is an effort to shift beyond the written record for which law is most associated—including police reports, autopsy records, verdicts, and appeals—toward a more embodied appreciation within legal studies in a reminder—no, a reprimand—that "*being human is a praxis*."[36]

I return to the perverse perlocution, "No Human Involved," as an omni-absence maneuver that reinvests in severance of body and flesh. This term emerged by the 1980s as a systematic categorization of non-white life. Abbreviated to the shorthand, N.H.I., the acronym first circulated within the Los Angeles Police Department (LAPD) as an internal code for black and brown Angelenos presumed by law enforcement to "belong to the jobless category of the inner city ghettos."[37] Its crude and exclusionary gloss, sensationalized in the wake of police brutality against Rodney King, exemplifies the ways in which the legalese of law and its agents negates a more complete rendering in which bodies and flesh might be indivisible.[38] By suggesting no human to be involved, the term distorts the obvious, fleshly presence of life in scenes of police violence. It intimates that there need not be attention to the potential for discolored bruises, open scars, or dried blood. There need not be attention to the disjointed angles forcibly choreographed by the police officers' billy clubs, or to the facial expressions of anguish which filled the scene even as video evidence circulated on loop. The jurispathic conceit of law pronounced this loudly when the state jury acquitted the officers of assault charges. Pursuant legal verdicts turned on the "reasonableness" of "excessive force"—that is, a discernment hinged on the *perceived* relationship between the rational and the kinesthetic.[39]

Therein lies the crux of this book, the invisibility of body knowledge before legal actors and legal logics. The stakes could not be higher. When rhetoric alone is allowed to classify legal personhood, nomenclature can obscure what choreographic attentions cannot overlook. Without more embodied methods such as those found in dance and performance studies, the silhouetted life of legal personhood continues its course. That is, in the absent flesh of law we find a legal negligence toward the kinesthetic, somatic, and moving body that supplements alternative modes of knowing and being. Following Anne Cheng's own interdisciplinary grappling, we might consider legal personhood as the "delicate slippages between bodies and their surfaces, essences and attributes" and add to this the gestural potential to move and move otherwise. Cheng initiates a parallel question when she notes the "dilemma of legal presencing: how to make bodies evident in the eyes of the law."[40] Although she writes of aesthetics and the ornamental rather than the kinetic *per se*, we both appreciate the forms of law which exist beyond the textual. The absence of the human then, or the overrepresentation of Man, echoes wider critiques of humanism as a liberal project of modernity and morality leveraged to justify violence elsewhere. It also removes attention to the sentient flesh, turning our collective gaze away from the animate form. What would it mean to pull at the loose threads of "juridical humanity" which produced the absent flesh of law?[41]

TOWARD A SOMATIC OTHERWISE

Scholarship in the legal humanities remains predominately bound to textual analysis, dismissive of dance studies' diligence toward the political potential of the body as a site of embodied knowledge, intellectual practice, and creative discipline.[42] Absent is an attention to that which exists *hors-texte*: the somatic, the kinesthetic, and the ephemeral. This linguistic predisposition saturates critical legal studies and its many epistemic branches which move through discourses of political theory, philosophy, history, sociology, and anthropology. It is, perhaps, an act of "looking for law in all the wrong places."[43] In turn, I am invested in rethinking legal application, debates, and actors *through* dance studies methods which hold the body and flesh together. This commitment toward the recovery of the "disembodied lapses" of law follows what I view as the intrinsic relationship between the legal and the choreographic, one longstanding yet long overdue in its address if we are to overcome our contemporary episteme's dramatic shortfall.[44]

Having bourgeoned in the 1970s, the law and literature movement exemplifies the potential of legal humanities to open toward the subjective, drawing upon literary methods to reconceptualize law: *in* literature and *as* literature. Such methods challenged the more utilitarian movement of law and economics that developed from legal realist debates. The idea of this field has been to push for greater moral sensibility, imaginative potential, and empathetic orientation for legal scholars and institutions alike.[45] Guyora Binder and Robert Weisberg's *Literary Criticisms of Law* at the turn of the twenty-first century and later Elizabeth Anker and Bernadette Meyler's *New Directions in Law and Literature* coalesce around these shared principles and highlight the immense value of (re)inserting the humanities into legal arguments.[46] Many other scholars, from within and beyond formal law, have contributed to this effort as critical legal studies began to extend its methodological impulse toward more capacious ways of knowing.[47]

As generative as such literary criticisms of law are for developing a culturally sensitive approach to law that values an empathetic maturity—a humanist commitment to ethical correctives, in the words of Julie Stone Peters—this movement, however, has hardened a larger trend of critical legal studies to center law as a textual practice.[48] The field's titular framing itself points to the privileged class of the linguistic that foregoes the embodied, leaving the field implicitly tethered to the science of the Word.[49] Literary methods of rhetoric, narration, language, translation, and interpretation saturate this set of scholarship alongside themes of status, character, identity, and oration. Even when performance has been introduced as a legitimate object of study in a broadening of the interpretation of law, culture, and the humanities, there remains a trend to occlude corporeal experience in favor of linguistic form. The more nascent subfield of law and performance frequently returns to rhetorical analysis, discursive logics, and dramatic plot points.[50] Script dominates the evidence analyzed as its scholars explore spectatorship, reception, plot, reaction—Aristotelian terms entangled in the legal—alongside repetition, spectacle, and legal subjectivity. Absent are alternative methods of the body that include kinesthetic attention, corporeality, proprioception, somatic memory, and touch, alongside thematic concerns of discipline, partnering, technique, improvisation, and rehearsal: the body of law, not only the letter of law.

Laws and verdicts are often pronounced—spoken aloud, held in the mouth, articulated via the body, and ultimately embodied, and as such always already require a physical manifestation in subjunction to the text. Implementation of laws, by definition, influence action, gesture, comportment, movement, mobility, and motility—that is, bodily performance. Laws are upheld through quotidian acts of repetition, sustained through bureaucratic actions that require personnel and papercuts, through life-altering verdicts that shift one's sense of place and self. It is necessary to allow for the integration of dance studies methods in order to better understand this bodied reality. Already Lawrence Douglas, Austin Sarat, and

Martha Umphrey, in their invitation to think law and performance together, note that "conceiving law through the lens of performance invokes legal realist claims" like that of critical race theory and legal anthropology. Continuing, they "assume that the meaning of law is articulated in its doings that are situated and embodied rather than abstracted into formal rules and principles inert."[51] Popular scholarship from other fields, such as Bessel Van der Kolk's *The Body Keeps the Score,* too reflects the potential for somatic histories to be taken seriously outside of dance studies, if not yet a mainstream norm for the American legal academy.[52] The argument of this book invites us to build upon that assumption to ground an emergent intuition which positions body knowledge as a central lever within legal frames.

Consider, for example, the following scenario: *Seated in the driver's seat, you are driving north on Palm Drive heading toward downtown Palo Alto. As Palm Drive turns into University Avenue, you come to the intersection of University Avenue and Emerson Street and, seeing the sign for public parking, you turn right. Before you consciously decide that your route involves a right turn, your left hand reaches for the blinker to indicate to the traffic behind you. Safely merged onto Emerson, you continue on your merry way—perhaps to Bell's Books or the farmer's market.* The destination, of course, is not the point. It could be Paris or Algiers, Baton Rouge or Washington, D.C.—any of the cities featured in the pages to come, not only the town from which I write. Rather, it is the reflex of the body to signal that grabs my attention, or more precisely, the somatic memory of the left hand to reach upward in order to comply with the law (not signaling during traffic being a traffic violation). In this way, the individual has internalized legal imperatives in a kinesthetic manner and, consequently, becomes a horcrux of the law itself.

The scene above points to the ways that the law is learned, somatically. These somatic repertoires as legal repertoires accentuate the ways in which law is socialized and made to live in the flesh. If my able-bodied white form unconsciously reaches for the blinker as I drive, such a reach might always be conscious for the driver of color who is ever aware of racial profiling. For someone raised outside the United States, for example in a British (post)colony wherein traffic flows inversely, these repertoires live differently and stress an outsider position when moving through the gestural landscape above. For someone who just learned to drive, or has not yet learned to drive, the kinetic knowledge of the law would not have yet submerged. Bodily inventories reveal our proximity to legal force. Positionality matters. To hold tight to the body *and* flesh, performance *and* choreography, in doing legal studies, is to embrace this specificity and forego the myth of disembodied objectivity and its dislocation to the page.

If words are thus internalized and made flesh, how does the law live within us, in our muscle and bone as much as memory and mind? Phrased otherwise, what are the gestures of law that create a legal repertoire for the State? I feel the law in my body when once, hiking in California, my heart rate intensified as I briefly cut across private property to return to the trailhead I lost. I feel the law in my body when, lining the street for a local parade, I hold my bladder in discomfort, not allowed to relieve myself in public. I see the law in other bodies when, along a crowded street, a couple walks to the end of the block to cross at the designated crosswalk rather than jaywalk directly to the bus stop across the way. I see the law in other bodies when, walking alone at night, a man averts my gaze to signal non-aggression, his hesitation of eye contact memory of law's racializing history. As Claudia Rankine charges in her lyrics on citizenry, "certain moments send adrenaline to the heart, dry out the tongue, and clog the lungs."[53] Consciously or not, the law becomes internalized in a kinesthetic process, to be felt, lived, embraced.[54] Ominously or not, I now contain the law in my own body. It exists in the live through my comportment, my own schema, not merely in doctrine: action, after all, materializes ideology. As a result, I—and by extension we—assume a new ownership toward the legal, in which response-ability takes on choreographic potential that spills to and beyond the body politic.

In calling for a somatic intelligence in legal theory, I do not mean to reinforce the Cartesian cut in which emotional and embodied intelligence are classed secondary. Embodiment reflects a "lexical band-aid for a 350-year-old wound," and we might do well to one day let it go.[55] Until then, however, I wrestle against the inheritance of the mind-body dualism that shapes many Euro-American concert dancers and legal theorists alike.[56] Against such Enlightened tropes of knowledge production, I write toward a more comprehensive view of legal theory that holds multiple modalities at once: absence/presence, body/flesh, choreography/performance.[57] When the category of the human remains indebted to the "taxonomical telos" of scientific empiricism and historical orderings, I find it imperative to articulate my choice as a recalcitrant one.[58]

Such internalization of somatically-held knowledge is a double-edged sword. In 2021, when police officer Kim Potter shot and killed civilian Daunte Wright, her police chief labeled this death of a black man by a white officer "accidental."[59] Citing "muscle memory," a habituated somatic pattern of drawing a weapon for a senior officer, a narrative was crafted in which Potter followed kinesthetic memory to reach for her taser *on her right*, not realizing it was a gun instead. While the question of why such force would have been required during a routine traffic stop at all remains, the potency of somatic memory left unattended reverberates through the scene. After all, officers are trained to carry their taser *in their left* holster and their gun *on the right* (for right-dominant officers) to avoid this precise confusion. To inadvertently invert the muscle memory, to unconsciously cross the sagittal axis of the body, seems unfounded. It calls into question the legal distinction between intent and culpable negligence.[60] As fate would have it, Potter was training younger officers at the time of the homicide. This racially charged example reflects only one news story, but it exemplifies the very real consequences for the law to appreciate, *with nuance*, somatic knowledge as evidence, as Potter's innocence or guilt rested on this very framing.[61]

Let me clarify: my intent is not to theorize laws *of* dance in the literal sense, nor laws *as* dance in the metaphorical sense. In both critical dance studies and the law and literature movement, we see a similar nuance rehearsed: law *as* literature distinguished from law *in* literature, dance *as* protest distinguished from dance *in* protests. Nor is it my intent to collate here the myriad of ways in which the law regulates bodily function, such as in medical settings. I am not even attempting to account for the ways in which law regulates the *dancing* body, though all of such digressions could be productive. The former encompasses a sprawling history that includes medical practices, reproductive rights, sexual identity, and racial formation: areas advanced by feminist legal studies, critical race theory, and other legal activists. The latter includes copyright law, religious conservativism, indigenous censorship, and ableist rhetoric, among other discursive norms. Both share an umbrella focus of property and ownership: the body to be tamed and conquered as a part of modernity's churn. Neither, however, feature the law and the choreographic as co-constituting ideologies which press back against one another in jurisgenerative and jurispathic manners alike.

To summarize the necessity of my proposed intervention: recall the infamous words of Justice Potter Stewart, "I know it when I see it," used to define his test for obscenity, itself an obscene artifact of the supposedly all-knowing court.[62] Now near-parody, this statement reveals many things to me: first, textualism, based on intent or otherwise, fails to produce articulate rule because even legal language can be profoundly vague and abstract. In this instance, the abstraction of the pronoun "it" leads to incredible ambiguity, twice over: I know *it* when I see *it*. Second, legal texts are especially prone to shortcomings when addressing concerns of the ephemeral or corporeal, in this case obscenity law. The justice does not seem equipped with the necessary vocabulary to discuss the body meaningfully, yet nevertheless assumes authority in the discussion. And third, even he subconsciously acknowledges that his process of rational legal interpretation involves the sensorial. Here the sense of sight and ocular processes of recognition that exceed language produce legally verifiable knowledge: I know it when I *see* it. Taken seriously, this phrase suggests that legally-relevant knowledge is contained in the extra-literary, or paratext—what Peter Goodrich has framed as minor jurisprudence and I point to as the choreo-jurisgenerative influence of the body.[63] It reflects my effort to move beyond a question of legal interpretation that once again returns us to the authority of the text and instead to think anew about where that center of authority lies—in spaces that exceed the lettered, the read, the formally documented. With the stakes so high—I think also here of willfully xenophobic misidentification of personal tattoos as international gang affiliation and resultant deportations[64]—such tolerance for ambiguity, uncertainty, and lack of clarity when addressing the corporeal, as well as the monopolization of power in which Justice Stewart monolithically embodies the I of judgement, continues to unsettle me in a profound, deep centered way.

Taking a step back, dominant methods of legal interpretation ground their arguments in either the methods used or motivating outcomes to a given scenario: across competing views of textualism, originalism, or the more unruly standards of purposivism, there is a shared sense that legal interpretation names a rational activity meant to extract normative meanings from a legal *text*. Rather than debate here the ideal process of interpretation, I hope that *Legal Moves* might shift our attention to what legal scholars attempt to interpret—namely, to unravel the bounded status of legal text as well as perceived sites (or bodies) of rationality. Specifically, I intervene to argue that the object of analysis of *texts* is too narrowly defined, such that the debate is not only how to locate meaning in a legal text, but what could and should constitute such a text in the first place. Viewed in this sense, the expanded methods of the legal humanities toward law and literature are not yet sufficient for opening toward a humanistic epistemology of legal thought, at least not an illiberal one, despite their productive foray into interdisciplinary grounds. Just as it is impossible to circumvent analysis of the law as word, it is equally impossible to not have to pass through the status of the human—body and flesh. A deeper approach holds both at once at the foundation.

I turn to dance studies to articulate this possibility for its vocabulary has always been poised to capture the jurisgenerative potential of the body in motion—its ability to name, value, and theorize the fleeting, the vanishing a hallmark of its form.[65] As a discipline, critical dance studies has moved beyond historical and biographical details of choreographers and performers to forcefully articulate the politics of movement as it takes place on and off stage.[66] This includes a deep understanding of the ways in which individual gesture, collective mobility, potential improvisation, corporeal memory, proprioceptive awareness, and kinesthetic empathy intersect with concerns of power, biopolitics, labor, agency, and freedom. It further acknowledges the body as the identitarian site on which processes of discrimination and exclusion occur—racism, sexism, ableism, nationalism, and more—and as an agent interacting within an eco-material world.[67] A mixed-methods approach of this manner also allows for the ephemeral to be taken seriously as formal evidence, beyond the culture of truth-making secured in legal doctrine that relies upon the linguistic and the archival. Summarized, I suture the field of dance studies with its robust theoretical, conceptual, and methodological offerings toward legal domains (rather than an abstracted reading of dance as metaphor or itself a category of analysis).

With this call toward the somatic otherwise of law, I want to pay homage to the existing works in dance studies which center the legal, even if they do not name themselves as furthering the project of the legal humanities. Anthea Kraut presents the history of choreographic copyright; Kareem Khubchandani critiques the dance ban in Bangalore within a history of moral anxiety; Jacqueline Shea Murphy reminds us of the 1978 American Indian Religious Freedom Act in which the US government reversed prohibitions on Native dance and spiritualities; Paul Siegal contributes a queer reading of the First Amendment via the dance floor; Hetty Blades et al. focus on the intersection of dance, disability, and law by centering differently-abled dancers; Victoria Fortuna discusses Argentina's national dance law; Joshua Chambers-Letson traces Asian-American selfhood through legal and aesthetic means.[68] Each of these works, alongside others yet unnamed, contrasts the desire to dance with the legal enforcement thereof, policing around sociogenic, economic, and moral incentives. These works are vital and exemplary, and give me permission in their precedent. They remain, however, bordered in their conversation with dance scholars and not yet taken seriously for their critical approach to legal theory, history, and practice. From legal studies, Sean Mulcahy begins a comparison between law and dance, but remains constrained to the literal stage and the courtroom in his "verbatim musilegal theatre" case studies.[69] Outside of dance studies proper but still within the frame of the extra-literary, scholars such as Fred Moten, Hentyle Yapp, Ann Pellegrini, Karen Shimakawa, and Michelle Castañeda's distinct scholarship reflects a twenty-first century response from performance studies, yet also remain at the margin in legal studies.[70] As a whole, however, these works do not yet compel legal studies to embrace a more capacious and fundamental sense of the choreo-jurisgenerative. Broader, more complete transference of the methods of dance studies to legal theory remains unexplored.

REFUSING GRAMMARS OF A BROKEN HUMANISM

In Sylvia Wynter's 1994 letter to the academic community, she draws our attention back to the epistemological violence which enabled N.H.I. to be used and legitimated in legal circles, from police to jurors to legal actors in between. As Wynter suggests, the "classificatory logic of the acronym" perpetuated by the American legal system following the acquittal of the LAPD officers who brutalized Rodney King excludes all but the normatively white, Euro-American figure.[71] For many, it reflects the perverted logics of a liberal humanism in which a false guise of universal being veils more pernicious justifications of colonial accumulations, racial hierarchies, rational ordering, and neoliberal structuring. For others, the veil was never present, with racial violence and typecasting rationalities openly coded into the founding systems of Western modern law. The vision of humanism bounded by the logic of this phrase remains a narrow one, as representation of an ecumenical subject persists as the collective white whale.[72] Following Wynter, the problem is fundamentally epistemological, rooted in the disciplinary paradigms in which order and hierarchy are institutionalized, reified, and normalized under the guise of objective truth. Frustrated and fed up, she lobs the question: "What is wrong with our education?"[73]

What is at stake in *Legal Moves*, then, is a disciplinary charge to rethink the fields, or ways of knowing, included within a wider understanding of Euro-American educations of legal theory. Against its discursive violence, can law ever be humanistic? In what moments has this potential already emerged, and in what spaces is it most necessitated? Suspicions abound, and I too remain cautious toward the liberal politics of the human which have been invoked to justify exclusion: less-than-human, sub-human, partially-human, non-human but never fully-human if inconvenient to the desires of law-granting powers. A misanthropy toward "Western thought's arrogant universalist assumptions, commonsense tautologies, and professed reforms to the category of the human" continue here.[74] The choreo-jurisgenerative frame positions the human otherwise, not centered on the fixed idea of personhood, but attuned to the movements between body and flesh.[75]

Against the way that language stabilizes, and thereby naturalizes, legal categories such as N.H.I., soma-kinesthetic acts uniquely and productively trouble this fixed status by turning attention toward the unstable, the fluid, the moving. Following Tiffany King and her assertation that humans *are* involved, I mean not an hostility to critical legal studies but an invitation to think again.[76] A dance studies intervention with legal humanities moves as an effort to account for the "errant grammars" of law, what King poetically constellates as "[t]hese extradiscursive and semigrammatical performances, defacements, and modes of living that confound normative modes of being must coexist with and work on the relations of conquest."[77] This builds upon related theorization such as Hortense Spillers's "American grammar," Denise Ferreira da Silva's "modern grammars," and Zakiyyah Iman Jackson's "modern grammar of representation" to index a bodily syntax of agency and accountability in a re-mattering of the flesh-made-object. It resonates too, aruably most proximately, with Frank Wilderson's foundational critique of the "Settler/Master/Human grammatical structure" in which Western logics erase the verb, the action, the praxis.[78] By refusing the grammatical hierarchy between subject and object within legal rhetoric and by turning from the anatomical to the kinetic, I underscore the potential for a body to be mapped with agency beyond frameworks of personhood which require *a priori* legal recognition.

I hope that this book, which invites dance studies and all its bodily figurations toward the legal humanities, can refresh a stalled disciplinary conversation—to shift narrow recognitions toward corporeal truths, to listen to the need to move with stillness, to locate the absent flesh of law across choreographies of race, law, and empire. At stake is a new understanding of how supposedly objective logics of law have masked its aesthetic and corporeal bias, past and present. This is an undisciplining of law in recognition of Katherine McKittrick's articulation that "discipline is empire."[79] The illiberal humanism of this project extends to its rather unruly sources of evidence. In the pages to come, I trace this possibility across examples of law and law enforcement, including vagrancy claims, traffic stops, protest demonstrations, and other public performances. I supplement archival material—of police reports, juridical documents, and constitutional revision—with embodied perspectives learned from more than twenty years as a disciplined body in a dance studio, including my own performance practice in select works discussed. Both are interpreted alongside artistic works, including but not limited to: performance offerings by niv Acosta and Fannie Sosa, mayfield brooks, William Forsythe, Jo Kreiter, and Rebecca Lazier, visual installations by Pélagie Gbaguidi, Pascale Mathine Tayou, and Sander van Bussel, and dramatic features of Eugène Scribe, Louis Clapisson, and Charles Fanny Reybaud. The tension of these pairings allows me to articulate what is lost when the law presumes linguistic form entirely. Each of the following chapters work toward this aim, suggesting alternative performances that center the body via the methods and histories of dance studies. My hope is that this project here, with its attempt to saturate the legal with a fuller choreo-jurisgenerative understanding, can be one of many attempts toward this epistemological redress.

Critique of Man and its bordered humanity is increasingly well rehearsed, if ever relevant. I find particular counsel in Tiffany King's "Black Notes on Western Humanism" as she elucidates this turbulent genealogy.[80] The coupling of dance studies and legal humanities gives entry to see the humanities "after Man" with greater clarity, and to better grapple with the implications: present, historical, and future. While the second half of this book returns to this question most fully through evaluation of the (un)becoming aesthetics of dignity and vulnerability associated with human rights discourse and international law, implications unfold throughout. This new sensitivity toward the corporeal is neither about correcting police bias, nor about charting the shifting lines of choreopolitics in a carceral state, or even expanding the category of the human, if all might feel implicitly called into question. It is, more foundationally, about a shift in epistemological orientation toward embodied histories, techniques, and aesthetics which inform the production of legal theory and its subsequent action—ways of knowing that have oft been left outside the bounds of legal studies if, as I will argue, have always been entangled.

This morass of legal and dance studies as an intervention on the genre of the human should not be construed as a plea for expanded recognition under existing frames, but a rupture of the category itself. It is not about infinite expansions of life forms into the category of Man, but rather critical attention towards the methods and epistemes used to carve this Man from Other. More specifically, while others critique the genre of the human from the field of science or the field of history and the respective domains of *universal nomos* and *universal poesis*,[81] I align more closely with Denise Ferreira da Silva, whose ethico-political attention drifts toward the rule of law and its juridical architectures.[82] By "asking different questions, methodological rather than ontological ones,"[83] I shift from an ontological emphasis found in many critiques of anti-blackness toward the methodological in amplification of those who write toward the praxis of being human. Intervening at the source, I insert alternative methods, ways of being, and knowing otherwise, open to what might shift as a result of this praxis. This approach "holds in it the possibility of undoing and unsettling—*not replacing or occupying*—Western conceptions of what it means to be human."[84] If still incomplete and ongoing, I hope this work might further disrupt the prevalence of monohumanist thought via the pluralization of methodologies. The crisis, after all, is not one of representation, mere inclusion into existing structures, but both epistemic and systemic.

Legal Moves is a part of the continual interrogation of our knowledge systems and hope that readers will embrace its invitation to continue the work.[85] That is, I tarry in this space to remind myself of the infinite intelligence of the fleshed body against the ventures of capital to invest elsewhere.[86] Toward a commitment to a ruptured humanism, one freed from its monohumanistic stratification of the world, I am indebted to the robust tradition of Black studies, French and francophone studies, Arab and Caribbean scholars, and postcolonial thought: Sylvia Wynter, Hortense Spillers, Saidiya Hartman, Tiffany Lethabo King, Zakiyyah Iman Jackson, Denise Ferreira da Silva, Fred Moten, Sora Han, R. A. Judy, Anne Cheng, Amber Musser, Jasbir Puar, Samera Esmeir, Aimé Césaire, Frantz Fanon, Assia Djebar, and Colin Dayan, amongst others. Although not always in smooth alignment, I find here not only vital critiques of governing epistemologies but also powerful articulations of new world orders continued by the creatives and critics gathered in these pages.

THE CHAPTERS

This book is structured in two parts, Part I: Keeping Score and Part II: Righting Wrongs with an interlude that serves as a portal from one to the other. The first section establishes the historical relationship between dance, law, and the conscripted body as entangled ideologies, tracing acts of discipline, absence, and refusal across French imperial order and Enlightenment thought. The second part pays attention to human rights concerns with particular attention to the embodied aesthetics at stake in vague scriptures of dignity, vulnerability, and relationality present in both anticolonial and postcolonial worlds. Part I's return to French courts and gilded palais, to histories now far removed (if still felt for many), is not meant to sever the reader from the present; each time I return to the contemporary significance and continued unfolding of the implications. Rather, I open with a reminder of those three words, "No Human Involved," even as I linger in archival spaces of francophone law precisely because of the way in which French legal theory has informed a long tradition of juridical thinking, from Montesquieu and Rousseau to the present. This is, after all, a book written by an American citizen *and* francophone scholar, an academic *and* a dancer in one. Transnational and transhistorical implications emerge for our understanding of the body's choreo-jurisgenerative capacity, as made possible by cross-cultural methods of comparison between France, its colonial states, and overseas territories alongside more contemporary, comparative scenes in American legal history.

Part I: Keeping Score features three chapters—"Con/scripting Law," "Fleshing Legality," and "Regulating Rhythms"—which compare the founding logics of French codes of conduct to dance notation systems established coeval during colonial order between the eighteenth and twentieth centuries. To open, chapter 1—"Con/scripting Law"—establishes the historical precedent for such a reimagination of legal theory, arguing that legal studies and dance studies have long been entangled ideologies throughout Western jurisprudence. I attune myself to the French courts of Louis XIV when he made his call for ballet's first notational system *and* the creation of colonial codes of conduct, sensitive to the shared logics of the representational body which move across both. Simultaneous investments in civil law tradition and dance notation invite us to read legal mandates as a genre of corporeal writing, scripting comportment and disciplining bodies of the Empire—a significant alternative framing of a canonical and oft-discussed period of dance history. While subsequent chapters take up more specific examples, and the implications of this pairing, I begin by taking the time to parse the distinction between dance notation and dance scores. I choose to make a distinction between the former *as retrospective* and the latter *as anticipatory* as a means to signal temporal difference in service to a larger purpose of this chapter, which is to theorize the temporalities of legal writing and the resulting praxes of its interpretation.

Throughout this chapter, I move toward a choreo-jurisgenerative capacity of the body. Through an attention to the score, I point to the *process* of being conscripted into State narratives and the *place* where language and action meet, where doctrine becomes animated. To reframe the law as a score invites a more pluralist understanding that considers legal codes as both noun (a score as printed document) and verb (to score a particular composition). It shifts attention toward the law as a process rather than a fixed object. This forces uncomfortable cohabitation between *bios* and *zoe*, the "registers of both sign and matter" summarized at times as the biocultural.[87] Here I intentionally point us toward the postcolonial thinking of scholars like David Scott, as the reading of law as score works against the conscripting project of European modernity.[88] In the second half of the chapter, improvisation and related practices of nonperformance serve as a way to maintain the possibility of moving otherwise within both jurisgenerative and jurispathic modes of legal interpretation. Although improvisation features a plurality of meanings—as a spontaneous act, a tactic of survival, or a practice of freedom—I center a more critically skilled interpretation of improvisation that produces an indeterminate temporality between the body and its notation. My own participation in the dance score, *There Might Be Others* (2014–2017) by Rebecca Lazier, allows for a personal and auto-ethnographic conclusion to this argument.

Chapter 2, "Fleshing Legality," pushes the geographic focus from the French metropole to overseas territories as it unearths fleshed memories of the *Code Noir*. A series of edicts essential to the construction of race and racial identity in the French empire, the *Code Noir* moved from Europe to Africa to the Caribbean islands of Saint-Domingue, Martinique, and Guadeloupe. This corpus defined the conditions of slavery in concepts of European modernity and reveals shifting legal orientations to the body and categories of the human which emerge following the edicts of Louis XIV. Most infamously, Art. 44 pivoted from feudal law to define the slave as a "thing," a material commodity for economic exchange scripted outside of the fully human. Alongside the formal legal archive, I turn to theatrical and aesthetic renderings of the *Code Noir*, including plays, operas, novellas, and visual works, to invite consideration of the codes and their fleshed experience wherein performativity takes on jurispathic weight. This paired reading of performance and law reveals the dependence of doctrinal development on the marked body. Ontologies are made malleable through the imaginative realm of performance: flesh as evidence, body as property, law as *coup de théâtre*.

Formulation of the body-as-archive appreciates the fleshly forms of law, inscribed on the body as notational flesh or encoded within via a disciplinary regime of fleshed notation. Its methods give sentience to flesh, animating critical attention to the epistemologies held within legal attention to the body while forcing scrutiny of the idiosyncratic and irrational behaviors of law itself. Review of the *Code Noir* and its afterlives—across its language, aesthetic making, performative events, and *advocats*—affirms this inverted order. This extends from anti-black sentimentalities held in Eugene Scribe's abolitionist *Code Noir* (1842) to reliance on kinesthetic empathy rehearsed by *Société des amis des Noirs* (Society of the Friends of Blacks), a Parisian abolitionist society in the 1780s. In sum, "Fleshing Legality" accounts for the aporia of legal persons bound up in the *Code Noir* that structured liberal humanism and continues to structure racial inequalities of the twenty-first century, revealed by the dis-membering and re-membering processes wherein wounds are made and healed and scars linger still.

Chapter 3, "Regulating Rhythms," concludes Part I by shifting from the *Code Noir* toward its rippling iterations of the *Code de l'indigénat* and the Black Codes as legal logics of the disciplined body spread throughout the French empire—the former which defined French political categories of subordination from French West Africa to French Indochina and the latter which manifested in the postbellum period of Louisiana and the American South. These transplantations allow us to trace not only the geopolitical reach of French civil law tradition in colonial and neocolonial spaces, but also the ways in which its implementation and choreographic strategy evolved in response to more localized repertoires of society. The first half of this chapter reads the soma-logics of the *Code de l'indigénat* to suggest a *hyper-kinetic jurisprudence of the body* in which the racialized other was cast at a perpetual distance to French citizenship under its system of legal pluralism. The second half reads the soma-logics of the Black Codes to suggest a *hypo-kinetic jurisprudence of the body* in which blackness was interpellated to quench capitalist appetites for unbounded productivity.

Rhythm emerges as an ambivalent metric to track the choreo-jurisgenerative body. Read together, these two transmutations of French legal code present opposing strategies for the ways in which laws metabolize its subjects to regulate the rhythms of the body, if in both we find stilled patterns and slow life produced by colonial law. I conclude with a turn to the aesthetics of rest, exemplified by contemporary movement artists and activists, as a practice of refusal in direct confrontation to the legal histories of the body scripted into perpetual motion. This includes review of niv Acosta and Fannie Sosa's *Black Power Naps* (2019) and Jo Kreiter's *The Wait Room* (2019) which both present alternative value systems for the horizontal body wherein rest for the supine figure emerges as a political act. The chapter unfolds to give texture to this embodied experience of legal time, including the contrapuntal tempos of legal pluralism and the ambivalent desires of colonial humanism. *In sum, the chapters of Part I serve to chart a history of legal documents which reveal a manifest attention to the body and body knowledges, moving from a founding moment of law and imperial order toward the iterations which ripple forward in time with different valences of force.*

Across the first three chapters, I seek to locate contours of the absented body, searching for its fleshly potential even when it has otherwise been written out. The interlude, "Sycorax's Alterity," serves as the fulcrum between Part I and Part II as her fictional figure travels as an a-legal and illegal foil to early modern, colonial worldviews that continue to motivate contemporary artists and theorists. Her absence defines the plot, and the interlude spills out as the missing link. Shifting to the second half of this book, I turn toward more contemporary locales in which the body appears more fully before the law. This extends in and outside of the courtroom, on and off the stage. Arguably, this shared orientation is nowhere more self-evident than in the legal theatre of human rights, a space defined and ambiguated by self-evident properties of dignity under universalist rhetoric.

The second part of this book unfolds in three chapters—"Policing Dignity," "Touching Associations," and "Un/becoming Humanisms"—to challenge the ambiguity in legal rhetoric when discussing the universal body. This extends across the human rights language of dignity and vulnerability, as illustrated in "Policing Dignity" and "(Un)Becoming Humanisms" respectively, toward slippage in constitutional language of individual protections, such as First Amendment rights to assembly in "Touching Associations." Protest, policing, and staged interventions complete the scenes as interpretation becomes contested under current rubrics of evaluation.

Chapter 4, "Policing Dignity" opens Part II by delving into the differentiated aesthetics of honor and dignity as status and rank confound within human rights discourse. Drawing upon original archival research conducted at the Paris préfecture, I feature the 1961 Paris Massacre which punctuated a turbulent month of conflict between Algerians living in France and the French police during the final months of the Algerian War of Independence. Recorded as "the bloodiest act of state repression of street protest in Western Europe in modern history," the event featured approximately 20,000 French Algerians in a pacifist protest; approximately 12,000 were wrongly arrested or detained, and competing sources estimate 20 to 200 were killed by the French police. I chart the divergent interpretations of honor and dignity that move throughout formal and informal records in which the language of dignity became racialized in its Algerian enactment and honor attributed to the French state—both imprinted in flesh yet denied before law. The striking ethno-national division suggests the limits of a universal understanding of dignity when identified via rhetoric alone. How is the choreo-jurisgenerative body perceived when coded as illegible within Western aestheticism of decorum? That is, when no longer presented as overtly dignified before the law?

To respond to these questions, this chapter challenges the self-evident relationship between dignity and human rights which emerge from French legal thought. Through embodied attunements, I chart an aesthetics of dignity across artistic and historical events as built upon aesthetics of decorum located in early court ballet tradition to argue for a more fluid, sensate interpretation of this para-legal category. This shift serves as an invitation to value that which occurs in surplus of the rational, logical, or rhetorical processes, including the physiological, affective, and kinesthetic. Although in its rhetorical form, dignity's logic may hold up to scrutiny, its corporeal trace has been especially lost and indeterminant. I suggest that dignity is not, as often upheld, a universal liberty but rather, in Foucauldian terms, a *regulatory ideal*. When dignity becomes seen as a narrow manifestation of reason and rational form, dignity becomes at odds with the charges of human rights. Recognition becomes a partial strategy toward the repair of the dignified body—to be seen and legitimated in one's very being. This question of recognition returns me to the founding logic of *habeas corpus*, to be legible *before the law*, rather than to more nascent discourses of visibility politics.

Remaining in the Maghreb and its diaspora, Chapter 5, "Touching Associations," refreshes the distinction between the right to assembly and the right to association, noting that the former has faded from court attention in favor of the latter in recent decades. For legal scholars who assume linguistics as communication's primary form, the right to association becomes a legitimate substitution for the right to assembly, and the right to free speech a logical next derivative. In this chapter, however, I turn to Melissa Ziad's circulation as the "ballerina of hope" during the Hirak demonstrations of Algeria to disrupt this shortsighted logic. Her performance draws attention to the role of protest, crowds, and assemblies as a constitutive voice. In contrast to assembly, association—as subsidiary legislation in Algeria and as primary status in the United States—shifts attention away from the corporeal protection intended for assembly toward the ideological and the linguistically related. That is, association implies a desire to *identify with*, but not necessarily a need to *be with*—to share space synchronously. To me, as a dancer and performance studies scholar invested in expressions of the public body, the historical process of conflating assembly with association and, subsequently, speech not only points to the absent attention to the gestural body as sociogenic formation, but to the larger negligence of legal studies to fully appreciate the distinction between body and text, a nuance of performative speech-acts theorized in and by the humanities *ad infinitum*.

Crossing American and Algerian legal histories where assembly's protections have slid from contemporary view, including close-readings of constitutional texts, "Touching Associations" argues for a corporeal understanding of crowds and crowd theory. This attention grounds assembly in the act of gathering together beyond mere associative solidarities. Ziad's international circulation facilitates this recognition—a literal snapshot of the individual intricacies that together coalesce to perform the crowd. In part due to the mob mentality that marks the logic origins of its theorization, crowds have traditionally been framed as impressionable, excitable, hysterical. The body, when assembled in front of law as Ziad's own figure demanded, may acquire violent potential, but fear need not be the default lens of interpretation. In doing so, this chapter follows the legal scholarship of John Inazu to amend the theories of Gustave Le Bon toward more embodied understandings of touch. The balletic ensemble—unlike other scriptings of assembled bodies that also serve as inciteful verbs (to crowd, to mob, to swarm, to gang up on)—casts a peaceable, trained, disciplined tone over the events, its coordination implying prior rehearsal and collective composure.

Bodies materialize laws as much as, if not more than, their written counterpart.[89] Such is the choreo-jurisgenerative nature of law; human rights are no exception. Cued by Sylvia Wynter, the final chapter concludes with an imagination of a more incipient humanism, one in which human rights are rooted in a politics of a disciplined vulnerability. Featuring William Forsythe and Kendall Thomas's *Human Writes* (2005) performance-installation, which both embodies and materializes the many paradoxes of human rights, this chapter calls attention to dramaturgies of vulnerability. I read this work alongside the *Human Rights Tattoo Project*, wherein law is unequivocally rendered fleshed. The conclusion is thus a beginning, an invitation to participate differently in the illiberal project of becoming humanisms. Read together, the chapters of *Legal Moves* embed the reader in corporeal narratives of the police state and epistemological violence, as well as the alternative communities produced, through its historical attention to the choreographies of race and law which traverse the French empire.

For readers in dance studies, I hope that this project invites agency to critically engage in concerns of the legal, beyond the familiar realm of the political where artists and humanities scholars so often remain.[90] For readers in legal studies, I hope it encourages a new perspective on the impact of law, in all of its diversity of application, and provides an alternative vantage point for considering its interpretation. For all, I hope it encourages a method of perceiving justly, outside of the discursive legal classifications which have perpetuated misrecognition and accentuated difference held up, as Sylvia Wynter and others argue, by our disciplinary standards in the Academy.[91] May we begin to locate the absent flesh of law, for those left behind and those yet to come.

PART I

Keeping Score

CHAPTER ONE

CON/SCRIPTING LAW

As European modernity settled into formation and its imperial project began a global rampage, a new attention to the body and its aesthetics emerged as a central concern for the securitization of the nation-state. By the late seventeenth century, a cascade of legal declarations flowed forth in France: in 1685, Louis XIV issued a decree that would set in motion the *Code Noir,* a series of legal codes that mandated conditions of slavery throughout the French colonial empire. The following decade, in 1698, he then issued a contract that provided a retirement pension to Opéra-ballet performers at age 42.[1] A year later, in 1699, at his mandate Raoul Auger Feuillet published *Chorégraphie, ou l'Art de Décrire la Danse* to codify a notational system for the dancing body that oft frequented France's royal courts. Unrelated on the surface, these three texts emerge from a shared era in which French culture and politics, ballet and national identity, dancing bodies and law were inextricably linked. All three of these texts crafted a future via gestural demands on the body: from the innocent call for a dancer's final curtain in retirement to the gruesome calls for corporal punishment contained within the *Code Noir.* Read together, they invite theorization of the myriad of ways that legalese has choreographed State bodies. The entanglement of law and dance emerged as a reciprocal force to conscript modernity's being.

In this chapter, I theorize legal forms—be they laws, codes, constitutions, decrees, or other articulations of juridical authority—as a choreographic project. Both genres share ontologies of corporeal notation, a writing of the body into being.[2] Louis XIV promoted this orientation toward movement as scripture when he invested in an unprecedented intellectual and political project of dance notation.[3] This attention to the notation of dance as a codified system played out as France transitioned from interdependent spaces of customary law to a more coherent, unified system of civil law. Yet this parallel timeline is not often read against the choreographic logics which simultaneously debuted. From this oversight I find it relevant and revealing to think of both together as counterparts to a shared logic, one providing space to rehearse the other. Legal code—in its pluralist genre as discursive *and* corporeal text, an utterance *and* enactment, a score *and* notation, bios *and* logos—established a sociological constitution of France through kinesthetic repertoires.[4]

For the dance scholar, there is a rich and robust tradition for appreciating this royal engagement, as many have attended to the corporeal politics of power, class, and gender manifest in the salles de danse. Entering from a legal studies perspective, other scholars point us toward the sociality of law, inclusive of its performative and kinesthetic dimension as much as its scripted lexicon. Yet the legal scholar does not turn to the choreographic origins of Western dance notation for understanding, although the king did himself, and the dance scholar rarely reaches beyond the political toward the legal.[5] The historical relationship between dance theory and legal form merits its own attention.[6] Each, while seemingly separate in scope and aim, reflects an effort to systematically and strategically define future happenings and imaginations via a codified notation system. Both set out to conscript European modernity through bodily regulation.

These forms converge around disciplinary understandings of the relationship between the body and writing, including vested ontologies of notation, temporal links between movement and its record, and manifest space for improvisation. I return to this historical moment wherein dance and law appear conjoined to ask: *How do temporal politics inform choreography's jurisgenerative and jurispathic potentials, not least as pressing upon understandings of legal interpretation and the authority of a text? What are the implications for understanding legal scores as both scripting and conscripting? How is agency amplified when reframing legalese as a framework of possibility, akin to improvisation and choreographic scores, rather than as a prescriptive and restrictive set of mandates meant to limit? How does rhetoric come to regulate the body even as flesh comes to instantiate its meaning?*

To respond to these questions, the first part of this chapter offers a brief overview of the convergent histories of French legal code and dance notation. I then parse the dance score as separate from dance notation to offer temporal clarity around the choreo-jurisgenerative and choreo-jurispathic. I extend this context to position improvisation as a rehearsal of agency within choreographic codes of law. The chapter concludes by considering a contemporary performance score, *There Might Be Others* by Rebecca Lazier, to imagine another way of configuring relationality between bodies and their scripted futures. Chapter 1 thus sets a theoretical foundation for Part I: "Keeping Score," which read together argues that laws have long operated as a societal score, scripting movements and conscripted citizens into racialized categories of (non)belonging. They therefore lend themselves to choreographic analysis from the methods of dance studies.

I begin with an attention toward the ways in which the body—as courtly dancer or conscripted subject, always both—was written into being through governmental pen. I chose to write of dance scores in lieu of a more capacious term of movement scores to more forcefully bind the disciplines of legal and dance studies, but I welcome a more protean interpretation in each instance. By score, I name the material source of a dance, oft in written prompts distributed between choreographer and dancer but sometimes more symbolically and abstractly cyphered. By dance score, I *do* mean that which scripts any bodily movement, and by dance I *do* mean bodily movement broadly interpreted. To speak of the dancing body, however, in lieu of the moving body, intentionally suggests a refinement—or confinement—at play through learned technique with a particular aesthetic standard, and thus a tension between movement and agency held in a singular figure.

The attention to the score allows me to point to the *process* of being conscripted into State narratives and the *place* where language and action meet, where doctrine becomes animated. With this formulation I intentionally point us toward David Scott's *Conscripts of Modernity*, in which he theorizes conscription as the coercion that obliges Euro-modernity's pre-determined narrative.[7] Like Scott, I too am concerned with the "conceptual problem of political presents and with how reconstructed pasts and anticipated futures are thought in relation to them."[8] In contrast to his commitment to literary genre, however, I invoke frameworks from dance studies, such as the score, to imagine choreographic futures not foreclosed by a particular teleological drive. This focus invites new avenues through which I articulate less rehearsed temporal contours of legal writing and the resulting praxes of its interpretation.

HISTORIES OF THE LEGAL-DANCING BODY

The French project of "juridical humanity" relied on extrajudicial spaces in the construction of Man, including the dance floor as a site of bodily aesthetics and authority.[9] At the height of the First French Colonial Empire, Louis XIV diverted his attention from international affairs to call upon Pierre Beauchamp to articulate dance on paper via a new writing system. It was, after all, in 1662 that Louis XIV declared himself King *and* established the Académie Royale de Danse with the express intention of increasing the homogeneity of French dancers by training new dance masters. As decreed in *Letters Patent of the King* (1662):

> Although the Art of Dance has always been recognized as one of the most honorable and necessary methods to train the body, and furthermore as the primary and most natural basis for all sorts of Exercises, including that of bearing arms, consequently it is one of the most advantageous and useful to our Nobility, as well as to others who have the honor of approaching Us, not only in time of War for our Armies, but even in Peacetime while we enjoy the diversion of our court Ballets.[10]

Slipped into this official discourse, the art of dance, especially court ballet, suggests a militant potential (named in this letter as training to bear arms) but also one of resistance (named as diversion). The desired notational system would be able to relay dances such that they could be interpreted "without need of personal instructions" from a dance master; more sinisterly, they allowed for the uniformed body to be created even when a regulating force was not present in the flesh.[11]

As noble bodies adopted required form in the salles of Versailles as a part of its newly mandated repertoire, France required compliance in the bodies of its subjects elsewhere, too, including overseas territories ruled by the *Code Noir.* The royal investment in baroque dance was not merely an indulgent project of excess and opulence, but a technology of the body, a Foucauldian project before Foucault. Dance masters, after all, were meant "to regulate and give the tone to the whole" of society, as expressed by Duc de Saint-Simon in *The Memoirs of Louis XIV.*[12] The titles dance *master* and slave *master*—in their Janus facing roots of sovereignty and suppression (to master a discipline and to master a body as expressions of dominance)—both imply the restriction of corporeal freedom. Read from this methodological vantage, the royal creation of dance notation and manuals reflects a philosophical project echoed in the use of civil codes to discipline a French public, citizens and subjects alike.[13,14] The coeval production of discipline and authority, exemplified by official documents of the early Enlightenment period across legal and aesthetic practice, transcended boundaries of public and private, stage and street, domestic and overseas. Louis XIV himself embodied this disciplinary crossfade as he demonstrated a relentless, and arguably all-encompassing, fixation with dance. He would feature in many of the ballets which animated his court; Versailles was a veritable theater with dance as the primary act and the Sun King as the *premier danseur.*[15] Baroque aesthetics of the sensuously lavish and overly ornate moved to the dance floor as the absolute figure of Man grasped for global power.

The fêtes of Versailles and its disciplinary practice of decorum propagated an "unwritten constitution of the kingdom."[16] Commissioned by Louis XIV and codified in *Chorégraphie ou l'Art de Décrire la Danse, par Caractères, Figures, et Signes Démonstratifs* (1699), the Beauchamp-Feuillet notational system met the royal demand to regulate the French body politic through written form. Rather than script the more affective and gestural vocabulary of the dancing body, the Beauchamp-Feuillet notational system primarily concerned itself with dictating the spatial and geometric shapes of the body from an aerial point of view—that is, the geographic circulation of the body via "geometric laws of movement," including positions of the feet and six leg movements in coordinated response to music.[17] For example, Figure 1.1 illustrates the flight patterns of different walks that can be done both forward and backward, while the accompanying page details side-steps and the proper placement of the front foot. Other notations at times

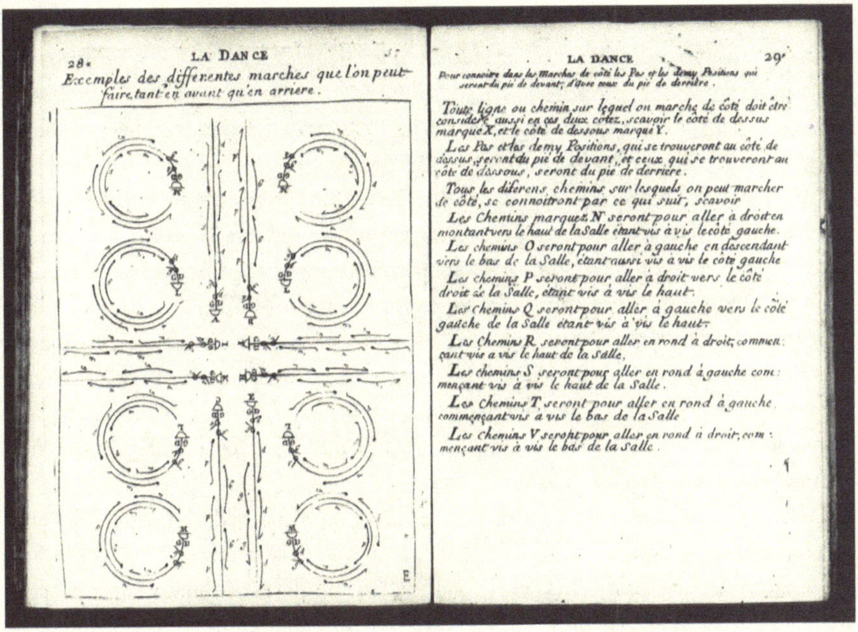

FIGURE 1.1 *Illustrations of Beauchamp-Feuillet notational system. Feuillet, Raoul-Auger, 1659 Or. Recueil De Dances. A Paris: L'auteur, 1709. Image. Retrieved from the Library of Congress.*

include instruction for the upper body, including small flourishes of the wrist, but the focus remains on the spatial politics of the dance floor.[18]

During this era of proto-ballet, and notably the first major effort to record Euro-American concert dance via a written notational system, Louis XIV frequently was seated on high with an aerial view, as the salles of Versailles featured a panopticon arrangement: ballet normalized (as) surveillance.[19] What emerged was a system seemingly as qualified to notate a court dance as a military promenade with a synchronized corps at the heart of both. "Notation hardened dance," writes dance scholar Susan Foster, "giving it a masculine status" as a dominating force that echoed State domination elsewhere.[20] By arguing that the Beauchamp-Feuillet system repeated a colonial imagery in its notation for the dancing body, she convincingly binds the rise of the dance notation system to the political ideology of France's colonial project of expansion. Foster and other dance scholars who write after her influence, however, do not go further to link notation to French legal codes of the same ideology as a symbolically coded order of the State.

I return to the late 1600s when the word *choreography* itself found widespread implementation *and* colonial desires acquired new force.[21] More specifically, I return to the period of baroque dance and its reconstruction, frequently defined as 1660–1750, when ideologies of law, dance, and the body were so clearly entangled by the monarchy.[22] Midpoint between the *homo politicus* (Man1) and *homo economicus* (Man2), this era marks a demi-epistemic revolution in which the rise of dance notation parallels the consolidation of legal logics with vested interest in the representational body. Gestural articulations of decorum rehearsed in the salles de danse and reproduced through dance manuals provided a clear aesthetic referent through which the category of Man could be identified.

While for the contemporary reader, "choreography" more commonly permeates popular discourse, its emergence as a critical concept reflects "a peculiar invention of early modernity, as a technology that creates a body disciplined to move according to the commands of writing."[23] Here the creation of a body reflects a wider "civilizing" project that occurred across legal, political, and socio-genic spheres. The Beauchamp-Feuillet notational system and its provocative line which cleaves the body from presence, "*de la presense du corps*/of the presence of the body," becomes not an anomaly of choreographic attention in legal logic, but a quintessential example of a more foundational inter-articulation.

The desire to conscript a public, to regulate national order, has never been a merely political project. Since the rise of the imperial nation-state, the aesthetic and the legal have been dual frontiers through which modernity choreographs and secures its borders. "Dance notations, like all writing, once confront the law," writes the French critic Laurence Louppe.[24] Dance manuals and the legal codes operated around a shared belief that the body holds social and political capital—for some, the former allowed its accumulation and ascension; for many, the latter precluded its progress, frequently around minoritized lines. Both sought precision in language as a linear instrument between reading and execution. As physical objects, both are visually similar with characteristic calligraphy, engendered with similar symbolic weight. In either case, the state became reliant upon the body's discursive propensity in a twinned ideological project whose shared origin has since faded from view. Such an overlapping history, part and parcel of one regime, foreshadows André Lepecki's more contemporary formulation of "choreo-policing" as the means through which bodies circulate in civil society.[25] But the relationship between choreography, police, and its refusal—what we might triangulate as a mapping of justice—exists well before this twenty-first century identification.

Ballet was hardly monolithic during the seventeenth and eighteenth centuries, and I do not mean to compress it as such. This period saw tremendous change, from early court ballet, to burlesque ballet, to comedy-ballet.[26] Dance historians have further noted the evolving relationship between dance and text throughout this period with text—speech, lyric, poetry, etc.—disappearing from the stage until "textless performances" emerge as the spectacle *du jour*. But the "dance—text differential" in court ballet moves beyond an aesthetic or political project toward a more ideological shift across disciplines, including the legal.[27] At the same time, choreography in France was "frequently likened to, and indeed contrived to suggest, a written text." Dance historian Mark Franko goes on to playfully but critically read *dance as text* and *text as dance* in a reminder of the reciprocal nature of the two: "textural gesture" and "gestural text."[28] I pair these small moments to synthesize historical social inquiries into the relation between movement and language, flesh and word, the ephemeral and the literary, that would structure epistemological orders to come.

More than a social occasion or diversion, this "becoming textual" of the body, its movements, and its coordinated aesthetic practice reflects a deeper logic of French political thought and resultant legal theory.[29] I am reminded of the lore of Thoinot Arbeau, a French cleric of the late sixteenth century who invented an antecedent to the Beauchamp-Feuillet system via his study of Renaissance social dance. His foundational dance manual, *Orchesographie* (1589), features a narrative of a young male lawyer seeking counsel from Arbeau, the priest/dance master. This scene arrives in contemporary theory from time to time, but attention tarries on the alloying of writing with dancing via the newly coined term "orchesographie," as well as the homoerotic relationship of the student and dance master, rather than the disciplinary suturing of the legal prodigy and dance notation.[30] But this tale captures my attention for its unexpected proximity between the legal profession and dance in which the logocentric ranking of disciplines momentarily invert: it is the lawyer who "begs his dance master" for lessons he deems vital to social success, not the embodied bending to the lettered. We have yet to contend fully with how the law receives the reply, how it submits and endows itself to dance. Nevertheless this scene highlights an exchange of dance and law that predates invocations of speech-acts and other contemporary formulations of law and performance.

Beyond the shared attention to conscripted bodies across legal and aesthetic space, French legal tradition allows particular entry into consideration of law as a form of bodily notation given its central feature of written rule as a part of its civil law tradition—the oldest and most widespread in the world.[31] Statutes, codes, and legislation serve as the primary source of legal authority in France, in contrast to jurisdictions primarily governed under local or common law. This value system, reflective of a literary epistemology rooted in the collected authority of the archive proper, reaches across the multiple periods of legal history in France: from periods of *ancien droit* (old French law) to *droit révolutionnaire* (revolutionary or intermediary law) to *droit nouveau* (new law, or as often glossed, Napoleonic law). Now discussed in teleological narratives, the movement across these periods reflects an effort for civil law to cohere toward a unification, rationalization, and centralization of state authority against the more patchwork affair remaindered from feudal society's distributed landscape.[32]

The Napoleonic civil codes emerge as a hallmark of this transition, intended as a consolidated and comprehensive system of law. But the process to extend a notational system for the representational body began long before, including under the Bourbon crown as prototyped via a set of regulatory laws, *La Grande Ordonnance de Procédure Civile* (1667), informally known as the *Code Louis*. This new philosophy of modern civil law is indebted to the contributions of Jean-Baptiste Colbert and Jean-Jacques-Régis de Cambacérès. It was Colbert who drafted the *Ordonnance pour la reformation de la justice* (1667) in an early attempt at a centralized French legal code as well as the *Code Noir* (1685). Cambacérès led the drafting process for the *Code de procedure civile* (1806), as well as *le Code civil des Français* (1804).[33] This genealogy of legal thought extends from the tradition of Roman law, which was prevalent throughout southern France and Paris during the medieval period (prior to the unification of the northern *droit couturier* and southern *droit écrit*) to the contemporary moment, still founded on this scribal effort. The period not only reflects the emergence of civil law's ambition as a uniform and unifying text, but the process itself included an immense effort to document existent legal practices. Phrased otherwise, it was a project of vested notation, in which new epistemologies were required for transferring gestural acts and performative histories into written form just as dance too moved into the record books.

This wider history shares a commitment to the letter of the law as the source of legal authority. A monovalent attention to the codes as a methodical writing system dominates the historiographic narrative of its significance. What slips from view, then, is 1) the unruly, incomplete, and impossible nature of the codes as even the written remains slippery, and 2) the equally pervasive ordering of bodies, that is, the way these codes were drafted alongside adjacent philosophies of dance notation as scholars from across disciplines and elite society grappled with articulating an aesthetics of national identity through the written delineation of corporeal acts. Taken at the macro scale and within the spirit of an illiberal humanism, the evolution of the French legal system reflects a shared project of developing a dance notation system: facilitating the transition of a feudalistic, medieval state replete with plural and competing legal bodies toward the consolidated logic of a more modern nation state with a coherent body politic performing a singular legal system.

SCRIPTED GESTURES, CORPOREAL WRITING, AND CHOREOGRAPHIC RECORD

> *La loi ne dispose que pour l'avenir ; elle n'a point d'effet rétroactif.*
> [The law ordains for the future only; it has no retrospective operation].
>
> —CODE CIVIL DES FRANÇAIS, *éd. Originale et seule officielle, 1804*

The conscripting force of law and its temporalities shift as bodily notation emerged as an evolving tool of the French empire. To understand how legal forms operate as choreographic force, I distinguish between dance notation and dance score. Both have been confounded into a shared paradox of archival futurity, a concept that points to the unruly keep of the ephemeral. The perceived temporal order between writing and performance slips, no longer unidirectionally fixed with causality. While this distinction is a technical one poised for the dance scholar invested in debates of temporality, it also provides an alternative entry into debates of the letter of the law contra the spirit of the law. In a special issue of *Dance Research Journal,* Mark Franko formulates the idea of "archival futurity" to encapsulate the oxymoronic sentiments of reconstruction in dance as simultaneously preserving the past while also prompting future movement. For Franko and the issue's contributors, the archival futurity of dance roots itself in a "radical reconsideration of the score: what the score actually is and what can be done with it."[34] A leading authority on dance notation, the Dance Notation Bureau, offers an even more elastic ambition with its expressed motto, "[p]reserving the past, enriching the present and securing the future."[35] This dictum points toward the multiple temporalities envisioned in the use of dance notation that parallels intent for civil law traditions. While I appreciate the generative entanglement of past and present, record and regeneration bound up in written records of dance, it remains necessary to have language for the differing properties of each, for what the score actually is beyond its polemical nature.

To find logic within this contradiction of archival futurity that at once points forward and backward on the horizon of possibility, I choose to make a distinction between dance notation *as retrospective* and dance score *as anticipatory* as a means to signal temporal difference in the constructed relation between text and body. It simultaneously invites a distinction in the relationship between the law as choreo-jurisgenerative (in the case of a dance score) or the law as choreo-jurispathic (in the case of a dance notation). If other scholars productively work against such a codified division between the document and the event, carelessly or intentionally interchanging the terms of notation and score, I hope that the distinction can serve a larger purpose in the context of this book for theorizing that which instigates movement—suggested here as legal prose—and an ability to respond.[36] While I respect that not all choreographers and scholars have followed this divide, one which is not impervious to chiasmatic crossings, I suggest it here for the sake of clarity (rather than corrective) in understanding the prefigurative conditions of law. Extending this logic to decolonial processes, David Scott's project of conscripted modernities similarly asks us to "re-think the narratological relation between colonial pasts and post-colonial futures."[37] With this in mind, I resist a symmetrical mapping of dance notations onto colonial pasts and dance scores onto postcolonial futures. Rather, the nuance of dance studies allows an entry point to resist a teleological interpretation of colonial time and its legacies.

Looking back, dance notation presents itself as record, archive, and publication, a document of that which has been (danced). Euro-American dance notation formally emerged in dance manuals to codify European courtly-social dance, including contributions from Jean-Georges Noverre, Thoinot Arbeau, Pierre Rameau, as well as Pierre Beauchamp and Raoul Auger Feuillet.[38] Later dance notation would take on more capacious forms.[39] Notable evolutions include that of Rudolph Laban, author of arguably the most well-known system of recording dance which emerged in the 1900s from fraught mid-century nationalist politics. Laban's notation is notoriously detailed in its ability to document weight transfer and momentum of the body with attention to space, time, and flow; geometric "alphabets" spell out movement series in careful ledgers of somatic units.[40] Working from the performing arts more broadly, the nineteenth-century orator François Delsarte catalogued a new system of bodily expression as related to gesture and emotion. His systematic development of bodily laws, which echo and influence instructions for proper oration in the courtroom, would go on to motivate American modern dance, including Ted Shawn's publication on the method, *Every Little Movement* (1954).[41] Julie Stone Peters presents the importance of bodily decorum as part of legal oration in medieval Europe, suturing Delsarte's career to a larger history of oration, bodily significance, and law.[42] These systems of bodily meaning, diverse as they are, point to corporeal codes rooted in European cultural legacy *and* corresponding logics in legal systems.

Dance notation functions as a choreo-jurispathic means of retrospective documentation and regimented discipline of the body-yet-to-come. It orders, standardizes, and consolidates: replication as a means to be exact. At the most fundamental level, dance notation functions as a note-taking record, the stenographic ledger of a danced movement, not dissimilar to the way written forms of music operate as a series of instrumentalizations meant to be executed for replication. Notation, figured as such, begets an orientation of futures past in which the "horizon of possible futures" wanes, collapses toward a precedent of what has already been.[43] In many ways, dance notation returns us to the double logic articulated by Rebecca Schneider, in which "the live is a troubling trace of a precedent text and so (herein lies the double trouble) comes afterward, even arguably remains afterward, as a *record* of the text *set in play*."[44] Attentive to these finicky temporalities of the live, dance notation offers a means of recapturing and even reenacting the past, for example, in the efforts to reconstruct Vaslav Nijinsky's lost *Sacre du Printemps*, the case study par excellence of lost writings of dance in the Euro-American concert tradition.[45] Writing about its retrospective value, Stephanie Jordan confirms that "[n]otation provides an analysis of movement that is a *prerequisite* for analysis and interpretation according to chosen frameworks."[46] Notation thus captures spectral traces of the corporeal residue of movement, a sort of ghost-catching that can be both playful and haunting.[47]

A dance score, in contrast, suggests future movements in a logic of choreo-jurisgenerativity. At its essence, it "leads to the creation of new work."[48] In a Derridean sense, the score "calls into question the coming of the future;" originalism fades in favor of more living forms.[49] By the 1960s, the practice of postmodern choreographers such as Trisha Brown, Yvonne Rainer, Simone Forti, and Steve Paxton increasingly engaged avant-garde score-based works to model alternative socialities. Robert Cover makes this connection between dance scores, law, and jurisgenerativity explicit when he writes that "[l]aw may be viewed as a system of tension or a bridge *linking a concept of a reality to an imagined alternative*—that is, as a connective between two states of affairs, both of which can be represented in their normative significance only through the devices of narrative."[50] The score, as law or dance, writes toward an imagined future, one animated and received by a wider public, audience, or society at large.[51]

The Choreographers' Score: 2020, a series of commissioned works from twenty-six choreographers, illustrates the many forms a score can take, often more abstract in form and function than dance notation. Curated by Kristy Edmunds in response to the suspended possibility of live performance during the height of the COVID pandemic, this collection features scores from luminary choreographers including Ann Carlson, Lucinda Childs, Deborah Hay, Ralph Lemon, and Alice Sheppard.[52] The series as a whole exemplifies the potential of a score as a site of activation, from directives of "Gather Here" to linear prose to bold colors left up to interpretation [see Figure 1.2]. Molissa Fenley wrote on a legal pad, unintentionally anticipating my coupled argument of law and scores. Unlike dance notation, which often attempts precision in the interpreted relationships between time, space, and action to allow for repetition and replication (in a codified reading practice from left to right or top to bottom and corresponding relationships to sequence, cardinal planes, or other fixed laws of physics, for example), dance scores frequently and intentionally abstract and obscure in their meaning: graphic shapes and patterns, splashes of color, and scattered words might inspire movement generation, but hardly conscript regulated bodily acts.

The open invitation to interpretation extends a sense of agency, generativity, and individualism to those inhabiting the score not bound in the politics of dance notation. The stanzas of Shamel Pitts's commissioned entry, "Touch of Red," resemble lines of a journal entry that call for "Help(!)" as "air swells and boils the blood" in an exchange of the formal and the regulated for the informal and the intimate. Movement can be openly imagined in response: *the rib cage freezes at the top of its expanse, arms flail out, smacking the wall behind.* Fragments layer in Zoe Scofield's contribution: "dizzying, swirly, whirl," "accelerate, rotate," annotate the page alongside six silhouetted figures each posed with heel popped and back slightly arched. These scores present not a disciplinary directive but an affective pool pregnant with interpretative possibility. They set the tone, not the conditions, of future action. In the score, the body is yet to come. Acknowledged but not present, we can prepare for its arrival.

My invocation of dance scores, then, differs from previous scholarship on law and music(al scores) in which theories of interpretation, authenticity, and originalism supersede those of activation, generation, and exploration.[53] When discussing authenticity and the Early Music Movement from a Western classical perspective, for example, legal scholars Sanford Levinson and J.M. Balkin rely upon a traditional interpretation of the score as a source from which musicians attempt accuracy, reconstruction, and replication (what I differentiate as notation).[54] A libretto becomes bound to historical articulations of "the best and most representative executants of the day" and legal studies as a hermeneutical-sealed practice reigns.[55] In contrast to this annotative sensibility that aligns more closely with the genre of dance notation, a dance score as a catalyst toward future potentials itself enables meaning-making rather than a record for meaning already-made. This temporal shift from notation to score allows us to move away from a language of interpretation rooted in textual fidelity towards that of responsibility, response-ability, and the agency which glides between. Consequently, we might view the dance score as responsive to values in the present rather than restricted to codified norms of the historical past that may linger as prejudicial rhetoric. If not careful, latent bias can manifest itself through the constant return to the past: *pre*-judicial thought animated as *post*-judicial action.

Consider the ways in which dance scores parallel theorization of legislation, in contrast to the linear temporalities of dance notation and originalism. As put forward by Jeremy Bentham in 1782, legislation can be summarized as:

> an *assemblage of signs* declarative of a volition conceived or adopted by the Sovereign in a State, *concerning the conduct* to be observed in a certain case by a certain person or class of persons, who in the case in question are or are supposed to be subject to his power; such volition trusting for its accomplishment to the *expectation of certain events* which it is intended such declaration should upon occasion be a means of bringing to pass, and the prospect of which it is intended should act as a motive upon those whose *conduct is in question* (emphasis added).[56]

Signs, conduct, events, and expectation converge for both the law and the score in this early modern formulation, with power and sovereignty implicit in each. That is, legislation and legal order can be reduced to, or most simply understood as, an interpretative set of *signs* that direct the *action* of a member of the public toward an anticipated *outcome* based on the authority of its creator.

This definition reads as a choreographic one, not least through the emphasis on conduct facilitated not only through language itself but a wider set of signs. Dance scores take this to an extreme, as the set of signs possible for a score can be abstract, obtuse, and playfully obscure [see again Figure 1.2]. But this extreme reminds us of the diffuse, omnipresent space of law that often exceeds the imagination in legal studies. Summarized, the dance score functions as a futuring, a catalyst, and an activation of a set of possibilities. So too does law generate an idiom for future gesture, if its ontology has shifted over time and under different regimes.

I recognize the fundamental elasticity of these categories. According to the Dance Notation Bureau, a dance notation presents the virtue of being simultaneously a mode of historical dance preservation and reconstruction, while also being the documentation that first made choreographic copyright possible. Its motto points to this multi-temporal ideal. Yet the rest of its mission is strikingly unidirectional: "[dance notation] allows the dances to continue to be performed long after the lifetime of the artist," and in the words of choreographer Anna Sokolow, allows for new dances to be made "without fearing for the life of earlier pieces."[57] Although a document itself might be both notation and score, bodied orientations shift it toward either a document requiring replication (named here as dance notation) or a document inviting yet-unrealized futures (named here as dance score). This is the distinction I point to when reading legal codes as either notation or score—a set of fixed ideals stabilizing past behaviors, or more undetermined directives rehearsing multiple possible enactments, determined by the authors, actors, interpreters, and judges alike.

While juridical thought holds careful and contested scrutiny to law as notation, the wider public often acts in ad hoc, improvisatory, and strategic ways under the more unruly logic of law as score. After all, our quotidian gestures remain bound in the legal scores that influence our choice in movement, including supplementary choices of costuming (e.g., public decency laws), music (e.g., public disturbance laws), and lighting cues (e.g., traffic and vehicle lights). Consider that Bruno Latour summarizes the temporal processes of French law and its epistemologies as "always consist[ing] in an *a posteriori* reconstruction of the rational core of the discipline."[58] What disappears, survives, and reappears—whether ideologies, subjectivities, or praxis of the body—functions as a subsequent excursion of these lawful texts that score the future for the conscripted body.

The temporal order which distinguishes between dance notation and dance scores gives entry into the violating problem-space of law.[59] There is an improper but important parallelism between law as dance notation and law as dance score, as I have framed it, and law-making and law-preserving violence, as Walter Benjamin critiques it. Legal violence, perpetuated under natural law and left uninterrogated, evolved as the legalization of violence. This extends, for Benjamin, to critical examples of the death penalty and the police wherein necropolitical consequence confirm jurispathic order.[60] But following the ambivalent temporalities of notation/score, the emergence of new legal code can simultaneously be read as a founding event, a discrete flashpoint that inaugurates a new order, *and* as the culminating crystallization of past repertoires of civil society already well-rehearsed. Score or notation, process or event, means or ends; temporalities of legal code confound again and again in a global game of call and response. The

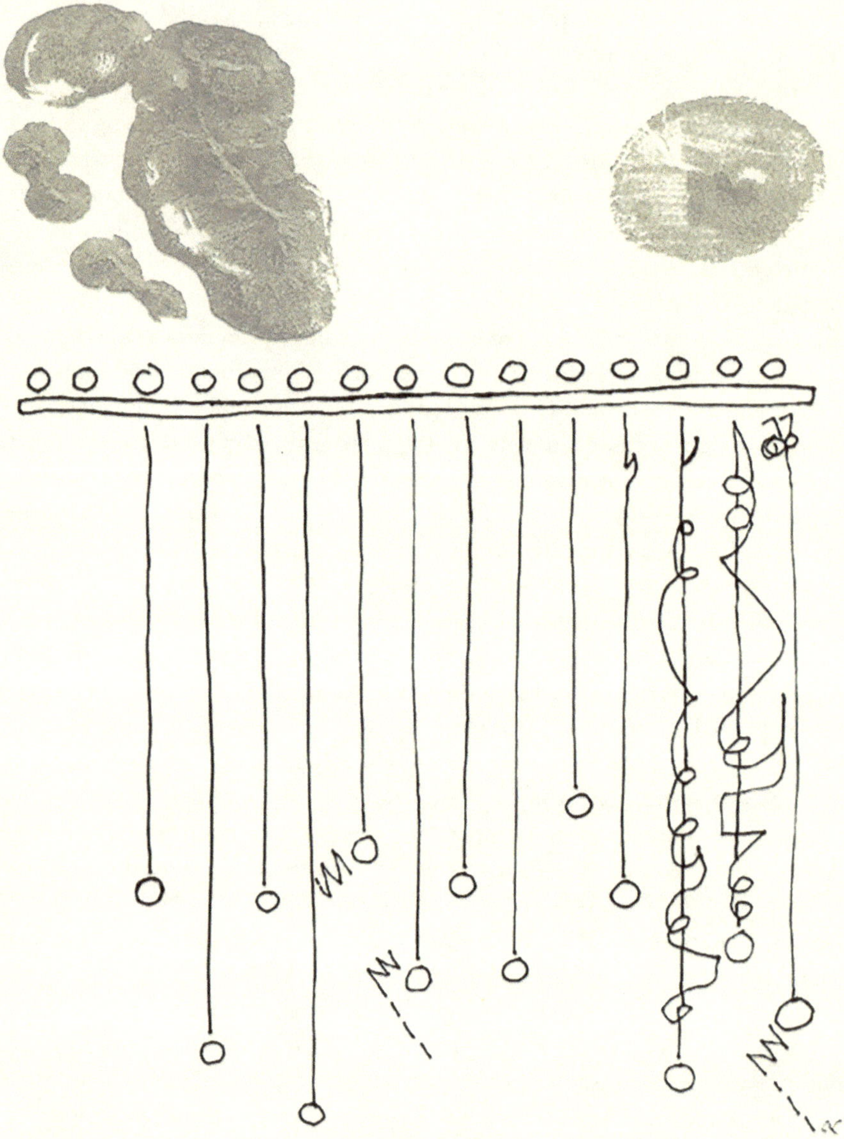

FIGURE 1.2 *Above: "Untitled," by Ann Carlson. Next Page, Top: "Untitled," by Zoe Scofield; Next Page, Bottom: "Touch of RED," by Shamel Pitts.* The Choreographers' Scores: 2020 *was commissioned and published by UCLA's Center for the Art of Performance in partnership with Pomegranate Arts, Lapis Press, and YoungArts. Courtesy of the artists.*

FIGURE 1.2 *(Continued)*

ambiguation names an uncertain relationship between body and text, flesh and word, nestled within genealogies of the choreo-graphic. Benjamin alludes to this corporeal foundation when he names the humanity of legal subjects as "bodily life . . . vulnerable to injury" in an emphasis of mortality and motility held in the absent flesh of law.[61]

While Benjamin's writing only alludes to the relationality between performance and law, by the end of the twentieth century, legal scholar Bernard Hibbitts surfaces a more direct comparison:

> The dynamism of performance is arguably reflected in the performative inclination to think of law not as things but as acts, not as rules or agreements but as processes constituting rule or agreement. A performative contract, for instance, is not an object, but a routine of words and gestures. A witness to a contract testifies not to the identity or correctness of a piece of power, but to a phenomena seen and heard. Likewise, members of performance cultures tend to think of justice not as something that simply is, but rather something that is done.[62]

Or I would argue, it is something yet to be done—a future action in response to a scripted formula, a temporal logic of the dance score. I linger with Hibbitts's careful use of "inclination" to describe the performative processes of law—not a directive or a fore-given, but a potential to trust in a way of knowing developed elsewhere. It returns us to a more fundamental understanding of jurisprudence as knowledge of law or skill in a legal area, honed and developed as a kinesthetic process, ongoing and ever-incomplete. In the practice of execution, then, emerges an equivocal space for response, a constant need to respond again to keep the authority of the text at play.

AN INDETERMINATE THEORY OF IMPROVISATION

The choreo-jurisgenerative logics of a score open an indeterminate relationship to the future. The dance score, now understood as distinct from dance notation, invites a politics of improvisation into the legal. With the future no longer prescripted but indeterminate, space emerges to explore, negotiate, interpret, or imagine otherwise. As Bruno Latour dramatizes in his ethnography of the French *Conseil d'état*: "An abyss suddenly opens up before the eyes of the researcher. Codes, with their clarity and elegant certainty, are no more: the commissioner of the law, whose voice acquires greater subtlety, enters into the infinitely more intricate fabric of the interpretation."[63] What to do? That is, what to do when we understand even the most textual of forms to contain an implicit plurality and porosity of paths not yet determined?[64] How do methods of interpretation shift, and for whom?

Improvisation occurs when we allow ourselves to understand form outside the jurispathic logics of notation. Movement improvisation trains the imagination as much as the body (unlike other dance techniques, such as ballet, in which exacting replication suggests mastery). Dancers are cued by qualitative directives: "initiate movement from your ear," "travel as if in a world without gravity," or "spiral." From a singular directive, dancers are tasked to respond expansively, imaginatively, uniquely (rather than conforming or replicating, as desired in accurate reconstructions of dance notation). Much of the work of improvisation emerges from the identification of the full range of potential (options) rather than from the execution of the movement itself. Trained to move openly in response to a given directive, the improvisor learns to find possibilities to move otherwise.[65] More than an articulation of the relationship between movement and politics, improvisation names the generative space of interpretation that shifts between writing, movement, and law. Rules are acknowledged, received, perceived, refused, reported, and reimagined. These are not errant acts; the improviser understands the consequences. Whether finding alternative rhythms internal to the body or rehearsing new edges of agency within jurisprudential space, improvisation breathes with calculated intelligence.

There is particular potency in the way in which Fred Moten legitimizes the rigor (and rigorous resistance) of improvisation within embodied legal contexts when asking if we might consider imagination as not "lawless but lawful."[66] For many, nowhere is this more clear than the fugitive performance of Harriet Jacobs.[67] She incarnates how legal actors—subjects and subjected alike—find ways to keep the future at play under conditions of duress. *To steal away*, to make *nothing out of something*.[68] Jacobs's fugitive flight from scenes of fleshly violence began with seven years in hiding nearby. Cloistered in an attic, she carved a physical space, a "loophole of retreat," outside the slave-legal system.[69] Her pause became a jurisgenerative moment as she entered her life into evidence. The performance of her absented self, strategically withdrawn, gave way to an abolitionist cause.[70] Jacobs's improvisation produced a legal provision: an alternative future whose ethics require (re)address. The constant return to her remarkable life acts, across decades and disciplinary gulfs, confirms its generative and generational performance.

I do not mean to suggest a false utopia by thinking of the law as a score. For some, creativity emerges from a space of limitation. But under the felt restrictions of law and anticipated discipline of law enforcement, creating otherwise emerges out of forced necessity. The acute pressures of the legal system override such an artistic point of view and keep the score in perpetual imbalance. To find movement from within constraint does not imply an infinite range of motion. It also does not reduce the possible violence of the constraint. For Jacobs, her pathway to freedom—now frequently glorified or romanticized as fugitive achievement—stilled for seven hard spent years in self-confinement. Her kinesthetic, durational score consisted of a practice of concealment and silence that contradicts the liberal values of freedom, liberty, and expression so often mapped onto movement's potential.[71] These terms are not unconditional; they each have expressly legal limits. Yet as dance practitioners *have* found opportunity, potentiality, and even possibility from the "tight places" of a score, so too can the hailed body locate alternative value systems of (non)performance that rupture forth from a pre-given future and challenge dominate, jurispathic modes of interpretation.[72]

Choreographer mayfield brooks gives fleshed form to this critical generativity through their praxis *Improvising While Black*, which lives in the "visceral felt moment" that profiles even as it invites.[73] As performance practice and movement research, *IWB, e ye double you be,* underscores a being in the world conditioned by the choreographic frames of legal codes that structure daily acts, routines, and rituals as quotidian as driving. brooks acknowledges that "I cannot escape the warped ontology of blackness, but I can shapeshift in and out of the warp. I can transform my own expectation of myself and live in the immersion of a beautifully improvised dance."[74] This praxis critically confronts the ways in which the score (violently) assumes a positionality—*while black*—forcing flesh in front of the body. *Their torso rides invisible pistons, pumping up and down, up and down, in cadence with their audibly labored breath. The hiss of the exhale presses their arms out, as if releasing pressure in a steam engine. Silver fabric refracts the light off of their partner, Mlondi Zondi, upstage left.*[75] If Moten's theory of improvisation binds blackness and performance in the break, the cut, brooks shifts the demand by dancing "in the hold": improvisation as a kinesthetic means to call attention to the nadir in the structure and its ancestral figurations, what Hortense Spillers wrote as the "enforced state of the breach" that arises from vestibular cultural formation.[76] The performance is not a way out, but a demand to look again, to return to the indeterminate somewhere between past and future if not quite present.

Following the imperative of contract law, Sora Han sutures improvisation to nonperformance as that "which cannot be contracted . . . but is nevertheless a legal form of being."[77] Her reading of *Betty's Case* (1857), which turns on the perceptions of contractual freedom for Betty, a Tennessee woman who elected to remain enslaved even after the court ruled her to have free will, inverts linkages between blackness and performance by inserting nonperformance as the "radically indeterminable" and "always present fugitivity."[78] Betty's refusal of the freedom to perform, to not perform freedom, defines the nonperformance of blackness as she refused to re-body her flesh into the anti-black logics of an abolitionist liberalism.[79] The disorienting logics fundamental to contact improvisation wherein destabilized orientations produce sites of learning, including as rehearsed in mayfield brooks's *IWB* practice, turns on its head: it is the judge as the score's arbiter who is left disoriented, not the performer.[80]

Contact or contract, the law presses against improvisation as nonperformance: a contraction of the flesh held tight. For Han, it is the unanticipated return to slavery that exceeds all comprehension from the legal and its desires for legal personhood. For Moten, it is the fugitive flight out that begins in stillness which gives rise to the outlaw. Across both opposing vectors of motility, it is the kinesthetic pathways, the movement potentials, which exist outside of legal reason and ground improvisation as a choreo-jurisgenerative theory even for no-bodies.

Improvisation traditionally denotes the simultaneity of performance and composition to name that which is generated in the beat of the live. Dance scholars, however, chart a longer shadow of production that challenges this immediacy and decouples the facile alignment of improvisation with naturalized notions of spontaneity. Movement improvisation instead encompasses the critical invention and transmission of corporeal techniques, structures, and body knowledges as a learned practice that performs alternatives/unwritten futures. Improvisation arrives from tremendous preparation. The temporal frame shifts from the immediate to the processual as improvisational success stems from movement generation rooted in preparation, not reckless impulsiveness.[81] Legal frameworks invests in this nuance, as the discernment of premediated acts of violence turns on the legibility of bodily acts in relation to its temporal choreographic construction. This orientation is critical to understanding Betty's decision as a calculated refusal, not an irrational anomaly improvised in the moment.

Not every application of the law opens toward the improvisatory; the choreo-jurisgenerative should not be read as synonymous with progress. Consider how "No Human Involved" articulates an alternative power of jurisgenerative grammars from a vernacular internal to law enforcement agents, in a reminder that the mappings of lawless and lawful, inside and outside, can be crossed. All sides of power are pressed into acute moments of improvisation, not just those performing from the undercommons. At the time of Louis XIV, for example, the proximity between dance and improvisation itself was an improper aesthetic. "Anyone who has studied baroque dance in the studio under the teacher's watchful eye," writes Franko, "can testify that it allows little or no place for spontaneity. The royal body dancing was made to *represent itself as if remachined* in the service of an exacting coordination . . . It was an early modern techno body."[82] European modernity crafted itself as a tightly conscripting present. But the future remains indeterminate, and the fugitive nonperformance of law continues to improvise otherwise.

Improvisation, as unruly as its ontology may be, synthesizes an alternative way of knowing and being beneath law's choreo-jurisgenerativity. Allaine Cerwonka and Liisa Malkki's *Improvising Theory*, for example, presents an intentional conflation of the intellectual jurisdictions between anthropology and jazz tradition, on the one hand, and collaboration and solitary reflection, on the other. Ethnography, she argues, like the non-literary traditions of performance and dance studies, maintains a nervous condition of perceived illegitimacy as it seemingly operates in the interstitial space of the live, ceremonial, enacted, embodied, ritual of being.[83] Centering improvisation as method, Malkki presents an interpretative approach to anthropology of the live as "simultaneously a critical theoretical practice, a quotidian ethical practice, and an improvisational practice."[84] Legal scholar Sara Ramshaw's argument, *Justice as Improvisation,* returns us full circle to the legal as she argues for the inevitable use of improvisation by judges and other legal authorities in positions to execute justice. Both legitimize improvisation in disciplined spaces of knowledge.

Ethnographies of French legal tradition already contain a gesture towards the expanded methods of improvisation. Latour reflects on the ambiguities and moral uncertainties contained within French immigration law. In a particular case of migratory expulsion in which the plaintiff's life is at stake (as repatriation consequates the death penalty), he notes the necessity of:

> degrees of freedom in the definition of our capacity of judgment, an aptitude to *unbind* which permits us only to *bind again* without attaching ourselves in any durable manner either to the brilliantly coloured multitude of external events to which we have little access or to the strict application of rules and texts which are never sufficient to define our task. If they [legal actors] consider themselves to be "too bound" they will never be able to exercise their faculty of judgment: they must then, through all this labour, effect some kind of "unbinding." Only then will they be able to stick to their position.[85]

The ability to perceive differently, unbounded by convention, tradition, or precedent, shares in its imaginative force the skills fostered through improvisation. Although Latour's account of society and political commitments diverges from my own, the critical grammars of the nonmodern which precede his socio-legal ethnography re-articulate the skepticism toward scientific authority expressed by so many scholars. Phrased otherwise, the revelation of improvisation in law extends beyond my own humanities center toward the social scientist.

I gather these wide-ranging scholars, artists, and histories here, admittedly poly in their philosophical and political views, to stress that scores create the necessary conditions for bodily improvisation, for a space to think, act, and move otherwise. It equally informs those acting in the name of law—the lawyer, prosecutor, judge, and jury—who "tend to consider themselves to be too bound" by the parameters of law.[86] The requisite shift in legal perspective is important. By understanding the law as score to be endowed with improvisatory demands, we finesse a more nuanced and grounded appreciation for the jurisgenerative practices which inevitably result. This shift emerges from the indeterminate relationship between the score and its enactment, wherein disciplined training, improvisatory practice, and individual (non)performance meet.

ON ONE CONDITION

I conclude with Rebecca Lazier's *There Might Be Others* (2014–2017), a performance which mobilizes a relational property within the choreo-jurisgenerativity of scores. Commissioned by New York Live Arts, *There Might Be Others* draws upon an intentionally international cast, including communities from Canada, Poland, Turkey, and the United States.[87] Through strategic use of a score, the performance event builds an open public of participation as it invites performers who might have learned the score in dislocated space-times. The score itself features forty-four modules and related instructions for structuring movement patterns, becoming iterative in its potential of "emergent composition" in real-time.[88] Each module contains a complimentary score for twelve musicians, composed by Dan Trueman in collaboration with performance ensembles Sō Percussion and Mobius Percussion. The structure calls for attention to tone, rhythm, humor, labor, distribution, and style. "Play with dominance. But also question these roles," suggests the score in the module "Box Drag: Dance." The question of agency and response-ability remains at play as the cast negotiates a new social order via collective action.

The indeterminate exchanges for the conditional. The title, *There Might Be Others,* repeats a politics at once inclusive and expansive, in which scores have the potential to open toward manifold possibilities in spite of prescribed notions of the (con)scripted body. In its acknowledgment that there *might* be others, unaccounted for or intentionally absent, the score confronts concepts of stable borders, porous, shifty, and ever in flux. The score invites inhabitation by others, with or without the explicit permission of its makers. *There Might Be Others* was published as an open-source document, becoming a text and a performance, an artifact and an activation "for any reiterations, reimagines, and repurposings."[89] Its politics are distributive, diffuse, and, arguably, democratic.

There Might Be Others scores a process for relationality that situated myself as one amongst many. The task was a collective one. Inhabiting this score myself in 2018, I grew attentive to the bodies around me.[90] The dance progresses as the cast moves through modules, allowing no more than three different activations to be performed at a time. Embedded in this shifting polycule, I learned to monitor (witness, surveil) gestures on stage so as to ensure my participation complied with the rules of the game, exiting an action if I realized the rest had moved on. Having been initiated to the score in one short morning for a university demonstration, I found inhabiting its contours dizzying, disorienting, and overwhelming in its potentials. Cast members begin with the shared directive, "begin seeing." In this first "seeing score," we entered with the express purpose of creating a responsive community. It was also "a mechanism to suggest a mode of viewership for the audience."[91] This process of active witnessing materialized an enacted sense of belonging, as imagined solidarities became both visiblized and internalized. And so I shifted into a newly heightened state of awareness of the relationship between my body and the laws at play that both motivated and limited the set of actions available to me. The newly sensitized attunement toward being-with reminds me that the relationships created exist not only between the performer and the text, the citizen and the law, but between the participants themselves: the cast, the public, the constituents.

What we see in *There Might Be Others*, from both the vantage of the audience and embedded within, is the creation of something from nothing; a community emerges where there was not one before. *Moments of unity surprise for their coordination. The in-sync toss of a leg across the cast produces a sign of the dancers' long training in the performance of live scores and spontaneous coordination. A single line stretching across the stage emerges from the unpattern of scattered bodies. Listening is seen; watching is felt.* The performance scores a rhythm of relationality made visible to the public in a way not otherwise apparent.[92]

The score challenges us to imagine this coalition, felt, choreographed, and put on full display. This shift from the indeterminate to the conditional, the singular to the collective, counters the absolutism seeded in the early modern civil code. At the time of Louis XIV, ordonnances were imagined as a direct line to the king, a vertical trajectory of proximity (or distance) through which a ruler could control his subjects. Louis XIV began his various proclamations, edicts, declarations, ordinances, and decrees of colonial violence with a future-facing address: *À tous presens et avenir* (*to all present and to come*). In contrast to this self-aggrandizing presentation that places the Sun King at the center of the universe, *There Might Be Others* diffuses that hold to gesture out to others omni-absent, unnamed, and unknown. Through the evolution of dance scores and notation presented above, we arrive here, a space where horizontal lines of relationality feature with equal prominence as opposed to the aerial view of surveillance which defined Versailles.

Participation in *There Might Be Others* reflects how methods of dance can intervene within legal theory: the ability to process the abstract, a means of honing attentions toward the corporeal, and a recognition that the presence of rules—legally-binding or otherwise—scripts realities and forecloses possibilities. Through the scaffolded sensing and attunements, I felt the directive of Katherine McKittrick settle into my being: a "realization of the living, then, is a *relational* act and practice" that "must be imagined as inviting *being human as praxis* into our purview which envisions the human as verb, as alterable, as relational, and necessarily dislodges the naturalization of dysselection."[93]

The work challenges normative ideas surrounding who is constituted through a singular, founding document.[94] This extends to the drafting process itself, as the performers were integral to the movement research and listed in the program as "in collaboration with." I am reminded of the ongoing initiative of Légifrance, an online platform committed to "the public service for the diffusion of law" and which contains the codes, constitutional texts, and legislative files of France since 2002, as it similarly diffuses its legal score against barriers to access that might otherwise restrict engagement. I wonder how I might relate differently to the legal scores which structure my everyday if I had participated in their formation, not just their re-articulation. But I do not mean to overstate this comparison. In the dance, I could exit the score at any moment, refuse to participate without significant consequence. There was no possibility for nonperformance of a given past or prescripted future because a binding contract did not exist.

For legal scholars, theorists, and movers needing to unlearn or unbind a narrow process of judgement, one might learn from *There Might Be Others*: the score teaches us a new orientation toward laws and the potential for the body to respond, and respond differently, "leaving us to imagine their interaction and shape it at the same time: to dream or to act."[95]

> There might be other instructions...
> There might be other scores...
> There might be other systems...
> There might have been other versions performed...
> There might be more.[96]

May we continue to allow for such indeterminacy and unknowing in spaces as codified as the legal sphere, where rules are taken as absolutes and verdicts are issued with supreme authority. *There might be more.*

This chapter has sought multiple aims: 1) to establish a historical record of the shared and entangled logics of the law and the choreographic dating back to Louis XIV as civil law became a unified norm for France, 2) to set up the distinction between dance notation and dance scores as legal interpretation similarly follows temporal logics of choreo-jurispathic and choreo-jurisgenerative variation, and 3) to introduce space for improvisation, indeterminacy, and relationality within these debates. Each text, be it notation or score, albeit in different scales and contexts, puts forward the body as matter and mattering, beyond its political rights of citizen and Man. The pathways provide alternative entry into our understanding of the function of a given law: as prerogative, as arbiter, as source, as guardrail, as obligation, as inspiration.

The jurisgenerativity of scores reminds us that the future remains open, indeterminate, and subject to interpretation. So often debates surrounding legal interpretation exist primarily in juridical spaces of hallowed courtrooms, sanctioned classrooms, and prestigious law review journals. They extend primarily to scholars, judges, prosecutors, and legislators clad in authoritative fabrics. The jurisgenerative body, however, frames it otherwise, as a more diffuse set of interlocutors ever contributing to the score. It extends, playfully yet critically, our pre-given understanding of who participates in such acts of interpretation.

Law lives in the body and moves through the flesh; it shifts, tumbles, hides, reveals, conscripts, expels, and stills. It choreographs. I hope that our methods might shift in order to better keep the score.

CHAPTER TWO

FLESHING LEGALITY

The scene shifts to 1720 Martinique where colonial conquest laps at the shore. A tattooed "R" under a ducal crown marks Donatien, the protagonist in *Les Épaves* (1838), a novella by Charles Fanny Reybaud, as known property. This scene of recognition transforms Donatien from an *épave*—a slave "who belongs to no one" and thus remains subject to sale under the *Code Noir*—to proprietorship by Cécile, an emergent love interest whose family name shares the enfleshed insignia.[1] The auctioning of Donatien comes to an immediate halt. In an execution of justice based on a technicality of legal code, the pair unites, protected from the pending sale. The scene will shift again toward a more liberated future through yet another invocation of the *Code Noir,* but I begin here in this moment wherein not only does law become a plot device, but flesh becomes fact: "*la preuve en est écrit sur son bras* (the proof of which is written on his arm)."[2] Branded in natal origin, the body speaks back through memory of the flesh. Arrested, assaulted, and auctioned, Donatien's future was prescripted to violence as his stigmatized subjecthood slid toward chattel object. But his body as living archive of law reminds those present at the auction of a different history, of a future-past which sets him free.

If this drama scripts a romanticized fantasy in the French Caribbean, its technical accuracy nevertheless unsettles an easy relationship between forms of body, text, and authority which undergird the production of Man. The letter of the law inscribes itself *on* and *in* the body through its tattooed form; scar tissue remains a permanent trace of corporeal provenance. In hearing the *Code Noir* invoked in his favor, "*Donatien se leva sans répondre. Il y a des émotions, des situations dans la vie où la parole est impuissante* (Donatien rose without answering. There are emotions and situations in life where words are powerless)," reflects the narrator, in which, speechless, the corporeal self becomes a truthful site of legal imprint.[3] I will return to staged adaptations in which this scene occurs to amplify the performative interplay of law and bodily agency, but I open with this scene for its depiction of carnal matter in which law becomes tattoo becomes flesh, and corporal punishment becomes corporeal evidence becomes legal rebuttal. Somatic discourses of skin, tissue, and flesh of the body surface racial violence as historical fact by centering itself as a site of both meaning-making and meaning-maintaining: the body as an archive and archivist in one. The scene reveals the dependence of doctrinal development on the marked body: not doctrinal corpus enshrined with archival purity, but a more viscous, embodied, kinesthetic, and sensate domicile of a living, legal history positioned here as the *épave, debris, flotsam* that floats between chattel and degraded human.

Throughout French history, several doctrines of colonial law exemplify the dependency between stagecraft and statecraft, dance notation and legal notation, in the construction of a new social order. This chapter extends the argument of chapter 1 to read the *Code Noir* as a notational regime yet pushes further to consider implications for understanding the body and its reproduction as a resulting repository of law. Even in historical-archival sites of law in which the body has been absented, dare I say especially in such sites, we might attune toward the corporeal to better understand the disciplinary logics, performative potential, and selective sentimentalities which emerge from its bodily relief. In the scene above, already we see imperial ontologies made malleable through the imaginative realm of performance: flesh as evidence, body as property, law as *coup de théâtre*. Law's choreographic propensity shifts from a merely framing device to a material product, the legal archive now found in living repositories of somatic histories.

Dance theorists move within a tradition that appreciates the sentient flesh and the bodily hull of the archive in a disruption to the authority of discursive forms of knowledge.[4] Its methods give sentience to flesh, animating critical attention to the epistemologies held within legal formations of the body while forcing scrutiny of the idiosyncratic and irrational behaviors of law itself.[5] In *The Sentient Archive,* choreographer Emily Johnson asks:

> Can this archive of living knowledge, body memory, and experience be of use? Can we learn to trust what our bodies know and remember as real information? Can others learn to respect this information, letting the stories and experiences held in our bodies be of good use to the world? Would it lead to an understanding beyond that which I can grasp?[6]

These questions arrive from the first person but extend across the field to challenge logocentric logics of Western modern law in which the lettered represents the stable and logical and the body insinuates the unruly and irrational. *Pace* Rebecca Schneider, performance remains. The ephemeral no longer lives for its disappearance, but antagonizes archival assumptions through repetition, re-enactment, and that which "remains differently." Review of the *Code Noir* and its afterlives—across its language, aesthetic making, performative events, and *advocats*—affirms this inverted order.

Ranging interpretations of the *Code Noir*—across the visual, performative, theatrical, and literary—reveal expansive, protean forms of bodily notation. The various works gathered in this chapter—from abolitionist playwrights, practicing lawyers, and decolonial artists—repeat with theme and variation the *Code Noir* to puncture the received and naturalized history of the law toward something else. Repetition returns us to the cut, as Saidiya Hartman writes, the jurispathic instance in which an otherwise was foreclosed.[7] The return is not a recuperative act but a rupture, she reminds us.[8] Repetition, *répétition,* the francophone dancer translates, is a rehearsal. Engagement with this wider archive of the *Code Noir* gives insight into the ethical and epistemic logics of modern law that would reproduce Man while codifying violence. As much as the code begets critique for its founding violence, attunement to the fleshly in relation to its rhetoric reveals the many paradoxes, contradictions, and illogics which riddle the code. The codes become messy, contradictory, and incomplete, no longer heralded for their precision, comprehensiveness, or unity as the legally-defined body shifts shape, meaning, and prominence. As Canisia Lubrin's fictions reminds in *Code Noir: Fictions,* these decrees are not relegated to the past even in their abolition; each code sets up a prerogative of racial violence that seeps into orderings of the present in startling and uncanny ways.[9] The conundrum is longstanding: "the transformation of categories—the double movement and complex relations between the extremes of flesh and mind, external and internal, and what can be removed and what must remain—gives the juridical order power to redefine persons."[10] Fundamentally a question of imagination and its limits, artistic otherwises offer critical insight into the role of the body under law and its social death, both as it was and as it could be.

By first establishing the *Code Noir* and its choreo-jurispathic origins as a regime of notation for fabricating the body of the legal slave, I move to review the fleshed contours of the kinesthetic body as an affected remainder of the laws. This includes performative reproduction of flesh scripted in the codes as well as presented on stage in plays, scripts, and operas in further evidence of doctrinal dependance on the body. I extend this critique to claims against the *Code Noir,* such as vocalized in court by the *Société des amis des Noirs* (Society of the Friends of Blacks), in which lawyering strategies leveraged the relational politics of kinesthetic empathy, if abolitionist sentimentality of both the adaptations and the *advocats* remain circumscribed by anti-black desire. I conclude with an attention toward the contemporary art of Pélagie Gbaguidi and Pascale Marthine Tayou, who visualize the code's bodily incongruency. In so doing, I read the *Code Noir* for its *minor jurisprudences of the flesh,* a centering of the body, its affective potential, and kinetic output beyond its scripted overture.[11] A minor jurisprudence of the flesh invites alternative consideration of the well-charted terrain of legal persons.[12]

It allows us to account for the aporia of legal persons bound up in the *Code Noir* that structured liberal humanism and continues to structure racial inequalities of the twenty-first century, revealed by the dis-membering and re-membering processes wherein wounds are made and healed, where scars linger as evidence of past harm no matter what other story may be told.

STAGING IMPERIAL CODES OF CONDUCT

The *Code Noir* emerged from two separate edicts by Louis XIV—most notably the Edict of March 1685—but was not solidified into a stable referent until around 1720 as its practice and form settled into state routine.[13] Its authority ended at the beginning of the Second Republic with the definitive abolition of slavery in 1848 (though it had been abolished across several iterations in previous decades in a non-spectacular cease). To date, the code circulates widely in French culture as a moniker of a dark history, not least for its imperative of corporeal punishment and denouncement of Jewish bodies.[14] It includes, in more than one instance, permissions to the death penalty, an act now recognized by the United Nations as "incompatible with the right to life" if still practiced in the United States and elsewhere. Louis Sala-Molins, a contemporary voice against naturalization of the *Code Noir*, labeled it "the most monstrous legal document of modern times;"[15] Voltaire wrote that "the Black Code only serves to show that the legal scholars consulted by Louis XIV had no ideas regarding human rights."[16] Others have named it a crime against humanity, calling for an "autopsy" of its post-mortem hauntings, mordantly personifying the text itself.[17]

The code forwards, unambiguously, the entangled praxis of racial capital, justice, surveillance, and authority in the framing of its address.[18] When adopted within the territory of Louisiana in 1724, the *Code Noir* began with an overt mission: "for the government and administration of justice, police, discipline, and the commerce of black slaves, in the province and colony of Louisiana."[19] While such elements of the political-juridical system are now often discussed under implicitly correlated terms, here the relationality was articulated with explicit form and new clarity. The body—as fleshed but not sentient—remained the central lever through which power was wielded, even as political, economic, and linguistic dominance has been theorized as signs of modern governance. An attention to the fleshed body reveals, with forceful clarity, the ways in which legal mandates choreographed race and racial hierarchies, shifting comportment and disciplining bodies through legal techniques in order to cohere a constructed nationalism.

Rather than a single charter, the *Code Noir* was a series of documents that defined the conditions of slavery in concepts of European modernity.[20] It would stand as the main legal text of French colonial enslavement. The corpus was essential to the construction of race and racial identity in the French empire that extended from Europe to Africa, the Caribbean and continental North America, but originally it only addressed the French island territories of Saint-Domingue, Martinique, and Guadeloupe. Summarized, its transatlantic reach conscripted an international community of subjects as non-French populations were interpellated into French structures through choreographic force. Historians, political philosophers, and legal scholars have approached these codes with nuanced attentions, but collectively typify an archival focus that leaves out the body, its sentience, and the choreographic logics which undergird its writing and performative afterlife.[21]

The codes feature a wide range of practices that center on a kinesthetic articulation of power.[22] The *Code Noir,* as issued in 1685, included scripting of marriage rights (Art. 8–11), baptism (Art. 2), and marooned futures (Art. 38–39)—that is, a pas de deux, a ritual, and limited flight.[23] Art. 11 in the *Code Noir* of 1724, issued for the then-colony of Louisiana, went as far as to dictate the site and hour of burials.[24] If not expressly choreographic, these articles demonstrate a legal preoccupation with the kinetic, notated as compulsory gestures, kinesthetic performances, and scripted movements of the subjugated body even in death. In this way, the codes present a logic of early dance notation, in which permissible repertoires narrow to produce and then reinforce a socio-aesthetic divide. The scripted gestures become means, not ends, to the colonial project of corporeal conquest.[25]

French modernity was thus defined performatively, consolidated through shared rituals and repertoires as mandated by law. As Joseph Roach reminds us in regard to French civil code, legal authority relies upon performative activation to secure its presence, force, and validity.[26] The *Code Noir* worked in tandem to produce Frenchness, on the one hand, and choreograph racial otherness, on the other. This includes performative acts of Roman Catholic tradition to incorporate conscripted bodies under its French empire; against this forced assimilation, corporeal punishment, absence of rights, and other egregious abuses simultaneously cast a stratified racial class. Kidnapped and colonized bodies were tasked with performing the totality of this impossible repertoire. For example, baptism and Sunday observance were required as a means to cohere a legible body politic through kinetic means and to designate othered bodies as French. Required rest on the Sabbath resourced the body as labor while simultaneously encoding with spiritual but not legal personhood. Such ambivalent understandings of the body cross figurations of legal authority, kinesthetic force, and religious observance cinctured by values of productivity and racial capital. The kinesthetic provided means of "difference being managed" as conscripts of modernity.[27]

Archival reviews in response to these racializing codes refute their totalizing force: stories of deviant passing,[28] of fugitive refusal,[29] and insurrection proliferate if one looks closely.[30] Illicit marriage, reburial, and the documentation of other acts of deviance remind us of the potential to respond with an alternative; Daphne Brooks confirms these dissenting acts in a performative realm of vitality.[31]

The evolution of black dance in the United States itself speaks to this potential, as the outlawing of crossed-feet and percussive instruments influenced the formation of rhythm tap during the antebellum period. People found ways to move otherwise against laws which limited licit modes of performance.[32]

Considering the law through this choreo-jurispathic lens does not change its lived history, but it does accentuate the governing logics of a particular regime or political period as the breadth of the legal repertoire suppressed other modalities of being. Expression of legal codes as the law (as opposed to the laws) bears a trace of the fantasy of oneness indicative of civil law's absolutism and jurispathic order which continued through France's *mission civilisatrice*. Manifest in the singular, *the law* slips toward the sovereign rather than a more distributed apparatus. Recognition of the *Code Noir* as a regime of notation moves us away from its canonized articulation as edict—that is, linguistic utterance drafted by the crown—to a more physical understanding imprinted on the flesh and inherited through corporeal violence with the kinesthetic at the fulcrum of enactment. That is, it refuses a disembodied severance between the political philosophies of statecraft and the lived impact of law, the cleaved divide between body and flesh, in recognition of the code's choreo-jurispathic demand.

Consider the following passage from Father Jean-Baptiste Labat, who in his reflections on Martinique around 1700 notes:[33]

> Laws have been passed in the islands to prevent these *calendas*[34] not only because of the indecent and lascivious postures of this dance, but also to avoid overly large congregations of slaves who, finding themselves so joyfully thrown together, usually under the influence of brandy, could stage a revolt, an uprising, or thieving raids. However, in spite of these laws and all the precautions that the masters can take, it is practically impossible to prevent them, because of all of their entertainments this is the one that pleases them the most and to which they are most sensitive. In order to make them forget this infamous dance, they have been taught several French dances, like the minuet, the *courante,* the *passe-pied* and others, as well as *branles* and round dances.[35]

Anxiety around the potential errancy of the kinesthetic, dancing body ensnared the *Code Noir.*

The above passage reflects a tripartite attitude toward fantasies of a choreo-jurispathic body: first as irrational, then as a sign, and finally as an archive. It acknowledges, in disambiguated terms, the power of kinetic expression that might move in excess to even the most comprehensive codes of legal regulation. In the first part, Labat reflects on how dance itself has been prohibited in the anxious policing of mobility, collective engagement, and non-linguistic forms of communication. This ideology positions the dancing body as conditionally unruly when not following aesthetic standards legible to European lawmakers. He continues to identify a second orientation toward the body as an investment in choreographic expression as a nationalist project. With specificity he calls out baroque dances with corresponding notational form. A third ideal follows in which disciplining movement practices serve to replace the perceived unruliness and racial difference of other repertoires. Rather than additive function, he proffers a displacement method for other corporeal histories stored in the body. This final clause implies the sentience of the body-as-archive centuries before such a phrase moved in vogue. Its choreo-jurisgenerative potential was understood but in turn suppressed in pursuit of a jurispathic move.

Labat presents an incoherent and contradictory logics of kinesthetic signification as always unruly *yet* capable of being disciplined *even as* a national archive. Read together, Labat's comments reflect discordant ontologies of "sentient flesh dancing" as he records dance as potentially incendiary, a volatile force if not otherwise controlled. As R. A. Judy theorizes, "the contestation of the flesh is between two distinct performative activities of signification."[36] If Judy develops this constellate term in regard to the specific sonic signification of Juba tradition, the duality of signification extends to the dancing body and law more widely, including under the notational regime of the *Code Noir* wherein choreo-policing externs body-movement as both errant and repository.[37] The oxymoron is not, as Judy first foregrounds, *sentient* flesh—a combinate of mind and body, albeit one in which the mind yet again modifies the body—but sentient flesh *dancing*, as if the affective, socio-kinesthetic proximity of expressive movement vexes the materiality of flesh. The phobia toward sentient flesh dancing, while far from inevitable, reflects a very real anxiety of modern colonial law. Assimilating practices emerged in response to discipline the hyperkinetic body in its many shades.

Bodily form, expression, and attention saturated a wider politics of the monarchy during the force of the *Code Noir*. French historians and dance scholars alike have marked the seventeenth and eighteenth centuries as the most body-centric era of French political thought. This extends from the proliferation of figure-forward rhetoric (such as "corps," "corporations," and the "long arm of the state") to the glorification of the body of the king (through symbolic acts, symbolism, and fixation in his health, fertility, and virility) to ritual activities and performance-based sociality at the heart of society.[38] Bourbon absolutism relied on a public appreciation of the duality of the king's body: as divine and mortal, as body natural and body politic. Never was this more emblematic than the moniker of the Sun King who professed the apocryphal utterance, *L'état, c'est moi*. He would elaborate, "In France, the nation is not a separate body but resides entirely in the person of the King."[39] The French body politic, then reaching transatlantic delineation, was formalized under the notational regime of the *Code Noir* and other *grandes ordonnances* as ceremonies, social behaviors, and daily circulations of the body became regulated toward a particular vision of assimilated Frenchness. Dance and law together united king and kingdom through repertories of action, a repetition of daily aesthetics formalized as French custom, code, and law.

If notation hardened dance, the codes hardened the public.[40] As much as the *Code Noir* choreographed reprehensible acts of violence upon black life, it simultaneously choreographed barbarianism for those executing the codes. Processes of punishment became internalized acts of justice carried out in somatic memory of the crown. While there may exist instances of harm executed per an individual's own psychic predisposition to racial injury, the disposition to inflict violence through bodily spectacle was influenced systematically by the juridical text of the *Code Noir* and the specificity of its notation. The human-to-human violence of the whip was quantified, "29 lashes" for offense of gesture and word;[41] freedom was counted in grains of sugar, "300 pounds of sugar for each day of refuge" offered to a fugitive[42], and 10 *ecus* fined for permitted assembly[43]—each score of violence settled in a dehumanizing calculus of the body. Just as decorum was rehearsed in the (legal and social) courts, "violence," writes Achille Mbembe, "becomes an element in manners," itself a trained repertoire.[44] One might learn intricate footwork on the dance floor or master repertoires of violence depending on fleshly standing before the law.

The text alone as material object was not enough to secure its authority. It was iterative, transient, and idiosyncratic in both application and ideology, dependent on bodied infrastructure. This more Hegelian understanding all too acutely reminds us of the ways in which scores are relational texts, constituting membership and Frenchness not just for its perceived subjects, but for the agents of law enforcement who upheld its violence and the lives who received its whip.[45] It challenges the divide between the choreographer and choreographed in a reminder that the relationship between law and its performance is not just reproduced through vertical extensions of text-to-body, but horizontal body-to-body. Body and law become co-constituting agents, touches of history pressed upon the other through a regime of notation.[46]

PERFORMATIVE RENDERINGS AND STAGED READINGS OF THE *CODE NOIR*

"When one is considering the crimes of slavery, the popular theater is as central as the courthouse," writes Saidiya Hartman in *Scenes of Subjection*.[47] While Hartman stresses that racial violence is no less cruel in theater than in law, I shift interpretation slightly to emphasize performance as no less imperative to the securitization of the *Code Noir* than the courthouse. To understand the codes fully, one must look toward its staged performance: not only for its sentimentality or affective reception, but as a vital site for its mechanics of reproduction. In the mid-nineteenth century, acclaimed dramatist Eugène Scribe (who preceded his theatrical career with education from a leading Parisian lawyer, Louis-Ferdinand Bonnet) dramatized the *Code Noir* as a score when he wrote a libretto for Louis Clapisson's opera, *Code Noir* (1842).[48] Based on Charles Fanny Reybaud's novella, *Les Épaves* (1838), and set in 1720, the opéra-comique's title extends not only the centrality of law to the performance but also the collapsed referent of the two. Not only did such reproductions, as re-performances, invest in the omnipresence of the *Code Noir* even when framed as abolitionist projects, but they also scripted the imaginative limits for bodily possibility and its maneuvers.

Iterability of the *Code Noir*—across time, place, and medium—begets review via a performative interpretation which, for Derrida, "transforms the very thing it interprets."[49] A brief moment of justification and grounding is required, however, as the term "performativity" moves in disjointed and haphazard ways across its innumerable invocations. If Butlerian performativity has since been diffusely taken up as a sociogenic theory of identity, it emerged from a jurisgenerative propensity: Butler confesses, without explication, that their concept of performativity arises from Derrida's (reading of Kafka's) "Before the Law;" Butler's more recent book, *Who's Afraid of Gender,* quietly harkens to Robert Post's essay, "Whose Afraid of Jurispathic Courts: Violence and Public Reason in *Nomos and Narrative*;" and, as J. Hillis Miller deftly reminds us, Butler acknowledges (if in a tucked away footnote in *Gender Trouble*) that their theorization of performativity came about as they taught Kafka's "In the Penal Colony"—a parable which tarries in the inseparable interplay between flesh, law, notation, violence, and the body.[50] Early premonitions of performativity, then, arrive out of a Kafkaesque scene which doubly gives both body and flesh to the law: to give a body as in to submit a subject, to hand over the prisoner to the State *and* to give flesh as in to instantiate, to materialize the letter of the law in sanguine ink. Taken together, the turn to understand legal moves via performance and dance studies is no turn at all; the law was always already bound up in the drive toward performativity and its bodily undercurrents. But if we accept performativity as iterative constitution, inclusive of its infelicitous acts (such as the colloquial equation of performativity as the insincere), then the maintenance propensity of performative investment emerges as an antithetical potential to its more generative reality. That is, performativity for Butler may operate with jurisgenerative valence, but in thinking with Derrida we cannot ignore its jurispathic weight.[51]

The *Code Noir as opera* was first staged in Paris in 1842 as created for, and performed by, predominantly white Parisian abolitionists. The narrative follows a French naval officer, Donatien, who upon his homecoming to Martinique, realizes his mulatto identity and uncertain maternal lineage render him an *épave* under legal provisions held in the *Code Noir. Les Épaves*, translocated as the title of a different adaptation of the *Code Noir,* translates from the French as "wreckage," but was also used at the time to name an enslaved person whose mother was unknown:

a figure whose status remained lost at sea, adrift in the indeterminate notation of *partus sequitur ventrem*. Without a known mother, the *épave* "belongs to no one and yet has no title to freedom," and becomes capital of the government, for sale and for profit.[52] Through dramatic revelation, the opera displays the interarticulation of rights, race, and reproduction that were central to the political and legal debates surrounding slavery in the French colonial empire.[53] In a different theatrical reproduction of the plot, *Mulatten* (1840) by Hans Christian Andersen, the racial hierarchies and marooned futures constructed by the *Code Noir* climax when the codes are read aloud on stage in the auctioning of Donatien (renamed Horatio by Andersen).[54] Performative interventions determine the resolution of the dramatized *Code Noir* in each variant. Flesh emerges as the space where the legal symbolic appears; an apparition of the marked body disrupts sedimented orders produced by the codes.

Stagecraft calls into question the performativity of statecraft, even as it operates on shared logics.[55] In a concluding scene of *Mulatten*, the love interest of Horatio interrupts his sale at a slave auction when she, Cécile, intervenes with an announcement:

> And the law is: that when a free-born woman
> Of noble ancestry marries a slave,
> Then he is free; all punishment which was threatening him
> Will be annulled, his crimes forgiven,
> His chains are hung in the church's nave.
> He is free! Free!
> . . .
> Let it be known this man no longer is a slave,
> No, he is my husband![56]

Cécile's interruption turns on the audience's understanding of Art. 9 and 13 of the *Code Noir* which set the status of freedom and its transference via manumission in relation to the matrimonial process.[57] In Reybaud's version, the direction is even more overt: "Read the article of the *Code Noir:* 'any slave who marries a white woman is free by law.'"[58,59]

Here a performative utterance, in a strictly Austinian, trumps the racist authority endowed by the letter of law and otherwise upheld through social attitude. Cécile's enunciation of the now-famed speech-act "I do," remixed as "No, he is my husband," transforms Horatio's condition of bondage. For Cécile, her profession of love transforms Horatio's position before the law. But the score remains intact as her speech reproduces the black body as available for white desire; nothing is abolished. She instead fortifies its authority and represents the limits of performativity as a bodily endowment. Privileged heroism of the individual evacuates agency and personality for the one. Her liberal abolitionist vision of a future relies on a limited understanding of the performative as a singular speech act, emptying the scene of bodily agency. As footnoted in the reprint of the opera *Code Noir*, "*comme dans la novelle de Fanny Reybaud, le Code noir se fait instrument de délivrance entre les mains du deus ex machina, après avoir été outil d'oppression* (as in the novella by Fanny Reybaud, the *Code Noir* becomes an instrument of deliverance in the hands of *deus ex machina*, after having been a tool of oppression)."[60] This utopic rewriting of the codes as anything other than oppressive falls flat as the codes transform into Savior, as if to reinforce their reception as divine authority.

Performative articulation of the codes rests on a form of speech acts that absents a more kinesthetic sensibility in which the body too is endowed with agency. For J.L. Austin and the landslide of scholars since, the performative shorthands a scenario in which a (linguistic) utterance transforms a body, notably here a raced, masculine body left passive. It takes a dance scholar, Susan Foster, to remind us that even Butler, for whom bodies matter, defined performativity as "forms of authoritative speech" even while opening to self-fashioning gestures.[61] Language dominates the body even as the discourse on performance and performativity was meant to recuperate agency. I mean this not as a critique per se, but a cautious reminder of the limits of understanding performance and liberation, performativity and jurisgenerativity, as conjoined discourse *especially when the body goes missing.*

Instead of the performative marriage announcement that voids Horatio's enslaved status, as in the excerpt above, Scribe follows a different legal clause in the *Code Noir* according to which the identification of Donatien's mother as a slave allows *her* owner to step in to claim proprietorship over Donatien as kin becomes rescripted as capital:

> According to the *Code Noir*, which you know better than I do, the sale of a masterless slave is void if the master presents himself, and the master am I![62]

The opera, then, does little to rupture the reproductive violence of chattel law and its matrimonial inheritance. Rather, the plot hinges on the continued legitimacy of *partus sequitur ventrem*.

Locution not locomotion again drives the scene even though the play tours Donatien's flesh as the centripetal force; the abolitionist future imagined remains circumscribed by preordained logics of the law's logocentrism. There is an added cruelty in staging the auction block as a scene of adoring confession. It reproduces a social kinesthetic wherein blackness is equated with stillness and labor, simultaneously relegated to the periphery while an object of desire. Donatien remains displayed on the platform of an auction block, static, passive, objectified. Without kinesthetic presence, his body disappears from the scene until only flesh remains. Centering the flesh of law and its performance, invocation of the *Code Noir* as a cause of liberatory celebration omits the wider choreographic order of the codes which continue to qualify, constrain, and wound life. In all three reproductions, performative mechanics undergird the socio-legal production of the body's conversion to flesh.

Theatrical concern reached only to the mulatto in systems of anti-blackness wherein slavery's injured party was positioned as not black. Donatien's fictional biography as an educated elite from Europe who served his country reinforces a hierarchical performance of the perfect victim; exceptionalized, Donatien's figure obscures the sociological reality that many, if not most, slaves were of mixed inheritance. In the original cast, the tenor playing Donatien, Gustave Roger, hesitated to darken his face in order to visibly signal his mixed-raced character.[63] If an internal moment, his inclination toward blackface underscores the ways that the legal logics of the *Code Noir* required an artificial presentation of racialized aesthetic in order to find coherence for the attending public. It also reveals the imaginative investments of white abolitionists in which sympathy was not extended for the black actor. It is not new to critique the violence of blackface.[64] But the performance, even in an abolitionist frame, gives clarity to the jurispathic force of law in narrowing not only the subjectivities held in the legal system but the imagined possibilities of its representation.

When law becomes spectacle, the empathetic limits of society come to the fore. The performances reflect back, as they participate in, the limits of empathy, not only for white abolitionists toward black captives, but also of white society toward the violence of law itself and its enfleshed reproduction. Re-read as a script, in the absence of a performed presence, one can only project a scene. The reader is forced to conjure a possible staging, to cast out an imagining of what might have been. This act of filling in implicates as it illuminates. Enjoyment is bound in property and proprietorship, as Hartman reminds, only to reinforce a legal othering in the theater and entertainment. She warns against an "affiliation of Blackness and performance" which transmutes terrorizing realities into "innocent amusements" as it recommodifies black life for the pleasure of others.[65] To enjoy, to partake in, to consume *extends* possession of the black body to the stage; it does not abolish. As liberally progressive as some scenes in *Code Noir* may have been, they press against the limits of a humanistic sentimentality implicit to the codes itself.

By returning to these scenes, I do not intend to proclaim that performative interventions hold the power to transform law, nor that they should. On the contrary, these scenes—reliant upon performative acts to drive a plot—serve to reinforce, not reimagine, the status quo. It is revealing that abolitionist stagings of the *Code Noir* failed to materialize the raced body as an agential body. Put otherwise, the agency coded in these scenes draws out the critical distinction between being *subject to* the law and *subject of* the law. These scenes are complex representations of the racial-legal schema of slavery, but they are also fictional scenes serving a dramatic plot function. In their imaginative force they present the limits of performativity and its social uptake when circumscribed by the logocentric logic of the speech act.

BODILY PAROLE AND KINESTHETIC EMPATHY IN THE LEGAL ARCHIVES

As I have argued in the sections above, the *Code Noir* as a *regime of notation* contains within it explicit choreographic features and bodily fixations. The *Code Noir* as *performative reproduction* secures an anti-black world through its iterative commitments that stabilize over time in dramatic unfoldings. The *Code Noir* as a genre of *bodily parole*—wherein speech expresses the limits of bodily extreme and parole as police force returns to its linguistic capacity—points toward kinesthetic investment in bodily extremes. Viscous language permeates the codes and its reproduction in divergent attempts to dis-member and re-member body from flesh. Attunement toward bodily language emphasizes the shifting temporalities of the body as given and the body as constructed in the *Code Noir.* Read again with an attention to not only how the body is pre-scribed but the ways in which it is described gives entry toward an interiority of legal logics that leverage the moving potential of kinesthesia. This dual attention allows us to grasp at the "anti-discursive and extralinguistic ramifications of power" that Paul Gilroy articulates within the space of the plantation, and which I view as implicit to a more complete portrait of law that allows us to hold law-making and law-preserving episodes at once.[66]

Erotic speculation of bodies out of line saturates the legal text.[67] Consider how the Louisiana *Code Noir* of 1724, Art. 32 prescribes desired actions and describes repercussions:

> The runaway slave who has been a fugitive for a month, counting from the day his master denounced him in court, will have his ears cut off and will be branded with the fleur de lys on one shoulder, and if he runs away a second time, again counting from the day of the denunciation, his hamstring will be cut and he will be branded with the fleur de lys on the other shoulder; the third time he will be put to death.[68]

The bodily language above moves with barbaric violence, a series of three hypothetical acts toward freedom reinscribed as cause for injury. Rather than a normative description, Art. 32 contrives a scene and imagines modalities for the infliction of pain. Discipline shifts from a retroactive application of supposed justice toward a suppositional becoming of an anti-black racial order. The codes feature a will to imagine in bodily extreme; its force contorts flesh into dis-membered positions of the pained body.

Bodily parole, as fixation on corporeal description, manifests a jurisprudence of the flesh rooted in the extreme. Hyperattention to the visceral, not its negligence or disavowal, defines the logics of the *Code Noir.* As much as legalese has come to be carefully swaddled as objective, impartial, and detached in its deliverance for its attention to the stabilized lettered over more emotive, personal, or fluid forms of reason, here it is the letter which is offensively affective, sensational, and suppositional in register and the body which is drained from feeling. Authors of the *Code Noir* wielded not a scientific, political, or legal lens of objectivity but a perversely choreo-jurispathic appetite as they imagined what and how flesh could perform.

The *Code Noir*, in its many permutations, revolves around a logic of visceral description in its disciplining of enslaved and colonialized bodies. Doctrinal language of law has evolved away from this genre of bodily parole that induces a kinesthetic response in the reader. But it returns to haunt/hunt again. *I react with a tightened reflex, my own abdomen constricts as it reads the bodily language so vitally macabre that it arrests and nauseates.* Scholars such as Hortense Spillers return to these "high crimes against the flesh" and wield the viscerality of prose to ensure that history's violences do not go unaddressed.[69] But if Spillers writes affectively to make a point, the codes deployed extremes of bodily parole to make a cruel profit. Interpellative address arrives through the violence of thick description, as the proliferation of bodily parole in the codes is not the scripture of recognition but of dis-memberment. Its address produces a new genre of circumscribed life: the absented body, the fleshed body, the body impossible. Consider how Judith Butler theorizes the production of flesh through the abjected body:

> one must imagine an impossible scene, that of a body that has not yet been given social definition, a body that is, strictly speaking, not accessible to us, that nevertheless becomes accessible on the occasion of address, a call, an interpellation that does not "discover" this body, but constitutes it fundamentally. We may think that to be addressed one must first be recognized, but here the Althusserian reversal of Hegel seems appropriate: the address constitutes a being within the possible circuit of recognition and, accordingly, outside of it, in abjection.[70]

The *Code Noir* imports this impossible scene of the body, the becoming of the flesh. The impossible body of law circulates as a somatic remainder alongside the law's illocutionary force.

If insidious language of the body defines the technical writing style of the *Code Noir,* such bodily parole returns, repurposed and reproduced, under the abolitionist practice of parliamentary spectacle. The *Société des amis des Noirs* (Society of the Friends of Blacks) pursued a rhetorical strategy of bodily parole when, in 1790, they presented to the National Assembly their *Reflections on the Code Noir and denunciation of an atrocious crime committed in Saint-Domingue.* To prove the "inhumanity of the master," the authors recount "excessive beating, not simply for mutilating his slaves, but for roasting them slowly . . . [and] the placement of red-hot irons and brands on the trembling limbs of these souls."[71] The strategy was clear. Lawyering practices of the time leveraged recognition of kinesthetic empathy and visceral evidence of flesh when advocating their abolitionist arguments.

Through discursive figuring of the body via thick description of trauma and distress, the *Société des amis des Noirs* named, documented, and visualized the overseas violence for the Parisian audience as if to re-member the abjected body, as if to piece together its presence from the contours of its relief.

Relentless attention to the visceral consequences of the codes denaturalizes the constructed class of legal slaves and civil bodies, flesh and body. Summarized with viscous overwhelm, a "monument of blood" was filed against the *Code Noir*.[72] This description, evocative for its refusal to sanitize violence, raises the question: Is its revelry in the violence of bodily parole any less grotesque?

For the advocats, this visceral presentation of mutilation and torture not only documents but accuses:

> Oh! Who can peacefully regard this monstrous iniquity, this collusion between justice and tyrants? Eh! How do we not see that atrocities multiply when justice, far from punishing them, either complacently closes its eyes or punishes them only lightly? We have been told that the judges' reasoning was well-grounded, that they ruled in compliance with the code. Well then, the code is barbaric.[73]

The argument shifts the standards of the debate: the law thus presented is not unjust, but irrational. Contemporary legal humanists have called for a new turn toward law and affect to circumvent the flaws of rationality.[74] We already observe in the 1790s an attempt toward this new approach wherein empathetic appeals were made at the somatic level of the body.

The approach, however, was limited. The *Société des amis des Noirs* posed the questions: "Can an assembly that demonstrated such great respect for the rights of man let stand a law in a part of the French Empire that authorizes, that encourages, the most revolting cruelties?"[75] The questions continue, prescient and poignant in formulation: "Does the law not obviously favor their inhumanity? Does it not favor it, when it orders cutting the hollow of their knees when they seek to recover their liberty by fleeing? Does it not favor it when it declares *immobile*, that is to say, inanimate objects, to be above these beasts that one can break or mutilate at will?"[76] Evocative and provocative, the sentimentality of this rhetoric of denunciation functions to avoid or repress the more fundamental paradox in which a democratic law could include the law of slavery. Flesh once again obscures; its opaque mass halts further lines of questioning as h o l l o w k n e e s reverberates loudly, drowning out concern for its undergirding logic. This time flesh conceals not the body beneath, but the law which surrounds. It turns attention toward the performance of the self and away from its choreographic frames.

We arrive at a critical impasse, wherein the liberal potential of kinesthetic empathy runs up against the politics of sentimentality. Susan Foster and Saidiya Hartman meet in an abolitionist crossroads. Kinesthetic empathy, so well theorized by Foster within dance studies as empathetic connection through kinesthetic experience even when retrieved through bodily parole, animates strategies of the legal archive.[77] Performances of kinesthetic empathy suggest that the onlooking public—be it present in the assembly or en face in the archive—*winces, shivers, clenches, inhales* when confronted with the pained body. But the stage of sufferance, however inverted for abolitionist aim, when wielded as legal strategy of *Société des amis des Noirs* belies the expressed commitments of abolitionists and their investments in the liberalisms of freedom and liberty. French *advocats* attempt a recovery of the kinesthetic, if woefully underprepared to do so ethically and comprehensively. The liberatory potential of kinesthetic empathy crosses into the sentimentality derided by Saidiya Hartman.[78] Parliament and other stages of legal reform become yet another scene of subjection. The body remains absent as flesh returns as fetishized surface of legal trauma.

The limits of kinesthetic empathy to give both meaning and form within abolitionist effort suggests the impossibility of the zero-degree of civil law. Produced as a suppositional becoming of a slave society, the *Code Noir* cannot stand outside of ideology and cultural imprint. Here I find it particularly useful to linger with R. A. Judy's rumination on formulation of flesh as he, via Spillers, returns us to Barthes.[79] If the zero-degree of writing is the emptying of meaning into form, transliterated to the theft of the body into the flesh, then the zero-degree of civil law, in parallel, becomes the absenting of performance into the choreographic wherein all that is left is the hollow (outline of what could have been). But law bears a trace of its somatic *a priori*, of the scar tissue left behind as hieroglyphics on the flesh, precisely because it relies on the simultaneous dis-membering and re-membering of body and flesh. Such a zero-degree remains a floating horizon, and the abolitionist vision continues toward a different form of negation, as a "complex term and not zero, neutral term."[80] Practices of kinesthetic empathy operate as an effort to reverse this flow, but its catalyst all too often relies on a sentimental frame that inhibits full uptake. If the abolitionist practice of kinesthetic empathy reaches toward a zero-degree of law, "a knowing driven by a desire to neutralize power," it fails to escape its own anti-blackness.[81]

Contrary to disciplinary logics which teach of the certitude of the written archive contra the ephemerality of the para, here the converse arises from corporeal epistemologies wherein practices of bodily language and investments in kinesthetic empathy press against sedimented legal logics.[82] If new directions in law and literature gesture beyond the novel toward affect and performance, the sentient body remains largely absent, a mythic signifier devoid of its own somatic method.[83] To study fully the cultural life of law in pursuit of an illiberal human, this liveness must be reinstated without the suppositional erotics contained within its most violating corners.[84]

Scars remain, wounds unhealed. When the *Code Noir* was officially abolished in spring 1848 at the direction of Victor Schoelcher, it had executed its force for over 160 years. Although this date marked the formal abolition of the French slave system, the anti-black slave society persisted, not least as imperial practices of violence continued outside of France's European territory throughout its Second Colonial Empire, including territory in North and West Africa. What is the remainder? Fleshed memories, traumas not recorded before the law but impressed upon it nonetheless. As Louis Sala-Molins pens, "In a few pages, with the aridity that befits the seriousness of laws, it tells us of the life and death of those who, in fact, do not have a history. In five dozen articles, it marks the road that was followed by hundreds of thousands, millions of men, women and children whose destiny should have been to leave no trace of their passing from birth to death."[85]

PARADOXICAL FACES OF THE *CODE NOIR*

Centuries passed and abolition remains only partial. The *Code Noir* and its performative afterlives rumble into the twenty-first century, leaving heavy footprints in the sand. Kinesthetic empathy from its bodily parole continues to produce a response. For artist Pélagie Gbaguidi, the encounter is one of disbelief, a non-comprehension that nevertheless propagates a series of drawings.[86] Gbaguidi's figures—vibrant abstractions of stilled life—rupture the myth of law as legible, orderly, or elegant as ugly lines swirl and amass in disorientating connection [see Figure 2.1]. Drawing in visceral response to the *Code Noir,* the Beninese multi-media artist refuses to aestheticize the ugly. Charcoal scrawls accentuate pastel figures laid to rest as a jaune figure looks on. The negative space surrounding the figures marks the absented flesh and its contours. I wonder what laps at their edge. A vine—no, barbed wire—stretches through the limbs of each in this hallow burial ground, tracing the violence that controlled and contorted life even in the grave and obscured boundaries between the natural and the constructed. Only one face looks back at me in scorn as if to say, *this body remembers long after the codes passed on.*

The work emerges from a series of 100 drawings which transmute the *Code Noir* in the context of a wider installation that appreciates the body as archive, inclusive of the art which adorns the cover of this book. Visual cultures of the body become an annotation to law, a "choreography of the sign," proffering a more holistic, more *human* interpretation.[87] Gbaguidi first learned of the codes as a child but only remembered them during a 2004 residency in Nantes that shuttled her back to the shores of French slave trade. She casts herself as a contemporary griot—a legend, cypher, or key to interpreting a fuller portrait of the law and its afterlives. Her process responds to the hauntings of "the memories of those who can no longer testify for themselves."[88] The debility, earnest in its motivating intent, ambiguates

FIGURE 2.1 *"Code Noir" by Pélagie Gbaguidi, 2005–2007. Courtesy of the artist, Fortes D'Aloia & Gabriel, and Goodman Gallery; photography by Peter Cox.*

the years-old debate of personhood. Can "they" not testify for temporal removal? Or can "they" not testify for lack of recognition? Is fear of consequence the cause of inhibition? Or is the question more ontological, asking if the flesh can testify when the body is missing?

The question hangs suspended in the air, particulates strung out to ask who comes to matter. Posed by an artist, its capacious folds invite an existential pondering around an ethical axis. Rooted in close readings of the legal doctrine itself, it wedges between the discordant logics of Art. 26, 30, and 31: with either irreverence, irrationality, indifference, or all of the above, the *Code Noir* offers pathways for those enslaved (and thus rendered nonhuman before the court of law) to both act as witnesses in trials and file formal complaints in a thin effort of "liminal incorporation."[89] The *Code Noir* in one breath endows the enslaved person with the right to "give notice to the attorney"[90] while exhaling in another breath that no slaves "shall be party either in judgement nor in civil suits, either as plaintiff or defense, neither in civil or criminal."[91] With even less rationality, it in one breath offers a pathway for an enslaved person to testify as a witness, while in the same breath—indeed the very same sentence—asserts that such dispositions would not be a "source of any presumption, conjecture, or proof."[92] The very code produced to govern and suppress the figure of the nonperson attaches pertinent characteristics of legal personhood in an idiosyncratic scripture; such is the duplicitousness of juridical humanity wherein vestigial conjoinment dangles as a begotten remnant of another life. These moments disambiguate the errancy of law and its unwillingness to be coherent in value and strategy. Gbaguidi's artwork emerges out of this vexed history, not as a means to reconcile the incongruency but to underscore—with long strokes held firm, emphatically—that an irrational legal tradition produced the harms which compelled her to create.

If Gbaguidi sketches the body in outline to draw attention to its porous legal construction, consider another contemporary response: a Cameroonian artist previously educated as a lawyer, Pascale Marthine Tayou created *Code Noir* (2018) to refract this historical flux through a monumental, seven-panel work. A series of silhouetted figures carved from the wooden surface—a redux of the commissioned sculptures of colonialist order, remixed here in blackened form—simultaneously constitute and distort the large-scale reproductions of the *Code Noir*.[93] Their silhouettes emerges not by carving around their edge to reveal their form but by carving out their bellies so that their outline emerges through hollowed absence, negation of space. The vertical, totemic shape, rendered in profile without a face, emulates a barcode, accenting the code's role in the commodification and retail of the body. Pleated pages of the *Code Noir* create a literal backdrop to the profiles in the matter that surrounds, in which law becomes as material as flesh (and flesh becomes as knowing as the law). The black hole of the silhouettes distort depth perception. It is no longer clear that before the body, there is flesh. Perhaps, as Judy writes, the flesh is at last with the body. Or perhaps we arrive at the ultimate inversion: body before flesh, wherein performance remains.

Retrieval of the codes, a re-membering repurposed for their materiality as salvage, float overtop. I think of Donatien cast as an *épave*, a different body of salvage life, adrift in the legal milieu of person, persona, and personhood, a floating signifier buoyed somewhere between being and nonbeing. The salvage aesthetic both "calls into question and refashions the objects and subjects of history, creating," as Angela Naimou theorizes, "from the wreckage of legal personhood."[94] These panels were mounted in the wider installation, *Colorful Line* (2018), whose quip on the economic apartheidic history of the United States blurs geographies of articulation and temporalities of experience of the French colonial empire. If the body is no longer for sale, the work cries out that its trauma most certainly remains traded as the spectacularization of black pain on the marketplace. Although presented as visual art, the work hosts a spatiality of the body akin to the foci of dance. The profiled figure—a void beneath the text of obscuring force imprinted upon—saturates with its obsidian darkness. Black redaction becomes a space to project imaginaries of the legal consciousness, recalling the unknowability and illegibility of the othered body before the law.[95]

Tayou's palimpsest—overlays of legal code, barcode, and body devoid of persona—reproduces the *Code Noir's* most infamous article: in Art. 44, the *Code Noir* rendered *the slave* a "thing," a material commodity for economic exchange rather than a human being replete with fleshy rights, motility, and improvisatory strategies.[96] The sub-human status was reinforced by a wider denial of legal (non) personality throughout.[97] Art. 44 regarded slaves as *meubles* (movables) as objects of ownership that could be transferred either via sale or inheritance. The body as available for transference turns on a kinesthetic sensibility. It marks a philosophical and ontological turn away from French feudal law, under which slaves and indentured servants were regarded as immovables, that is property attached to land, a distinction elsewhere summarized by French language as *choses mouvantes* (moving things) and *meubles* (movables) that emphasizes the kinesthetic postures of personhood.[98] While the shift in category from objects associated with real property to fungible commercial objects may seem merely rhetorical, weaponized to conscript labor under forms of racial capital, it indexes a cultural and epistemic shift in the ontological perceptions of the body. The shift emphasizes the fleshed body as racial capital, valued for its laboring potential unmoored from a given place or rooted belonging. The body becomes a consumable, not a resource. On the one hand, this construction shifts the body into the discourse of disposability, rather than the perpetuity and immortality suggested by property; on the other, it defines the subject through animacy. Both exhaust life, if differently. This duality creates a vacuum, in which the body that lives a civil death remains ever in motion.

The attention toward the body as a commercial object severed from its place is hardly surprising from the pen of Jean-Baptiste Colbert. His strategy of mercantilism defined his economic and political philosophies as First Minister of State. The *Code Noir* was published posthumously following his death in 1683 after a gloried career balancing trade, commerce, and tariffs. This includes the publication of several ordinances, including consolidation of existing edicts and laws into: The Commerce Ordinance (1673), the Forestry Ordinance (1669), Civil Ordinance (1667), The Criminal Ordinance (1670), and the Naval Ordinance (1681). The Colonial Ordinance, or what is known as the *Code Noir*, arrived in 1685 after decades of careful notation of the circulation of material goods and commodities. The *Code Noir* follows in this era of civil logic and logistics, scripting the colonially-enslaved body as yet another object of French imperial wealth.

The visual works of Gbaguidi and Tayou reveal new contours to the absented flesh of the *Code Noir*'s many bodies. The *Code Noir*, exemplar of a paradoxical law that inscribed barbaric violence while standing on the thorny laurels of a circumscribed humanism, writes the body in nonsensical tension. Materiality of the body morphs per the whims of the code. "The law kills and the law resurrects," writes Colin Dayan in a critique of modernity's false exchange of the religious for the rational. "Legal practice thus conflates symbolic control and the inscription of that control on real bodies."[99] Contemporary visual culture attempts to map out this incongruency.

Post-Renaissance and post-Enlightenment thought all too readily tolerated the idea that someone could have a body containing a soul (in need of salvation) all while refusing recognition of that same body as a full person with human rights. This fracture reinforces the Spirit/Flesh divide that Sylvia Wynter critiques of modern epistemes and further serves recognition of the corporeal vitality of the body.[100] At each instance of the paradoxes in the *Code Noir*, the fault-line comes in a dismemberment of the body from legal personhood, a willingness to turn into the fleshed as the central concern of the human. It facilitates what Dayan might call a "double-movement" that engenders juridical order and authorizes "the power to redefine persons."[101] I look toward the errant logics propped up as rational, fractured by a new order of being/knowing/sensing refracted back in these visual pieces.

More than emphasis on the obvious ethical critique and contradictory logics of the *Code Noir*, its performative life underscores the body as sentient and law as illogical in a reversal of juridical-epistemic order. The veneer of legal persons as articulated in the era of freedom begins to crack. There, the body slips between positions of subject and object, persons and nonpersons, life and death. It slides as an agential force and malleable commodity. This ambivalence of being becomes both hypervisible and invisible before the law—sketched as an outline or shaded in black, but not with a face. As scholars before me have noted, "the site of slavery in the colonies rendered material the conceptual, giving a body to what had been abstracted."[102] What is left to do but to conceptualize the material remainder? To re-member its history, abstracted back through artistic means so as to draw attention to its intellectual incongruencies and ethical failures.

If legal personhood is understood to have been constructed through the socio-political apparatus of law, scrutiny of the *Code Noir* reveals how legal nonpersons were equally constructed through legal action rather than its non-address. When we understand the law as choreographic notation, the distinction between legal bodies and biological bodies dissolves: even the natural body has been legally defined, and both have been crafted through robust notation, juridical processes, and constant pronouncement.[103] Dayan holds this tension at play by naming the civil body and legal slave as twinned artifices of juridical making, each at the precipice of social death. In each instance the immense project of juridical humanity extends to aesthetic constructions and kinesthetic reproductions, which must be accounted for in the legal violence that maintains bare life.

Legality emerges through its repeated performance. For the *Code Noir*, this performance was notated in explicit terms, and later propagated on the abolitionist stage. Throughout these historic events of statecraft and stagecraft the raced body was disciplined through attention to the flesh in which the visceral was coopted for violence. Reading the *Code Noir* for its kinetic fixation invites a more nuanced understanding of the temporal interplay between the text, the body, and the resulting movement of authority. This includes attention paid to its performative acts, reliance on bodily parole, and limited potential for kinesthetic empathy. Attunement toward these minor jurisprudences of the flesh hones our attention to keep the question of the human, irreducible to Man, open to the demands of the absent flesh of law. It points us back, with specificity and expertise, toward the moments of contradiction contained within its pages. Fleshly attunement accentuates the inherent polysemy of the law, belied by the *Code Noir* and its reproduction across various aesthetic responses. I point to the performative afterlives of the *Code Noir* in its various modalities to challenge the narrative of law as pristine, fixed, and organized, but no less mercurial than the live.

CHAPTER THREE

REGULATING RHYTHMS[1]

> **The violence which has ruled over the ordering of the colonial world, which has ceaselessly drummed the rhythm for the destruction of native social forms and broken up without reserve the systems of reference of the economy, the customs of dress and external life, that same violence will be claimed and taken over by the native at the moment when, deciding to embody history in his own person, he surges into the forbidden quarters.**
>
> —*FRANTZ FANON,* The Wretched of the Earth

Legal moves continued to shift. Logics of the *Code Noir* consolidated into future iterations of penal law and civil code for the French empire to produce new rhythms of colonial humanisms.[2] The entanglement of corporeal notation and law which began under the reign of Louis XIV continued under new rules as legal texts travelled to the African continent while also reaching across the Atlantic into the continental Americas. In this chapter, I press forward in time from the *Code Noir* toward the *Code de l'indigénat* in Algeria and the Black Codes in the Southern United States to sit with the rhythms of kinetic regulation and resulting temporalities of slow life choreographed by the law. In one scene life was cast aside as troublingly foreign, held in a state of suspended life with mobility restricted. In another, flesh was folded in with an insatiable appetite toward industrial progress and perpetual labor: stillness countered the legalized violence of racial capital. The body remains the still object of law in both. These manifest forms of regulated rhythms, "repeated and patterned," index not only the geopolitical reach of the French civil law tradition in colonial and neocolonial spaces, but the ways in which its implementation and choreographic strategy evolved in response to more localized repertoires of society.[3] Oceans apart, the body scripted outside of humanity moves in abject tempo to legal time, perpetually disjointed and out of sync.

Rhythm emerges as an ambivalent metric to track the choreo-jurisgenerative body. It keeps time of the collective force of colonial violence as well as the liberatory praxis of anticolonial futures. This chapter makes space for both through by tracing stilled patterns and slow life produced by colonial law. For Sylvia Wynter, an attunement toward the "rhythmic interplay" of bios-mythios frictions shuttles us between nature and narrative, science and poetics—that is, it frames the vibrations produced in the interaction between the body and the law.[4] It names the internal mechanisms through which the legal score becomes animated, the science of the word made live. This kinesis resides not in domains of the body or in the law itself, but in the temporal relay of activation—the doing, the praxis—whose constant shuffle destabilizes a biocentric linearity and teleological narrative of the human. While Wynter emphasizes the double interplay at an abstract, historical, and esoteric level, the sociogenic principle moves in an embodied locale, too, via performances of the fleshly body.

Roland Barthes ruminates on the communal textures of rhythm in *How to Live Together*. His arrival at rhythm as rhuthmos through Ionian philosophy opens up an alternative:

> Prior to the Attic period, *rhuthmos* never meant "rhythm;" it was never applied to the regular movement of the waves. The actual meaning is rather: a distinctive form, a proportioned figure, an arrangement; very close to and yet very different from *schema*. *Schema*: a fixed, fully developed form that's set down like an object (statue, orator, choreographical figure). *Schema* ≠ form, the instant it's assumed by something moving, mobile, fluid, the form of something that lacks organic consistency. *Rhuthmos* = the pattern of a fluid element (a letter, a *peplos*, a mood), an improvised, changeable form.[5]

Kinetic orientations of the body ground his theorization: *choreographical figure, something moving and improvised* hint at schema as choreographic notation. More precisely, temporal flows bind elements of a choreographic order imposed by a schema, evoked here as legal codes. It is not just that the body is scripted by law, but how and to what affect.

Idiorrhythmic practices move alongside the smoothing counters of rhythm, from individual acts of resistance to swells of revolutionary force. "Since *rhuthmos* is by definition individual," elaborates Barthes, "idiorrhythm is almost a pleonasm: the interstices, the *fugitivity* of the code, of the manner in which the individual inserts himself into the social (or natural) code."[6] I center slow rhythms as the routinized effect of settler colonial codes in order to emphasize the imposed time of law as an induced state of kinesthesia, not merely punctuated events of juridical action. In so doing, I do not mean to suppress a history otherwise, wherein coordinated revolts and spontaneous resistance repeatedly mark the horizon.[7] The archive yields counter tempos, syncopation, and improvisation as "new rhythms" of Fanon's anticolonial becoming and Derrida's new world order.[8] Expressed rhythms, alternative rhythms, and nonrhythms play on and against one another.

Scores amassed in the late nineteenth and twentieth centuries, figuring not only the individual but also larger soma-logics of settler legal time. These flows include *hyper-kinetic* and *hypo-kinetic jurisprudence of the body,* which respectively traffic in exclusionary or inclusionary patterns.[9] Akin to biological processes of flow, hyper- and hypo-kinetic movements suggest (im)mobility over a national membrane and resulting flows for peoples brought into or excluded from the populus. Dance and performance studies invite us to view, critique, and reimagine this dramaturgy in which legal orders that hail the individual cohere toward a wider repertoire of existence. Phrased otherwise, while the law-as-score (as I argue in chapter 1) produces the body-as-archive (as I argue in chapter 2), it also conscripts fuller ensembles in meta-movements of hyper- and hypo-kinetic juridical order. Against the disembodied pen of legal theory, attunements to the body and its rhythm reveal a juridically constructed "constellation of potential mobilities that," as Jasbir Puar theorizes within the modern state, "condition the consciousness of mobility disability."[10] Circulation stilts and bodies traffic in historical waves as laws build out an infrastructure of the human.

Soma-logics—juridical orientations toward the body politic, not the political body—name and give texture to this embodied experience of legal time, including the contrapuntal tempos of legal pluralism and the ambivalent desires of colonial humanism. Tracing the soma-logics produced by the *Code de l'indigénat* and the Black Codes underscores rhythm as, per Wynterian logics, "collaboratively navigating racial infrastructures": it scales us from the singular archival body toward the plural body politic and also illuminates the praxes between the ethnoreligious formations.[11] Following the ethics of Mark Rifkin, this chapter moves beyond a pluralist expansion of colonial time to instead account for the *processes* of temporal domination engendered by settler colonial law.[12] This sensitivity nudges us to read the rhythm of law, which is the rhythm of multiple temporalities, as embodied. Scaled to the macro choreographies of society from the intimate portraits of the flesh, a wide lens gives narrative clarity to broader socio-legal tempos that conscript peoples into relational striations of race, labor, and capital.[13]

Resulting movements cut across the lexicon of comparative colonial violences of race: dispossession, enslavement, confinement, assimilation, and removal.[14] Against black, indigenous, and colonized life, time has been weaponized to become a disciplinary regime and legal artifact of difference. This extends from discrete codes, articles, and ordinances to more sweeping temporal logics that presume authority for settler-racial law. While distinct, in practice and theory, traces of legal transplantation bind this chapter as the *Code Noir* iterated at transnational and transhistorical scale.[15] The coupling of the *Code de l'indigénat* and the Black

Codes puts pressures on the suggested affinities even as it invites cross lateral amplification as we attune ourselves to the divergent rhythms produced.[16]

The first half of this chapter reads the soma-logics of the *Code de l'indigénat* to suggest a *hyper-kinetic jurisprudence of the body* in which the racialized other was cast at a perpetual distance to French citizenship under its system of legal pluralism. These exclusionary practices reified the Algerian constituent as abject and set in motion a colonial legal time in which the colonized body ossified in a suspended state, addressed but not of the nation.[17] In this analysis, abjection codes for the ways in which the settler-colonial *Code de l'indigénat* fetishizes performative difference. To focus this argument through the choreo-jurisgenerative body I center the ways in which spines articulate a posture of being out of time, literally and metaphorically disjointed by regulated rhythms. Written into the colonial force of the code as the "exceptional body," the addressed "*indigène musulman*" navigated stagnated rhythms as a "feature of both colonial world and colonized body."[18] I go on to read closely for shifted rhythms in which the French codes cast Algerian life into a state of delinquency by anticipating deviance in lieu of prescriptive measures.

In the second half of this chapter, I read the soma-logics of the Black Codes to suggest a *hypo-kinetic jurisprudence of the body* in which blackness was interpellated to quench capitalist appetites for unbounded productivity. The apparatuses of re-capture, in the wake of a wider history of slavery, absorb the fleshed, leaving life behind.[19] White desire for labor consumption leads to perpetual motion; being idle was made a crime. Across the Atlantic, attention reifies around the movement politics of the black body as mobility becomes increasingly bounded under the Black Codes. Legal anxiety extends to the stilled, the vagrant, or unproductive body and stillness codes as biopolitical refusal. The desire to exhaust the racialized body bleeds into the contemporary moment.

Read together, these two transmutations of French legal code present opposing strategies for the ways in which laws metabolize its subjects to regulate the rhythms of the body. The comparative structure edifies the need to embrace a shift, as dance scholar André Lepecki emphasizes, "toward a kinetic subjectivity, informed by choreography's tandem encounter with Modernity."[20] I conclude the chapter by reviewing aesthetics of rest as a practice of refusal, situating this emergent force of the arts and activism in direct confrontation to the legal histories of the body scripted into perpetual motion. niv Acosta and Fannie Sosa's *Black Power Naps* (2019) and Jo Kreiter's *The Wait Room* (2019) present an alternative value system to the stilled, horizontal body wherein rest for the supine figure emerges as a political act. "Beneath these time-maps are the grids of empire and the moving terrains of trauma and memory," argues Vilashini Cooppan in her imaginative guide to soft time. "Beyond them are intimations of other ways of thinking" that includes rhythms of the corporeal.[21]

STASIS IN THE REGIME OF EXCEPTION

Issued as a provisional "regime of exception," the *Code de l'indigénat* operated as a penal code or "law of violence" for those recognized as *sujets* under French colonial order.[22] The set of laws, regulations, and punishments, sometimes shorthanded as *l'indigénat*, projected French power throughout the second colonial empire in spite of its erratic legislation.[23] This administrative authority of the French state was formally established in 1881 in Algeria, with specific decrees pre-dating this synthesis. It would eventually extend throughout French West Africa to French Indochina, including Senegal, Togo, Cameroun, Mayotte, Madagascar, Polynesia, and Cambodia until its dissolution in 1946.[24] Similar to the *Code Noir* that scripted the conditions of enslaved individuals, the *Code de l'indigénat* determined the political status and underprivileged categories which developed in relation to the colonized. In the settler-colonial context, the *indigénat* distinguished between French citizen and French subject to legally ascribe a hierarchy between the settler and the native in a dualism that flattened existent nuances of social order into a monolithic other.[25] The violence of the regime includes the tiered categorization of human life, this time not of human and non-human but of European and Other (non-French Europeans in Algeria were not subject to its discipline). Eventually the exception—of legal violence, differentiated rights, choreographed publics, and hyperkinetic jurisprudence—became the rule.[26]

Playing on the double entendre of corpus, Algerian philosopher Sidi Mohammed Barkat features the body in *l'indigénat* when he coins the codes as "*le corps d'exception* (body of exception)."[27] This exceptional body, as both juridical text and embodied figure, exemplifies colonial soma-logics of abjection. Barkat summarizes the suspension of the exceptional body as an entire group of people not admitted to citizenship but still a member of the nation, "*de sorte qu'il est contenu dans cette société, inclus en tant que non compté, inclus en tant qu'exclu* (so that it is contained in this society, included as not counted, included as excluded).[28] Contained by exclusion, the exceptional body moves as the omni-absence of legal alterity, there but removed. Its tempo is never in line. Aporetic politics of the abject, riddled with orientalizing overtones, lead to its polarity, which repels as it draws in. The double movement, a double bind as "consigned to the past" or "inserted into a present defined on non-native terms," emerges in *l'indigénat* wherein the proliferation of codes defined non-French, non-white life only to name it as out of time.[29] Settler sovereignty operated through rhythmic regulations, weaponizing the authority of temporal order and legal time. Abject and excluded even while addressed, the body becomes the exception for French colonial law.

Attention to absence, presence, and erasure in Algerian settler-colonial formation leads Anne-Marie McManus to theorize the "petrified subject" as "distended, immobile, sentient."[30] In more visceral imagery, she suggests the "body rendered into topography."[31] She comes to this theoretical entry through a comparative reading of Frantz Fanon and Kateb Yacine, two iconic scholars of race and anticolonialism in Algeria. Rather than read this subjective absence and perpetual suspension through the anticolonial psychoanalytics of Fanon, as offered by McManus, I attend to the choreo-jurisgenerative forces which ground Fanon's observations. The "*indigène*," frozen outside of European modernity as a result of imposed legal maneuvers, moved to a rhythm of slow life as a suspended subject: "a viscerally felt, agonizingly slow and perhaps imperceptible motion of annihilation that the subject nevertheless lives."[32] I draw forward this theorization of the petrified subject not to further drain agency from categories of subaltern life but, refigured as *suspended*, to underscore that the temporality presented emerged as a choreographic effect of the codes. Legal alterity holds the *suspended body* aloft, but not fixed, in a metaphysical state and carceral act that continues to push targeted life outside the temporal flows of a State-sanctioned "good life."

In the Maghreb, the *Code de l'indigénat* induced a stalled temporality that cast the Algerian body "at once intimate *and* foreign" in a jurispathic fantasy of legal order.[33] More nominally, it operated under impressions of legal pluralism, offsetting Muslim, Berber, and Mosaic law with newly imposed French colonial law. Art. 1 structured this order from the outset as it recognized pre-existent laws but prioritized rights only for French citizens.[34] In so doing, it collapsed the plurality of non-French identity into a singular subaltern status, the "*indigène*," policing Jewish, Arab-Muslim, and indigenous identities under its authority while often inducing conflict between these groups.[35] If not directly racialized like the *Code Noir*, it allowed for *de facto* discrimination along ethnoreligious lines, leveraged as crude synonyms for nativeness and authentic Frenchness.[36] But the lines were blurry, as Muslim personal status came to rub against French civil status, not least in instances of mixed marriage that forced recognition of the entangled religious, racial, and sexual difference held in the plural legal system.[37]

Assimilationist efforts attempted to absorb colonized publics into French society by erasing traces of precolonial culture. By the early twentieth century, however, this ideological approach began to transition toward theories of association, which increased flexibility as colonies were (supposedly) treated with greater (cultural) autonomy. Whereas the *Code Noir* promoted forcible assimilation to the Roman Catholic ideals of France, the *Code de l'indigénat* produced the abject local, scripting the Other in perpetual distance from the European citizen: legally, culturally, and aesthetically. Rights were suspended for the non-Christian, who were rendered temporally other until willing to performatively declare a new identity through adoption of religious rituals (or shedding of previous customs and beliefs). In so doing, the codes induced a native absence, the Algerian figure suspended from within. This absence functioned "not [as] an arrival point, but [as] a sustained state in repetitive motion where presence is repeatedly denied, where the subject is continually re-excluded from the category of Man."[38] Suspended, the laws reinforce the legislators' orientalist views of the Arab body as indolent, disinterested in civil participation.[39] The choreo-jurisgenerative body was cast as inappropriate, a moral impediment, and out of sync with imperial hegemony.

Judith Surkis exposes French colonial oppression and discrimination as built and maintained on "fantasies of sexual difference."[40] She goes on to frame this sexual desire as the "corporealized conception of Muslim law."[41] For Surkis and other historians, this corporealization is largely limited to sex and marriage rights—polygamy, repudiation, and child marriage. My attention to the body traffics and circulatory flows of (im)mobility induced by the *l'indigénat* extend this frame toward wider rhythms of hyperkinetic orderings. Corporeity remains the foci. Consider how Surkis suggests the "colonial legal construction of Muslim 'personal status' and its differences from a secular Civil Code elaborated a corporealized conception of Islam. The legal status of French citizens, European nations, and Algerian colonial subjects or *indigènes* increasingly took on bodily attributes and qualities."[42] I quote at length here to underscore the subtle but intentional creep of the body in historical analysis of the law. As much as legal studies may turn to late modern legal code as a site of the philosophical grounds of personhood and race formations, the material body cannot be ignored. Corporeal implications abound.

While legal pluralism produced inevitable hierarchies across its differentiated constituents, some colonial administrators narrated an alternative reality in which the plurality was offered out of respect for difference and local custom under an Enlightenment era conception of universalism.[43] Justifying its violence, French senators and state councilors, such as State Councilman Flandrin, purported that the "full exercise of the rights of French citizens' is incompatible with the 'preservation of Muslim status and its provision.'"[44] I tarry with the word choice, preservation, and its temporal ambivalence—exclusion from an unprovincialized modernity masked as acknowledgment for cultural difference. Disguised as an invitation to pluralism out of respect for difference, the operative forced individuals to negotiate a ranked priority between religion, ethnicity, and nationality, with biopolitical implications on sexuality, domesticity, and reproductive life.

The penal code existed alongside a wider swathe of French colonial law that evolved across the nineteenth and twentieth centuries to accommodate shifting political realities. The Crémieux Decree (1870), for example, allowed for the strategic disassociation between nationality and citizenship through enforcement of cultural difference, attention to embodied repertories, and policing of bodily vernaculars as citizenship was conferred upon the majority of the Algerian Jewish population without opening this pathway for Algerian Muslims.[45] Three years later, the National Assembly introduced the 1873 Warnier Law. This new law established pathways for French nationals to acquire land previously held by a local community. On the one hand a straightforward law of dispossession now all too familiar in its settler-colonial narrative, it indexes the tense negotiation between body and property under legal personhood. Summarized, the Warnier Law reflects French desire for the "assimilation not of Algerian people but Algerian land."[46] Land became French, while bodies remained Algerian-Muslim.[47] Disjointed from both land and country, those hailed by the *l'indigénat* were forced outside the rhythms and narrative of modernity. Coupled with differentiated mobility, this severance produced a world in which "mobility is the personal property of the body, a procession of the self."[48] The exclusion—more than territorial sentiment of place—produces the violent logics of "colonial humanism" which would come to define the French imperial nation-state.[49]

Hyperkinetic mobilities, in which Algerian life was partitioned outside of French modernity, define the codes. Jasbir Puar writes that the "cordoning of time through space contributes to an overall 'lack of jurisdiction over the function of one's own senses' (Schuller 2018: 74) endemic to the operation of colonial rule, as well as a sense of being 'stranded in time' (Lagerquist 2008)."[50] Although she writes of a different space of anti-Arab force, the logic precedes in the *Code de l'indigénat.*

Counter-rhythms emerged against the imposed French legal hegemony. Many Algerians chose to remain under Muslim law and refused to divorce themselves from cultural-religious values in exchange for French citizenship. This rejection of the naturalization process subverted colonial expectations; national homogeneity remained an elusive myth for the French state as resistance took on layered forms. But even those who decided to convert to Christianity were often still denied French citizenship.[51] And those who did convert nationality were cast as the *évolué.* This term, suggested for those who had ceded customary law for European standards, insinuates not merely a merging as in the grammar of assimilation, but convergence toward progress—a temporal mark of having come into time with the Westphalian tempo of modernity. Species hierarchies, naturalism, and animacy saturate this moniker for the newly legal position, pairing nationalism and evolutionary theories and further linking anti-black and anti-Arab grammars of racialization.

Through strategic legal pluralism across ethno-racial, linguistic, and religious orders, the *Code de l'indigénat* occasioned a soma-logic of stasis, the exceptional body suspended in disjointed time and stagnated in the framework of colonial law and order. Regulation of soma-logics in which foreignness is suspended reinforces a temporal alterity in which ethnicity is positioned alongside the still: immobilized to the a-temporal past and withheld from futurity.[52] Following Roland Barthes, Hortense Spillers observes the myth of ethnicity for its "powerful stillness" which "embodies nothing more than a mode of memorial time." Clarified as "a signifier without movement," that is, suspended in temporal distance to Western legal time, she draws attention to the disarming propensity of ethnic labels to write over the body as absent from a subject position.[53] The force is both rhetorical and physical, bios and mythos, in a return to the regulating rhythms that intend to stall sites of choreo-jurisgenerativity.

REGULATING TEMPOS OF THE EXCEPTIONAL BODY

Reading the *Code de l'indigénat* as a score challenges a linear mapping of conquest as presence, erasure, absence, and aftermath. Formalized in the late nineteenth century, half a decade after the French invasion of Algeria, the codes were not a law-founding violence. French occupation had already arrived. Rather, the codes served to legalize—and make permanent—*de facto* discrimination already been well-rehearsed. Sidi Mohammed Barkat summarizes the temporal purgatory as "*le report indéfini d'une pleine inclusion annoncée* (the indefinite postponement of a full inclusion yet to be announced)"—a denial of legitimate recognition by the State.[54] This temporal framing of a law as the postponed future, as scripture of the not-yet-here, challenges easy understanding of the temporal order of law discussed thus far in which we find symmetric mapping between the past and the future. If law-as-notation points to the reenacted past, and law-as-score as the future potential, the *Code de l'indigénat* suggests scripture of a perpetual meanwhile—neither law-founding nor law-making but in the break. It also scored a colonial condition of moving that set bodies in motion without the intent of progress wherein *being* mandated *being-in-time*. "Rhythm," as Barthes reminds in regard to modern living, "acquired a repressive meaning."[55]

Scripted offenses in the *Code de l'indigénat* extend from vague threats against French authority to the specific refusal to respond to administrative summons of the State to daily bans on night travel.[56] It extends toward more affectively amorphous spaces such as the performance of an "insulting attitude" in the presence of French officials.[57] Punishment includes administrative internment, forced labor, capitation, and other violences that center the body and its labor. Religious affairs received heightened scrutiny, with prohibited assemblies for ziara or zerda, and prohibited gestures for celebration, inclusive of weddings, births, and circumcisions.[58]

Article after article aggregates to reveal a state of anxiety toward control, an articulation of who, what, and where "native" bodies belong even as they are cast aside. These logics of hyper-kinetic scripture include:

> *Habitation isolée sans autorisation en dehors de la mechta ou du douar, campement sur des lieux prohibés ; Départ du territoire de la commune sans avoir, au préalable, acquitté les impôts et sans être munis d'un permis de voyage ; Infractions aux instructions portant réglementation sur le mode d'émigration des nomades ; Réunions sans autorisation pour zerda, ziara ou autres fêtes religieuses ; coups de*

> *feu sans autorisation dans des fêtes ; Mendicité hors du douar, même pour les infirmes et les invalides, sauf cas d'autorisation* (Isolated dwelling without authorization outside the mechta or douar, camping on prohibited sites; Leaving the territory of the commune without having first paid taxes and without having a travel permit; Violations of the instructions regulating the mode of emigration of nomads; Meetings without authorization for *zerda*, *ziara* or other religious festivals; shooting without authorization at festivals; Begging outside the douar, even for the infirm and disabled, except in cases of authorization).[59]

Stasis and motility link these individual offenses. They each interrupt a familiarized rhythm, oft with attention to sleep and scenes of the night. This extends from the prohibition of providing asylum, camping on prohibited grounds, vagrancy, gathering without permission, and more generalizable restrictions to movement and mobility.[60] Internment suspended the body from public space through house arrest and detention alike.

These regulations reveal an anxious attention toward the circulation of native life, what colonial administration prefigured as liable to spill out of their "proper" place in the colonial hierarchy. The inscribed territorial boundaries and restricted curfews parallel the spatial and temporal directives exercised in the *Code Noir* as bodies were set in motion or otherwise stilled through highly regulated circulations in daily routines. The *Code de l'indigénat* also featured corporal punishment and execution, emphasizing the ways in which the body of the subject was differentiated from the body of the citizen. The abject body lingered, politically immobilized and stagnated in perpetual counterpoint to Western scriptures of modernity, yes, but very much present as a physical force and in the psychic anxiety of colonial administrators compelled to write against forecasted action. The suspension of potential mobilities along ethnoreligious lines as a legal strategy reads with contemporary familiarity.[61] *Hyper-* and *hypo-kinetic jurisprudence* become familiar refrains of legal history if we train ourselves to attune to the body at scale.

The listing of offensives teeters between minutia and the exhaustive, but never fully both. The inability to write in larger, categorical, generalizable terms of the body marks the codes such that vagueness inevitably slips into its notational system. "Acts of disorder" and "disrespectful acts or offensive remarks" against French authority, for example, prescribe a legal attitude of censored speech and conduct, but do little to describe what gestures rise to the level of illegality. The body, as central as it is to the choreographic thrust of the codes, is left hollow and ill-defined.

Exemplifying the bodily coercion of the codes "as a culture of commandment" as expanded throughout French West Africa, Gregory Mann details that when "men and women spent long nights along the marshes of the inland delta of the Niger slapping the water with their hands in order to quiet the frogs that troubled an administrator's sleep, the indigénat was at work."[62] He draws attention toward the scripted actions imposed by the codes, a strange scene of compelled labor in the dark when night gathering was otherwise banned. This historical recount underscores the ways in which the codes produced a particular rhythm with sleep, rest, and stillness as kinetic and biopolitical motivators. Not only did the code engender quality sleep for the colonial administrator, but it also produced insomnia for the colonized figure. Anthropocentric desire for control defines the choreographic logics wherein environmental domination was predicated on othered labor. Ideas of control quieted the frogs and suspended the *sujet* in a state of stasis—not stillness as rest, but the constant, repetitive slap of the water that tethered the laboring body to a fixed location along the water's edge. The historical account also reminds us that colonial rule was more often than not messy, incompetent, and inefficient, all while maintaining a façade of law and order—a fantasy of legal orientalism punctured through a return to body and earth, hands touching water, amphibians quelled.[63]

Evocative on many levels, this vignette captures a particular posture of colonial humanisms. Consider the scene again with attention to the spinal curvature of a body crouched along the riverbed. To stoop, to bend, the vertebras sweep in a convex overture toward the water in antithesis to the vertical spine of Man. A Vitruvian axis of life is refused, made illegal. In chapter 4—"Policing Dignity"—I return to the failed sign of the vertical body within human rights discourse. But here the coding of the supine figure as Other emerges through legal regulation. Erect postures code for "power, certainty, individuation . . . language and rationality," writes Susan Foster in regard to phallic desires that manifest in bodily aesthetics of European modernity.[64] By conscripting low postures, the *Code de l'indigénat* choreographed an alterity as outside these values. Kinesthetic regulations indenture postures of colonial and neo-colonial order. Rhythm is bodied, curved in the night.

The postures induced by the code recur, transplanted from the code's origin in North Africa to the Indian Ocean. In another scene of forced labor, spines contort in rounded architectures of the body, their plane disjointed from the vertical axis of modernity. Under *l'indigénat,* administrators could convert fines and incarceration into sentences of forced labor. Six hundred thousand such conversations were recorded between 1898 and 1910 in Algeria alone; enforcement often exceeded the letter of the law.[65] As petitioned to the Governor General of Madagascar against the conscription of the codes, "It is with worrisome frequency that these acts of arbitrariness are multiplying . . . the native is arrested, imprisoned for months without trial, without interrogation; and this with all the fewer restraints that the inmate is always used as an economic workforce."[66] This petition exemplifies the tension in which the native is cast as unproductive even while vehemently extracted from labor and the scale of these postures.

A photograph captioned "MADAGASCAR—Construction de la Voie Ferrée du Lac Alaotra" arrives on a postcard circa 1908 to capture this scene [Figure 3.1].

FIGURE 3.1 *Manipulation of colonial postcard, originally captioned: "MADAGASCAR—Construction de la Voie Ferrée du Lac Alaotra." Overlay by Anna Jayne Kimmel.*

Seven indentured laborers bend under the codes in the construction of a railway. Their spines angle ever lower toward the horizon, made one with the landscape. I have blurred its face, disinterested in the reproduction of racial violence and tropes of oriental travel cards. Instead, I trace the contours of the spines to document the bodily figurations and their anatomic geometries of legal alterity. Grey arches of interned laborers stoop under the weight of colonial law; overseers stand tall in perforated lines as they surveil. The erect spines wear a breasted coat and brimmed hat, ivory linen pants unmarred. The curved spines glisten bare in the sun, further encoding an aesthetics of power differential. Experiences of time emerge as relative motion, an embodied frame of reference, that positions bodies alongside or in (dis) relational line.[67]

Such scenes of racial violence, as Kemi Adeyemi deftly observes, orient around white supremacist obsession with the 90° angle that reaches up without acknowledgement of the ground beneath. Adeyemi arrives at this theory through police violence and black death in the United States and charts its historicity through Judeo-Christian order into Enlightenment thought and colonial occupation.[68] Its truth radiates in global order, including under the settler violence of the *Code de l'indigénat*. If endemic to capitalist colonial legalities, the aesthetic dis/alignment of the spine as a social signifier consolidates under the scrutiny of the dance scholar. Reflecting on the "hegemony of the vertical," Ann Cooper Albright charges: "The Christian/capitalist complex insists that what is up is good (stock markets, tall buildings, bank accounts, and other assorted 'fill in the blanks') and what is down is bad."[69]

The *l'indigénat* translates this vector onto embodied form as a choreo-jurispathic force of body, labor, and posture.

Legal codes frequently articulate an idealized way of moving, a suggestion for legalized behavior—of religious conversion, nationalistic responsibility, or other codified gestures—in a positivist attempt to choreograph a vision of compliance. This includes scripture of gestural limits of the body, as well as its affective orientation toward the subject. The *Code de l'indigénat* defaults from this rhetorical strategy. Instead of scripting behavior as what one ought to do, as detailed extensively in many articles of the *Code Noir* via its calls for naturalization and apostasy alongside other imperatives, the *Code de l'indigénat* frequently defaults to a series of ought nots. Closer scrutiny reveals an affective orientation in which the body of alterity is already presumed as non-compliant—both out of line and out of time—spawning the score to be one of regulation rather than proscription.

For example, the 1874 *Code de l'indigénat* issued in the prefect of Algiers featured the following rules (with support from penal code 465 and 466):

> February 9, 1875. – Decree of the Prefect of Algiers. Considering the decree of September 11, 1874 which declares applicable, in all the civil territories of Algeria, the provisions of Art. 17 of the decree of August 29, 1874;
>
> 3. Negligence to provide information on a crime or misdemeanor whose suspected perpetrators are not among those in respect of which the testimony of the witness is not accepted in court, and which are listed in the first 5 paragraphs of Art. 322 of the Code of Criminal Procedure;
>
> 4. Negligence to appear on simple invitation, even verbal, before the justice of the peace carrying out an investigation;
>
> 5. [. . .]
>
> 6. Disrespectful act or offensive remark vis-à-vis a representative or agent of the authority, even outside his functions, and even though this act or this remark would not meet the required characteristics to constitute a misdemeanor or an offense of insult;
>
> 7. [. . .]
>
> 8. Refusal or non-execution of guard, patrol and lookout services, placed by virtue of an order from the authority; abandonment of a position or negligence in the same services;
>
> 9. Refusal of transport services and authorized camp guards for commissioners-investigators in charge of applying the law of July 26, 1873;
>
> 10. [. . .]
>
> 11. Refusal or failure to comply with the summons of the investigating commissioners to assist as witnesses or as interested parties in the operations relating to the application of the said law;
>
> THE PREFECT: BRUNEL[70]

Refusal, negligence, and denial motivate this text. Read collectively, the codes anticipate deviance, projecting delinquency onto othered bodies while recognizing the vital force of bodily insurgency.

The different rhetorical strategies reveal a shifting attitude regarding the regulation of choreo-jurisgenerative bodies. These codes did not so much police colonial difference, but reinforce it, as a self-fulfilling prophecy through its "deeply circular connection between the colonial legal order and racial thinking."[71] Rather than affirming the potential for a model citizen (however harmful or racist that model could be), the *Code de l'indigénat* presumes defiance, anticipating and reinforcing rebellious attitudes.[72] It projects an ethnoreligious theory of behavior while also shifting the temporal register into a hypothesized future. This anticipation marks a temporal shift in our understanding of the performance of legal violence. As James McDougall summarizes, "Colonial violence was encoded, in Algeria as elsewhere, as defensive, preventive—even, already, as pre-emptive—a necessary response to the putative, and very really feared, instinctive, unpredictable and unlimited violence that the 'native' supposedly bore always within his breast, and of which his occasional self-assertion in rebellion was simply proof."[73] McDougall's interpretation underscores a historian's perception of anticipated time—"preventative—even, already, as pre-emptive," while furthering identity as bound in resistance—"self-assertion in rebellion."[74] Legal time, far from linear, skipped a beat.

I do not mean to suggest the absence of resistance, disobedience, and violence prior to the writing of the codes. Pre-colonial and colonial Algerian history alike feature anticolonial action as both individual and collective, spontaneous and organized since the French invasion in 1830. Samira Benhaddou reinforces this inclusion of resistance when she concludes her study of the *Code de l'indigénat* with the local contestation, protest, and insurrection that occurred in response: from peaceable acts of petition and debate to more active forms of refusal and disobedience to comply with French conscription.[75] The *Jeunes Algériens* further exemplifies the success of these tactics, including the Jonnart Law of 1919 which extended voting eligibility to Algerian Muslims under French governance.[76] As recently as 2025, Algeria confirmed a parliamentary commission to draft a bill to criminalize colonization, which followed upon similar efforts introduced in 2005.[77] Such a law, if passed, would shift the temporal rhythm of the legal score yet again. It would not only mandate future action, but rewrite the narrative of what has been done.

I return to these histories to underscore the multiplicities of time scores held in the code as a muddling of law and order wherein past events, or rather stigmatized perceptions of past events, leap past the present to define the future. The *l'indigénat,* anticipating future actions, shifts from a purely notational practice—a marking of what has been. It also deviates from a purely scored practice—a marking of what might be. It instead uncomfortably straddles the reiterative and proleptic at once. It is this biopolitical function of the "racialization of temporality," as Puar writes, that "puts under duress ascriptions of the past, the present, and the future."[78] Legal times warp. Such differentiated times include the suspended and exceptional body, but also the collapsed horizon of proceeding and preceding time that stall for the meantime.

CODING BLACKNESS, VAGRANCY, AND THE IDLE BODY

If the *Code de l'indigénat* suspends the ethnoreligiously other as perpetually disjointed from colonial time through a hyperkinetic jurisprudence of the body that at once stills and expels, then the Black Codes insatiably consumes black labor through the disavowal of rest in hypokinetic strategy. Phrased otherwise, if a dominant rhythm of *l'indigénat* moved bodies into positions of legal stasis, the Black Codes activated the policing and capture of those deemed to be too still through the proliferation of vagrancy acts. Stillness and (im)mobility politics saturate the kinetic subjectivity of modernity in each case, if in divergent form, setting in motion the "tick-tock of bodily time" that straddles anti-black, anti-Arab, and anti-native logics in Western ideals of humanism.[79] In the second half of this chapter, I turn toward the American transplantation of the *Code Noir* to consider legal anxieties centered around the idle body and resulting performance installations which vision alternative values to stillness as rest and rejuvenation.

Following the Civil War, the French *Code Noir* of Louisianna regenerated across the American South.[80] Although ubiquitous in the antebellum period, with prior adoption of the codes occurring as early as 1806 in Louisiana, the Black Codes are most strongly associated with laws passed in southern states in the postbellum moment (1865–1866), between the period of legal abolition and the establishment of Jim Crow laws. These laws transplanted racialized logics of the *Code Noir* to maintain the socio-political dominance through the classification of race by restricting the civil and political liberties of free black Americans. The Black Codes reflect a history of "*de facto* and *de jure* systems that have restricted the movement of black bodies in space."[81] As such, the codes undermined the efficacy of the 13th amendment that abolished slavery in the United States and gave cause to the ratification of the 14th amendment that called for equal protection under law.[82] As the French colonial logics of the *Code Noir* transferred to the American post slavery logics of Black Codes, the notational regime continued as a mechanism for discipline of the choreo-jurisgenerative body.

A *hypo-kinetic jurisprudence of the body* defined the Black Codes. Attention to the idle body became legal recourse for choreographic maneuvers as an "apparatus of capture."[83] Central was a reinforced attention to vagrancy laws whose essence criminalized both presence and rest for bodies deemed illegitimate.[84] Restrictions on the still body proliferated. Throughout the nineteenth century, southern legislatures passed codes against loitering and idleness that legitimized a practice of arresting freed people and committing them to involuntary labor. Nine southern states amended vagrancy laws immediately following the Civil War, the majority of which added clauses to allow for convict leasing and other prison labor projects; other states, such as Maryland, already had such codes on the books. As argued by Risa Goluboff, vagrancy laws—and the related policing of loitering and suspicious bodies—became a prolific tool of the State and, by 1950, were in existence in every state and Washington, D.C., illustrating the pervasiveness of this particular legal score rooted in racial anxiety.[85] Douglas Blackmon elaborates this history in *Slavery by Another Name,* asserting that the practices of convict leasing, sharecropping, and forced labor gave rise to the US prison-industrial complex that propels itself into the mid-twenty-first century.[86]

The social landscape in which American legal tradition emerges has a long history of conflating concerns of stillness with errancy, bodily need with the profane, corporeal aesthetics of rest with the unsanitary. Origins of policing in the United States can be traced back to a white supremacist desire to legally contain, as the proto-police force of the slave patrol was used to recapture and detain those who dared to run away.[87] The "kinetic project of modernity" defined within the aesthetics of dance extends to the State and its legal arm, as peoples are kept in perpetual motion in the name of labor, productivity, and capital gain.[88] "Keep moving" becomes the refrain as the codes name the unproductive body as always out of place. Consider Florida's Black Codes (1865), wherein "any able-bodied person who was 'wandering or strolling about or leading an idle, profligate, or immoral course of life' could be arrested."[89] Being idle became a crime as the State forced movement and perpetual motion for bodies deemed deviant or suspect.

Consider the following iterations of the Black Codes and the way in which they script race, labor, and stillness in tension:

> Section 1, An Act to Amend the Vagrant Laws of the State: Be it enacted by the Legislature of the State of Mississippi, that all rogues and vagabonds, idle and dissipated persons, beggars, jugglers, or persons practicing unlawful games or plays, runaways, common drunkards, common nightwalkers, pilferers, lewd, wanton, or lascivious persons, in speech or behavior, common railers and brawlers, persons who neglect their calling or employment, misspend what they earn, or do not provide for the support of themselves or their families or dependents, and all other idle and disorderly persons [...] shall be deemed and considered vagrants under the provisions of this act; and, on conviction thereof shall be fined [...] and be imprisoned.
>
> —*Mississippi Black Codes (1865)*

> An Act to Confer Civil Rights on Freedmen, and for other Purposes
> Section 2, An Act to Amend the Vagrant Laws of the State: All freedmen, free negroes and mulattoes in this State, over the age of eighteen years . . . with no lawful employment or business . . . shall be deemed vagrants.
>
> —*Mississippi Black Codes (1865)*

> An Act to Confer Civil Rights on Freedmen, and for other Purposes
>
> Art. 96, Vagrancy and Idleness: All persons who have not some fixed and known place of abode, and some lawful and respectable employment . . . shall be deemed vagrants, and be liable to the punishment hereinafter prescribed.
>
> —*South Carolina Black Codes (1865), "Some Misdemeanors"*

> Art. 98, Vagrancy and Idleness: The defendant, if sentenced to hard labor, after conviction may be hired for such wages as can be obtained for his services, to any owner or lessee of a farm, for the term of labor to which he was sentenced.
>
> —*South Carolina Black Codes (1865), "Some Misdemeanors"*

In each instance of the articles above, the racialized body becomes legally defined through its laboring potential and commodified value. Productivity stands in for personhood; stillness becomes criminal.

There is particular confoundment in Section 1 of the Mississippi Black Codes, reprinted above, in which the rogue is conflated with the juggler, and pilfering equated with game and play, as if the slide across these genres of gestural acts should be self-evident. This conflation was a common feature of US vagrancy law more broadly, in part an inheritance from early modern English law (not least the Theatrical Licensing Act of 1737, a censorship measure for plays and public performance which was written as a vagrancy law). Itinerant dance and theatrical performance punctuate corners of legal histories in surprising but consistent ways, wherein the body deemed wayward in its aesthetics becomes susceptible to scrutiny.

Beneath the surface of anti-vagrancy and anti-loitering laws and their related anxieties toward the still body simmers assumptions of idleness with unproductivity. This symmetry extends from Virginia's 1866 Vagrancy Act which opens by lamenting the rise in "idle and disorderly" persons, as well as "vagrancy and idleness."[90] The first pairing suggests that the idle body is disorderly—coded outside the bounds of order, logic, or reason and thus inherently ambiguous. The second pairing implies the vagrant body to be an idle body—coded outside of capitalist frames of productivity. Bodily gestures became economic signifiers. Economic disenfranchisement coded for racist orientations, as the codes provided the means for returning the formerly enslaved into similarly indentured positions of labor and servitude. Following the Vagrancy Act of 1866, the resting body continued to be coded as at odds with productivity. In Florida, for example, the vagrant was defined as one who relied on income elsewhere.[91] Stillness, idleness, and unproductivity became further sutured together.

Vagrancy, a catchall for the "out-of-place" body, has long centered performance and its ephemeral ambiguity. In 1960, a dance floor became the overt centerpiece of legal debate. In *Thompson v. City of Louisville,* the black petitioner was found guilty of both loitering and disorderly conduct.[92] His defense? He was dancing.[93]

As a manager would testify, he saw Sam Thompson, the petitioner, "standing there in the middle of the floor and patting his foot."[94] An officer nevertheless "baselessly" arrested Thompson for loitering.[95] Choreographic attention, and the inability (dare I say unwillingness) for legal actors involved to meaningfully and objectively discuss the body, led the case to be deemed "so totally devoid of evidentiary support as to be invalid under the Due Process Clause of the Fourteenth Amendment."[96] That the body might be read so differently points to the inherent and ongoing difficulty in objectively discussing the body when perceived as idle.[97]

More than a singular instance, this example of corporeal ambiguity at the center of juridical debate would repeat itself. Just a year after *Thompson,* the US Supreme Court ruled on a second case involving conviction without bodily evidence: *Garner v. Louisiana* involved allegations of disturbing the peace when black defendants sat at a public lunch counter.[98] That sitting or "passive presence" might give cause to citations of "disturbing or alarming the public" again underscores the lack of meaningful gestural interpretation found in the courts and the anxieties surrounding hypokinetic jurisprudence.[99] As discussed at the time:

> Thus in their essentials, the two cases were identical: they both came from the lowest state court without a clarifying opinion by the state supreme court; they both involved breach-of-the-peace type laws firmly embedded in our common-law heritage; and in both cases, the Supreme Court supplied a construction of the law demanding evidence which it found had not been produced.[100]

Both cases also center the still body, one quick to be read as out-of-place for the aesthetics of racial difference.

While racial bias and other discriminations repeatedly play a significant role in the differentiated interpretations and their motivations, a continued permission to corporeal ambiguity in legal theory underlies the tolerance for such prejudicial enforcements. Reflecting on *Thompson v. City of Louisville,* Justice Black writes it best: "Decision of this question turns not on the sufficiency of the evidence, but on whether this conviction rests upon any evidence at all."[101] His opinion reveals a very real shortcoming of evidentiary capacity and ways of legal knowing when it relates to the body and its gestures. It simultaneously underscores how many legal actors are willing to push forward even without legal evidence of bodily fact. The versatility of loitering laws, as Goluboff identifies, not only "represented an approach to policing, a vision of society" but a fundamental willingness for the law to misunderstand the objectivity of the body and its gestures.[102] While the eventual reversal of these laws reflects shifts in socio-cultural values of the 1960s and 1970s American political landscape, it also reflects an epistemological gap of the courts: namely, a continual lapse in rigorous and meaningful vocabulary when addressing the corporeal.[103]

To be a "disorderly person" requires evaluation of gesture, comportment, and more ephemeral interpretation of the body in motion.[104] Rhythms matter. The discerning eye of a choreographer seems paramount to objective analysis, above and beyond the historically-profiling gaze of police trained otherwise.[105] Without tighter attention to corporeal interpretation, legal rhetoric slips between the permissible policing of conduct to the impermissible policing of status. Race, class, and labor shift in and out of focus in these codes, leaving discriminatory ambiguity in its wake.

Loitering and idling, after all, are often defined against the litmus test of "purpose" or "object," a *raison d'être* deemed worthy by society (or at least the onlooking authority).[106] Recall that loitering laws restricted the presence of the body for an extended duration "without a clear purpose."[107] This definition thus acknowledges and presumes the ambiguity of the corporeal while nevertheless seeking to delimit it. The "clear" confounds twice over. Without *clear* purpose, on the one hand, suggests that the existence of purpose itself is not enough. Rather, it must be rendered visible and knowable to the onlooking public—present in the visual realm. At the same time, without clear purpose also suggests that visibility of purpose itself is not sufficient. Rather, the purpose must come into ready focus. It must be *clear*. This reading of visible returns us to a question of the aesthetic valence of law as it relates to the body and the resultant ambiguities. People who practice repertoires less mainstream might not be *clear* in their purpose, but this should not render their bodies less legal.[108]

The policing of rest, which finds historical foundation in these codes, ripples forward into the contemporary now in subtle yet pervasive ways. This history includes both banal and malicious legal codes at the local, state, and federal level in the United States, extending from anti-vagrancy laws and anti-loitering laws to more politicized restrictions such as the passing (and eventual repeal) of the "Walking While Trans" ban which disproportionately targeted trans women and women of color.[109] Consider also the 2024 Supreme Court ruling in *City of Grants Pass v. Johnson* which the court reversed and remanded a previous decision such that the right to sleep in public space became a criminalizable act.[110]

The codes converge. In a hypokinetic juridical structure, this wayward figure glosses for the unproductive body.[111] Stillness is either positioned as unproductive or in anticipation of violation. Legal theory rarely positions the still body as resting, recovering, or rejuvenating—three states of being which are undeniably productive if viewed at a larger scale. Rather, these vital signs are misrecognized as mere idleness, as wasted breath and dangerous potential. Across both we find, as Puar does elsewhere, "titrating control over temporality: by foreclosing or suspending access to speed, the immediacy of forms of contact, and the space-time compression so coveted in modernity and crucial to the circulation of goods, ideas, and bodies."[112] While some people have been conscripted to legal stasis, under logics of the Black Codes, passive rhythms are annulled.

REST AS REFUSAL OF THE SCORE

Against the prohibited rhythms of the idle body, slow rest emerges as a strategy of refusal.[113] Artists script rest as resistance to a system that has otherwise exploited labor from bodies of color and criminalized the reparative act of staying still. Theorized within the aesthetics of contemporary dance, "[t]he still *acts*," writes dance scholar André Lepecki, "because it interrogates economies of time, because it reveals the possibility of one's agency within controlling regimes of capital, subjectivity, labor, and mobility."[114] This orientation extends from the aesthetic to the legal, in which the body at rest becomes unduly bound in suspicion. As emphasized by Lepecki, the still body produces these anxieties in the onlooker as it seems to trouble hegemonic tempos of labor and capitalism which otherwise structure the neoliberal order. For others, such as Shabari Rao, stillness "disrupts what it means to perform" productivity, productively.[115] Stillness, as the antithetic rhythm of movement, refuses a politics of ableism, capitalism, and colonialism so deeply entrenched within some legal codes in which the model citizen has been narrowly constructed as a productive one. Stillness acts out against a national history which has propagated intolerance for downtime for communities of color. Through modulated realities and refreshed perspectives, performance works shift attention away from *what* the body does, toward the equally urgent consideration of *how* the body does.

The perpetuation of the body in motion as a socio-legal undercurrent has generated momentum in the call for the right to rest. In *Black Power Naps*, multi-media artists and activists niv Acosta and Fannie Sosa offer an immersive alternative to the hypokinetic jurisprudence, in which futuristic beds crafted in amathyst hues and luxurious sheen shimmer with their invitation to care [see Figure 3.2]. First presented at the Museum of Art and Design, Miami Dade College (2019) and later restaged at the Ford Foundation Gallery (2020) and Museum of Modern Art (2023), the space as library-cum-resting space-dreamland presents as a sanctuary for rest. Scale matters, as the invitation to rest arrives for the collective against the anti-black legal history which wrote against gathering without a pre-ordained purpose. Neon colors jolt the senses. Stillness can be loud. Stillness can be vibrant. Lying prone can be overwhelming.

Otherness and its anti-black violence, for Kemi Adeyemi, continues to be reproduced at the 0° and 180°, in direct opposition to the 90° of Man.[116] Sarah Dowling similarly builds out a literary history of the supine figure, "splayed out, laid low . . . ground down" as the murdered, the poor, the tired, sometimes named as the "prostitute, the protestor, the murder victim, the invalid, the layabout, the

FIGURE 3.2 *Image of* Black Power Naps *installation, by niv Acosta and Fannie Sosa. Photograph by Da Ping Luo. Courtesy of the artist.*

depressive: all . . . associated with lying down."[117] Hershini Young extends this posture to the floating body in search of a differential movement practice which might open from African diasporic performance.[118]

A piece built around care politics of the horizontal opens up new angles to the future in refusal of the white/normative/state line that suggests it as grounded, run into the ground. The abolitionist humanism of *Black Power Naps* finds itself oriented around the 180°, a revaluing of the horizon and its grounding frame, not an expansion of those included in the vertical reach of the 90°. The space for rest presents soft surfaces on which to lie recumbent. Acosta and Sosa invite bodies to occupy the horizontal plane, to allow the disciplining politics of the vertical spine to recede in favor of a more supportive environment. Creative world-building frays the "spatio-racial coordinates" which bind the relation of horizontality and black death in refrains that continue to be reproduced in our contemporary slave society.[119]

Napping assumes a critical edge that forces a rupture in time's linearity. Whereas we are frequently exposed to narratives of the active body as resistance, *Black Power Naps* interjects with the political potential of the passive body as an act of temporal sovereignty. The horizontal figure lies still, refusing a relentless pressure of temporal advancement. It reveals a break, a rupture, a suspension, a hiatus. For Fred Moten: "The hiatus is a stage, a break, a performative occasion, the ordinary irruption of the extraordinary in the ordinary: *blackness*—the black mass in all the richness and diversity of its becoming-object, its interior interobjectivity—*thinking* in the wrought social informality of imagining black things."[120] His rumination, indebted to Hortense Spillers, inverts dominant world orders wherein a hiatus suggests relief, nondoing. Rather, as Acosta and Sosa suggest through the nap space, the interval between—amid rest and leisure, stillness and animation, life and death, past and future—is an active construction.

Black Power Naps presents an inter-generational project of redress as it choreographs invitations of rest, care, and recovery within an oppressive national legal history. "It came from understanding that the American dream is a sleepless one," Sosa said. "We inherited this exhaustion."[121] Acosta and Sosa frame their project as an intervention into a historical lineage in which the colored body has been forced into states of exhaustion and fatigue:

> Departing from historical records that show that deliberate fragmentation of restorative sleep patterns were used to subjugate and extract labor from enslaved people, we have realized that this extraction has not stopped; it has only morphed . . . As Afro Latinx artists, we believe that reparation must come from the institution under many shapes—one of them being the redistribution of rest, relaxation, and down time.[122]

Although the *Code Noir* and its iteration into the Black Codes are not named, the legacy is most certainly addressed. Through the transfigured space, rest becomes political. "It's really the white man's worst nightmare," continues Acosta with forceful conviction, "to have a fully rested Negro who is fully self-possessed, to literally have the legendary clapback which we all need, and in order to do that, we need rest."[123]

Black Power Naps was originally presented as part of the "No Series" curated by Jenny Schlenzka at Performance Space. As named by participating artists, the wider series tarries in the legacy of Yvonne Rainer's "No Manifesto" (1965), a defining postmodern dance score drafted as a series of refusals. On the floor, the installation offered its own contemporary score, coding refusal and rest alike as a practice of choreo-jurisgenerative resistance:

> To the beings that come into the space
> Here we tell you the laws of our land.
> Continue to mind that the space is to be enjoyed without extracting or hurting.
> Leave everything intact when leaving. . .
> If you see a Black person resting, don't call the police!
> Never.
> Put your mobiles on silent and leave your shoes in the entry.
> Don't eat.
> Don't drink during this experience.

Don't disturb others' dreams or rest.
Collaborate.
Respect this sacred space.
Little ones alone without adults, not recommended but supported.
Blessings.

Race, labor, and religion again blur, rescripted once more as an alternative law of the land. A coy tension emerges between the creators' ethos of care and the named bodily demands. Acosta and Sosa assert their own laws of invitation and restriction, restructuring sociogenic norms while playing on familiar order. Rehearsed and enacted, if nonetheless real.

Or so it aims. When installed at the Museum of Modern Art in New York in 2023, museum staff ejected a woman of color at the suggestion of a white visitor who found her to be "aggressive" when asking for quiet in the space. "Basically, they told me: You can never rest!" reflected Heather Agyepong, the British Ghanaian artist in question.[124] The exchange labeled Agyepong as too much, too kinetic when removing her from the space that invited rest and stillness. In this scene and others, the policing of the idle body continues well past the racist formation of the Black Codes even in the privileged space of the museum.

Rest as a counter tempo to hypokinetic force extends beyond metaphor. Rather, the scientific impact of sleep deprivation extends wide and deep. Biomechanical metrics—of heart rate, life space, blood pressure, immunodeficiency, and more—reveal the all too real impact of legal codes on the body itself, not only on its access to personhood. These biometrics diverge along racial lines, revealing a sleep gap rooted in historic disenfranchisement.[125] Wellness becomes impacted by the score, if the body is rarely understood holistically in these terms. "Power naps" signal this vitality, while "Black power" places this biological project within a specific genealogy of activism and resistance. "Black power naps," then, as an aggregate title of the biopolitical, counters the constricted view of body knowledge.

Rest as resistance extends as a critical force for many artists, activists, and academics. Others elsewhere are quick to share in this disposition, an alternative association and appreciation for the body at rest. bell hooks, Trisha Hersey, Luke Williams, and countless more labor to share—in verse, in prose, in visual design, in performance—of "that glowing reminder that, at times, the most amazing things can emerge from a place of leisure."[126, 127, 128] As Hersey poignantly and publicly offers, rest can proffer a "*healing mechanism* for cultural trauma and a *form of resistance* against oppression."[129] For Hersey, the subversion comes in the form of a quartet of imperatives—Rest! Dream! Resist! Imagine!—as her Nap Ministry offers a more internal score for rest as resistance. It begins with an intergenerational memory of meditation, a posture of stilled lids often illegible under Western epistemologies. Her project of rest honors a "refusal to donate my body to a system that still owes a debt to my Ancestors for the theft of their labor."[130] Adam McKinney, now artistic director for the Pittsburgh Ballet Theatre, extends this politics into the realm of concert dance. In 2022, McKinney offered a creative rest session for the Jewish Studio Project, which invited the community to "look at the topic of rest and creativity through the lens of somatic practice and embodied healing."[131] Both amplify a critical, creative investment in slow rhythms as a refusal of a hypokinetic order.

As a final performance example in which flightlines flee from the temporal regime of modern discipline, Jo Kreiter's *The Wait Room* (2019–2022) confronts the historical links of stillness, blackness, and carcerality from another angle. *The Wait Room* is the first part of Kreiter's "Decarceration Trilogy: Dismantling the Prison Industrial Complex One Dance at a Time," created in partnership with the Oakland-based ESSIE Justice Group, an organization of women with incarcerated loved ones that addresses the rampant injustices created by mass incarceration.[132] The outdoor performance, choreographed as an aerial work, animates the physical and psychic experience of waiting for incarcerated loved ones, emphasizing the gendered violence of legal time experienced by those on the outside. The trope of stillness for communities of color most impacted by the prison industrial complex turns on itself: the waiting room accentuates the system of criminal law as itself the cause of delay.

A hydraulic stage fashioned as a clock dial marks the time as aerial dancers perform overhead. Their sweeping rotations carve the night sky before they rebound off the clock's face and back out again. *The harness holds her tight, bounded force as security, as she tumbles through empty space. She inverts, hanging head under heels, ankles bound by an industrial rope, a chair left vacant beneath.* The aerial dance produces an alternative aesthetics of stillness that returns us to the relative motion of suspension—bodies sail in onto-kinetic flight over the surface of the clock under which gravity, not only time, moves differently. The platform tilts; the horizon shifts. Vertebras reorient, then disorient. The dancers refuse to be mapped within the temporal frame of relative motion that dominates scientific time. Suspended, their aerial arcs destabilize the authoritative politics of 90°. Rhythms continue to be regulated, not least in the carceral setting staged by Kreiter. Whether hyper-kinetics suspend the body in a legal double bind of stasis, or hypo-kinetics compel movement by disavowing stillness, rhythms of law continue to order its publics at the scale of the masses.

Much more can, should, and has been written on these legal codes, as their structured violence created a system of dominance that requires continuous dismantling; my aim is not to offer that history here. Rather, in Part I I gather each of these three texts—the *Code Noir,* the *Code de l'indigénat,* and the Black Codes—to exemplify the project of legal writing as a choreographic one. Comportment, conduct, and the disciplined form cinch these two separate forms of law and dance, as both seek a body: to regulate, monitor, produce, or animate. As Susan Foster writes, they "operated to confirm the existence of an absolute set of laws to which all bodies should conform."[133] That the "they" in her sentence could refer to either the legal codes or dance notation is precisely the point.

From the *Code Noir* to the *Code de l'indigénat* to the Black Codes, theories of the choreo-jurisgenerative permeate legal history. As French legal theory consolidated into its civil law practice, attention to the body and its kinesthetic potential saturated the codes. Dance notation, developed in the courts, parallel governmental attention to the body. If the particular zeal of Louis XIV faded, a national norm for legal coding was set in motion. Century after century, this entangled attention ripples forward with profound consequence: law as score, body as archive, legal time as racially coded rhythms of humanity. Violence, discipline, and refusal surface as common practice, collectively rendered banal through the dehumanizing rhetoric which centers the body, abjected or consumed. In spite of the intellectualization of law, its rational processes remain plagued by irrationalities as the fleshed slip from full articulation. From the metropole of France, to the expanded empire across the waters of the Atlantic and the Mediterranean, to the islands of the Caribbean and the Gulf shores, the epistemology of the choreo-jurisgenerative body spread, whether acknowledged or not.

INTERLUDE

SYCORAX'S ALTERITY

In the lore of Sycorax, we know few objective facts. She arrived on the fictional island in 1588, or thereabouts. She is the contoured, absent flesh that nonetheless returns. Her legacy plays out from the periphery. In Shakespeare's *The Tempest* (1611), the Algerian mother of Caliban births the antagonist but never receives any lines. Even though her character becomes a felt recurrence, this single mother appears only through hearsay. The audience learns of the sorcerer's exiled life through secondary commentary: the chastising tongue of a Conquistador villainizes her past while her son champions her authority. She is a body without voice, already deceased when the play begins. She remains an enigma, "depicted as a subject without language, and therefore without humanity."[1] We must settle for her description by Prospero as the "hunched back foul woman," "physically loathsome," and "filthy, obscene, and discolored."[2] She stands in as the absented body of the outlaw, the blackened and darkened contour in Shakespeare's early modern worldview.

The making of the island order turned on the "jurisgenerativity of no-bodies" as Sycorax's absent presence defined the terms and conditions of future play.[3] Shakespeare positioned her outside the law, made geographically peripheral through her exile *and* intellectually unknowable to the socio-legal orders of the day. She was ostracized for dark magic, witchcraft, and occult praxis that undermined the authority of more narrow ways of knowing. Phrased otherwise, her embodied, non-literary expertise was presumed as suspect, aberrant, and deserving of expulsion. She became both illegal and a-legal, her mythical ways of knowing too much for legal frames. Others push further to suggest her pregnancy as a deviant act of legal procedure to avoid execution, placing her closer to the "Frenchwoman Joan of Arc, who also tried to save herself from the law by claiming she was pregnant with a bastard; Joan simply wasn't as successful."[4] This built lore, based on fact or fable, condemns the mother while essentializing the reproductive potential of her form. She was thus scripted, scored, and inured into a rhythm of alienation. She has since been silenced, disciplined, and erased. Yet she moves. Even along the periphery, she is central to the story if not centered in the text.

The void from which Sycorax persists has become a rallying point for black feminist, Caribbean diaspora, and Native studies. For Hortense Spillers, Sycorax confirms the "unrepresentability" of Caliban as an anagram of the cannibal and brutal figuration of the Caribbean—the beastly other that the genocidal formation of the New World Americas necessitates. Her "not-sayable offers a strategy for describing the 'future,' which is always a pregnant possibility in the now."[5] For Abena Busia, Sycorax's "unvoicing" casts the woman's voice as void, and debates about Caliban and Ariel "are in danger of continuing the lie that tells the story as if Sycorax had no part, and as if her voice were absent from the debate."[6] For Sylvia Wynter, "Caliban's woman" is Miranda, not his mother. In her reading of the play Sycorax slips even further from view as foil to Prospero.[7] Wynter reads an "epistemic absence" in *The Tempest*, not only of Caliban's non-desire for a woman—reproducing a hetero-ablest orientation to humanity—but of a wider knowledge system altogether that embraces something beyond the lettered arts. In each iteration, Sycorax stands for the silenced and speaks from the edge. Reinterpreted in plays, operas, sculpture, film, and other media, her myth continues to reverberate.

I linger here in the absent, and arguably misunderstood, body of Sycorax whose visceral self never quite appears but who nevertheless symbolizes various structures, ideologies, and histories for centuries to come. Shakespeare's final mother births something else. For the argument made in this book, Sycorax comes to represent an alternative way of knowing—not just a separate positionality cast aside, but a separate way of being in the world—whose orders and logics unsettle conceits of legal formation that continue to date.

> *What would shift if we allowed Sycorax to remain, to have a body even after her moment of* habeas corpus? *That is, if legal theory attended as much to the corporeal aesthetics and bodily movement of Sycorax's mythology as it did to the language and the literary authority of Prospero? How can these black and indigenous femme forms—these Sycoraxian modalities of being, living, and becoming—come to script legal studies differently? What would it take to make present the impact of her absence and alienation? If her body slips from view, what recourse do we have to reconstitute it and thereby reinsert her?*

I pose these questions as a dancer and performance studies scholar committed to the legal humanities so that we might together imagine a theoretical landscape in which Sycorax can "buck against [the] kinetic normativity" circumscribed in an imperial frame of jurisprudence.[8] *Legal Moves* adopts a method by which, borrowing from Irene Lara, one makes an effort to position oneself (and one's discipline) "alongside Sycorax."[9] My refusal to turn away from the material body, to allow a discourse to speak for and through the flesh, credits the maleficent legacy of Sycorax.

It has since become common practice to suggest that *The Tempest* narrativizes and normalizes a colonial drama, presenting a European vision of Man driven by a domineering appetite for land and body.[10] The island play spills from its imaginary dot into Mediterranean and Atlantic spaces alike, intertwining Italy and Algeria, Tunisia and Bermuda, and stormy cosmographies through crisscrossed sea voyages.[11] Shakespeare himself was influenced by the real-world events of discovery captured in travelogues of Renaissance explorers, not least historical recounts of the 1609 *Sea Venture*'s wreckage in Bermuda while en route to Virginia. Beneath these violent worldviews—dark European fantasies of ecological imperialism, anthropocentric comedy, and indigenous erasure—percolates two ideologies less often addressed: the tandem modes in which the body and its knowledges are scripted for the Other, not least in Sycorax's omnipresence. These other ways of knowing and moving cohere through Sycorax and ripple forth into lasting configurations of body and knowledge that continue to structure narratives of global legal orders, including questions of governance, sovereignty, property, and personhood.

Western epistemological anxiety features the unwritten, the embodied, the fleshly ways of knowing that counter rhetoric's hegemony in legal spaces. *The Tempest* hinges on this ideological thrust and epistemological ordering. In one instance, the originary criminalization of Sycorax turns on her possession of a knowledge system deemed threatening to the status quo. Proclamations of "[t]his damned witch" and her "sorceries terrible" justify her position as exile (1.2.316–320), as if trans-corporeal and para-literary knowledge is dangerous and its possession by a woman of color to be feared and punished. Juxtaposed, Prospero self-presents as "the prime duke, being so reputed/In dignity, and for the liberal arts/Without a parallel" (1.2.90–95). Edification confirms his stature. Yet in his fervor for "secret studies" outside the literary empiricism of the liberal arts, he lost Milan to his brother (1.2.95). This scene leverages education to simultaneously reinforce the duke as the superior being while also blaming other intellectual pursuits outside the canon as reason for his political fall. Ways of knowing outside of empirical study transform into sites of blame and dark influence.

At the same time, the New World Order was constructed through bodily differences and corporeal aesthetics. The play relies on deforming language to invoke Sycorax as an ethnically crip other. Prospero brandishes a critique of the figure of "that foul witch" who "with age [she's] grown into a hoop," elsewhere calling her "hunched back" (1.2.309–310). More than an ageist quip on the elderly, this line binds colonial understandings of human anatomy, corporeal aesthetics, and criminalized personhood. Her spine becomes the focus, an anatomical attention paralleled at the time in rhetoric of decorum and the dancing body as court dances and prototypes of ballet stretched across European spaces of rule. Shakespeare positioned Sycorax's inhumanity against the vertical line, her supine spine withheld as the sign of European refute. From the atlas vertebrae to the coccyx, attention to the carriage of the body—gesture, stature, and comportment—creates the foundation of the play. Her child's dehumanization takes place in similarly corporealized discourse, exaggerated to such an extreme that a servant, encountering Caliban's body, incredulously ponders: "What have we here, man or fish? Dead or/ alive?" (2.2.25–35).

Wynter emphasizes this rift in her analysis of *The Tempest*: "A new notion of the world and 'idea of order' was being mapped now, no longer upon the physical cosmos. Instead, the projected 'space of Otherness' was now to be mapped on phenotypical and religio-cultural differences . . . as a 'law' that allegedly functioned to order human societies in the same way as the newly discovered laws of nature served to regulate the processes of functioning of physical and organic levels."[12] *The Tempest* builds upon socio-political imaginations of the ideal body founded in the Renaissance tradition of humanism to carve its colonial fictions. "The disruptive potential of carnality" cohered as European mainstay.[13]

Moral geographies of an old-world order, alongside more empirical geographies of new world discovery, continued to be produced on and off the stage. Ballets in the salles of Versailles repeated similar exotic fabulations and allegories to power as Louis XIV manifested European absolutism. The making of Man was well underway, swelled by the French Renaissance period which pushed toward its apex. Renaissance humanisms uplifted the masculinely coded projects of scientific, geographic, and imperial pursuit of Europe. In the precipice of the French Revolution and its sweeping reform, difference lay at the heart: culture and nature, mind and body, self and other, Prospero and Caliban, Sycorax and Miranda. "I think, and therefore I am," not "I move, and therefore I know" was the cogito *de jure*.[14]

Modern law served as the lynchpin to the worldmaking of colonial order, configuring the human through absences and presences, in which Sycorax was included only as a foil in the making of Man. The French Revolution produced a global epistemology of rights and Man with transhistorical implications: liberal European humanism codified itself in the 1789 Declaration of the Rights of Man and the Citizen, its limited scope critiqued but enduring in the 1791 Declaration of the Rights of Woman and the Female Citizen; the United States ratified its own constitution the same year; the Haitian Revolution moved toward successful insurrection (1791–1804); and the *Code Napoléon* (1804) formalized a system of civil law based on Enlightenment value and prior iterations of the *Grande Ordonnance de Procédure Civile* (1667). Modernity thus arrived.

Legal studies similarly calcifies a stratified view of language over the bodied, in which the linguistic and the literate reign supreme within its logocentric methodology. Even the legal scholar James Boyd White would ask, in response to *The Tempest,* if we can imagine an "actual legal system without rules."[15] The textual authority of law, akin to Prospero's command of language that distinguishes him from the "monstrosities" on the island, continues to be reproduced. Such an occluded domain formalizes a worldview "half-starved" and impoverished, forever in deficit of a fuller truth.[16] The fault line of disciplinary logics found in the legal humanities, in which the book is valued over the body, reflects a wider trend in legal studies and broader figurations beneath the human. Ironically, this includes early discourse of legal humanists too, in which its Italian Renaissance intellects exalted textual analysis of Roman law, including the more performative space of speech and oration. Read again in a time wherein trust in legal authority as an objective matter has been eroded, its language and procedure manipulated, Sycorax's alterity proffers a lens through which we might reconsider the limitations of the literary acumen of the law.

As Samera Esmeir argues, the entangled relationship between the rise of positive law, colonialism, and the human precedes a "juridical humanity," a conceptual phrase which names the law's central role in constructing this fabricated order of humanisms.[17] The seventeenth century saw the expansion of the first French colonial empire as European reach pressed into the Americas, the Caribbean, and Southeast Asia. In that century, occupation was had, genocide waged, cartographies remapped. Sycorax's home of Algeria would come to define the second French colonial empire. France's *mission civilisatrice* leveraged cultural, theological, and linguistic differences to justify military intervention and conquest. These historical dramas unfold not quite in parallel, but nonetheless spill out a new world order shaped by concomitant values of enlightened/science/white/dominance. Far from a French-specific history, implications flow into the Americas, not least through the Louisiana Purchase and the hangover of French law into the United States. The Black Codes, a transplantation of French law into US civil law tradition, structured postbellum legal racism and enabled the ongoing practice of police brutality.

I linger with *The Tempest* not for its historical accuracy, but its "prophetic" summary of the epistemological blind spots which served to structure the New World of particular British, French, and Spanish formation.[18] Although the play is fictional, its imports are no less true. As Lara asks of Sycorax, "Absolute accuracy of representation may not be possible, nor is it necessarily the goal." The intervention in these ongoing discussions is "to imagine the possibilities of 'her' missing or distorted subjectivity in the modern-colonial imaginary and the ways that making 'her' *present* may help us to better understand the unjust legacies of similar underrepresented and misrepresented subjects."[19] Sycorax, this fictional figure, continues to haunt our world orders and ways of knowing. The erasure of her being and flesh outlines her presence, acting as a mirror to the failures and restrictions of law's logocentrism. Instead of reading Sycorax's muted presence as confirmation that the subaltern cannot speak, the artists who reimagine her potential instead suggest that she speaks in alternative, non-linguistic communication "illegible to Western forms of narrative."[20] This follows from Charmaine Lurch, a visual artist and sculptor whose wirey presentation of Sycorax performs a disruption to habituated ways of viewing, mapping, claiming. Lurch instead presents a Sycorax who "evokes a dancing grace and beauty."[21] She produces a "different way to see, think, and perceive" rooted in an appreciation of corporeal and bodily ways of knowing.[22]

Alternative knowledge systems require alternative methods. "She abolishes," writes Kamau Brathwaite of Sycorax, "the traditional margin and the boundaries of books," or in this case, the four corners of law and its black-lettered hegemony.[23] Motivated by Sycorax to take seriously the need for a methodological shift away from the linguistic and toward the corporeal processes and events which undergird legal logics, I suggest the coupling of critical dance and legal studies to reinsert the body as a source of knowledge and as a disruption to the proto-liberal humanism modeled in *The Tempest*.[24] As Tiffany King reminds us in *The Black Shoals*, "new worldmaking practices require pores, skin, bone, touch, erotics, and new haptic modes that change our relations to the notion of the human as an ordered sovereign, bounded, raced, and settled individual."[25] Sycorax, exiled for her alternative ways of knowing and powers which unsettle a status quo, becomes absented from future categories of the human. "Occupying Sycorax's position," writes King, "overturns the order of Man and refuses the aesthetics, orders, and structures of the violence of conquest."[26] *Legal Moves* aims to center this alternative way of knowing, one historically peripheral in spaces of academia and so-named institutions of higher education, calling for a richer tapestry of legal methods to supplement (but not displace) existing norms. I shift us toward viscerality in addition to visibility, the corporeal over the anatomical, the felt beyond the forensic, the physical over the discursive, the body as sentient rather than merely sensitive.

The chapters which surround begin to answer the questions posed here. They probe an epistemological shift, a pressing together of body and law, colonialism and the choreographic, literary ways of knowing alongside more moving forms. I invite the reader to occupy Sycorax's position, or at least to imagine a world in which legal studies is positioned alongside.

PART II

Righting Wrongs

CHAPTER FOUR

POLICING DIGNITY

> ***Le 17 octobre 1961, alors qu'ils avaient tenté de manifester contre le couvre-feu décrété quelques jours plus tôt par le préfet de police, une véritable chasse à l'homme s'était déchaînée contre eux. Alors qu'officiellement on avait d'abord parlé de 2 morts, la réalité était très supérieure : sans doute environ 200 victimes. Ce 17 octobre 1961 avait été le paroxysme d'une répression sanglante. Très vite ces crimes avaient été dissimulés et l'oubli les avait recouverts.***
>
> **(On October 17, 1961, when they had tried to demonstrate against the curfew decreed a few days earlier by the prefect of police, a real manhunt was unleashed against them. While officially there was first talk of 2 deaths, the reality was much higher: probably around 200 victims. This October 17, 1961 had been the paroxysm of a bloody repression. Very quickly these crimes had been concealed and oblivion had covered them up.)**[1]
>
> —*JEAN-LUC EINUDI,* Octobre 1961, Un Massacre à Paris

On April 2, 1998, the Assize Court of Gironde found Maurice Papon guilty of crimes against humanity for aiding and abetting the unlawful arrest of Jewish persons in 1942, thereby assisting in their deportation to Auschwitz.[2] During this longest trial in French history, a trial within a trial emerged: questions were raised about Papon's good character for his role in the 1961 Paris Massacre, an event described in the epigraph above (which transpired the same year that Papon received the Legion of Honor medal, in near satire of a commitment to human dignity and demonstration of "tolerance" by a necropolitical state).[3] After WWII, Papon, the former secretary-general of the Gironde prefecture during the Occupation and a part of the de Gaullist regime, went on to become the prefect of the Paris police (1958–1967). During this tenure, he oversaw the violent and fatal suppression of French Algerian resistance by the Parisian gendarme, including leadership during the 1961 events. Notable for several reasons, the massacre evidenced the use of colonial tactics of torture, detainment, and death carried out within European borders.[4] As an expert witness called to testify, historian Jean-Luc Einaudi confirmed Papon's responsibility in the massacre, alongside testimonies provided by archivists Philippe Grand and Brigitte Lainé. By associating the events of 1961 with those of 1942, the trial staged a complex narrative of genocide and postcolonial order, once again correlating Algerian and Jewish positionality as per the *Code de l'indigénat* in a modern practice of ethnoreligious othering.[5]

The trial lays bare the monolithic authority of transitional justice and its Western hegemony at a time when repartitions and re-judication efforts gathered critical mass more globally. The trial itself played out in what Lisa Yoneyama theorizes as a post-Cold War global order, the decade following the collapse of the Soviet Union in which international affairs settled into new political, economic, and socio-cultural formations.[6] The scrutinized events themselves fell any pretense of the narrative wherein France assumes an untarnished, heroic position of moral victor against the Axis powers. Papon's culpability on the world stage names France as complicit with the pan-European Nazi Holocaust and extends the inheritance of the postcolonial condition to include similar atrocities. The trial bares the contradiction of 1961 as Europe championed a commitment to human rights in 1948 while continuing to perpetuate colonial violence, not least the mass casualties and tremendous brutalities of the Algerian War for Independence then seven years, and an estimated one million deaths, in an accumulative toll. By 1961, the mass migration of *pieds-noirs* further tested the limits of cosmopolitan hospitality in Europe's center.[7] The distinction between law and justice, as Jacques Derrida reminds, remains "unstable."[8]

Scholars return to this moment in which bodies were rendered absent before the law in a geopolitical "economy of affirmation and forgetting" in liberalism's archive, noting the violation of French-Algerian bodily integrity and subsequent historical erasure.[9] Fatima El-Tayeb reflects that the "connection between colonial and metropolitan violence that Papon personified" is "persistently suppressed in European discourse."[10] Randall Williams broadens the argument to identify the "secret intimacies" between the *Universal Declaration of Human Rights* and the European desire to contain anticolonial momentum.[11] Although crimes against humanity for which Papon was charged operate on a separate legal plane from human rights, both presume a universalized image of the human who is meant to be protected in embodied terms. Built upon pillars of European modernity, subsequent expressions of dignity as corporeally manifest turn on provincialized norms of scopic appeal, not universal truths.

As a concept, dignity has been theorized extensively from a legal, moral, philosophical, and political position: as virtue, as right, as autonomy, as inviolable.[12] It has taken on diverse and divisive meanings, strongly bound up with concepts of rank, value, respect, merit, and honor.[13] Conflicting interpretations create a circular telos, in which dignity is both an inherent property of being human and yet also something that requires vigilant protection as dignity's tautology shifts between intrinsic-being and active-doing. It simultaneously calls for yet eludes embodiment. Dignity becomes, then, a "public, normative practice" but arguably one that is also, in many ways, performative, and for other scholars still, "nothing but a phrase."[14] Dignity thus takes on a vacuous meaning, nearly void of a significant referent as its porous interpretations drain it of stable force.[15] A return to the archive of human rights atrocity in 1961 Paris gives space and form to theorize the embodiment of dignity, a capacious signifier rarely pinned down in legal terms in spite of its reaching presence and global significance. At stake is an understanding of dignity not as a universal ideal, but a provincialized aesthetic of the body.

Theories of bodily being inform legal, discursive figurations of the dignified body, even when those epistemological underpinnings often go unnamed. Sans acknowledgement, this figuration becomes cast as neutral, objective, natural: legal, self-evident, and inherent, as in the preamble of the declaration of human rights. But within this mainstreaming of human rights discourse, there exists a liberal paradox regarding the body that has yet to be fully reconciled, a paradox suggested by Elizabeth Anker as an "ambivalence toward embodiment" indicative of Eurocentric ideals of knowing, a "decorporealized vision of the subject."[16] But as I argue throughout this book, bodies materialize laws as much as, if not more than, their written counterpart.[17] Dignity accrues through vast repertories of social, political, and religious norms. Although dignity's logic may hold up to scrutiny in its rhetorical form, contours of its universal corporeality is anything but inherent. When this attunement falls from view, implications can be deadly; the aporetic relationship of law and justice reifies. Might we unbind human rights and their corollary aesthetics of dignity from a choreo-jurispathic center?

Throughout Part II, I feature the choreo-jurisgenerative body refracted through the aesthetics of ballet, as its its repertoire of French nobility offers particular clarity into the blurred lines between aesthetic, epistemological, and legal projects of social order. Its techniques, values, aesthetics, and practice saturate law in both central and oblique ways. This normative body asserts a soft power, as those held outside of its reified anatomy are cast as disfigured, illegitimate, and as I argue, at times illegal. As anthropologist David Scott suggests in an interview with Sylvia Wynter, "[t]he anticolonial assault, then, is one fundamental moment in the dissolution of Europe's idea of itself as the embodiment of humanity's ideal."[18] This holds ongoing purchase not only in French legal tradition, but international courts as well. If human rights ideologies have become (or always were) severed from a universally-embodied articulation, the chapters in this section analyze their underlying hierarchies of aesthetics while simultaneously pointing to their vital consequence.

In this chapter, I return to the 1961 Paris Massacre in which the language of dignity reared itself as provincial.[19] On the precipice of French colonial rupture, the performance of dignity—through expressions of non-violence, orderly conduct, and the vertical spine—was not enough to prevent atrocity. This chapter opens with close readings of a photography series by Elie Kagan of the Paris Massacre to exhume the entangled logics of dignity, embodiment, and kinesthetic signs as documented October 17. I situate this historization within a wider history of the embodied aesthetics of dignity through which human rights have come to be both defined and regulated, one I trace through kinetic logics of comportment and nobility with particular attention to the vertical line of dignity as an orienting geometry of the body. I argue that residual expectations of the dignified body continue as an embodied aesthetic of French nationalism and hangover of the reign of Louis XIV. Read together, I show how these embodied aesthetics make visible the exclusionary logic beneath the purported universality of human rights. With this trajectory in mind, I return to police records from the Paris Préfecture to challenge assumptions of representation and recognition as duelling assertions of dignity contra honor compete for legibility within the official reports of the massacre. I conclude by considering a contemporary protest in Paris in which scenes of the overtly balletic body, as a hallmark of dignity's sign, seemingly neutralized a violent response. At stake is an understanding of the corporealized legibility of dignity as a provincial signifier as well as of the limits of its declared universalism.

1961: A CHALLENGE TO DIGNITY'S VERTICAL LINE

The Paris Massacre of 1961 was an evening of bloodshed that punctuated a turbulent month of struggle between Algerians living in France and the French police during the final months of the Algerian War of Independence. Recorded as "the bloodiest act of state repression of street protest in Western Europe in modern history,"[20] the event refers to a night of pacifist protest by French Muslim Algerians.[21] Approximately 20,000 French Algerians participated in the protest; approximately 12,000 were wrongly arrested or detained, and differentiated accounts estimate 20 to 200 were killed by the French police under the leadership of police chief Maurice Papon.[22] The scale of brutality is impossible to ignore, notwithstanding the fact that cover-ups and national narratives of history write it otherwise.

The protest aimed to demonstrate support for the Algerian *Front de libération nationale* (FLN) in France in an act of anti-colonial sentiment, although formally it was a retaliation against a curfew policy imposed on French Algerians as abjecting codes continued across the mid-century.[23] Protestors assembled throughout Paris, with main gathering points along the Grand Boulevards from Place de l'Opéra to Place de la République. Shots were fired by the French police at Pont de Neuilly, and additional deaths occurred at Pont Saint-Michel across from the

Police Prefecture. Those detained were brought by the *Régie Autonome des Transport Parisiens* (RATP) to *Le Parc des Expositions de la Porte de Versailles* (Palais des Sports), where torture and beatings led to additional deaths in the coming days. Demonstrations continued, including coordinated events by the FLN, student organizations, and female-powered resistance. No police deaths were ever reported.

October 17 was the culmination of police violence and Algerian resistance. Most Algerian deaths by police violence in Paris 1961 occurred before October 17, even if that fateful date was the singularly most fatal.[24] In the weeks preceding the demonstrations, countless bodies were recovered from the Seine and other channels of water—the identification of the deceased eroded over time without means of identification.[25] Disintegrated and decomposed, bodily integrity was not a priority for the police. The aggressive police reaction was without justification that evening, however, as the police were notified in advance of the pacifist and unarmed intention of the protest, including the anticipated presence of women and children. It was, rather, a result of more entrenched State anxiety toward foreign terrorism and Arabophobia that built upon actions taken by both the FLN and *Organisation armée secrète* (OAS) in Paris in the preceding weeks. The FLN's *Fédération de France*, led by Mohamed Zouaoui, came to be viewed as a counter-state to French authority.[26] Anxieties in the metropole reflected escalating atrocities overseas during the Algerian War for Independence, including mass exodus of *pieds-noirs* migrating from Algeria into France.[27] I name this context to situate this localized event in a much larger history of anticolonial revolution and vindication.

The draconian treatment of French-Algerians during the Algerian War of Independence—both in France and its overseas occupation, including the discriminatory curfew that precipitated the massacre and followed activities of detention, exportation, and death—was promoted in the name of national security and public order as a "state of exception."[28] But the perverse ordering of humanity was anything but exceptional. Racialization in 1961 was colonial, but as Michael Rothberg argues, also imbued with historical practices of antisemitism to which Papon was formally linked.[29] Only those with North African heritage—whether Algerian or not and including those with legal French citizenship—were targeted under Papon's regime. This "inconsistency," as the FLN named it in their *Déclaration Sur la Répression et les Mesures policières dans la région Parisienne,* included the "racist humiliation" of French police tactics against French Muslim Algerians, which escalated throughout 1961 up to and after the event of October 17.[30]

When discussed at all, the historiography of the event presents multiple, contradictory perspectives. Papon eventually filed a libel suit against historian Jean-Luc Einaudi for his representation of the event which, effectively dismissed, presses into questions of memory, evidence, and recognition. The French government has yet to offer a formal apology to the families and communities of those most impacted.[31] My aim is not to re-historize this event or to attempt to locate a new level of truth from the remnants of a partial and hazy narrative. The event, its death toll, its economic damage, and its emotional trauma have already been catalogued by scholars like Einaudi. Rather, I intervene to name the aesthetic ambiguity of the choreo-jurisgenerative body and the way anticipated violence punctuates legal discourse involving its bodily description. Surrounding reports evidence an ethnoracial bias in dignity's performance and call into question the universality of human rights discourse.

Consider the following descriptors of the 1961 Paris Massacre, which lend the language of dignity to an embodied and corporeal form:

> The marchers set out for the central boulevards with an unmistakable sense of release and a pride in their ability to assert their dignity as Algerian patriots—a pride that Papon and his lieutenants found insufferable and were determined to punish.[32]
>
> —*HISTORIANS JIM HOUSE AND NEIL MACMASTER*

> I was struck by the impression of discipline that reigned throughout the procession.[33]
>
> —*DISTRICT COMMANDER GAVEAU*

> They marched in good order, the leaders at the front, with an inexpressible dignity.[34]
>
> —*JOURNALIST RENÉ DAZY*

These three reflections, offered from a historian, an officer, and a journalist in transhistorical positioning, summarize an affective orientation toward a dignified body as simultaneously disciplined, insufferable, and inexpressible. An air of stateliness circulates, as pride, patriotism, and other militarized language frame what is regarded as the dignified body within nationalistic terms.

One word catches my attention above the rest: what is so *inexpressible* about dignity? And what are the consequences of its inexpression? The inexpressible body pulls at my senses and demands refinement in its corporeal articulation. It suggests a lack of precision even when the stakes are most high. I hear an echo of Justice Potter—*I know it when I see it*—which then, as now, excuses State/white/national hegemonic preference to ensure the opinion of the court as fact. Discernment transfers to the witness as judge, the moving body displaced from its own frame of reference.

Few photographs of the 1961 massacre exist as evidence, as film and cameras were intentionally destroyed by the police throughout the bloodied night. The most circulated photographs come from Elie Kagan, a freelance reporter for *L'Humanité*, who documented the night alongside René Dazy.[35] In one image, a sea of young men arranged in an orderly group fills the street beneath a sign advertising the star Jean Gabin in a juxtaposition of French dreams. *Protestors file in orderly procession, walking upright with strict postures and arms pressed to their sides. Faces are bright, expressions calm. Collared shirts, buttoned high, peek beneath long overcoats, dark ties, and groomed mustaches.* The protestors might as well be queuing for entry to the theater. The crowd faces toward the cameraman in a choreographic front with clear rows spilling out. Two men oppose the masses with arms raised as if to conduct the traffic of human forms. No one seems jostled, off-kilter, or uncertain: there is a systematic line and design, a repeated motif of order that haunts the photograph. With spines straight and shoulders squared, the protestors presented an "inexpressible" rank of dignity. "Dressed in their Sunday best" of pressed shirts and knotted ties, the dignified body of Paris 1961 seems to be synonymous with the disciplined body, an aesthetic associated with Western European cultural tradition and ethnoreligious hierarchy of cosmopolitan non-belonging.

The bodies in Kagan's photographs adopt a posture of dignity that refuses the retroactive discourse of agitation, violence, and volatility offered in the massacre's coverage. French historian Lia Brozgal repeats this interpretation, affirming on the opening page of her monograph that the demonstration was "dignified and peaceful."[36] The crowds cohere in a vision of dignity as theorized by Ernst Bloch as "walking upright" and later by Jeremy Waldron as "a sort of moral orthopedics," emphasizing dignity as ambulatory and terpsichorean, a bodily architecture of philosophical force.[37] In a similar vein, Derrida's writing on law returns his reader to Freud's theory of the origin of moral law wherein affective sensibilities of shame lead *homo sapiens* to walk upright in postures of the vertical Man.[38] The line—taken as the vertical spine in anatomical performance of dignity, an upright vector—distinguished one's moral and physical stature as peaceable before the law, a sign and request for dignified treatment and human rights standards to apply.

The embodiment of upright postures of "*proper* citizens" became a strategy for non-white life in the Arabophobic state.[39] Such verticality, a corporeal articulation of rank and highness, deployed in scenes of anticolonial protest work against the derogatory status French-Algerians were demanded to occupy under colonial world orders. It plays into the Eurocentric imagination of rights that, in a post-World War II era, declared itself the standard for universal human rights discourse. No arms of any sort were allowed to be carried at the October 17 protest, as explicitly and publicly announced to French police in advance. The tactic of deployed dignity extended to a politics of non-violence that linked the Algerian effort in global solidarity.[40] In the same year, across the Atlantic John Lewis recounts civil rights era sit-ins: "It was like going to church, I guess. You would put on your church-going clothes, Sunday clothes, and we took books and papers and did our homework at the lunch counter, just quiet and trying to be *as dignified as possible*."[41] Performed just a few months later by French-Algerians, a similar aesthetics of dignity was modeled in an attempt to be regarded as fully human under discrminatory frames of law and order.

But the sign glitched, willfully unheeded. Violence surrounds the vertical body when signals of the raced body fail to extend beyond the flesh.[42] In these scenes, choreographic assumptions override close reading of the performance. Consider, by extension, that the gesture demanded in "Hands up! Don't shoot!" asserts a verbal cue to perform a *port de bras,* to compel the body upward into a sign of dignity and a vulnerable posture of surrender. Hands raised above the head, palms facing out: the sign of compliance and non-threatening life is built upon an exaggerated performance of the vertical line. But too often the line falters and life splays. "Blackness is what lays bare the limits of this kinesthetic sign," writes dance scholar Anusha Kedhar, "what turns this universal gesture of submission into a gesture of guilt, criminality, and culpability."[43] If this sign so often fails as a universal referent, especially in the anti-black demos of the US police state, the intuition still exists to script the body into vertical comportment in recognition that sociogenic disavowal of dignity might arrive through embodied repertoires.

I wonder, though, whether the sign failed in 1961. Or rather, if shifted to the onlooking officers, the surrendered posture of dignity signaled space to exercise racial violence. Perhaps the vertical line of the body signals non-violence, but raced flesh signals in higher frequency in an anti-black, anti-Arab, ethno-humanist world. In the contemporary era, murders of black and brown lives by US police all too frequently occur in response to the most mundane of activities: sleeping, holding Skittles, walking home. In France, civilian fatalities from police brutality during traffic stops have enflamed the nation, including fatal force against youth of Algerian descent. French President Emmanuel Macron acknowledged these recent events as both "inexplicable" and "inexcusable," the former term glossing an eerie echo of the "inexpressible" dignity of French Algerian demonstrators in 1961.[44]

The vertical line travels across theories to reproduce the category of Man and its ethnoreligious exclusions. This line pierces through historical arcs of Judeo-Christian custom, Enlightenment thought, colonial order, and capitalist logics to become, for Kemi Adeyemi, "intimately entwined with beliefs around subjectivity, rationality, civility, and, ultimately, one's capacity to fit in the category of Human."[45] The line as oppressive vector saturates posthumanist figurations, including non-representational forms of Deleuzian "lines of flight" which, per Tiffany King, nevertheless "resurrect the human through the geo-epistemology of the 'line'" even as they attempt to escape exclusionary orders and colonial-genocidal logics.[46] "Even the 'line of flight,'" writes King, "establishes a linear/nonlinear structural opposition that demarcates the 'order' of the invisible white 'self' in opposition to the 'chaotic' realm of the dead Indigenous and Black 'nonbeing,'"[47] Phrased otherwise, the "geometry of line" understood from within the theory of Gilles Deleuze and Félix Guattari reproduces, rather than refuses, the hierarchies it writes against.[48] King's sharp skepticism toward the utopic potential of post-humanist, nonrepresentational politics returns us to the line as a moral barrier, a geometric shape, and an aberration of inclusion made possible only through no-body's death, underscored by the events of October 17. This is the jeopardy, I argue, in the close association between verticality, universality, and descriptions of the dignified.

Not cast in the armor of classical form, the choreo-jurisgenerative body becomes vulnerable before the law. From this slippage, the inherent status of dignity presumed by human rights comes into question. "When I search for Man in the technique and style of Europe, I see only a succession of negations of man, and an avalanche of murders," concludes Frantz Fanon in *The Wretched of the Earth*.[49] Since human rights have become endowed with concepts of dignity, their representation, embodiment, and enactment reveal an understanding of what it means to be dignified, to have dignity, or to risk the indignant and the undignified. For Carolyn Dean, "The destruction or mutilation of the body is now a metaphor for the violation of human dignity and the destruction or 'unmaking' of the civilized world."[50] Can we imagine the recognition of dignity outside of assertions of universality written in the techniques of Europe? Can humanisms exist beyond the vertical? Can they embrace horizontality as an "aesthetic modality and an egalitarian gesture," per Telory Davis's call, rather than the antithesis to the power held in upright being?[51]

Extending the critique of the vertical line of Man and its fatal failures, I suggest that dignity is not, as often upheld, a universal liberty but rather, in Foucauldian terms, a regulatory ideal. When dignity becomes seen as a narrow manifestation of reason and rational form, dignity becomes at odds with the charges of human rights. To understand dignity as an aesthetic code and embodied repertoire, once applied as a condition to human rights, extends the interpretative force of law to the embodied. Once dignity's visual and embodied form are considered, its efficacy begins to unravel. Even a return to the spine, the skeletal vector that binds flesh and body, cannot overcome the raced overtones of human rights' first order of dignity, named for all but granted only to the few. To police dignity is a jurispathic logic and choreo-jurispathic force—a delimitation and negation of rights based on corporeal aesthetics that is all too often fatal.

BALLETIC LEGACIES AND PROVINCIALIZED AESTHETICS OF DIGNITY

Dignity sits as the *a priori* concept of human rights. In a now familiar refrain, the 1948 *Universal Declaration of Human Rights* begins its preamble by foregrounding this concept and repeats this priority in Art. 1: "All human beings are born free and equal in dignity and rights."[52] The insertion of "dignity" into the opening lines directly amends the previous standard that "men are born and remain free and equal in rights" found in Art. 1 of the 1789 *Declaration of the Rights of Man and of the Citizen*.[53] Either by negligence or intention, the language of dignity was fully absent from this foundational constitution. Absent too was an expression of the human at the species level, replaced by "Man" and "Citizen," by which the body became bound in State jurisdiction and gendered formalism.[54] Since 1948, countless other charters, constitutions, and legal texts center on the ideal of dignity.[55] But despite its historical reach and conceptual breadth, dignity only came into contact with legal frames after WWII as human rights consolidated as a universal concept under the liberalist project of the United Nations and the fraught politics of global reconciliation.[56] As a result, dignity is often eclipsed by the coeval discourse of liberalism: individual sovereignty, rationality, and liberty before the law.

Such are dignity's purported universal, and universalizing, standards. French legal scholar Muriel Fabre-Magnan summarizes that dignity does not aim to "protect a particular person, or even a category of persons, but humanity in general."[57] Instead, dignity accounts for "what exceeds man, what remains a transcendence despite what we have called the disenchantment of the world."[58] Yet this diffuse status of dignity, at once generous and egalitarian, risks dissolving entirely when not held to more particular standards of expression. Put more sharply, approaches to dignity as a universal value mask its Eurocentric aesthetic hold. Movement toward the vertical degree of Man is not transcendent but assimilationist. Choreo-jurispathic orders lead to provincialized aesthetics of rights and man, but when glossed as universal, fail in their protections. Dignity, as performed by an ethnoreligiously othered body, becomes "inexpressible."

Empire claims for itself "morally upright behavior," furthering the metonym of the dignified body as a sign of righteousness.[59] With the body at the center, dignity embodies an aesthetic position previously theorized under socio-economic terms of class. Jeremy Waldron, scholar of law and philosophy, features an embodied potential when theorizing dignity from the perspective of rank and nobility, taking the literal language of "your highness" and other markers of the dignified. Waldron writes:

> The high character of dignity also has physical connotations—a sort of "moral orthopedics" of human dignity;—what some Marxists, following Ernst Bloch, used to call "walking upright"; Dignity has resonances of something like noble bearing. In one of the meanings the Oxford English Dictionary ascribes to the term, it connotes "befitting elevation of aspect, manner, or style; . . . Stateliness, gravity." When we hear the claim that someone has dignity, what comes to mind are ideas such as: having a certain sort of presence, uprightness of bearing, self-possession and self-control, self-presentation as someone to be reckoned with, and not being abject, pitiable, distressed, or overly submissive in circumstances of adversity.[60]

This interpretation stems from a twentieth-century discourse indebted to ancient concepts of *dignitas* that centered social and political status, rank, and etiquette in place of more contemporary theorizations of a universal human nature.[61]

Here it is easy to imagine Waldron's words, read out of context, as the description of the balletic body, the disciplined choreo-jurispathic figure which has been afforded legal protections in spite of its animatedness. Bloch's invocation of walking upright invokes the vertical spine, an aesthetic and anatomical choice that has often distinguished ballet from other dance forms, especially those taxonomized as non-Western or non-classical. By extension, this definition then places the balletic body in direct opposition to the "abject, pitiable, distressed" body and reifies an ableist perception. The classical form of Louis XIV's court becomes the gold standard for the dignified.[62]

Consider the parallels between Waldron's formulation of dignity and dance scholar Brenda Dixon Gottschild's classification of ballet:

> In traditional European dance aesthetics, the torso must be held upright for correct classic form. The erect spine is the center, the hierarchical ruler from which all movement is generated. It functions as a single unit. The straight, uninflected torso indicates elegance or royalty and acts as the absolute monarch, dominating the dancing body. This vertically aligned spine is the first principle of European dance, with arm and leg movements emanating from and returning to it *[demonstrating]*. The ballet canon is organized around this center. In fact, this structural principle is a microcosm of the post-Renaissance colonialist worldview. Like the straight, centered spine of its dancing body, Europe posited *itself* as the center of the world, with everything else controlled and defined by it.[63]

But unlike mainstream discourses on dignity, Gottschild continues to challenge this embodied advantage: "As assessed by Africanist aesthetic criteria, the Europeanist dancing body is rigid, aloof, cold, and one-dimensional. By Europeanist standards, the Africanist dancing body is vulgar, comic, uncontrolled, undisciplined and, most of all, promiscuous."[64] Here, perspective makes all the difference, as point of view determines criteria in spite of the supposed universality afforded dignity.

The aporetic definition of dignity arose alongside an aesthetic lineage of Man, both produced and secured in theatrical spaces, performance venues, and dance manuals—that is, while dignity moves plurally through discourses of politics, philosophy, and religion it simultaneously coheres through bodily acts and state repertoires performed by and for the model subject, the proper citizen. When Louis XIV established ballet as "one of the most honorable and necessary means to train the body [and] our Nobility," dignity cohered as regulation of rank and status.[65] The embodied form of the dance floor seeps into public imagination elsewhere: the chin slightly lifted as a line of elegance, shoulders firmly squared as a site of authority, footwork deftly controlled as both grace and good health. Ballet consolidated the idea of the dancing body as the dignified body par excellence, endowed with royal aesthetic in the divine image of a king. Subsequent legal code built upon this logic to conscript a subject of modernity through repertoires of decorum. This corporeal coding of the French body emerged in parallel to the structures of French ballet as coded in the courts. Reaching an apex by the twentieth century, the classical form exemplified a vision of the humanistic ideal. The preeminence of the balletic body perpetuates an understanding of the ways in which aesthetic trends of the body have produced and reified some of the most divisive presentations of difference, especially along the colonial-modern fissure, including in legal spheres and the jurisdiction of human rights.

This parallel between techniques of ballet and philosophies of dignity proffers an embodied aesthetics often left unnamed. In *The Frail Social Body,* Carolyn Dean translates this argument on movement aesthetics to a wider argument on the aesthetics of human rights: "Universal personhood and the universal body that houses it is an ideological fiction: one that renders mostly white, masculine, heterosexual, and upper-class bodies the standard against which all others are judged."[66] But I raise this parallel for a more pressing thesis: if dignity reflects the aesthetic norms of ballet, and if ballet has been demythologized as a provincial, ethnic form, then dignity stands to have its own aesthetics interrogated for its false universalism. The claim for ballet as an ethnic form arrives from Joann Kealiinohomoku's essay, "An Anthropologist Looks at Ballet as a Form of Ethnic Dance," wherein she catalogues the flora and fauna, customs and celebrations, mythology and narratives which regularly play out in story-ballets so as to locate ballet in provincialized space-time rather than atemporal mark of high art.[67] *Consequently, the dignified body as an* a priori *value is much more culturally specific than the universalizing language of the human rights declaration proports to be.*

The collapsed distance between ballet and dignity suggests an aesthetic value to the presentation of human rights rooted in a shared attunement to corporeity that leaves little room for bodily alterity. Precisely because ballet suggests a specific decorum associated with a Eurocentric vision of nobility, rank, and grace, dominant human rights imaginaries fail to extend elsewhere. The balletic body then becomes a metonym for the inviolable body, exemplifying the domineering reach of a Eurocentric aesthetic tradition in legal terms. Such is the larger sophism of human rights, in which the efficacy of universal claims fails to be fully felt when its provincialized aesthetics remain uninterrogated.

A turn toward the embodied attunement to dignity is not new, if its aesthetic inheritance in other realms is not often drawn in shared formation. Following Enlightenment theories of dignity established by Immanuel Kant, Friedrich Schiller related dignity to conduct, mannerisms, and comportment. In his 1793 essay "On

Grace and Dignity," beauty and aesthetics entangle again and point us toward a repertoire of ballet in surprising and uncanny ways.[68] Schiller offered a preliminary formula for understanding the relationship between the embodied and the intellectual, suggesting that "[d]ignity relates to the *form* and not to the *content* of emotion."[69] He summarizes that "grace lies in the *freedom of willful movements, dignity* in *mastery over unwilful movements.*"[70] The former clause draws us toward embodiment in human form; the latter clause of mastery over unwilful movements reads close similarity to the definitions of ballet as described by Gottschild. It invokes the aesthetics of self-restraint, sovereignty, and bodily control—values rehearsed in the ballet studio as the human figure contorts itself into hyperextension and rotation in the name of virtuosity. Dignity becomes a technique of presenting the self as "calm in suffering," tethered to gracefulness in service of a larger aim.[71] Comportment, seen as self-control, sutures legal ascription of dignity to ballet's aesthetic tradition in contrast to more ecstatic forms. Contemporary scholars repeat this concept of agency and autonomy within their discourse of dignity—the self-disciplined figure that the techniqued body so clearly presents under provincialized lines.[72]

Dignity maintains its embodied foci when approached from outside this particular tradition. R. A. Judy, for example, emphasizes an Arabo-Islamic center of dignity in modernity's origin, in which dignity and imagination are the wanted couplet. For Judy, human dignity—كرامة الإنسان *kāramat-ul-insān*—emerges via the literary domain of the poetic as traced through the pages of Qur'anic verse.[73] He arrives at this point through Giovanni Pico della Mirandola's 1486 "Oration on the Dignity of Man," which opens with an expression of the "theater of the world"—an aesthetic, scripted space of live performance and embodiment.[74] The genealogy of dignity traced back through Euro-Arab crossings still presents the embodied aesthetics of dignity, if that overture has become lost along the way. As important, Judy notes that such orientations toward dignity are "foundational to the 'humanist' tendency of modernity . . . an anthropocentric *studia humanitas*," in further recognition of the provincialized history of dignity's false universalism.[75]

HONORABLE MENTION

Against propositions of modern sovereignty, concepts of dignity have been nefariously invoked as a means to regulate, restrict, and enforce conformity to national ideals across public and private divides. Within the French political and legal contexts, for example, dignity has been appealed to in the regulation of religious head coverings, the condemnation of surrogacy, and the challenge of rights pertaining to homosexuality and other identities. Policies of *laïcité* distinct to France inflect how dignity is understood, transmitted, policed, and performed, as state structures define it in relation to secularity. Bound in a strategy of assimilation rather than an approach of inclusion or integration, it has been wielded as a biopolitical force within discourses of national indignity in order to make claims on the relationship between dignity, belonging, and citizenship.[76] In short, dignity has been used to script assimilation toward a singular aesthetic possibility.

Elizabeth Anker summarizes this choreo-jurispathic conceit:

> As liberalism scripts the human, the dignified individual in possession of rights is imagined to inhabit an always already fully integrated and inviolable body . . . *At the same time, it posits a dangerously purified subject, one purged of the body's assumedly anarchic appetencies*: its needs and desires, its vulnerability and decay. And when the body cannot be thus ignored, the liberal tradition generally treats it as an *entity that must be repressed, quarantined, or otherwise mastered by reason.*[77]

In this poetic excerpt, Anker raises a potent question: beyond the dignified body, how do we view the undignified body, that is "defiled, decaying, or broken," the very body recovered from the Seine but neglected from history?[78] Under liberal legal frames, can the dignified body, in its material form, extend to the shamed, the harmed, the sick, and the otherwise non-normative figure?

When consulting the formal police archives of the 1961 massacre, I sought traces of dignity, or its absent flesh, to understand the event within a larger paradigm of human rights and human rights abuses and the ways in which consequences of its slippage became most fatal.[79] Toward that aim, I spent countless hours rifling through paper trails of violence. The official records housed in the *Archives de la Préfecture de Police* contain: boxes of paperwork with police memos, records of the FLN, family inquiries into the status of the disappeared, attempts at finding their location, duration of hospitalizations, and narratives of death. Scattered within these folders are also: autopsy reports, he-said-she-said accounts of gunshots and violence, and dehumanizing justifications of the atrocity. At the time of my research, the boxes had to be swept under general derogation prior to my viewing; the files had been opened to Einaudi for Papon's trial but resealed to the public for sixty years per French law.[80] I do not know how to account for the absent flesh of law when censorship leads to erasure and amnesty leads to political amnesia. "Colonial unknowing" and disremembrance facilitate artificial inroads to history with the humanity of some populations entirely eclipsed.[81] The desire to enflesh dignity from hollowed State language blurs text and body into a simultaneous effort of maintenance and re-membering.

Perhaps we ought not expect to find the rhetoric of dignity from law enforcement in its official records of the deaths. And yet these documents contain innumerable examples of correspondence to grieving and distraught families in search of information about their loved ones, to the press, and to the National Assembly—public and private areas in which the expression and acknowledgement of human rights could be expected to frame action. Nevertheless, a pattern did emerge: countless expressions of "honor" were iterated by French State actors, including Papon himself. A catch phrase of "*J 'ai l'honneur à vous faire connaitre que*... (I have the honor to let you know...)" saturates archival remnants as Papon and other officials responded, in dozens of letters, to inquiries on the whereabouts of individuals present at the protest. Speaking internally to the police force, he emphasized "*votre fidélité à nos traditions de discipline et d'honneur* (your loyalty to our traditions of discipline and honor)."[82] By framing his own sense of honor alongside institutional legacy, the dignity of an individual victim was eclipsed when human rights were forgotten as a universal responsibility.[83] Those endowed with State rank were presumed honorable, while those cast outside of State recognition (with an emphasis on Algerian origin regardless of citizenship status) were dismissed altogether, allowed to have been disappeared without a trace. In the 1998 trial of Papon, Einaudi turned the tables when, on the witness stand, he said that Papon's responsibility in the Paris massacre "dishonored the police."[84]

In contrast, statements of honor rarely appeared from French Algerian voices, which were instead replaced by calls for dignity: "*Nous avons conscience d'obéir à de nobles préoccupations, de préserver notre dignité d'hommes* (We have a conscience to obey noble concerns, to preserve our dignity as men)." For example, a declaration of the FLN slipped in these files concluded with a call for "*les objectifs humains de justice* (human objectives of justice)"; days later, student protestors repeated the refrain as they announced "*la revendication du peuple algérien à la dignité et à la liberté* (the demand of Algerian people for dignity and liberty)."[85] The FLN leader Zouaoui himself had ordered Algerians to demonstrate "peacefully, with dignity and an absolute calm," paralleling the language of grace and dignity amplified in the term's political-philosophical genealogy.[86] More importantly for my argument here, however, is the way that Zouaoui implies that dignity has an aesthetic element to its enactment, as if one could choose to perform dignity in protest (rather than it being a static fact of being as is often taken for granted under international law). By attending to the performative properties of dignity as a value secured through bodily acts, not intrinsic to being—first in the directive and then in its instantiation—he calls attention to the universal falsehood of human rights' first *a priori*.

Although this national division between the French expression of honor and Algerian expressions of dignity may be a linguistic bias of the small sampling at the *Archives de la Préfecture de Police,* or a nuance lost in translation, the striking division suggests the limits of a universal understanding of dignity when identified via rhetoric alone. Legal scholar Orit Kamir offers an important insight into the differing cultural and legal tones of dignity and honor, two concepts with distinct valences that are often used with flippant interchangeability or mutual constitution. "Like honor," writes Kamir, "the concept of dignity synthesizes (or confuses) human nature, noble sentiment, and claims to social respect and legal rights with actual 'natural,' social and/or legal rights. Like honor, dignity is thus generally treated as simultaneously empirical and normative, natural and social, both a source and a consequence. Its specific features, however, remain largely vague."[87] Distinguishing these two terms, she elaborates that "'honor' refers to the social status acquired by individuals in reference to the norms of an honor culture they belong to, whereas 'human dignity' is an innate, human attribute that is equally imprinted in every human being and commends reverence by all."[88] Honor, articulated as status, arrives through past accolades, accomplishments, and inheritance whereas dignity accrues in the present based on postures, bodily moves, and corporeal aesthetics. Honor lacks the embodied and aesthetic imprint suggested by dignity—an aesthetic I have traced through dance studies methods, imprinted in somatic repertoires yet at times denied before law, as the events of 1961 remind.

The divided attention to the body in official state reports surrounding 1961 underscores the raced connotations of dignity according to which it is presumed for some and thus without demonstrative expression, whereas for others it is a disavowed reality that requires constant re-enunciation in order to secure its future. Autopsy reports of October 1961 signal their own categories of Man, in which identifying classes descend from man, to subject, to deceased, to cadaver. This ordering scales from the bodily vitally of the human to the localized form stripped of life. It holds in residual effect the impact of Darwin's taxonomy still in need of *decolonial scientia*.[89] The body slips into flesh. Personhood ceases for the inanimate, as dignity becomes detached from the cadaver on grounds of its lifeless form.

A brother's careful description of October 17 illustrates a stark difference in attentions:

> *Le corps de mon frère était bleu, tout couvert d'ecchymoses, du sang avait coulé de son nez et de sa bouche et était coagulé. Il avait la tête ouverte, deux balles dans le flanc, un pansement sur les parties sexuelles et des traces de liens aux chevilles et aux poignets* (My brother's body was blue, all covered with bruises, blood had flowed from his nose and mouth and was clotted. He had his head cut open, two bullets in his side, a bandage on his sexual parts and traces of restraints on his ankles and wrists).[90]

Harrowing in its detail, the sheer recognition of the inhumane treatment affords a sense of dignity, of acknowledgment, of the violating acts. In contrast to the State legalese that merely tabulated a minimum body count and attested to the honor of the officers at the scene, the language of Amar Mallek's brother forced my own body to pause and recollect itself. Violence toward the body, previously erased by the weight of the archive and the bureaucracy of paperwork, re-emerges for the demand of accountability. As this note was titled, "*MALLEK n'est plus un 'disparu': il a été tortué et assassin* (Mallek is no longer a 'disappeared': he was tortured and murdered)." The passage extends a recognition rooted in the flesh, not assuaged by bodily absence. I return here not with a pornographic consumption of violence, but to sit with the aesthetic conditions at stake (or at risk) when rhetoric does not extend to fleshly descriptions.

Mallek's name was not the only one. Names unfolded before me, creating an affective forcefield in the archive, implicating me alongside the paperwork. These names felt out of place in this official Parisian prefecture scene. With their Arabic and Tamazight origins, such names had not often been included in official French discourse outside of narratives of colonial violence. But their legal record became an official trace of having been, even as their flesh was rendered absent before the law. Page after page, memo after memo, names were signed with a date of birth and marked with FLN association alongside language like "disappeared since," "marked urgent," and other stamps of anxiety. Marcia Siegel might have written that dance exists at the vanishing point; these individuals danced a tragic lack under provincialized aesthetics of law, perpetually at the vanishing point of public memory and state recognition.[91]

Jean-Luc Einaudi opens his history of October 17 with an epigraph by the Algerian author Kateb Yacine:

Peuple français, tu as tout vu	(French people, you saw it all)
Oui, tout vu de tes propres yeux.	(Yes, saw it all with your own eyes.)
Tu as vu notre sang couler	(You saw our blood flow)
Tu as vu la police	(You saw the police)
Assommer les manifestants	(Strike unconscious the demonstrators)
Et les jeter dans la Seine.	(And throw them in the Seine.)
La Seine rougissante	(The blushing Seine)
N'a pas cessé les jours suivants	(Did not stop the following days)
De vomir à la face	(To spew in the face)
Du peuple de la Commune	(Of the people of the Commune)
Ces corps martyrisés	(These martyred bodies)
Qui rappelaient aux Parisiens	(Who reminded the Parisians)
Leurs propres révolutions	(Their own revolutions)
Leur propre résistance.	(Their own resistance.)
Peuple français, tu as tout vu,	(French people, you saw it all)
Oui, tout vu de tes propres yeux,	(Yes, saw it with your own eyes)
Et maintenant vas-tu parler,	(And now are you going to speak,)
Et maintenant vas-tu te taire?	(And now are you going to fall silent?)[92]

In this excerpt, dignity is denied by those who refuse to look. The refrain "*tout vu de tes propres yeux* (saw it with your own eyes)" names and accuses in a familiar moral stance; at a more onto-epistemic level, the line suggests that dignity operates in the visual realm, that it has an evidentiary aesthetic value rooted in the proprioceptive. But the "it" that was seen remains elusive, fleeting from collective figuration when not more carefully held in embodied terms.

Under these conditions, the dignified body becomes one that is recognized—seen and legitimated in its very being. To be seen, to be witnessed, to have an audience. I write this not as an assertion but in caution. There is a thin line between the "witness and the spectator," recognition and voyeurism in scenes of global atrocity.[93] When dignity hinges on recognition, it becomes conditional and contextual, no longer universal (if it ever was). Aimé Césaire sutures these terms when he writes: "*en combattant pour la dignité de nos peoples, pour leur vérité et pour leur reconnaissance . . . nous aurons aidé à fonder l'humanisme universel* (by struggling for the dignity of our peoples, for their truth and for their *recognition* . . . we have helped to found a universal humanism)."[94] This conditional status harkens back to the opening words of the 1948 Universal Declaration of Human Rights (UDHR): "Whereas recognition of the inherent dignity and of the equal and inalienable rights of all."[95] Dignity, no longer a self-endowed value, requires visual receipt, embedding the body in relational form. Inversely, non-recognition swells the absent flesh of law.

Reflecting on October 17, Jacques Rancière amplifies the ways in which dignity turns on presumptions of the visibility of the body before law or absented as flesh:

> That day, with its twofold aspect (manifest and hidden), was a turning point. . . . The crucial thing about the effect of that day was the way in which the questions of the visibility and invisibility of repression became interwoven. . . . The police cleared the public space and, thanks to a news blackout, made its own operations invisible. . . . A phrase used by Sartre in his preface to *Les Damnés de la terre* helps us to understand, *a contrario*, the meaning of that twofold disappearance: "The blinding sun of torture has now reached its zenith, and it is lighting up the whole country." Now, the truth is that this blinding sun never lit up anything. Marked and tortured bodies do not light up anything. . . . On the contrary, *it was an invisibility*, the removal of something by the action of the police . . . *a form of intervention which prescribes what can be seen and what cannot be seen*.[96]

Frustrations with the lack of State acknowledgement of the massacre, then and now, underscore this orientation as the disappeared and disavowed were erased from the official French record and diminished as a mere incident. Rancière relies on the ocular, perceptions of the body, drawing attention toward the cleavage between the body and its flesh as legal systems and state rhetoric police "what can be seen and what cannot be seen." Therein lies a double-bind of recognition politics, wherein dignity is extended to the body visible before law, but the invisible body without dignity is never receipt of a stage to appear.

Recognition politics which hinge on perceptions of dignity fail as both a sensorial gesture and as a legislative force. That is, recognition politics fail to account for the body *and* its flesh, the choreographic frame *and* its performance. This question of recognition returns me to the founding logic of *habeas corpus*, to produce a body *before the law*, rather than to more nascent discourses of visibility politics. "To be before" is not only a temporal antecedent, but a relational construction of the body. State officials and historians alike have viewed this reciprocity as a partial remedy, even retroactively; others remind us that recognition is never enough while the exclusionary category of the human remains.[97] In all cases, recognition is not merely a legally ascribed status, but a kinetically produced aesthesis that situates both parties in contextual socio-political lineages. Recognition comes with ambivalence, at once a call for radical inclusion along abolitionist frames and a fraught politics with the potential to "replicate and reinscribe colonial regimes of knowledge/power."[98]

Despite these shortcomings, practices of acknowledgement and remembrance can serve in the dismantling of reified categories of life under law in extra-judicial efforts of reconciliation—be it the testimony of French conservationists at Papon's trial who violated policy in order to bring public awareness to the history, or the many cultural works produced in the tragedy's legacy. Benjamin Stora calls attention to this difference in intent:

> *Tout en connaissant la torture, elle ne la reconnaît pas officiellement. Il faut faire la distinction entre connaissance et reconnaissance. Dans l'espace public commémoratif, il n'y a rien: le 17 octobre 1961 n'est pas la rafle du Vél d'Hiv* (While in awareness of the torture, she did not recognize it. A distinction must be made between awareness and recognition. In the commemorative public space, there is nothing: October 17 1961 is not the Vél d'Hiv roundup).[99]

Stora's careful parsing between awareness and recognition turns on a distinction of physio-somatic nuance, as dignity becomes articulated in the eye of the beholder.

If names "would surface in journalism," in a macabre pun of language, traces of corporeal violence were minimized in lieu of more symbolic acts of remembrance.[100] In 2021, French President Emmanuel Macron announced a process for the recognition of French colonial violence in Algeria, including the events of 1961 in Paris. Stora, in a report commissioned by Macron, also called for a Truth and Memory Commission alongside other acts of memorialization.[101] But just as the call for "truth and memory" leaves behind the action of repair, most cultural memory produced about the event also eclipses the felt-senses of the body. Instead, linguistic and visual forms abound, including literary and graphic novels, poetry, and films. But as Sidi Mohammed Barkat reminds us: "*Rien, jamais, ne remplacera le témoignage de ceux qui ont vécu dans leur corps le drame du 17 octobre 1961*

(Nothing, ever, will replace the testimony of those who lived in their bodies the drama of October 17, 1961)."[102]

Tucked into the northeast corner of Pont Saint-Michel, a plaque commemorates the lives lost during the Paris Massacre of 1961. "*A la mémoire des nombreux algériens tues lors de la sanglante répression de la manifestation pacifique du 17 octobre 1961* (In memory of the number of Algerians killed during the bloody repression of the pacifist demonstration of October 17, 1991)," reads the sign. A "number of Algerians" weighs as an empty euphemism for the lack of State regard for the particular lives and bodies lost; the passive construct of "Algerians killed" side steps responsibility as it obscures culpability. Above the plaque, a metal statue communicates loss. Seven rows of seven silhouettes have been cut from a steel sheet, cut-outs of the lives lost, bodies rendered present through negative space [Figure 4.1]. "Missing persons" takes on a whole new meaning. Standing on the bank of the Seine to view this memorial, I am forced to peer through these hollow faces into the river into which some were thrown. The Paris Préfecture stands not even a block behind, though archives of this event have been removed to the east of the city, the distance a not-so-subtle metonym for the geo-spatial politics of histories deemed central to the capital city's mythology.

Until recently, the memorial was much less formal. "*Ici on noie les Algériennes* (Here they drowned the Algerians)" read a graffitied tag on the Pont Saint-Michel, painted but quickly scrubbed in an effort to effect colonial amnesia.[103] Photographed in the 1960s, the black and white image and its script produce but a trace of a graphic history marked upon bodies. Other images of its aftermath, such as those produced by Anne Tristan in *Le Silence de Fleuve,* reveal the body itself, offering insights into the (in)dignity performed through visual means.[104] The location of the bridge, one scene of many crimes, shimmers as a site of transit without memory as tourists pass nonchalantly by, unaware of the scene that was truly violent. I suspect many remain unfamiliar with this history, with that fateful date somehow too close and too far. This trace of the absent flesh, forgotten before the law, draws us back as the marked labor of violated bodies remains against a constitutional guarantee of dignity.

SWANS IN THE STREET

On the eve of Christmas 2019, Paris Opéra ballet dancers gathered outside Palais Garnier to perform sections of *Swan Lake.* Tchaikovsky's score swirled across white practice tutus as the dancers cautiously performed the petit allegro and the elegant arms of the emblematic ballet.[105] The unity of their movement in the *corps de ballet* scenes reflected solidarity, their multiplicity a refracted body politic anonymized by their uniform. With an arm raised and wrists folded gently, their heads bowed demurely into their shoulder to create the silhouette of a swan.

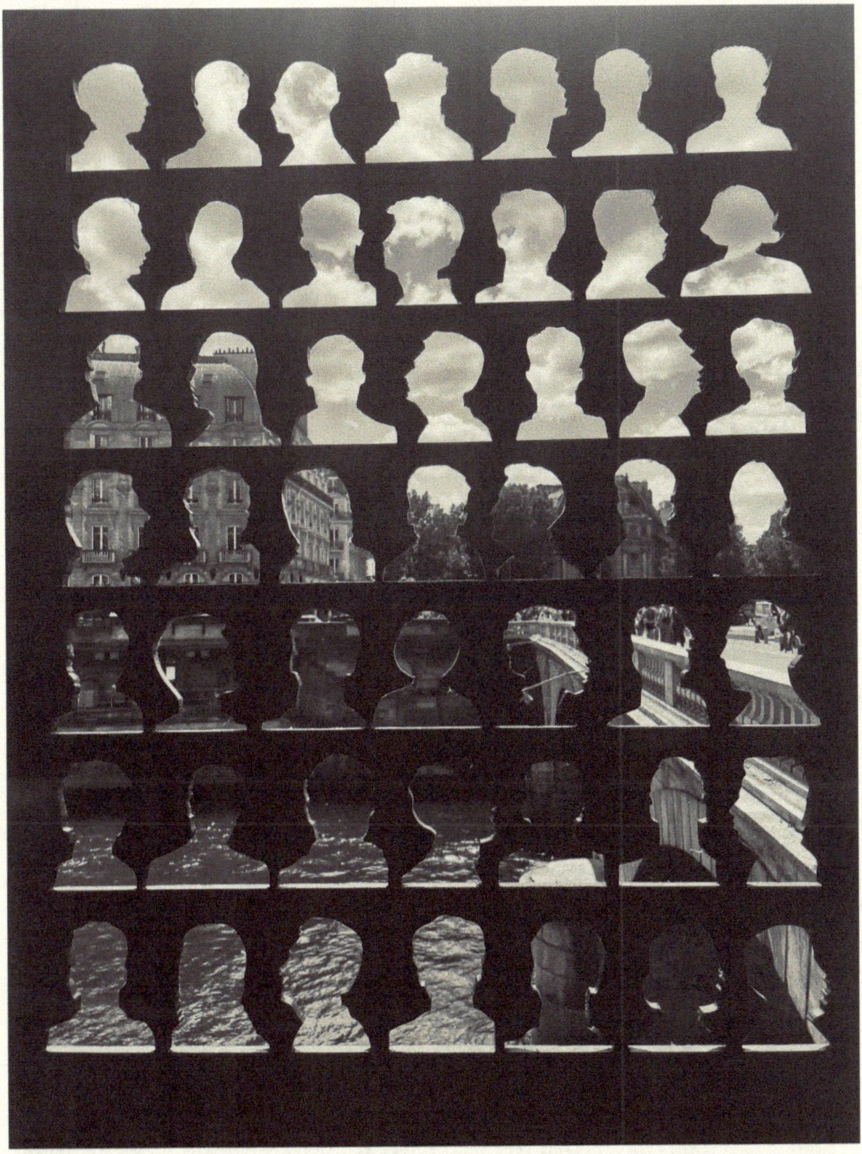

FIGURE 4.1 *A memorial to October 17, 1961, in Paris, France. The steel cutouts were added in 2019 alongside the plaque from 2001 which reads:* à la mémoire des nombreux Algériens tués lors de la sanglante répression de la manifestation pacifique du 17 octobre 1961. *Photograph by Anna Jayne Kimmel, 2022.*

"Culture is in danger" read the signs of artists and other civilians gathered to strike against a proposed retirement reform affecting French employees, including everyone from transportation personnel to healthcare workers to prima ballerinas. Implementation of the proposed universal pension plan would have unilaterally raised retirement to age sixty-four across professions, merging a system that has historically recognized the differences in aging bodies across employment sectors. Ballet dancers from the Paris Opéra stood to be the most effected, as retirement was previously mandated at age forty-two—retirement privileges that carry over from that seventeenth-century contract issued by a king.

"Even the Ballet Dancers are On Strike," published *The New York Times*, reflecting on the longest strike in France since the extraordinary efforts of May 1968.[106] Indeed, the protest functioned as a significant act of solidarity between the ballet dancers and all occupations at the Paris Opéra (as well as the next generation): the protest continued even after the government affirmed that current dancers would not be affected by the proposed changes. *Swan Lake* unfolded outside the Palais Garnier as an apology was issued to a wanting audience in light of performances cancelled by the strike; meanwhile, rehearsals continued inside for *Raymonda*.[107] Contracted principal dancers could not participate in the protest as a result of the contingent need for a potential performance. Instead, they were asked to train as if the show would go on. The "even" of the headline, though, suggests that ballet dancers would otherwise be excluded, as though the labor of their bodies was not included in the labor unions' address. *Even the ballet dancers are on strike* suggests that ballet dancers are not viewed as political, dissident, or as if the politics of the times were provocative enough for *even the ballet dancers* to strike. Ballet becomes an alibi in this neo-Enlightened aesthetic order.

But ballet dancers, especially in France, have long been entangled in political concerns. When the contract was first issued in 1698, the regulations, edicts, and ordinances that surrounded this State contract addressed marine and militant protections, soldiers in French colonies, the establishment of regulated commerce on Saint-Domingue, seminary initiatives and religious fugitives, indicating that the vast preoccupations of the State included attention to *even* the Opéra and its performers.[108] More than three centuries later, political and financial concerns about ballet continue to be raised, not least the reality that the pay of the historically female-majority company remains approximately half of that for the musicians of the Paris Opéra, a historically male-majority company.[109] The idea of a standardized retirement age, forty-two or older, fails to account for the particular demands of a dancer as related to specific repertoires, even as it scripts their life's trajectory. Étoile Léonore Baulac suggests that while the three-act classical ballets may be too demanding for anyone older than forty-two, many dancers could execute contemporary pieces and other select works of a repertoire that need not center on fantasies of the pre-pubescent body.[110] An increased retirement age also dismisses the labor performed during childhood (typically accrued by ballet dancers but not necessarily employees in other sectors who follow a more traditional pathway toward the labor force), one often glorified as a willing sacrifice.

I conclude with this scene not to support or critique the proposed pension plan, but rather as counterfactual to the aestheticization of the events of 1961 and to draw attention to the ways in which ballet as protest secured a protection for the bodies made vulnerable. Somewhere between the white tulle skirts and repertoire of *port de bras* and *pas de bourrée en pointe*, police were not called to the scene. In spite of the rank and file formation and sonic penetration, the language of agitation, unrest, or violence did not define the demonstration. Instead, the associative proximity between ballet and dignity offered a valence of protection and cultural capital. As I have argued elsewhere, repertoires of ballet seemingly cast the protesting body as peaceful, compliant, and demure, even when flagrantly breaching public ordinance.[111] Given that court dance and subsequent evolution of ballet originated in France as an extension of State values, such a gloss of the apolitical ballerina seems either innocently naïve or intentionally derogatory to performance labor, corporeal fatigue, and fleshed responsibility.[112] It only affirms the trend established in *Legal Moves* for the body to be neglected, cast aside, or made peripheral as mere or *even*.

Universal humanisms, articulated from the UDHR to crimes against humanity articulated under international law, have yet to be provincialized. Differentiated interpretations of dignity and related aesthetics which undergird human rights discourse have only been reinforced since the negligent recognition of the 1961 atrocity. Representations of violence and scenes of rupture for the dignified body become an imperative site of rethinking the public imagination of human rights and its protected subjects: a will toward bodily alterity beyond the choreo-jurispathic demands of dignity's embodied line.

CHAPTER FIVE

TOUCHING ASSOCIATIONS[1]

> **The young man tries to resolve the problem; what was the feeling he had that made him join this crowd, he who has never liked crowds? "These are my people," he says quietly to himself. And again he realizes clearly: "I have no friends, I've never had any friends, but I have people like me. This crowd, these men, are my people.**
>
> —ASSIA DJEBAR, *Children of the New World*

> **It is only in a crowd that man can become free of this fear of being touched. [. . .] The crowd he needs is the dense crowd, in which body is pressed to body; a crowd, too, whose psychical constitution is also dense, or compact, so that he no longer notices who it is that presses against him. As soon as man has surrendered himself to the crowd, he ceases to fear its touch.**
>
> —ELIAS CANETTI, *Crowds and Power*

In May 2019, Melissa Ziad danced alone. The Algerian ballerina posed *en pointe* in a street of Algiers. In a black leather jacket over a crimson leotard paired with dark-washed jeans, her *retiré en pointe* was both pedestrian—in the lexicon of ballet—and striking—outside of the studio and staged in the context of the Hirak demonstrations.[2] Her eyes cast downward to the camera in a confident expression of willful defiance as her torso obscured a national flag. Several men stood behind, most with their gaze directed toward her, the center, as though both surprised and impressed. Their attention mimicked the scrutiny of the world that recognized her grace and elegance. A "ballerina of hope," labeled the news.[3] "Poetic protest," posted the photographer Rania.[4] She added to her caption: "You can only gain your freedom by showing the enemy that you're willing to do anything to achieve it." In a world ravaged by grief and grievances, a pointe shoe facilitated her political potential.

Elsewhere in the capital city (and later that same street), the Hirak protests continued in an unprecedented durational event that mobilized against the fifth term of then-president Abdelaziz Bouteflika. Scenes unfolded en masse as avenues filled with bodies assembled in the name of change, protesting normalized corruption, elite authority, and soaring unemployment. Each Friday for more than two years, hundreds of thousands demonstrated throughout the country. Row after row, avenue after avenue, bodies jostled tightly together in improvisational unity. The movement forced Bouteflika's resignation and spawned a series of fraught elections and constitutional reform that, among other changes, restricted Algerians' right to assemble.[5] At its peak, several million gathered. At times it was an international affair with protests in diasporic solidarity across Europe and the world. There were moments when peaceful co-occupation erupted into flames, moments when the numbers waned, and moments when a ballerina danced.

If performed simultaneously and for a common cause, these two interrelated events expose a more rooted difference. For Ziad, the solo performance was scripted as a utopic utterance of hope, a docile dance that could mobilize public morale but was defanged of political danger. In contrast, in the mass moments of the Hirak, arrests proliferated, and human rights were violated by government authorities. According to the *Comité National pour la Libération des Détenus* (National Committee for the Liberation of Detainees), several thousand protestors, journalists, and activists were detained, often for arbitrary and uncited causes, despite Algeria's constitutional guarantee of freedom of speech and assembly. Both actions centered on peaceable conditions of street occupation, but the right to assemble was forgotten when the dancing body became charged as an ensemble.

Motivated by this contrasting reaction, this chapter considers the legal anxiety toward the plural body as opposed to the individual performance presented by Ziad. Specifically, it considers the blurry parameters surrounding the right to assembly, first constrained by a history of crowd theory and then by the more nascent introduction of associative rights. Assembly, in this context, signals the moment at which the public becomes constituted, rendered both legible and visible, to itself and to a governmental gaze. Ziad's international circulation facilitates this recognition—a literal snapshot of the individual intricacies that together coalesce to perform the crowd. Assembly also accounts for the tightening of political controls at that juncture, not least as evidenced by State violence in response to the Hirak. In legal and social theory alike, this anxiety towards the collective plays out with nefarious motivations and pernicious consequences as rights ebb and flow at the whim of the leading authority. Yet the balletic figure holds the potential to bridge these two states: individual performance and public assembly, disciplined body and unruly mass, constitutional form and constituted power. To simplify a collection of protesting bodies into an anonymized mass is to discuss an ensemble work without describing the individual dancers who, together, execute the choreography. Such reduction allows for the flattening of lived experience, personal motivations, and unique repertoires such that the crowd can be discussed in the dehumanizing terms so frequently invoked. Motivated by the need to reconcile these contradictions, I invite a conversation between legal studies and lawful forms, on the one hand, and dance studies methodologies and perceptual frames, on the other.

Throughout, I follow a comparative study of assembly in the United States and Algeria—two countries where assemblies' protections have slid from contemporary view. In the absent legal attention toward the former, assembly has been covertly (if perhaps innocently) lost to the freedom of speech; in the latter, more overt and flagrant breaches of human rights have led to its zealous appeal despite constitutional guarantees. Both countries, though, share revolutionary histories in which public assembly of the people—violently or not—marked a founding moment on their respective timelines of self-governance. Noting this discontinuity, this chapter begins with a critical return to crowd theory and its fear of touch to understand the stakes of being able to gather, *together*. This framing sets the stage for values of proximity that motivate me to parse the right to assembly from the right to association, two terms blurred under legal interpretation yet distinctly separate when viewed through the lens of dance studies. I then elaborate this distinction via a discourse of co-presence and the composite body, in order to challenge the anxieties entrenched in concepts of crowd theory that extend back to the legal. The body, when assembled in front of the law as Ziad's own figure demanded, may acquire violent potential, but fear need not be the default lens of interpretation.

Dance and protests have often been studied hand in hand,[6] and Ziad gives us an unequivocal excuse to take seriously the entanglement of the two. After all, they share many common elements—choreographed movement in a shared time and space, expressive gestures, a distinction between performer and audience, and often a rhythmic pulse and durational experience. However, there is necessarily a distinction to be made between protests and dance, one I choose to draw on lines of objectives and audience, rather than on movement or aesthetic. A dance is, in most cases, intended to be viewed by a live public—a collection of individuals, be it 2,400 interested individuals at the Lincoln Center or twenty-four obligated friends in the park. A protest, on the contrary, is intended to be viewed by an institution—often a government authority, but also economic and corporate institutions, for example during the Occupy movement. The implications are important: to view the Hirak as a dance, for the individual gaze, would be to view it for Boumediene alone. Rather, it was mobilized against a system of governance that allowed for certain precarities to be normalized. Algeria is not an isolated example; at the time of my writing, it would also have been misleading to view the protests of 2020 in Minneapolis as directed only against Derick Chauvin, or even for George Floyd. They were, rather, against a system of racism in the United States that allowed for police violence to be protected under the law. Thus, while I use dance studies to deepen our reading of crowds, demonstrations, protests, and assemblies, I do not mean to cast dance as an umbrella term for all events which involve the body. A performance, after all, is necessarily ephemeral. But a protest, at its best, has a lasting impact. The Hirak may be a perlocutionary performative, but it is not a dance in spite of Ziad's image. Rather, it is an activation of constituent power contra the force of constitutional forms.

A TOUCH OF LEGAL ANXIETY THAT ECHOES CROWD THEORY

Legal ambivalence toward the right to assembly permeates Algerian history—an oscillation between legislated permission and legitimated policing, at times an ominous conflation with freedom of speech that eclipses the body entirely. In reviewing records from Algerian detainment throughout the Hirak, there was a glaring absence of descriptions of actions and experiences of the physical bodies of those present, let alone an attempt at gestural interpretation. Rhetoric alone was enough to condemn; more than 1,400 individuals were detained on vague charges under the Penal Code.[7] As of May 2021, demonstrators' routes *and* slogans had to be pre-registered for the assembly to be deemed legal, echoing this logocentric preoccupation that saturates legal methods. An anxiety about language continued to sweep policies of assembly beyond the corporeality of those there and then, as journalists in particular were arrested as a means of censorship before any violence or escalated behavior. To be interpellated by the Algerian State then, in light of these policings of the right to assembly, suggests an anxiety of expression that at once privileges the logocentric and yet also presumes inciting behavior that could "harm national unity" under Penal Code Article 79 or "offend public officials" under Penal Code Article 144. The body of the people became both too much (to control) and not enough (to effect change).

This State anxiety toward the protesting crowd reflects a broader discourse on crowd theory in which the body is misunderstood. In part due to the mob mentality that marks the logic origins of its theorization, crowds have traditionally been framed as impressionable, excitable, hysterical, which is to say, affectively illegible to scholars and legal practitioners alike. First theorized by French socio-psychologist Gustave Le Bon in the end of the nineteenth century, crowd theory set up two axioms: 1) that the crowd should be theorized from the psychological (as opposed to a physiological) framework, and resultantly 2) that in the crowd, the individual loses his sense of consciousness and becomes part of an unruly, impulsive, and immoral mass that operates outside of rationality.[8] Absent has been the question of the somatic, the fleshed experience of its citizens which leads to kinesthetic knowledges. Le Bon's title, *The Crowd: Study of the Popular Mind,* itself points to this duality with which he articulates the crowd via the popular mind rather than the public body.[9] From this discourse, an unbridled fear of the agitated body exudes public discourse and the right to *assembly*—functionally the right to form a crowd—has been repurposed as the psychological or at least ideological protection of the right to *associate with.*[10] Ironically, legal scholar Larry Kramer's *The People Themselves* reveals how judicial announcements have historically triggered celebration and "extravagant marks of joy and exaltation," including bonfires, festivities, and other carnivalesque behavior, showcasing how the law is both caustically and correctively involved with the crowd.[11]

Le Bon, writing from the end of the nineteenth century alongside theorists such as Charles Darwin and a young Sigmund Freud, wrote in the shadow of the Second French Empire, when revolt from the working class led to social revolution and the stability of the elite was under assault by the masses. Le Bon's study of the mind was later repurposed by fascist leaders including Adolf Hitler and Benito Mussolini, casting his work in a trajectory of malevolent use. When formed, crowds have consequently been read as violently ecstatic even when clearly choreographed and contained on/by a formal stage. Printed at the time of the Hirak, reviews for *Les Indes galantes* (2019) reflect this predisposition, with Clément Cogitore's subversion of the colonial gaze via krump circles at the Paris Opéra read as angry baroque spectacle, never mind the historic use of collective action in Vaslav Nijinsky's *Le sacre du printemps* (1913) that startled and upset its public.

Updating this ominous forecast that condemns the assembled body to a frenzied fate, literary scholar Elias Canetti would cede that "without a doubt criminal crowds exist, *but virtuous and heroic crowds, and crowds of many other kinds, are also to be met,*" thus pivoting from Le Bon's overwhelmingly critical view of crowds toward a more democratic, and even docile, potential.[12] But the dividing line between the "malevolent 'mob'" and the "righteous protest"[13] frequently defaults to the desire of political end-games, despite the fact that their differing gestures seem overtly distinguishable to a choreographic eye.[14]

In 1960, Canetti first published *Crowds and Power* with the prophetic opening line: "the fear of being touched."[15] For a society now familiar with pandemic limitations, this fear reads claustrophobically familiar; the possibility of a return to pre-pandemic postures feels increasingly out of reach.. The fear of contact—both physical and residual, with specters of touch lingering in radial zones of six feet—penetrates deeply into post-2020 norms, including in the Hirak during which assembly was restricted in the name of public health. From the heated flames of rampant wildfires that devastate the landscape; to the aggressive hold of police brutality that sustains systemic racism; to the contamination from an unseen virus that spread worldwide, the fear of being touched has been negotiated on individual and governmental levels as we seek collective respite. For many, these new rituals of distance that rescripted values of proximity remain at play and intimacy remains as politicized as ever. The ability of people to gather in protest emerges marks the time.

Yet conjoined in the crowd, "in which body is pressed to body," Canetti posited harmony and surrender, a sublimation of mind and matter that contradicts both historical and contemporary anxieties of proximity. He begins to theorize crowds within the logics of affect that, as Brian Massumi writes, operate "in excess of any narrative or functional line."[16] Further articulating the affective entanglements in her notes on the performativity of assembly, Judith Butler suggests the inevitable relationship between fear and hope manifested through public display.[17] This excess becomes an entry point for reconsidering crowd theory and its relationship to the right to assemble; be it an image labeled a "ballerina of hope" or others elsewhere as nefarious rioters and looters, where affect theory and dance studies collide, the legal must follow with diverse attentions that can account for the nuanced range of possibilities.

Elias Canetti did not write of dance, and his work has not been frequently invoked in the realm of dance studies, but the parallel motifs are more than implicit.[18] Trained as a dancer since childhood, I appreciate the inherent joy of movement and desire to move with others that extends from the professional performer to the passing pedestrian, including as so-often replete in protest. I acutely understand the ability to satiate curiosity through physical participation, finding answers through kinesthetic enactment rather than more passive observation; through physicalizing the movement, I can approximate the experience of those around me.[19] Touch becomes central to how the dance is built. The dancer trains to make her body available to contact, anticipating that at any moment someone may reach out to touch, hold, grab, and offer their weight in a gesture of trust, not aggression. The fear of being touched, ironically assuaged by proximity, dissolves when in the presence of others as skin-to-skin contact becomes remapped as a site of care, information, activation, and support. For the touch of proximity in dance bolsters one's sense of privacy as boundary becomes mapped, rather than assaulting it (though violent touch unfortunately saturates dance spaces, too). Yet this knowledge remains absent from the dominant psychologies of crowd theory, in which violence has been scripted as inevitable (and police force thereby a requirement).

Linking dance rehearsals and crowd performances, there is a pull to relinquish oneself from the individual. Touch becomes an imperative for knowledge production, stability, and tranquility. It is precisely this seeming-spontaneity and improvisational logic that dance studies clarifies (perhaps most overtly in the domain of contact improvisation but not exclusively), such that compulsion can transform into carefully learned behavior and fearful anxiety can dissipate.[20] "It is by walking that we learn to make the revolution," offers a slogan of the Hirak, affirming the need for somatic education within political activity.[21] The unity within crowd formations echoes the satisfying unison moments in dance—a hallmark of the *corps de ballet* tradition, flash mobs, and other forms—as a choreographic trope known to animate the appetite for participation in the non-dancer, the spectator, the public. Yet the spectacularism of the spontaneous crowd exceeds the stage, and the tantalizing questions of *Who choreographed that? How did they appear? How did this coordinated action come into being?* often remain unanswered, or at least uncited and unseen. "And as usually happens with a crowd that feels alive," wrote Algerian novelist Assia Djebar, "no one can say who was the first to take the initiative."[22]

I digress into dance studies to underscore the kinesthetic imagery that permeates Canetti's logic, against understandings of protest as representation or mere amplification of "the people" in visible form. Rather, the connection with skin, flesh, and desire rings loud in my head when reading his words of negotiation between distance and proximity, indexing more contemporary scholars from my field.[23] If affect studies, cued by the centrality of fear, provide a rich tannins to Canetti's work, then an under tone of cognitive reception, cued by the dual emphasis of touch, suggests overtones of kinesthesia and corporeality. The need for dance scholars in this domain is implicit. Bodies pressed to bodies, the fear of being touched dissipates as more knowledge is gained and communicated, "the body as sensible and the body as sentient."[24] To articulate fear (affect) and touch (corporeality) via the methods of dance studies allows us to balance the paradoxes of proximity and distance, individual and collective, density and equality that animate legal policies of crowd tensions and otherwise perpetuate anxiety (not least as seen in the contrasting receptions of Ziad's individual image versus the larger protest).

Yet Le Bon's writing often supersedes Canetti's, and crowd theory unintentionally sets us on a trajectory to treat assembly not as a welcomed right, but rather as an excuse to perpetuate fear and violence. The fear surrounding assembly remains deeply wedged in society as the fear of being touched seemingly matters more than ever. This anxiety consequently forecloses the possibility of non-violent dissent—or legal and peaceable assembly. In *The Protest Psychosis,* for example, Jonathan Metzl reveals how civil rights protesters were categorized as schizophrenic so as to be institutionalized for their disorder.[25] We see this fear played out in the Hirak in moments of escalation, as well as the summer of 2020 in the United States as tensions fatally rose between protestors and police, as violence was anticipated in advance of actual evaluations of the gestures at play. There, in assembly, the mercurial personality of crowds exemplifies a site of legal performativity and State authority, as naming a crowd violent, uncivil, or disobedient sparked retaliating behavior that only fulfilled this agitated prophecy. By 2026, United States Immigration and Customs Enforcement extended this tactic at unprecedented scale. This sentiment echoes André Lepecki's reminder that "'body' and 'presence' trigger additional disturbances in critical and artistic fields: incrementing agitation, instability, and divergence."[26] With assemblies lodged in the public mind as a site of threat, recent calls to defund the police articulate a desire to defund fear.[27] In this affective economy of justice, theories of touch and being touched assume heightened importance. Future research on de-escalation techniques is merited, but for now I simply attest that before the methods of crowd theory can shift a legal perception of assembly, the field must be revived as initiated here, having waned decades prior.

Returning to Ziad's Hirak image, her legibility as a technical body of ballet resists the distorted and predisposed fears of crowd theory. This specific performativity, which begets a European classical tradition, works against conventional understandings of crowd psychology that center on a theory of agitation, irritability, and impulsiveness.[28] It instead indexes discipline, control, and restraint. To remain suspended in that moment, such that it is her hand that blurs and not her retracted foot, requires muscular control of the leg, a kinesthetic and proprioceptive awareness awarded only after years of training. Through the visibility of ballet technique dislocated to the street during a moment of demonstration, I am confronted with the indication that the dancing body and the protesting body are separate but related. She reveals the shared strength of physicality, willingness to be seen, and the command of space demanded of both. Her choice to perform *en pointe* indexes her form as a technical body that resists the narrative of both the collective crowd and the singular protesting body as unruly, disorganized, and inevitably violent.

To foreground Ziad as a ballerina, as the pose welcomed and the media followed, not only rescripts the protesting body as trained rather than disorderly and disobedient, but the reproductive body as a technical one. The "hopeful" label positions her as a participant in reproductive futurity even while her technical command *en pointe* demands recognition as a trained professional operating outside of such gendered logics. Randy Martin articulates the complex politics of such a technical body:

> For mastering a technique develops the fluency in practice that loosens the mixed hold on the body initially commanded by that very technique. Surely this contradiction does not necessarily translate into a politics that challenges state authority, particularly if the pleasures of accomplishing a given bodily practice are identified with the law of technique—the juridical structuring of opportunity—that assigned credit to the existing state order for what the citizenry accomplishes by dint of its own collective labors.[29]

Yet precisely because of the tension of her figure—of a colonial form presented as radical in a postcolonial world—Martin's words catch on themselves, slightly choked by the possibility of Ziad's scene. In contrast to other peaceful protestors among the Hirak who were arrested instead of lauded, her pointe shoe signals a law of technique that, in Martin's words, opened a "juridical structuring of opportunity."

Yet once amplified toward a crowd, nuanced comportment seems lost to legal authority, and anxieties around crowds, masses, and mobs amass instead. Ironically, US laws have instead criminalized the still and resting individual through a racialized introduction of vagrancy and loitering laws that police the idle body. But the balletic ensemble—unlike other scriptings of assembled bodies that also serve as inciteful verbs (to crowd, to mob, to swarm, to gang up on)—casts a peaceable, trained, disciplined tone over the events, its coordination implying prior rehearsal and collective composure. In reviewing Nicola Conibeire's *Assembly* (2013), Ramsay Burt notes that "rather than being separated from each other by the tape, dancers and spectators could both feel involved in and mutually responsible for the way *Assembly* proceeded. Each change altered the rhythm pattern of the space so that the room was the scene of a dynamic series of ever shifting processes of interactions."[30] Affirmed by this language that underscores the collective responsibility and participation of assemblies, I read crowd studies within the intellectual terrain of dance studies to further bridge the quotidian and pedestrian alongside trained and stylized gestures of crowd behavior; that is to say, to offer legibility and articulation to the surplus energy and emotion of crowds, beyond a reductive label of frenzy.

The anxiety reflected in originary crowd theory echoes critiques of Dionysian fervor, in which frivolity and excess were mapped onto the manic.[31] I want to keep an alternative possibility aloft, for as I write crowds are preemptively scripted as riots, charged with danger, and controlled by a curfew.[32] The whimsical or compassionate, technical or obedient potentials seem forgotten, weighed down by more graphic and racialized histories. As we turn from this history of crowd theory to the legal right to assembly—both of which purport to center the people as mass—critical understanding of touch falls from view, but the anxiety remains behind.

BETWEEN ASSEMBLY AND ASSOCIATION, ALGERIA AND THE UNITED STATES

In the final days of the 2021 term of the US Supreme Court, judges ruled a six to three decision on *Americans for Prosperity v. Bonta,* effectively deeming required donor disclosure a burden on a non-profit's First Amendment rights. In his opinion notes, Justice Clarence Thomas made reference to the right to assembly, reminding us of the First Amendment's constitutional language that Congress shall make no law "abridging the freedom of speech, or of the press; or *the right of the people peaceably to assemble*, and to petition the Government for a redress of grievances."[33] Although Thomas quickly moved into a related discussion on the right to associate anonymously, this gloss is significant: the US Supreme Court has not addressed an assembly claim since 1982, and has only mentioned it in briefs a handful of times since.[34] Rather, in the United States this corporeal freedom has been rescripted as the more symbolic right to association, and then further elided with the freedom of speech: a corporeal concern lost, if not disavowed, too.

John Inazu, a leading legal scholar on the right to assembly, noted this new attention with eagerness, having written nearly ten years before that "recovering the vision of assembly remains an urgent task."[35] That same year, academia's Hayden White quizzically mused: "Am I wrong or has anybody else noticed that police clearing of Occupiers and Flash mob participants violates the First Amendment—not the Freedom of Speech or Right of Petition parts but the Right of Assembly?"[36] Yet if a judge, a legal scholar, and a literary critic accent the necessity of the right to assembly, fewer scholars, if any, from performance studies, theater, or dance have spoken out about the urgent nature of the legal misinterpretation of the right to assembly in spite of its clear performativity. An exception may be Judith Butler's notes on assembly, although in their own words, they do not attend fully to its legal nature and only mention the related laws of association in their footnotes.[37] To me, as a dancer and performance studies scholar invested in expressions of the public body, the historical process of conflating assembly with association and subsequently speech not only points to the absent attention to the body under the law, but to the larger negligence for legal studies to fully appreciate the distinction between body and text, a nuance of performative speech-acts theorized in this field *ad infinitum*. Notably, speech act theory emerged as the right to assembly began to recede in legal attention, superseded by association and later by free speech itself.[38]

In contrast to assembly, association—as subsidiary legislation in Algeria and as primary status in the United States—shifts attention away from the corporeal protection intended of assembly toward the ideological and the linguistically related. That is, association implies a desire to *identify with*, but not necessarily a need to *be with*—to share space synchronously. Returning to *Americans for Prosperity v. Bonta* in which financial traces associate donors, or to the Algerian State's anxiety toward the formation of new political parties,[39] association implies an affiliation that has little to do with coordinated activity in public space. Through this lens, we might view association as relationality severed from the body, a detachment from the live. From this legal parsing, then, assembly becomes the unique right to gather together, to share public space, a protection of the *polis* and a manifestation of the Arendtian belief in the space of appearance.[40]

It is then apt to state that the right to assembly is neither speech nor association, but both at once: to freely express and exchange ideas, together. As a verb, assembly exemplifies the process of coming into being with; as a noun, its meaning shifts to signal the multitude that exists even when not together. It includes the opportunity to be affirmed in one's beliefs, intuitions, and experience; to sense hesitation, scarcity, and dissonance; to respond and engage in real time, rather than as discrete, autonomous individuals. Contra the isolation felt during the social distancing precautions of pandemic life, assembly allows us to sense the needs and precarity of the collective, to feel each other, to touch and be touched. It is politics as collaboration. The irony is that, against language that villainizes the mob, proximity can allow for more intimate readings that break us out of an isolated echo chamber or algorithmic feed that sows division.

The distinction between assembly and association serves as an instance in which constituent form and constitutional power come into tangible conflict. Scholars have theorized this paradox between law and power as the relation between the *constitutional* identity of a people, on the one hand, and the separate but related (and often entangled) *constituent* power of the people on the other.[41] Put simply, constitutional form centers on the rhetorical authority of a legal document whereas constituent power attends more to the material force of power: the constitution and its constituents as inseparable democratic parts. Ambiguity falls not only in the boundary between these two groups, but in the resulting distribution of agency and authority. The subsequent conflation of association and assembly, as charted by Inazu, is not isolated to the American legal context. Rather, it reflects a wider phenomenon of the lack of rhetorical rigor when discussing the political valence of the public body. Nowhere is this more obscured than in Algeria, where the very anticolonial government instated by the people perversely discriminates and suppresses them, leading to Ziad's performance that opened this chapter.[42] Writing from the field of dance studies, Susan Foster and Randy Martin confirm the constitutive potential of flesh when they articulate bodily matter as a signifying agent.[43] Discussing protests and the political, respectively, Foster and Martin's critiques transfer readily to the legal realm, asking us to parse speech from conduct, language from action, assembly from association and free speech.

For legal scholars who assume linguistics as communication's primary form, the right to association becomes a legitimate substitution for the right to assembly, and the right to free speech a logical next derivative. Yet as Butler notes, "[t]he assembly is already speaking before it utters any words," and the question of speech acts explored in *Excitable Speech* returns to the legal arena front and center via a turn toward constituting acts.[44] Speech and conduct cases more broadly elide this distinction as they rescript understanding of speech acts—at least a performance studies understanding via performativity—as all-encompassing forms of expressive conduct, inclusive of symbolic speech and action alike.[45] Consider that US Chief Justice Earl Warren and Justice John Marshall Harlan II affirmed that sit-in behavior was speech, and thus permissible and protected in their ruling on civil rights protests (*Garner v. Louisiana 1961*). If this ruling offered bodies new legibility within the law, dance scholars resist the idea that expressive conduct is synonymous with language as it functions in a separate domain of spectatorship, ephemerality, and subjectivity (among other imperative distinctions).[46]

To offer a bit of historical context: in contrast to the United States where the right to association does not appear in constitutional text, association and assembly were both written into the Algerian constitution as separate freedoms, although often appearing side by side as if no distinction in practice was required. The right to association first appeared in Algeria's 1989 constitution alongside freedom of expression and assembly (having previously appeared in heavily qualified terms in 1963).[47] In 1990, this right was more thoroughly articulated as distinct from assembly in the Association Act. This twilight year corresponded to the first time in Algeria's postcolonial era that it allowed for multi-party elections but was soon followed by a ten-year civil war when votes for a new political association called for the reigning regime to be ousted. Some 150,000 lives were lost, the inestimable losses are only further indicative of State inattention to the body. Following this civil war and the events of the Kabyle Black Spring, a ban on demonstrations was enacted in 2001. Although this state of emergency was formally lifted in 2011, expressive freedoms in Algeria remain conditional on religious, cultural, and national values.[48] The State's relationship to assembly continues to carry latent memories of violence and loss contra the experience in the United States where First Amendment rights have been viewed as imperative for revolutionary causes against British colonial forces and thus protected from the outset.[49] Without belaboring this turbulent history, conflation of language and the body as equivalent forms of expression continue to occur in spite of the separate historical orientations toward assembly by the United States and Algeria.

This absent flesh of law reflects a larger trend of legal humanities to privilege the linguistic, rhetorical, and literary methods over the contributions of dance studies: of ephemerality, kinesthetic knowledge, somatic memory, corporeal legibility, rehearsal, performance, presence. This distinction seeps into media representation, too. For example, NPR published an article, "Critics Say Anti-Protest Bill in Florida Threatens Freedom of Speech," referencing a 2021 anti-mob bill signed by Florida's Governor Ron DeSantis. This title once again omits the significance of the right of assembly as separate from speech.[50]

But the grammar matters, as bodies and their distinctive presence become eclipsed by their linguistic shadow. As Jacques Derrida writes:

> In these situations said to found law (*droit*) or State, the grammatical category of the future anterior all too well resembles a modification of the present to describe the violence in progress. It consists, precisely, in feigning the presence . . . It is precisely in this ignorance that the eventness of the event consists, what we naively call its presence.[51]

In anticipation of the violence of the crowd, the anti-mob bill assumes a future scripted as violent before ever made present. "Law is the projection of an imagined future upon reality," echoes legal scholar Robert Cover in his writing on violence and the word in legal interpretation.[52] To resist this inclination to imagine violent futures in line with the anxiety prompted by crowd theory, I suggest a constant return to the present: the actual event, the performance, the live, the dance that operates outside of literary and psychological logics. From the codified site of the dance studio, we can begin to reconcile the paradoxical fear of being touched yet desire to participate that propelled Canetti's scholarship and distinguishes between the permissible laws of association and heavily policed moments of assembly. Subsequent values of spectatorship, dance reception, and audience practice lend us a less escalatory method as they rehearse legal interpretation rooted in the actual, not the anticipated.

These trends carry over into analysis and interpretation of legal language, not least in ambiguous terminology surrounding both assembly and protest: obedience: disobedience, peaceable: non-peaceable, violent: non-violent, lawful: unlawful—binaries of criminalization discriminatorily left to the subjective interpretation of law enforcement, without nuance of gestural legibility or appreciation for the choreographic element implicit to each. Legal scholars and critical theorists alike repeat this bifurcated understanding, failing to include alternative methods of the body. Cover asserts that "we inhabit a 'nomos'—a normative universe. We constantly create and maintain a world of right and wrong, of lawful and unlawful, of valid and void.[53] Writing from a European context, Walter Benjamin summarizes this accepted ambiguity: "the meaning of the differentiation of violence into legitimate and illegitimate is not immediately obvious."[54,55] More specific to the context of crowds, legal scholar Tabatha Abu El-Haj underscores the arbitrary nature of "peaceable" in US legal tolerance for "peaceable assembly," and public researchers at Amnesty International decry the arbitrary policing opened by the added constitutional requirement of protest permits in Algeria in a critique of the interpretative commitments of law.[56] Such legalized rhetoric, with its rigid categorization that inevitably evokes bias so often along racial, gendered, and class-based lines, forces an antagonism when it fails to follow the poststructuralist logics of performance and dance studies that allow for the fluid, the fleeting, and the indeterminable.[57] Not everyone can wear pointe shoes; not all bodies look like swans.

In spite of these ambiguously defined categories of comportment, legal frames still assert the potential for neutral taxonomy, including the Algerian legislation prohibiting "unarmed gatherings that disrupt public tranquility."[58] The phrase "public tranquility" leaves room for interpretation: Whose public? Whose tranquility? Here violence is implicitly defined as violence against the State, not as violence that the State itself carries out, whether physical or verbal. Such neutralization of the location of violence allows for structures of power to remain in place (as *tranquility* becomes synonymous with *status quo*) and for transgression to be transferred to the individual even in moments of assembly.[59] Abu El-Haj notes that "crowds that form to respond to perceived abuses of governmental power are always disruptive," foreclosing the very potential for a legal, protesting body under this rhetoric.[60] Absent from this language is the need to protect the unfamiliar and the unstable, to allow for discomfort as a process of civic and civil growth; protestors at the Hirak paid the consequence when they failed to conform to codified aesthetics like the "ballerina of hope." Rather than reject any and all instances of such language, however, my aim is to interject with a greater attention toward the body such as those learned in the dance studio so as to recover the constituent power of the assembled and overcome the fear associated with the crowd, as Ziad's form demonstrated.

"Something important is lost," writes John Inazu, "when we fail to grasp the connection between a group's formation, composition, and existence and its expression. Many group expressions are only intelligible against the lived practices that give them meaning."[61] To rethink the value of assembly as discrete from association, I choose to attend to the dancing body, contra the distributed, virtual, and even anonymous expression correlated with association—the lived practice emphasized in Inazu's citation.[62] The fraught interpretation of the right to assembly during the Hirak was further compounded by the manifest presence of COVID-19 that, worldwide, led to the disavowal of gatherings under the name of public health. While some countries, including the United States, allowed assembly-as-protest under COVID restrictions, others, like Algeria, banned assembly altogether. Yet the continued desire to gather together in spite of the nascent fear of transmission, as well as the fervent legislation against assembly, suggests a shared understanding of the potential for the body to signify in excess of mere association or language, legitimizing what performance studies has long known to be true: that something magical happens in the live.

Ziad might have danced alone in Avenue Didouche Mourad, but armed with the repertoire of ballet where the disciplined body historically emerged from the ensemble, her powerful stance indexed a legacy that exceeded her individual form.[63] Although we more commonly associate ballet with Paris, Moscow, or New York—rarely Algiers where it signals the legacy of colonial import—her pose conjured a solidarity of bodies with a vocabulary shared worldwide.[64] Protesting in the lexicon of ballet, with its implied citation of a plural body, transforms the seemingly solo, poetic, and delicate figure; she lands with more political force and risk as an action of protest because her individual body implicitly beckons assembly. I squint my eyes and the anonymous males of the background join in the dance: a semi-circle of the *corps de ballet* in matching dark pants swirls behind, someone holding the flag to offer the framing of a curtain, the red of her leotard in pithy repartee with the red star and crescent of the national symbol. With her hair down, it could be the end of Act I in a street performance of *Giselle*, but her caption articulated another intention:

> Subversive art is the artform known by societies during revolutionary periods and intended to modify the existing system by illustrating its faults or by promoting different or even antagonistic values. An alternative to the dominant system can be expressed through artistic creativity, thus initiating a revolution of the modes of thought.[65]

A performance became a call to action, an invitation to dance that echoed a common idiom to a plural address of societies: if we can't dance, then we don't want your revolution. A call to assembly; a call to the many in the one.

ONE HERO, THE PEOPLE: THE COMPOSITE BODIES OF ASSEMBLY

When Judith Butler, Eve Sedgwick, and other critical theorists posit performativity within the context of identity formation, the individual is centered. Perhaps this singular attention originates from J. L. Austin's illustration of a performative utterance, not least in the matrimonial words, *I do,* in which the first-person assumes precedence.[66] But Randy Martin, by framing the performativity of a movement (in this context, assembly), takes an important step to extend its solo status to the ensemble and the possibility of collective action of the people: "Production is what dancing assembles as a capacity for movement, and the product is not the aesthetic effect of the dance but *the materialized identity accomplished through the performativity of movement.*"[67] There lies, then, a nuance between performative language and plural performativity. The latter requires *shared or distributed* maintenance for stabilization, unlike the former, which can create new world orders in a single utterance by a single individual.

With weekly repetition for more than two years, the reiterative performance of the Hirak exemplified a performative power of collective gathering. The embodied action more than stabilized a democratic identity for the State *if and only if* permitted, but its ambiguous status follows a blurred distinction between theory and practice, between articulation and action, between "collective right of assembly [and] the individual right of free expression."[68] The singularity of the event as unified across its weekly components suggests a generalized performativity, while the mass of bodies in assembly amplifies the repetition (or replication) into a plural production. In each moment of assembly, an utterance was made not once but many times over, one often so political and powerful that the State felt compelled to police even in the absence of physical escalation.[69] There exists, then, in assembly, an illocutionary force regardless of the perlocutionary effect.[70]

This force is at the distinction between assembly and association as it manifests itself through collective performance. Assembly, whether forgotten altogether or heavily policed, rears itself as the liminal or ephemeral revolutionary moment noted by Derrida, "in which the foundation of law remains suspended in the void or abyss, suspended by a purely performative act": the democratic distinction between being present or represented, how we are made manifest.[71] Beyond processes of representation, however, assembly becomes a performance of being-with, and as dance scholars would assert, a physical means of solidarity, corporeal labor, and technique of both improvisation and liberation.[72]

Viewed in this manner, the Hirak demonstrates the right to form an ensemble, or a troupe if we follow the French translation of *attroupement* designated in the Algerian penal codes (simply التجمهر, *al-tajamhur*, or "crowd" in Arabic). This process of linguistic translation itself speaks to the affective ambiguity of a crowd, as *attroupement* connotes a mob event whereas *al-tajamhur* has a more neutral connotation. Be it a troupe or an ensemble, though, it is *the body* that becomes protected via the right to assemble and its ability *to move with*, to be in coordination with other bodies: a *corps de ballet* protected as a universal right to take the stage. The durational element of this appearance repeats Mark Loughlin's pressing question from the perspective of legal studies: "If the people is treated as an active agent of change, is the agency merely momentary, or is it of continuing significance?"[73] Performance studies proffers an answer, attending not only to the afterlives of performance despite its ontological ephemerality, but also its constitutive potential, its ability to create change in its gesture, named by Austin, Tambiah, Butler, and others: its performativity.

"One hero, the people" has been the repeated refrain of Algerian nationals since its decolonial movement. It was revitalized in 2019 throughout the Hirak, centering people and their corporeal possibility as the central lever in their democratic processes of resistance. This phrase, while galvanizing, features the unity of the ensembled people, bringing a plural collective into a singular address while also bridging the historical past and contemporary moment, the people made one.[74] But there remains legal and grammatical ambiguity surrounding who and what is allowed to signify as "the people." Algerian Law 91–19, for example, prohibits gathering or demonstration of "any prejudice towards national constants, or to the symbols of the November 1 Revolution, public order, or public morals," as though such signs would be outside of the (national, peaceable, lawful) people. The surrounding legal language does little to define these symbolic terms of Algerian history, leaving it to the discretion of those in power.

This ambiguity towards constituent force spurs the need to retheorize assembly as co-presence via the choreographic, so that the distinction between association-as-ideological and assembly-as-corporeal may become more clear, and each thus more protected. By co-presence, I point to the values of being present *alongside* someone, rather than being present *before* someone, as is often the case in staged performance. In the case of the Hirak, where the right to assembly was encroached as threatening the State and its "national constants," this division between the symbolic and the bodily grew increasingly clear (Law 91–19). Laws of assembly in Algeria have further implied a suppression of Amazigh culture, restrictions that carry into the present: for example, during the Hirak, Amazigh flags were prohibited and over forty arrests followed for those sighted with such displays—even when Tamazight has been listed as a national language since 2002. In short, non-violent dissent was not extended to the non-conforming, and assembly was permissible only via assimilation. In a crowd, after all, one can blend in or stand out—or both simultaneously. Andrea Khalil describes a crowd as a "utopian moment of consensus" in which "the co-incidence of diversity of the crowd and its unity of political purpose," rather than its hegemony, "made it capable of change."[75] The Algerian government's anxiety towards linguistic difference and materiality signification evidenced here suggests a narrow understanding of the politics of the body, including its presence and performativity, theorized exceptionally well by the contributors to *Of the Presence of the Body*.[76] Instead, law and order fetishize the errant body much more than the errant comma, the tense body much more than tense poorly conjugated. Corporal punishment, after all, features more dominantly than corporal justice, and legal injury may have nothing to do with the body at all.

My definition of assembly as requiring a choreographic co-presence is not to further fetishize the live, but to emphasize the geographic and spatial relations implicit to theories of assembly frequently neglected from surrounding scholarship.[77] Association lacks the physiological coordination of being-with and instead extends to non-embodied relationalities that, as argued by John Inazu, "extend across time and place—groups like clubs, churches, and civic organizations," rather than relying on the synchronicity of the live. Consider, for example, Hilary Clinton's 2016 US presidential campaign: "I'm *with* her" as an associative statement of being in political alignment contra a more physical manifestation of being with her, literally speaking. While the former demonstratively or performatively asserts alliance, it falls short of physical coordination and the choreographic. In this way, the tension between assembly and association points to the distinct and collective affect allowed by live co-presence, when bodies come together to transition from one hero to the people beyond the symbolic.[78] Proximity emerges as a crucial element of assembly, such that contact, touch, and kinetic relationality are central to its formation. That is to say, elements of dance previously feared under crowd theory.

Phrased otherwise, the right to assembly uniquely protects, and thus values, the plural performative or what dance scholars have called the "composite body." Defined first by Randy Martin, but later taken up by Thomas DeFrantz and others, the term emerges from a discussion on nationalism, multiculturalism, and racialization to reveal "how difference is associated among those assembled in the nation, rather than being forced to sort out one body from another."[79] Martin elaborates that "[d] ance both appears in the conjuncture of imaginary and performative spaces and puts the constitutive features of a composite body on display. For dance is both a bodily practice that figures an imagined world and a momentary materialization through performance of social principles that otherwise remain implicit."[80] Ziad's unlikely performance exemplifies a singular composite body within the larger collective of the Hirak as she herself contains difference: a feminist performance overlayed with colonial techniques repurposed for the national liberation of a formerly colonized country, all in the denim symbolic of American masculinity and Western expansion. More than the punctum of the viral image, her pointe shoes on rough pavement rather than smooth Marley floor meant for dancing accentuated her as being out of place. Not of non-belonging, per se, but of intended to be elsewhere. She disrupts, in this uncanny performance, a normalized image of the event. It productively unsettles the expectations of what, where, and who this protest represents. She is but one participant in the larger moment, and the millions alongside her scale the texture we find upon close analysis of her one image. Spread globally in diasporic solidarity, assembly features not *a* composite body but composite bodies of the people; the plural made singular without deflating its diversity. *One hero, the people.*[81]

The idea of the composite proposes its own politics of being-with, one that acknowledges the multiple and layered histories that manifest into the singular present without discrediting the necessary moment of dissonance, the frictional point of contact found in every encounter. It may not be peaceable for Ziad to perform such conflicting histories in a singular pose; to balance *en pointe* requires the body to actively push into the floor through the supporting leg in an act of grounding while simultaneously to lift up through the carriage of the body, including the arm gracefully reaching up and the retracted knee suspended to the side. This tension extends to the collective identities presented within the Hirak movement, as protestors pooled from young and old, male and female, Arab and Amazigh—contra the history of more homogenuously masculine publics in North Africa. In the context of crowds, we might call this unlikely cohesion *asabiyya,* as suggested by Andrea Khalil in the wake of Ibn Khaldun and derived from the Arabic root of "to bind" (عصب).[82] While often translated as "solidarity" or "social cohesion" in processes of group formation (including tribalism), this root can evolve into verbs that imply healing—to swathe or to bandage, for example, that indicate an implicit carefulness—or into nouns that reflect the body's intrinsic capacity for such—a nerve or sinew, for example, that establishes the corporeal essence of assembly that predates mere association. The touch of crowd theory that was never meant to invoke fear; a gesture of *consent not to be a single being* that invites interpellation into a political event.[83]

In contrast to a narrow concept of legal assembly whose language preempts violence, the Hirak performed this transgressive togetherness of *asabiyya* as the consenting bodies cared for one another as though in a palliative process. The demonstrations rehearsed proximity in a direct choreography of care, a compassionate crowd that attended to the bodies on the line rather than succumbing to its volatile stereotype or differing from its imagined nation. For example, Lazhari Labter, an Algerian journalist and poet wrote a manifesto of eighteen commandments on how to use the body during these protests.[84] The loss of individualism within this composite body of the people yielded not to unruly behavior as theorized by Le Bon, but toward compassionate acts for others. Touch, then, has the chance to stem from gentle roots, and our fears may rest allayed.

The manifesto echoes dance scores, scripting the body with clear choreographies to anticipate moments of tension and reduce the uncertainty of the response. Gestures of the manifesto include offering a smile to police officers, a rose to a woman, and water to the thirsty. Outside of this particular score, the demonstrators collectively created a demeanor such that the Hirak has been called the "Revolution of Smiles." But rather than a demure mask, Assia Djebar reminds one of the potent defiance possible from the microchoreography of curved lips: "Cherifa was facing him; her eyes were not lowered; a simple movement of her head shook back a lock of dark hair; her mouth opened slowly only to trace a mercilessly gentle smile, the smile of triumph."[85] A subtle curve of the composite whole. Writing about Algeria's War of Independence, Djebar's pages are at once historical, fictional, and speculative animations of the crowds and the people. They are simultaneously made resonant as corporeal traces, the presence and viscerality made known through her poignant pen. But it is through such attention to these micro gestures, whether Cherifa or Ziad, that we can find possibilities to imagine the crowd as not just monolithically fearful.

These gestures of care, be they on Djebar's page or at the Hirak, exemplify the protest's peaceful methods of revolutionary practice, a system of non-violence (initially reciprocated by the State and police in their surveillance of the scene, though quickly dismissed).[86] In many ways, the eighteen commandments resist the anxieties attached to crowd theory, choreographing new language for what and how it means for a crowd to form—one that resists both the legacies of crowd theory as well as Algeria's fraught memory of violence and loss attached to histories of protest in which the racial imaginary, ingrained by centuries of systemic violence, conjures turbulence from still water: an entanglement, to carry forward Achille Mbembe's word.[87] This entanglement of plural performativity, spatiality, and composite bodies works together to emphasize the material and ideological differences between assembly and association that both recuperate the values attributed to constitutive power and motivate my writing.

AGAINST A UTOPIC VIEW OF ASSEMBLY

By erasing the distinction between speech and assembly as association, the law misunderstands what performance and dance studies already know: that the expressive potential of performative acts and corporeal gestures exceeds linguistic frames, and subsequently requires distinct attention to protecting the moment—in the archive, yes, but also for the vulnerability of bodies present there and then. This conflation of assembly and association, even when framed more specifically as expressive association, suggests that lawmakers, legal scholars, and legal authorities view the assembled body as gathered for the purpose of associating.[88] One and the same, where the virtual and the vital collapse into one. Yet to assemble requires liveness, whereas to associate suggests membership that may be nominal, financial, or political only—a box checked or annual dues sent. By articulating the absent flesh of law via the choreographic, including the ambiguous grammar between association and assembly, I demonstrate the need for further intervention into the methods of legal humanities, one that finally centers the live figure and leaves behind a unilateral fear of demonstrative bodies. Such collective and corporeal attention theorized via constituent power allows us to challenge the monopoly of constitutional jurisprudence.

A permission to violence percolates under my writing which I want to go both unendorsed and unaddressed, as my attention lies elsewhere. Yet it remains necessary to articulate: while caring crowds are possible and violence need not be assumed, pernicious potentials can manifest in an assembly far from innocent. There is a danger to laud the assembled body, to disavow the predisposed unruliness suggested by Le Bon and others. There exists a fine line between oppression, suppression, and insurrection, and the law understandably struggles to distinguish between just and unjust forms of mobilization. After all, the *Declaration of the Rights of Man and of the Citizen* of 1789 includes the right of "resistance against oppression" and following the Jacobin Convention of 1793, insurrection was listed in Article 35 "as the most sacred of the rights."[89] In this relationship between body and law that anticipates and fears collective violence, we must also remind ourselves of the legal violences that Jacques Derrida, Walter Benjamin, and others have critiqued, alongside the dual necessity that violence has ported throughout history's revolutionary causes.

To define the force of law, as Derrida does, as "the relation between force and form, between force and signification, performative force, illocutionary or perlocutionary force, of persuasive and rhetorical force, of affirmation by signature" is to understand the multifarious ways in which constitutional form is upheld.[90] Equally capacious are the forms of constituent power: strikes, demonstrations, protests, riots, and more. The general strike receives significant theoretical attention within this discourse, such as in Walter Benjamin's *Critique of Violence,* in which law is presented as factum. Benjamin emphasizes the split between constituent and constituted power in terms of the relationship between divine and mythic violence, concretized in the form of a general strike and the police, respectively. That is, for Benjamin, the mythic violence of law suggests its rupturing origins, a founding violence of the constitution upheld by the force of the police. In contrast, divine violence suggests law-conserving tactics via the general strike in moments of constituent power.[91]

However, to accept the strike as the exemplary constituent power once again fails to acknowledge the unique power of assembly. Discussion of constituent power via the strike mirrors but does not repeat the logic of assembly. Assemblies suggest presence whereas strikes connote absence—of bodies, of labor, of shared space. To strike is to refuse to participate; to assemble is to refuse not to participate. Strikes, then, may seem permissible, docile, inert. Assemblies, in contrast, no matter how non-violent, signify kinetic potential, possibility, a formation dense with energy, potentiated but not volatile, malleable but not unstable. Yet beyond presence alone and its performative potential, assembly requires co-presence and thus operates as a disavowal of neoliberal demand for self-reliance, a willingness to stand within the collective (or to operate in collective action).[92] Association, too, gets toward this need for collectivity, though historically associations form in positive identity *with*—in fraternity, in boy scouts, as academics affiliated with conference bodies—rather than gathered for the purpose of calling for change, or of identifying *against*: an interpretation that allows us to understand why association as mere identification *with* and assembly as protest *against* were scripted separately in the Algerian constitution. Being-with, after all, is a precondition of being human, a universal need even if no longer a universal right.[93] I take time to parse the opposing ontologies of a strike and an assembly in order to recenter accepted critiques of violence back toward the very bodies of the people at stake.

Rather than condone or condemn violence and revolution *by any means necessary*—in the profound legacy of Fanon and Sartre and Malcom X—my aim has been to underscore the legal ambiguity in the very definition of violence that has seeped into law.[94] Care and violence can coexist in the same act of bodies pressed together, and sometimes caring for others might imply violence towards the State. By emphasizing a linguistic and psychological frame for understanding these actions over gestural nuance, biases saturate reactions to the event, such that some protestors are deemed criminal while others remain innocent ballerinas.[95] This violence, however, does not justify the resulting ambiguity between association and assembly, as the fundamental rights in question are fundamentally different.

By June 2021, Rue Didouche Mourad was empty for the fourth Friday in a row. While previous weeks brought failed attempts to gather in protest, this first Friday of the month no one showed up but the police, as fear of arrest kept the public cloistered inside. The 120th repetition of the Hirak had to persist elsewhere, in Bejaia and Tizi Ouzou and likely other places in between. The somber tone proliferates. Melissa Ziad's Instagram has returned to one of a teenage youth, her photographs an aesthetic realm of neon pink. It was the efforts of two ordinary youth that captured the attention of the world, who unwittingly revealed the dichotomized right to assembly, and their lives inevitably must go on. A ballerina of hope, she was called, against a backdrop of fear and anxiety that too often frames a crowd as otherwise. A knotting of the virtual and the vital that demands we ask: When do we associate? Where do we assemble? How far apart can we stand and still be touched?

CHAPTER SIX

UN/BECOMING HUMANISMS

Metal tables fill a cavernous room, their surface covered in a sheet of parchment. On, around, and under each table, performers labor to sign the paper [Figure 6.3]. Covered in charcoal and sweat, and visibly exhausted, the skin of the dancers also becomes marked as inscriptions slowly begin to appear on available surfaces: "rights," "everyone," "free," alongside more illegible traces of writing. Bodies writhe to accomplish this seemingly pedestrian task as obstructions have been introduced to impede progress: for some, the body is contorted into disjointed positions, writing upside-down in a hyperextended backbend or with the charcoal held in the toes of a *développé* extended overhead. Others are restricted in more material ways, with rope or other forms of bondage constraining the dancers' form. Others yet ask the audience to interfere, physically interrupting the choreographic actions that fill the room.

In 2005, William Forsythe and Kendall Thomas premiered *Human Writes,* a performance installation that "reflects the history of human rights and the continuing obstacles to their full implantation."[1] This collaboration between choreographer and legal scholar, respectively, continued to be performed for the next seven years across European cities as the cast of dancers toiled to write the 1948 *Universal Declaration of Human Rights.*[2] The durational work questions the boundaries between writing and movement, declaration and legislation, law and performance as it calls for a "participatory human rights education."[3] For legal scholar Martha Minow, rights "as words and forms—structure attention."[4] Forsythe and Thomas shift this attention from the content, or linguistic field of interpretation, toward the drafting process—the un/becoming facilitation which takes place as Robert Cover writes, "in a field of pain and death."[5]

The hyphen finally takes center stage. The slim dash which has held together the choreo-jurisgenerative body, pulling disparate fields into a singular entity, merits an instigating role. The field of human rights, where law takes the global spotlight,

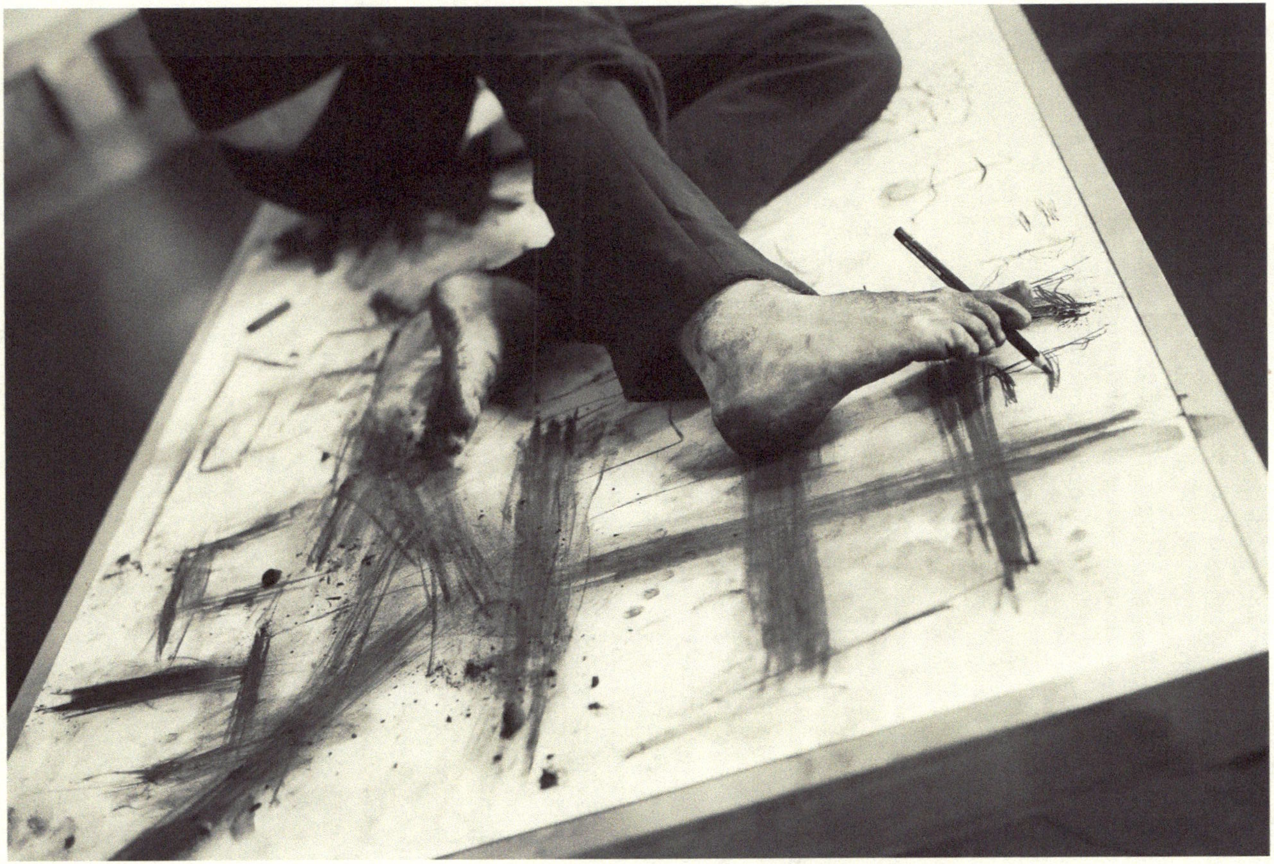

FIGURE 6.1 *Photograph from opening performance of* Human Writes, *Zurich 2006. ©Dominik Mentzos.*

becomes the final site of scrutiny for this interdisciplinary query. Vertical lines of Man rotate toward a new horizon. In Forsythe and Thomas's performance *Human Writes* (2005), the legal-dancing body arrives in the most literal fashion. Through the choreographic and material choices of the installation, law becomes both impetus and afterlife of performance, a charter animating a dance only to be written on and by the dancers, only to be performed again in a ceaseless cycle of implication. When dance scholars Lisa Doolittle and Anne Flynn champion a call to "dismantle the framework that has set up dance and rights as apparently unrelated," it is easy to wonder: what does a performance about human rights reveal about legal conceptions of the body?[6] A final return to choreo-jurisgenerative force as dramaturgical imagination affirms the mutually constituted relationship between body and law, upheld through kinesthetic repertories of participation.

As a public identity, Man occupies the global stage as visible but not viable. *Human Writes* moves as a critical coda to this European concept of humanism that emerged alongside liberalism and held high the idea of the individual, rational, and secular Man. In chapter 4, I articulated the argument that an embodied aesthetic of dignity is precedent to human rights' jurispathic binding; this chapter confronts the interrelated dilemma of vulnerability, a concept which cohered as a legal category in the early twenty-first century. What happens once we have arrived at the rhetorical dead ends to vulnerability, precarity, and related rights discourse? When the liberal conscription of law has been critiqued but not resolved? Might we still imagine a more becoming humanism—an un-becoming of our present order—as a viable legal move?

Unbecoming humanisms, then, project an alternative future for human rights, staged after the Eurocentric hold of colonial-racial violence foundational to its origin story. Eunjung Kim presents an unbecoming humanism as the embodiment of objecthood in a challenge to normative prescriptions of objectification and dehumanization.[7] I write of unbecoming humanism in a slightly different register, with emphasis on the double entendre of unbecoming as both a kinesthetic refusal of our present aesthesis *and* an active deconstruction, or undoing, of its built logics. This praxis is simultaneously an undisciplining, or unlearning of discipline. At times ambivalent, at times utopic, this unbecoming frays at the edges of the otherwise whitewashed promotion of human rights discourse.

I open this chapter with a close reading of *Human Writes* in recognition of both the paradox of human rights and the underbellied contingencies of vulnerability wherein the body becomes flattened, submissive, or stripped of its agency. The installation's ambivalent archival propensity gives entry to the body repositioned as a co-constituting force of law. Surfaces exchange marks, as skin and paper chafe in the production of rights and violence of the word. I supplement this reading with an attention toward the interpretative relationalities replete in the work's embattled humanism. Masochistic power dynamics, which elicit liberal empathy for the negligence of human rights while investing in the impossibility of their upkeep, emerge in the politics of this performance. More than the demanded verticality of dignity, a disciplined vulnerability indexes a horizontal claim to personhood as a non-rigid and non-linear understanding of bodied conditions. Injury invites alternative entry into the discussion of a vulnerability as a bodily wounding, a disciplined conditioning, and an intrinsic status of rights. I conclude by turning to my own body and its participation in the *Human Rights Tattoo Project*, in which the marked surface returns as an evidentiary site of legal form.

At stake is an unbecoming humanism—a kinesthetic project and participatory reality. This nascent attention—in performance repertoires, academic spaces, and legal discourse alike—charts a subtle but significant shift in the liberal subject from the self-contained, autonomous, and private figure into a more relational biosphere. An unbecoming humanism emphasizes the active and ongoing process required in its security rather than static endowment or natural property. An unbecoming humanism is one untethered from the ugly histories of humanism that defined Enlightenment thought and its manifestations of violence, subjugation, and perversion. An unbecoming humanism is the doing of illiberal humanism. It is beautiful, too.

HUMANS WRITE HUMAN RIGHTS

Body languages: I observe this as both noun and verb, something that corporeity *is* and something that corporeity *does*. Body languages. Body languishes. Cast members of *Human Writes* shift through postures of the curved, crushed, and exhausted; the condensed, inert, and contained; the extended, suspended, and supine. They refuse good standing—balanced force and weight without sway, without inertia. The postures yield to surfaces, flesh on flesh, body on table, ground pressed into fascia, palm against paper. A heel, dredged with carbon, smudges in parallel to the writing utensil gripped by toes [Figure 6.1]. Partial words emerge, but the text remains a garbled transcription [Figure 6.2]. The resulting fonts summon belabored strokes of writing etched in errant spaces under surveillance: the rebellious tags of graffiti thrown up quickly in the night or the marred desktop in a classroom from a fidgety student in need of an outlet. The performance installation leaves behind the large parchment sheets now inscribed, at least partially, with text from the *Universal Declaration of Human Rights.* Messy, incoherent, and illegible, the remnants challenge the black letter law's presumed formal clarity and temporal priority.

A focus on the artifact offers an image of the event which suggests a particular duality of the legal body: one fleshed with trauma, and one archived in lettered form. Existent interpretations of *Human Writes* feature subsequent archival implications on writing, lauding the visual artifact as proof of the performance. Dance scholar Gabriele Brandstetter offers a deep reading of the archival capacity of this work, arguing for a distinction between *Schrift* and *Schreiben* (that is, writing-as-text versus

FIGURE 6.2 *Photograph from opening performance of* Human Writes, *Zurich 2006. ©Dominik Mentzos.*

FIGURE 6.3 *Photograph from* Human Writes. *Photograph by Julian Gabriel Richter. Courtesy of the artist.*

writing-as-physical act).[8] Following Roland Barthes, Walter Benjamin, and Jean-Luc Nancy, she articulates compelling distinctions among the transcription, the materiality, and the signature of writing revealed in this performance. Forsythe's own fascination with dance notation as reflected in his wider portfolio furthers this impulse to view the tableaus and the dancers as two separate entities, wherein the *task of writing* separates itself from the residual artifact of the production. This attention, however, obscures an ontological confoundment engendered by the work, wherein the production of justice blurs as a conditioned conditionality.

I want to push against such a discrete ontology in which the flesh of law can be parsed separately. Many of these artifacts now live in the protection of museums as donated gifts, whereas the location, well-being, and care of the dancing bodies of the performance remain unknown—the live still too unruly for the wellsprings of museums' archival propensity.[9] Is the most significant takeaway, materially and intellectually, really the twenty pieces of parchment paper that surface the tables? As Édouard Glissant reminds us in his theorization of *le Tout-monde*, "writing no longer is, nor does it appear to be, any guarantee of transcendence."[10] What about the dancers' bodies, their fatigue, and the violence of the wor(l)d thrust upon *their* surface? The way in which the performance blurs the edge between "discursive-material plasticity of black(end) flesh" and the letter of law itself?[11] That is, once written, is it really so obvious that the only product of law is its written form?

The dramaturgical imperative of obstacles in *Human Writes* lead to the inevitable counter- and self-inscription beyond the more literal themes of inhibition and censorship. While the dancers labor to transcribe human rights onto the tables in a reminder of the "movement of the body as a graphic act," their bodies become increasingly marked, bound up in the archival residues of charcoal, their skin a canvas too.[12] From the process of writing and its forced movement, fusain transfers onto the flesh of the dancers as much as the canvas. These contra markings lead to a different type of relationality, an intrusion of legal force onto the body. In this performance, a legal world is not built only to the extent that bodies are on the line; the body is the line.[13] Law manifests through the reinforced processes of the conscripted body.

The dancers undergo a slow process of decay from the fresh and clean individuals who began the durational work to the exhausted and marked performers who emerge by the end, five to six hours later. In that endurance the dancers and audience members alike have time to feel, and to sense, the effort behind the articles as their bodies absorb the weight of the declaration. For cast member Anna Tenta, the force of the thirty human rights articles was triggered once felt, once inscribed on and in flesh rather than inanimately written in ink.[14] Photographer Dominik Mentzos captures this palimpsestic fatigue in his portraits of the dancers as they exit the installation with soiled faces, hands, and limbs marred in a graphite sheen. This material transformation of the human form to canvas neutralizes the body as yet another medium alongside the materiality of carbon, rope, fiber, parchment, and metalloids that together comprise the installation. Residue from the charcoal contaminates the space like an invasive species and signifies the residual traces of exploitation, toil, and commodity of the body as labor force, the very residue Lisa Lowe theorizes as traces of slavery, colonial extraction, and settler-colonial occupation that lingered during the rise of modern liberalism.[15]

The graphic performance of *Human Writes* undoes what Tiffany King terms "conventional moves of Western modernist writing" that elides violence and the word.[16] Its slippery ontology returns us to the distinction between legal notation contra legal scores; the temporal order between the textual matter of law and its materialization blurs in this performance, too. Anonymous bodies come together to write out a set of codes already written. The choreography appears simultaneously "as an answer to a call from and for the law;" flesh after bone.[17] The kinesthetic labor extends theorization of the blackened writing as not only a "modality of alphabetic script but as an ensemble of life practices," bios and logos, to the global stage of international law.[18] Sardonically, the actual text of the human rights declaration remains the most elusive part of the performance installation as its inscription is half-legible at best. Rather, the choreography more squarely showcases an aestheticization of violence on the bodies of those endeavoring to transcribe it. To view this work in terms of unbecoming humanisms, then, is to understand that the *Universal Declaration of Human Rights* is already written on the dancers in their gestural vocabularies regardless of whether it becomes transcribed. While the body operates as archive of law, *Human Writes* suggests an emergent potential in which the human writes back: body as techne of law.[19]

Whereas vulnerability has been cast as an interior, deep, and embodied sensation, *Human Writes* moves on the surface. I do not mean to conflate this epidermal fixation as shallow. Movement on the surface pushes cognition to the visible, the irrefutable, the knowable. Here, flesh does not obscure the body but becomes the surface which produces it. Bodies press against one another, contorting on carbon sheets to produce a surface of human rights that otherwise evades capture, perverting the established order of law and the body; they produce the flesh of law that was otherwise made absent from Man. Law becomes the exterior which hides wounded marks, an outer casing that obscures. The body (of law) becomes written through the flesh, in an inversion of Hortense Spillers's critical assertion that before the body, there is the flesh. To locate human rights on the flesh pushes discourse of the charter into the realm of the previously abject, cleaved from the disembodied state of the body. Flesh turns inside out. The inversion is not a reconciliation; those looking on are left queasy. Law's multi-graphic life is put on full display.

This interpretative ouroboros of human rights arrives through collaboration between a choreographer and a legal scholar—specifically two of the most prominent of the twenty-first century. Together they model the potential of an illicit, unbecoming humanism in which the body moves beyond its position as an archive of law toward a more complex arche-writing. Thomas's first encounter with Forsythe's choreography, at the suggestion of Gary Smith at the American Academy of

Berlin, was a performance of *One Flat Thing, Reproduced* (2000)—a dance of fourteen dancers on twenty tables in which the metal tables of *Human Writes* appeared as prop, platform, and instrument for dancing alternative orientations toward the horizontal plane. For Thomas, the poly-use of the table by the dancer mirrored historical narratives of the inscription of law and its codification on tablets, in which codes, materiality, and the practice of writing co-emerged to create a new system of social discipline. From this initial introduction, collaboration between Forsythe and Thomas interrogated the relevance of culture to human rights. Its subsequent analysis frequently bends, however, toward the written-body-writing divide of the fleshed archive as if there were anxiety around the discussion of human rights within critical dance studies.[20] In spite of the obvious parallels between human rights and dance, not least the fleshed body as the subject of concern, existing scholarship at this intersection continues to occupy a rather anemic presence.[21]

Trained within a postmodern and post-structuralist foundation of thought, Thomas's particular orientation to human rights foregrounds them as a way of organizing social life: neither a codified body of law, a legal system, or an institutional creation, nor a reference point of argumentation and advocacy, but as an active practice of representation (in confessed homage to Stuart Hall).[22] In this generative space of meaning-making behind both categories of human and rights, there is a pull to view human rights outside of the cultural relativism debates that saturated discourse in preceding decades. For Thomas, this interdisciplinary orientation solidified itself during a Literary and Society seminar encouraged by Gayatri Spivak at Bard College, "Human Rights and the Question of Culture," as taught by Thomas Keenan in 2001. From this seminar, Thomas was struck by the force of the arts—particularly the performing arts—in the South African Truth and Reconciliation Commission as an interdisciplinary legal response to atrocity. Four years later, Thomas and Forsythe jointly asked another interdisciplinary question to produce *Human Writes*: how can art be used, specifically the movement arts as a language of the body, as both a tool and a site for "building a culture of human rights"? Inherent to this question is a jurisgenerative appreciation of the body and its kinesthetic repertories as co-constituent to the legal process that diffuses both agency and responsibility across the various corpuses of law.

Debuted in Zurich in 2005, *Human Writes* emerged in a time when both terms—the category of the *human* and the legitimacy of *rights*—were acutely scrutinized across academic and public contexts alike. By the end of the twentieth century and early twenty-first century, "human rights" was an ambivalent signifier. On the one hand, it was an emergent moment for transitional justice in the wake of the seemingly-successful Truth and Reconciliation Commission of South Africa. Yet on the other hand, this contemporary moment also signified the continuation of violence and atrocities that challenged the narrative of human rights as a utopic and unifying force post-WWII.[23] Ideals of the sovereign, the rational Man, and tropes of common humanity found in liberal humanisms were challenged by the political realities of perpetration. Fundamental to this origin story, *Human Writes* was created from a space in which the status of human rights was always uncertain. When the UDHR was drafted in 1948, the world was a drastically different world order. Bandung was yet to be, and the question of who was to be invited to the table remained (at least partially) open. Human rights, then, built a kinesthetics of futures-past, preserving a passé world order of conquistador humanism even after other structures elsewhere entered into postcolonial progress. The extreme US violations of human rights during the War on Terror loom large, not least in New York City where Thomas lived and worked. *Human Writes* was created on intellectual, moral, ethical, and political grounds of both reflection and imagination. It is from this state of ambivalence, which annulled of a prior global consensus toward human rights, that surfaces between law and the body collapse into each other.

The days leading up to the Zurich premiere of *Human Writes* included a pre-rehearsal viewing of *The Specialist: Portrait of a Modern Criminal* (1999), a quasi-documentary film on the Eichmann trial in Jerusalem directed by Eyal Sivan. This film probes concepts of memory, the production of truth, and the aesthetics of law by manipulating footage, subjecting it to technical, visual, and acoustic distortion. Thomas selected this film for the cast's viewing as an example of movement of another kind—digital and two-dimensional without a centering of the body—to encourage a reorientation toward one's own practice of dance.[24] The non-documentarian video practice also undermined a linear narrative of the Eichmann trial, opening a new temporal orientation towards the relationship between justice, human rights, and the role of kinesthetics. *Human Writes* built upon its own documentarian form, soliciting from its dancers their individual experiences of human rights abuse. For example, a cast member recalled being forcibly taken from his family and community in his youth, displaced to a national school of the arts.[25] This dancer's testimony emphasizes the tension of Art. 27 of the UDHR which only ambivalently protects the cultural life of the community.[26] Such a compulsory, political view of culture enforces a jurispathic association between dance and law as it underscores the force of somatic pedagogy as a site of ideological indoctrination and domination. Shrouded by this violence, transcription of Art. 27 in *Human Writes* disrupts the idea of arts as a peaceful, pacifist, and humane initiative without lethal force. As the stained bodies of *Human Writes* invoke, the declaration and its articles remain vulnerable to cooptation and contamination, telegraphed by the residual carbon smeared on the space, page, and person alike. Law emerges through the body and its unbecoming, not only its disciplined form.

Following the debut, a legal scholar, a dance historian, and a human rights expert gathered for a public conversation at the New York Public Library for the Performing Arts: Kendall Thomas, Mark Franko, and Thomas Keenan joined to reflect on *Human Writes*. Franko troubles easy interpretation of the performance installation with the idea of "corporeal (W)*RI*(gh)*TE*s," a neologism which contorts writes, rights, and rites into shared articulation.[27] This conversation draws a parallel between

Human Writes and Kafka's *The Penal Colony,* the latter in which an apparatus inscribes legal decisions in the flesh. The reference is fleeting, but significant. Kafka's wit in the short parable invokes the sentence as both a legal verdict and a grammatical unit, a performative event translated by Forsythe and Thomas as a durational performance. The sentence measures time and pronounces force. "Our sentence does not sound severe. Whatever commandment the prisoner has disobeyed is written upon his body by the Harrow," pronounces the officer in *The Penal Colony.* When asked if the prisoner knows his sentence, the officer elaborates: "There would be no point in telling him. He'll *learn it on his body.*"[28] Kafka's penal colony turns flesh inside out, marking a condemned body as legal rhetoric punctures his figure. In this dystopia, the text of law is sanguine, fleshed, and somatic, learned *on* and *in* the body. This compression of law, flesh, and the body into a single being returns in *Human Writes* as letters of law become inscribed on the surface. That human rights might be performed in counterpoint to the animus of Kafka's language should leave us all unwell.

On the one hand, we may view the work as an entry into how law becomes abstracted, its legal prose refracted in the frictional resistance inherent to the writing process as a nib presses firmly into paper. On the other hand, it reveals how legal texts become necessarily embodied, labored, and exhausted, calling attention to the kinesthetic force behind both the intellectual formation of law and its legal enforcement. As Thomas and Forsythe reflect in the program note: "Any and every mark that contributes to the formation of a single letter must be the result of physical restraint, encumbrance, or resistance. To take a phrase from Jean-François Lyotard, we might say that these limit-rules force a recognition that 'humankind continues to be inhabited by the inhuman.'"[29] The duo points us back to a postmodern position of the inhuman, one circumscribed by techno-scientific critique. At first read, the comparison feels odd, a misreading, for Lyotard positions the inhuman as the mechanical interruption of humanisms, not a subaltern status of life. Read again, however, with more radical capacity, the note positions law as the inhuman, a technology of society that exists alongside the human. This second interpretation denaturalizes law and radically shifts the conventional acceptance of its many violations. *Human Writes* announces this fleshed relationality as violent, kinesthetic, and ongoing. It stages the techne body as instrumental to (but not an instrument of) law's articulation as a co-constitutive reciprocity. The line flips—a vector that extends laterally, the bar [-] of the hyphen, rather than a vertical ray of epistemological and sociopolitical hierarchy.

RELATIONAL RIGHTS, OR THE MASOCHISM OF "EMBATTLED HUMANISMS"

Amidst a rainstorm of contemporary legal and political skepticism, *Human Writes* tarries in the "shadow side of human rights," that is, how human rights discourse has been used to justify and legitimate human wrongs.[30] The performance dons a harrowing, bleak, and decidedly austere aesthetic, its soundscape deafening in the cacophonous clangs, scrapes, and industrious tones. This greyed forecast corporealizes the affective tenor of many scholars who argue that liberalism and its economic, political, and cultural commitments have been deeply and problematically entangled with global projects of racist and imperial order.[31] In conversation with Sylvia Wynter, David Scott reminds us that European ideals of humanism emerged coeval to the dehumanizing project of colonialism, showing the dark other side of the same project.[32] As blackness became weaponized as an antithetical concept to support the securitization of whiteness, and the colonized invoked as a shadowed figure to support the colonial, victims of human rights abuses who have been rendered non-human in their status have been used to fund the mythic category of the fully-human. In this reflexive negativity of the self, akin to a Sartrean-Fanonian logic of being, atrocity serves as a project of self-realization, a violent relationship between Self and Other that many throughout history have been anxious to dismantle.

This narrative is now well-rehearsed in academic and activist circles. Outcries amass: Sumi Madhok challenges the universality of human rights and instead offers local theories of difference via vernacular rights culture; Samuel Moyn critiques the economic injustices inherent to human rights in the neoliberal welfare state; Samera Esmeir more broadly proposes juridical humanity as a colonial process within the postcolonial world, alongside other calls to decolonize human rights; Zakiyyah Iman Jackson dismantles ontologies of Western science and philosophy which undergird this global structure.[33] If once meant as a standard for peaceful engagement, human rights have since paradoxically been held aloft as an alibi to justify war, death, and international violence as pretexts for necessary military interventions, perverting and distorting their claims to justice as they became subordinate to political aims contra a post-WWII idea of transcendence.

Physical antagonisms staged in *Human Writes* call attention to this exertion. The body, per Forsythe, is "folding and unfurling towards and against itself."[34] *A dancer hangs suspended by three straps under a table; in another corner, a table falls, rattling the space with its metallic echo and edging the audience toward heightened sensations.* While some see in the exhausted forms a labor to uphold human rights, I see a greater wrestling with the very ethics of human rights in the first place, far more than a Sisyphean commitment to their continuation. Dramaturgical obstacles and paradoxical relation to obstruction, destruction, and production propel the audience to reconsider an embattled humanism, defined by Scott as a "profoundly agnostic relationship with the aspiration to humanism" and supported by Wynter as one that "challenges itself at the same time that you're using it to think with."[35] Tangled bodies perform an ambivalence. *In a scene, a woman grasps at the foot of her writhing partner to quell his kicks as she holds a blunt writing instrument in the other hand. Legs enmeshed in a scissored embrace; the gesture is intimate and violent. His erratic movements jolt, disrupting the task.* It is unclear if this interruption antagonizes her quest to secure human rights or reminds her that she deserves better. Their limbs and their futures are, however, unambiguously entangled and uncertain. Unresolved, the violence continues indefinitely.

Bodies move in *joint motion*, a mutual pursuit of relief by opposing parties. We see the pressing, rubbing, chaffing, resisting bodies over, on, and against each other in pursuit of a global project of individual rights. This tandem act, what Sora Han theorizes through Fred Moten as *consent motion*, is both non-sensical and sensual.[36] As Han reminds us, submission follows a dual sensibility as both the authoritative "to propose or tender" and the compliant "to surrender and comply."[37] Submission, without further context, thus obfuscates the primary location of agency. In *Human Writes*, we are tasked to witness not only the bound body, but also its binding. Those acting in pursuit of the declaration's inscription enact their own delay: alone on a table, the dance makes the task of writing seem arduous, and I take the bit. Tension arises in the slippage between coercion and consent.[38] No matter how hard I search, both verbal and non-verbal affirmations recede from recognition. Imposition of human rights as a dominant and dominating discourse leads us here: the *friche* of power, bodies, and society bound in antithetical postures. Scattered limbs and toppled tables, *Human Writes* is a graveyard of broken promises and contracts breached.

The "erotics of submission" press beyond a generalized pleasure principle, as Han argues, toward the masochistic.[39] This position of masochism adheres not to a purely Freudian sense, but the Fanonian condition which turns on pleasure found in (the ongoing condition of) suffering rather than the condition of violence.[40] Pleasure is produced not from a direct act of violence, as in the founding violence of law, but in the secondary form of guilt or shame in its sustained endurance, an unwillingness for dominate powers to imagine it otherwise. Eyes glance over contorted scenes, acts of restriction, and bodies at their ends.

A hesitation to look again, to linger on the violence, to take pleasure in voyeurism generates a fog of guilt throughout the room. Few step in to intervene. This force of constraint and regulation, against more utopic properties of liberation frequently mapped onto the dancing body, sets up an uncomfortable mirror to the practice behind human rights and the violence endured in order to secure their performance. *A dancer holds the charcoal in his mouth, choking on the words meant to protect. Suffocated by their impossibility, he calls attention to their limitation even while writing them into existence.* "Relations of enmity," not altruism, define the performance.[41] The participatory framing of *Human Writes*—in both the dancers' authorial contributions of writing the charter and also the non-proscenium setting that interpolates the audience as witness and perpetrator—amplifies the tandem demands of domination and voyeurism. Its somatic formula maps a new relationality in which participation implicates.

Scopic violence haunts the performance. Re-staged in the United Nations Offices at the *Palais des Nations* in Geneva 2012, the intergovernmental organization—as architecture and people—is made to bear witness to "figures of sovereignty whose central project is not the struggle for autonomy, but," as Achille Mbembe confronts, "the generalized instrumentalization of human existence and the material destruction of human bodies and populations."[42] Audience members weave somberly through the industrial tables as if in a gallery, a factory, or an auction house, observing the scene of commodified bodies from a space of uncomfortable proximity. It is impossible to watch without being watched oneself. As Thomas and Forsythe suggest, "[i]n staging a collaboration between performers and audience, 'Human Writes' [sic] seeks to engage both the performers and their audience-participants to reflect on the role of art in building a culture of human rights, and to experience the difficulties of 'righting' human wrongs in a world in which we human beings have yet to become fully human."[43] The spectacle includes the spectator to disrupt a tradition of passive audience engagement in dramatic and distressing ways. This collapse suggests a particular type of complicit spectatorship that echoes the global witnessing of human rights violations perpetuated daily, akin to the Traveler in Kafka's penal colony. It also probes the line between aid and interference as a matter of perspective, for when the audience complies with the dancers' demands for obstruction, they become a perpetrator to those viewing from afar.

Rights shift to a horizontal plane, adopting a new slant. These tensions play out on cold metal tables, an ahistorical plane of negotiation in public, private, global, and corporate spheres alike. Attentions to the minor jurisprudences of law, including the table as apparatus and site of political negation and drafted legislation, carry weight too. The familiar surface on which these frictions play out transforms into a metaphor of negotiation, where power and decisions wrestle for the future. The use of the table as a platform for human atrocity repeats a familiar motif: within the Euro-American dance theater lexicon, it conjures *Der Grüne Tisch* (The Green Table). Choreographed by Kurt Jooss during the Weimar Republic, this 1932 work presents caricatures of the diplomat and Death amongst its eight scenes on the futile episodes of war. These personas parade power over, on, and around a table in a reminder of the localized site of command behind global acts. Brushed steel frames of *Human Writes* shuttle this macabre performance iconography toward the sterile—the operating room, or at least the adjacent space of scrubbing in, looms large. Signs of reproductive human rights violations as well as war-grieved histories sublimate from within the steel architectures. The table, as much as the gestures, implicates human rights for its genocidal and medical biopolitics.[44] The charter might have emerged from a series of table negotiations, cohered onto paper, but ongoing collaboration and maintenance are required for the continued realization of its longevity. International law requires the kinetic injection of constant performance even in its ambivalence.

Thomas, a professor and pedagogue, intended the piece to educate and engage its audience in participatory elements. This investment in an amplified "rights consciousness" suggests a more harrowing assumption: that human rights remain invisible and without participation in spite of their asserted universality.[45] It reveals that human rights slip from public view when not attached to an embodied form. This "critical praxis of being," in tension with the more romantic sweep of postcolonial promises, saturates the ethos of *Human Writes* even as its creators point toward the postmodern rhetoric of the inhumane.[46] It animates a refusal of a system built to harm. Bodies isolated and entangled, implicated in shared postures of subjugation and emancipation. From this deep paradox of human rights and embattled humanisms, the morass of legal bodies takes on a new meaning: not one of aesthetic production or ontological claims on the archival, but a presentation of the unresolved stakes of human rights and the indeterminate possibility of their reimagined future.

Through the durational struggle, the dramaturgy stages "the intransigent, recursive, self-referential, and (re)animating power of abject" life as per Zakiyyah Jackson's call in *Becoming Human*.[47] Inclusion is not the goal, as she argues, for those cast as external to the figure of the human. Rather, a more disruptive reconsideration of the category in the first place is required: tables overturned, flesh marred, unkempt disarray as remnant of the performance's long duration.

ANATOMY OF A VULNERABLE RIGHT

In the same year that *Human Writes* premiered, vulnerability formally entered into international legal discourse when UNESCO adopted the Universal Declaration of Bioethics and Human Rights. Intended for the scientific community, this charter establishes bioethical commitments for member states, governing "respect for human dignity, human rights, and fundamental freedoms." Art. 8 declares "respect for human vulnerability and personal integrity."[48] This declaration follows separate articles on dignity, autonomy, and consent, parsing out the entangled values in discrete terms. Vulnerability in this context was scripted as an antidote to the problematic ethics of scientific research and biopolitical discrimination.[49] Two years later, the European Convention on Human Rights adopted a vulnerability criterion in regard to discrimination under Art. 14, shifting the bioethical vernacular into a more socio-political sphere.[50] *Human Writes* prefigures this injection into legal discourse, as the cast negotiates vulnerable, relational, and risk-bearing environments in both aesthetic and material form. The performance simultaneously exposes the vulnerability of rights themselves.

Theorized under liberal humanistic frameworks, vulnerability frequently collapses in kinesthetic value toward its root etymology, *vulnus*. Latin for "wound," this origin imports a physical impression, a marked body, into the legal category, even if we know that vulnerability lives in spaces that exceed visible descriptors. The origin extends an aesthetics of the injured, the maimed, the weak, often around an arbitrary and inconsistent application which reproduces difference as hierarchy and bodily alterity as abject. Temporality once again ambiguates: are the vulnerable the wounded, or those susceptible to being wounded? If it is the latter, as defined by *Black's Law Dictionary*, what happens to the former?[51] Stigmatized and marginalized, vulnerability slips to debility and then disability. The able-bodied figure of Man returns as normative logic in legal discourse of rights even as vulnerability enters the scene.[52]

Debility—what Jasbir Puar defines as the state production of bodily injury and social exclusion via social, political, and economic force—marks the kinesthetic overtones of the installation. Thomas and Forsythe place this form on full critique as human rights emerge only through extreme force, "inadvertently yet presciently mapping the liberal elision between disability as an exceptional accident or circumstance and disability as intrinsic to the function of colonial war machines."[53] Bodies amass over the metal tables in a manufacturer landscape juxtaposed by flesh. Time and again, the aesthetics of the vulnerable have been leveraged to justify securitization, heightened surveillance, patronizing intervention, and acts of isolation. In the United States alone, human rights violations escalate under the Trump administration at global scale in debilitating moves that produce vulnerable populations.[54] State parties continue to practice the "right to maim"—to injure, to wound, to make vulnerable—in a repertoire of habituated violence even as they tout themselves champions of human rights.[55]

Human Writes reveals how vulnerability is made operative through Western aesthesis of the body. The choice to present human rights violations devoid of standard perceptions of dignity becomes, as I argue, the most political choice of *Human Writes*, as it provincializes dignity as Euro-American and vulnerability as situated beyond this geopolitical center. Consider the bodily lexicon deployed by Forsythe in this work: asymmetrical, exerted, depleted against more hyper-virtuosic performances for which his company is renowned, including aesthetics of contemporary ballet. To leave balletic body behind, then, marks a refusal to center European standards within supposedly universal rights. Yet in doing so, it perpetuates a myth that the violated body is always already non-European.

I want to challenge vulnerability and dignity as a zero-sum game. Dignity too often becomes exchanged for vulnerability when telling tales of the failures of human rights wherein the vulnerable body is one deprived of dignity. But the two concepts need not be so dichotomized. Might the former be positioned as a radical extension of the latter? Such that dignity is projected not via the vertical "geometry of the line," but the lateral line extended by relational and hyphenated forms of the choreo-jurisgenerative body of *Legal Moves*?[56] Can we imagine it not as a discrete figure bounded by individual rights, but something more situated, entangled, and collective?

Human Writes stages an ambiguous entry into an economy of vulnerability akin to what Rey Chow might call a "defiled image" or Judith Butler has expressed as a "precarious life."[57] Choreographic choices made by Forsythe presume the characteristics of human rights violations as counter to the normative body—as bound, restricted, and not fully-abled, as exhausted, blackened, and violated. As Gabriele Brandstetter reflects, the performance presents a logic of "exscription, of dysgraphia" as if the inability to achieve a normative vision of dignity in human rights permits a parallel interpretation of damage and disease.[58] Yet such vulnerability does not need to suggest the absence of dignity.[59] Coexisting representations of vulnerability and dignity in the same figure become an expression of embattled humanism, in which human life lives on a spectrum of both-and, rather than a state of either-or.

Forsythe dancers exemplify the lithe, creatively and intellectually. His companies have become synonymous with a hallmark of contemporary concert excellence wherein the dancers are renowned for their versatility and virtuosity. Beyond *Human Writes,* his repertoire tessellates balletic lines into unfamiliar geometries of the body in a deconstruction of the classical form to produce, in his words, "lines in space that could be bent, or tossed, or otherwise distorted": a familiar *épaulement* of the shoulders folded at the pelvis, an orthogonal placement of arabesque arms lowered to the floor, a quintessential circle of arms *en haut* translated across the body to a new resting position.[60] Movement generation, for Forsythe, emerges through a highly cerebral, nearly algorithmic, space as "a series of distorting operations."[61] The physical demand extends toward an intellectualism, wherein fast-twitch movements and improvisations must always be preceded by faster-twitch cognitions of spatial imaginaries and recursive flows. High virtuosity, in a Euro-American standard, remains.

The Forsythe dancer is trained to be open, not at the wounded level of the flesh, but as a somatic potential of the body to open (to possibility). This technique, displaced in *Human Writes,* turns on Forsythe's understanding of ballet as "maintaining decorum under extreme physical stress."[62] Phrased again with greater acknowledgement of the masochistic element, he "created a new 'paradigm of rigors,' in which the dancers maintain very complex torsions during physically antagonistic events."[63] His aesthetic emerges through the highly trained, technical dancer. If his works depend upon the improvisational propensity of his dancers, a contradiction emerges: there cannot be improvisation without intense, hegemonic disciplining that first familiarizes the body with the set of movements available in the score before it can move through a process of unbecoming.

The vulnerability put on display in *Human Writes* is a disciplined one. Disciplined vulnerability punctures facile imaginaries of the wounded as passive. *Disciplined vulnerability is not merely conditional, but highly conditioned.* It moves outside figurations of the vulnerable as "weakness or disadvantage."[64] It instead positions the vulnerable body as a technical, trained, and virtuosic one but still in relation and interdependent. This approach toward a disciplined vulnerability moves alongside what dance scholar Sariel Golomb observes as the kinesthetic becoming of the refugee: in response to Crystal Pite's *Flight Pattern* (2017), Golomb finds "something provocative about staging it [the category of the refugee] as a *universal* experience, primarily defined by movement."[65] But what is the provocation? If, for Golomb, the kinesthetic becoming of the refugee lays bare a "strategic obfuscation of the political", it does so in tandem with the wider legal apparatus and discursive landscape of human rights, too. Both *Human Writes* and *Flight Pattern* operate with a disorienting mapping between balletic body and bare life that scales between the individual subject and collective demos.[66] Forsythe and Pite (herself a former dancer of Forsythe's Ballet Frankfurt) alike challenge decades of biopolitical discourse through movement vocabularies laden with histories of occlusion. Yet both end up at ballet's rigid form and fraught grounds that have long disciplined modernity's anti-black body. But when Pite stages on the proscenium the refugee as "a body that signifies but does not testify," Forsythe and Thomas present a different dramaturgy in which violence does not originate on the figure before the law, but in the co-constitutive dependence of law on the body.[67]

Yet all too often, vulnerability emerges as ambivalent othering. Contra the images of youthful ballerinas so often associated with the physical ambition of Forsythe's choreography, studio director Julian Gabriel Richter expresses consideration for an ineffable maturity in the participating dancers for *Human Writes*. Although maturity does not translate directly to age, Richter noted that the "lived experience of the performer had an impact on the intensity of the performative act," in which older bodies (often) had a stronger expression.[68] Youth becomes an especially sticky category in both the context of ballet and human rights, as the former has frequently defaulted to a pre-pubescent aesthetic while the latter has devoted special attention to the category of women and children. As such, *Human Writes* reveals the inherent ageist and ableist predispositions held within normative aesthetic embodiments of dignity and human rights that exist beyond the performance space. Intentionally or not, this orientation maps the balletic body onto the dignified body, and inversely the unballetic body onto the undignified body (meant here as the body vulnerable to violence and without protected dignity).

Vulnerability thus simultaneously extends to the status of human rights itself, not just those moving through its protection. For Martha Minow, the vulnerability of rights emerges through law's interpretive turn as the field is critiqued from both ends of the political spectrum.[69] Forsythe and Thomas present this fragility as the bodies of *Human Writes* contort expectations and destabilize future becomings of the most formative rights charter. *Seated, a dancer's back rests against an overturned table. Contact with the surface mars past writing. The more she labors to unbind her ankles, the more she erases the declaration just produced. Sweat contaminates. The more she shines, the more the writing smudges.* Once written, rights remain vulnerable to distortion, transmutation, and grafting. Interpretation—as a struggle in and against power and authority—plays out on the surface of the body, in the fleshly matter of law.

By choreographing into being the "condition of precarity" of rights themselves, the performance sutures human rights to vulnerability even as this relation remains unarticulated in legal form.[70] Robert Cover's formative essay, "Violence and the Word," which demanded a new recognition of the violence of legal interpretation, builds its argument on Elaine Scarry's understanding that pain "does not simply resist language, but actively destroys it."[71] *Human Writes,* as a critical manifestation of the relationship between violence, rights, and word, furthers this argument through the transitive property to reveal that pain effaces rights. Endured pain from the violated body, the wounded figure, is the undoing of rights as it calls out the paradox of justice.

If dignity operates as a floating signifier, so often devoid of embodied grounding, rhetoric of the vulnerable often conflates the material conditions and aesthetic realm of positionality.[72] An alternative definition emerges through a politics of relationality: an attention to doing, not being. Whereas dignity occupies a self-contained status of the individual, vulnerability shifts toward a relational politics.[73] Performance studies scholar Jisha Menon identifies this as the "embodied intersubjective self" in which a liberal legal personhood unbinds from its autonomous self toward a lateral, relational, and interdependent model that we see in the intimacies of *Human Writes*.[74] From legal theory, Martha Fineman's theories of vulnerability similarly call attention toward the relational properties of personhood.[75] This extends from the grammatical construction of the transitive term, in which one is "vulnerable to" someone or something in contradistinction to dignity's intransitivity. It also scales toward the collective wherein vulnerability as a legal category often names the status of a group with special protections.[76]

Judith Butler parses this relationality:

> If we accept that part of what a body is (and this is for the moment an ontological claim) is its dependency on other bodies and networks of support, then we are suggesting that it is not altogether right to conceive of individual bodies as distinct from one and other or the conditions of their possibility. Neither are they blended into some amorphous social body. . . . What I am suggesting is not simply this or that body is bounded up in a network of relations, but that "The Body," despite its clear boundaries, or perhaps possibly by virtue of those boundaries, is defined by the relations that make its own life-in-action possible. . . . *[W]e cannot understand bodily vulnerability outside of the relations by which it is constituted.*[77]

If legal discourse tolerates the ambiguity of vulnerability for its slippery interpretation, only recently penning it in international courts, Butler presents one alternative in which the ontology of vulnerability grounds itself in bodily relationality, outside of the autonomous liberal legal self.

This move, at once familiar and radical, plays out in *Human Writes* in its interdependent dramaturgy between subject and object, dancer and audience, body and law. Rather than an aesthetic label, Thomas and Forsythe invest in the disciplined vulnerability of human rights as a relational proposition and bodied condition. It extends an understanding of rights as "interdependent and mutually defining" phenomena that "arise in the context of relationships among people who are themselves interdependent and mutually defining."[78] But relationality, far from a utopic referent, contains a mutual valence of risk and care.

FLESHED RELATIONS, SKIN DEEP

Let me conclude with my own vulnerability, extending relationality between author and reader. If I often feel too far removed from my hours in the ballet studio and no longer lithe enough to self-proclaim as a ballerina, those years in front of a mirror moving through Cecchetti technique still influence my daily postures, and that history still influences a more personal orientation toward my scholarship. It reminds me of the potential for dance, as well as of its very real limitations. My mother first enrolled me in a ballet class when I was five years old; in Reno County, Kansas, she was convinced that my commitment to this space would ensure that I grow up to be "a dignified young lady" in spite of the "rough-and-tumble" cowboy culture around me. I highly doubt she intended to invoke the language of a human rights charter when she recounted her motivation to me years later. I also doubt that she intended for ballet to serve as an aesthetic valence of rank to propel me in society. But even from her untrained perspective, ballet would function as a means of stylization and comportment which could benefit my social status—that is, she understood dignity in terms of its class-based origins and intended her daughter to benefit from the system by learning to dance the dance.

Years after I began ballet, and seven years after *Human Writes* premiered, another performance installation commenced that also endeavored to interrogate the somatic responsibilities of human rights. Led by the Dutch artist Sander van Bussel, the *Human Rights Tattoo* project seeks to write out the *Universal Declaration of Human Rights* in ink on skin, one letter and one participant at a time. Skin becomes canvas to law in an uncanny and uncomfortable proximity to a history of tattoos used to dehumanize the body, mark it as property, or otherwise abuse [Figure 6.4]. Consent makes all the difference. As a result of my own participation in this project a slight S now marks my wrist.[79] This particular letter contributes to Art. 24: "Everyone has the right to re<u>s</u>t. . . ." An assistant on site laughed at the irony of a dancer's surface being assigned to this article of the UDHR, but I found it fatefully apt. Amidst ascriptions of grace and dignity, the ballerina only succeeds via rest, through the off-stage moments of care carefully hidden from view. Vulnerability again touches dignity, not as separate logics but intrinsic properties of one another.

With the permanence of a tattoo, the project inscribes on the skin a legal memory (simultaneously a legal future), akin to how dancer Anna Tenta's body

FIGURE 6.4 *A visual representation of the* Human Rights Tattoo *project: the Universal Declaration of Human Rights, tattooed letter by letter on 6,773 people worldwide. The Scrolls of Rights, by Sander van Bussel—ongoing since 2012. Photographed by van Bussel. Courtesy of the artist.*

holds memory of her participation in *Human Writes.* Memory of human rights became scored into the body, visible to the self at all times in contrast to the ways in which atrocities fade from public attention—if ever visible at all on the global stage. The permanence of this memory matters, as ongoing investment becomes central to an unbecoming of humanisms. The body shifts from a dismissed site of the ephemeral too unruly for engagement toward a site of permanence, caretaker, archon. These hieroglyphics on the skin, rather than marking what has been indecipherable throughout events of violence, as Hortense Spillers emphasizes, index a collective effort to show what could be via self-afflicted labor. It transforms the site of the wound into a networked project of distributed responsibility, consensually and jointly produced. While I acknowledge critiques of the work for the lack of material reform to a broken system, its undergirding logics remain significant for the shift in perspective. The body becomes an annotation of law alongside more diffuse visual cultures assembled in this book.

While van Bussel does not cite Forsythe and Thomas directly, it is difficult to overlook the shared ethos between these performance pieces: both demand physical labor in the execution of human rights and involve a reconfiguration of bodily notation. As two creators presenting work in Western Europe within a handful of years of one another, they circulate in similar spheres of participation. Both translate human rights into an embodied aesthetic from within a particular Eurocentric imaginary. In both events, the body becomes marked, with remnants of the UDHR inscribed on the surface (if not deeper too) in permanent pigments or temporary transgressions. *Human Writes* and the *Human Rights Tattoo* project alike present not only an embodiment of law, but an understanding that the aesthetics of law is always-already embodied. Law archived in flesh, once and for all, manifests as the "critical point of intersection between writing and practice."[80]

The dramaturgical choice of marking the self refuses the aesthetics of ballet, as professional classical dancers have long been viewed as bodies that should be unmarked, especially not visibly by a tattoo. Indeed, an entire industry of body paint tint covers has been developed for performers, especially Euro-American concert dancers. This industry exceeds the stage, enlarging its reach to touch on wider conversations on Eurocentric norms of professionalization in which the politics of covering replicates the politics of passing.[81] And yet, the tattoo has a much longer history of global circulation, reminding viewers of the cultural specificity of this doctrine that challenges frames of modernity. Ink submerges beneath the surface, the dermal plexus where rights ambiguate between essence and auxiliary. Made central to human rights, the tattoo challenges long entrenched standards that the modern surface is clean, blank, and unadorned.[82] Through literal materiality of the skin's surface, van Bussel makes it impossible to overlook the category of the human delineated by human rights. By alloying writing to flesh, bodily integrity becomes endemic to law.

I tarry with this performance art piece as it amplifies the stakes of both participation and relationality intrinsic to the global project of human rights. In total, the project requires 6,773 individual participants with one participant per letter of the UDHR; over 5,625 have participated as of 2025. Through this collective effort, van Bussel demands human rights' relational property as bodily integrity and archival memory become upheld through a lateral network of distributed participation. Rather than an intrinsic, individual property inherent to all, vulnerability and related rights discourse can be better understood in this relational view—a value afforded the individual but only through a collective, lateral network of bodies. Recall the second sentence of Art. 1 of the UDHR: "All human beings are born free and equal in dignity and rights. They are endowed with reason and conscience and *should act towards one another in a spirit of brotherhood*." The reciprocal becoming of human rights defines the law, even when this latter portion of the article is often dropped from citation.

For others thinking deeply about dignity, humanity, and humanisms, relationality is already central, if not always at the center. Wynter, for example, articulates this need by a linguistic shift to the first-person plural:

> The problems that we confront—that of the scandalous inequalities between the rich and the poor countries, of global warming and the disastrous effects of climate change, of large-scale epidemics such as AIDS—can be solved only if we can, for the first time, *experience* ourselves, not only as we do now, as this or that *genre* of the human, but also *as* human. A new mode of experiencing

> ourselves in which every mode of being human, every form of life that has ever been enacted, is a part of us. *We, a part of them.*[83]

In the tattoo project, the dissolved boundary between performer and participant, constitutional author or constituted individual, performs a possibility of this logic of suspended difference: we, a part of them. Vulnerability—the micro-wounds of a tattoo gun's needles which puncture the skin—rests at this center, a fulcrum understood in relation to a larger (societal) whole beyond static aesthetic categories of (individual) being—6,773 individuals for one text. I wonder where the others are.

A deeper reading of these participatory kinesthetics suggests that vulnerability extends to all or none—that by witnessing violence a viewer becomes entangled in the same status of vulnerability. Such a politics reflects the proverbial voice of activist Lilla Watson, who asserts that "your liberation is bound up with mine," alongside the famous words "until we are all free, we are none of us free." These relationalities are at once interpersonal and global but entangled within a larger project of modernity. Wynter begins to transfer these relational and reciprocal qualities back to human rights when she writes: "But if you move outside these limits," of Eurocentric politics and philosophies of humanisms, "look at other cultures and their other conceptions, then look back at the West, at yourself, from a trans-genre-of-the-human perspective, something hits you. . . . This at the same time as we repress from ourselves that that is what we *are* doing: that we are, as humans, **self-inscripting and inscripted flesh.**"[84] May we learn to read our own inscriptions, the letters hidden (sometimes overtly) in our flesh.

Embodiments of vulnerability and the vulnerability of rights alike can carry perverted and fetishized meanings. Human rights become diluted in their application, but human wrongs stand as a clear juxtaposition. In aggregate, these scholars, artists, and activists working across fields of dance, law, history, and politics gathered here suggest an embodied imaginary of a disciplined un/becoming that exceeds the language of dignity. From the stage of *Human Writes* to the tattooed skin of anonymous strangers, the illiberal praxis of unbecoming humanisms allows for human rights to contain the vulnerable, the precious, and the para without falling into categories of the infra-human. A new planetary humanism, responsive to Wynter's call, invites participation, recognition, and relationality.[85] By holding contradiction and incompletion within our values of vulnerability and bodily integrity, we can shift toward a new millennium of the human that takes seriously the body and its flesh, not only the letter, as both jurispathic and jurisgenerative. And so the legal moves, bit by bit.

> *Everybody has the right to freedom of movement...*
>
> *—Art. 13, Universal Declaration of Human Rights, 1948*

EPILOGUE

BODIES NO LONGER/NOT YET HERE

We move to live,
to survive,
to tribe,
to connect,
to exchange,
to celebrate,
to mourn,
to protest,
to escape.[1]

In January 2020, the Dance Studies Association published "A Statement on the Inviolability of Movement as a Human Right." It expresses a collective "deep concern for those moving across borders who seek safety from violence, slavery, military occupation and poverty resulting from colonialism, disaster capitalism, and trans-border exploitative economic policies."[2] Published by dance scholars and practitioners, its language suggests an underlying relationship between movement as kinetic expression and movement as a political right. It does not state, directly, if it intended either to critique or to amplify the 1948 *Universal Declaration of Human Rights* (repeating most directly Art. 13, which concluded the previous chapter), and it does not mention the legal as a necessary terrain of this imperative. This statement entered the public domain as I began to settle my ideas for this book. It is, in many ways, both the beginning and the end of what I aim toward: a conviction that movement matters. More acutely, that movement matters before the law. Signed by a collection of dancers, artists, and scholars working across institutional and departmental settings, the statement also points to the interdisciplinary need to take this deep concern seriously.

Borders—both the geopolitical mapping of entrance and exclusion, but also the boundaries between more conceptual orders, including academic disciplines—shape our movements. They have shaped mine in material and affective ways that still linger in my bodied corpus. The border between dance studies and legal studies has long been ingrained in institutions built for higher learning, the creative siloed from the jurisprudential. Yet just as cartographic borders can be erased and redrawn, so too can we alter the categories that segregate our ways of knowing. By understanding the choreo-jurisgenerative body as a site of this transgressive cross-pollination, I place these disciplines in proximity to begin to trouble their prior separation. "It is only when such a category moves out of its negated place," argues Sylvia Wynter in her letter, "No Humans Involved," "that the grammarians of an order (as in the case where the lay humanists intelligentsia refused their liminal role in the Scholastic system of knowledge) can be freed from their system-maintaining structural models and prescriptive categories."[3] What is required is a movement otherwise, out of bounds and beyond borders.

Throughout *Legal Moves*, I have attempted to express the necessary entanglement between legal and dance studies, including both historical precedent and future implication. I want to conclude these thoughts by gesturing out toward the work that has yet to be done. By writing this book I wish to present not a conclusive response to the intersection of dance and law but rather its emergent possibilities. I want to invite others—artists, scholars, and lawyers, all practitioners of their own craft—to this shared endeavor. Much of this project has centered on the individual—the kinesthetic body whose corporeal choices open an array of legal implications. It has centered movement as sign, as memory, as archive, and as knowledge. From within the drama of *Les Épaves* wherein law become a *coup de théâtre* to the assertive posture of a *retiré en pointe* in front of an Algerian flag in which the colonial vocabulary of the repertoire signaled a poignant postcolonial defiance, movement matters for the individual. Through careful attention to this individual dancing body, stifled histories, texts, and imprints can be surfaced.

And yet movement before law can also be understood in a more planetary context, as the flows of human migration and circulation of bodies worldwide transition us to a worldwide scale. The relationship between body and law extends to entire communities, diasporas, and settlements as State projects of border enforcement, citizenship designations, and (non)belonging result in the constant renegotiation, and reperformance, of corporeal status. Movement can be understood in its absence, too, as this universal necessity becomes forbidden for those deemed illegal. Containment, detainment, and confinement were and are historical and contemporary punishments, restricting people into stillness and interrupting the choreographic flight patterns of human life. The need to attend to the kinesthetic and the corporeal in these moments of legal contention does not fade simply because the subject becomes the masses rather than the individuals, or even if they are disappeared from public attention altogether.

These questions arrive to me now as all the more pressing. In the United States, public trust in legal institutions has reached an all-time low. Skepticism, fear, and uncertainty saturate public consciousness as the courts and justice system redraw boundaries of power and drop artifices of impartiality. The illegibility of the body before law reaches a new inflection point under tactics deployed by US Immigration and Customs Enforcement: reminding of the Fourth Amendment's pledge to protect individuals from arbitrary interference by law enforcement, Justice Sonya Sotomayor dissents in *Noem v. Vasquez Perdomo* (2025): "After today, that may no longer be true for those who happen to look a certain way, speak a certain way, and appear to work a certain type of legitimate job that pays very little."[4] New legal moves toward corporeal interpretation are needed, grounded in a rigorous appreciation for the veracity of the flesh. This critical absence arrives as universities and the wider institutional landscape for higher education come to a tipping point, not least for the arts and humanities disciplines which elevate histories of moving otherwise.

I end with a provocation from Emily Johnson, a choreographer and movement artist based in Mannahatta in Lenapehoking committed to the project of re-worlding. She asks: "Can we learn to trust what our bodies know and remember as real information? Can others learn to respect this information, letting the stories and experiences held in our bodies be of good use to the world? Would it lead to an understanding beyond that which I can grasp?"[5] *Legal Moves: Choreographies of Race, Law, and Empire* is my answer, as I seek to interrupt any convenient omission of the body, to reinsert consideration for the humans who have always been involved.

So moved,
Anna Jayne Kimmel

NOTES

Acknowledgements

1. Randy Martin, "Introduction: Iterations of Dance and Politics," in *Critical Moves: Dance Studies in Theory and Politics*. Copyright 1998, Duke University Press. All rights reserved. Republished by permission of the copyright holder, and the Publisher. www.dukeupress.edu.

Introduction

1. Foucault, *The Order of Things*.

2. Spillers, "Mama's Baby, Papa's Maybe: An American Grammar Book."

3. Quashie, "The Fineness of a Sentence," in Crawford and Snorton, *The Flesh of the Matter*, 43.

4. Cover, "Nomos and Narrative," 10.

5. Cover, "Nomos and Narrative," 9.

6. Moten, "Jurisgenerative Grammar (for Alto)," in Piekut and Lewis, eds, *The Oxford Handbook of Critical Improvisation Studies*.

7. Olson, *From Law and Literature to Legality and Affect*, 6–7.

8. For example, see my critique of *City of Grants Pass v. Johnson*. Kimmel, "The Right to Stillness."

9. Barak and Bashi, *Purposive Interpretation in Law*, 3.

10. Grey, "Do We Have an Unwritten Constitution?" 12.

11. Goodrich, "Specula Laws: Image, Aesthetic and Common Law," 233–35. See also: Esmeir, *Juridical Humanity*, 105–6.

12. Judy, *Sentient Flesh*, 179–199.

13. This translation arrives from Samera Esmeir. For a more detailed genealogy, particularly through Immanuel Kant and Marcel Mauss, see: Esmeir, *Juridical Humanity*, 99 and the wider second chapter.

14. Harney and Moten, "Michael Brown," 81.

15. Spillers, "Mama's Baby, Papa's Maybe: An American Grammar Book," 67.

16. Scholars such as Zakiyyah Iman Jackson push beyond a linear production of flesh into body, refusing that flesh as biological matter exists outside of, let alone prior to, the cultural construction of the body. R. A. Judy affirms that "flesh is with and not before the body and person, and the body and person are with and not before or even after the flesh." Judy, *Sentient Flesh*, xvi.

17. Silva and Spillers, "Sending Language into Battle: Interview with Hortense J. Spillers," 22–23.

18. Spillers, "Mama's Baby, Papa's Maybe: An American Grammar Book," 67.

19. Fleetwood, "Excess Flesh: Black Women Performing Hypervisibility," in *Troubling Vision*; Judy, *Sentient Flesh*; Musser, *Sensational Flesh*; Ahmed, *The Cultural Politics of Emotion*; King, "Humans Involved"; Weheliye, *Habeas Viscus.*

20. Saidiya Hartman names flesh as the "elemental level." Hartman, *Scenes of Subjection*, 4.

21. Judy, *Sentient Flesh.*

22. Spillers, "Mama's Baby, Papa's Maybe: An American Grammar Book," 67.

23. Hyde, *Bodies of Law.*

24. Spillers, "Mama's Baby, Papa's Maybe: An American Grammar Book," 67.

25. Foster, "Choreographies of Gender," 5.

26. Lepecki, "Choreography as an Apparatus of Capture," 120.

27. Ife, *Maroon Choreography*, ix.

28. Lepecki, *Of the Presence of the Body*, 2–3.

29. Siegel, Marcia B. *At the Vanishing Point: A Critic Looks at Dance.* New York: Saturday Review Press, 1972. Print.

30. Judy, *Sentient Flesh*, xiii.

31. Hartman, *Scenes of Subjection*, 129–30.

32. Hartman, *Scenes of Subjection*, 131.

33. This French maxim names a tension in which ongoing participation in slave trade and colonial domination was masked under domestic articulations of the "Freedom Principle." Sue Peabody's analysis of the substitution of *esclave* for *nègre* in the 1777 *Police des Noirs* is particularly relevant here. For more, see: Peabody, *There Are No Slaves in France: The Political Culture of Race and Slavery in the Ancien Régime.*

34. Silva, "No-Bodies: Law, Raciality and Violence."

35. Moten, *Stolen Life*, 15.

36. Wynter in McKittrick, ed., *Sylvia Wynter: On Being Human as Praxis,* 23.

37. Wynter, "'No Humans Involved,'" 42.

38. While Wynter cites its routine use in the judicial system, origins of the term NHI remain uncertain.

39. *United States v. Koon*, 833 F. Supp. 769 (C.D. Cal. 1993); see also: *Koon v. United States*, 518 U.S. 81 (1996).

40. Cheng, *Ornamentalism*, 37.

41. Samera Esmeir articulates juridical humanity as the "governmental operations of the association between person and human, law and the human," in which marginalized peoples are recognized into legal systems only for discipline, governance, and control. This thesis nuances debates in which marginalized life is seen to be excluded from legal recognition and gives necessary context to the duality of absence/presence presented in *Legal Moves*. Esmeir, 78.

42. For foundational texts, see: Binder and Weisberg, *Literary Criticisms of Law*; Anker and Meyler, *New Directions in Law and Literature.*

43. Constable et al., *Looking for Law in All the Wrong Places.* This quip also echoes *Looking for Rights in all the Wrong Places,* a reminder of state versus federal power in the United States. Zackin, "Looking for Rights in All the Wrong Places."

44. Ife, *Maroon Choreography*, ix.

45. Binder and Weisberg, *Literary Criticisms of Law*, 4.

46. Binder and Weisberg, *Literary Criticisms of Law*, Anker and Meyler, eds., *New Directions in Law and Literature.*

47. I am refreshed by the emergent space of law and affect, not least demonstrated by Greta Olson and the related special issue of *Law, Culture and the Humanities.*

48. Peters, "Law, Literature, and the Vanishing Real," 444.

49. Aimé Césaire, and subsequent scholars such as Sylvia Wynter, advocate for the science of the Word as counter-narrative to the rigid formations of scientific knowledge. While I appreciate this initiative, it centers on the lexicon of poesis at the expense of a more manifold future. See: Aimé Césaire, "Poetry and Knowledge" in Richardson, *Refusal of the Shadow*, 134–146.

50. Meyler, *Theaters of Pardoning*; Peters, "Mapping Law and Performance" in Stern, *The Oxford Handbook of Law and Humanities*; Read, *Theatre & Law*; Sarat, Douglas, and Umphrey, *Law and Performance.*

51. Sarat et al., *Law and Performance*, 1.

52. Van der Kolk, *The Body Keeps the Score.*

53. Rankine, *Citizen: An American Lyric*, 7.

54. I think here with the familiar definition of habitus defined as "a subjective but not individual system of internalised structures, schemes of perception, conception, and action common to all members of the same group or class." Bourdieu, "Outline of a Theory of Practice," 86.

55. Maxine Sheets-Johnstone, cited in Foster, *Knowing as Moving*, 56. For a wider review of the upsurge of the adjective "embodied" across various scholarly discourses, see: Foster, *Knowing as Moving*, 56–77.

56. Foster, *Knowing as Moving*, 1 and "Embodying the Decolonial."

57. The special issue of *Law, Culture and Humanities* on law and affect, published in response to Greta Olson's *From Law and Literature to Legality and Affect*, best illustrates this potential. The articles included primarily commit to an attention to media, emotion, and optics in its conceptualization of affect over the physical body, however, and thus there remains a continued need to turn to dance studies for its extended vocabulary on performance and choreography. Christ and Schniedermann, "Towards Legality and Affect," 248–56.

58. Jackson's critique of the history of Western science grounds much of my thinking on this matter. Jackson, *Becoming Human*, 83.

59. "It is my belief that the officer had the intention to deploy their Taser, but instead shot Mr. Wright with a single bullet. This appears to me, from what I viewed and the officer's reaction and distress immediately after, that this was an accidental discharge that resulted in the tragic death of Mr. Wright." Sanchez et al., "Officer Who Fatally Shot Daunte Wright during Traffic Stop Meant to Use Taser, Police Chief Says."

60. The distinction between intent and negligence determines applicability of first- or second-degree manslaughter charges, respectively (in some jurisdictions, voluntary and involuntary manslaughter).

61. Potter was convicted on two counts of manslaughter and sentenced to two years in state custody, a lesser sentence than recommended given the circumstances. For more, see: *State vs. Kimberly Potter* 27-CR-21-7460.

62. *Jacobellis v. Ohio*, 378 US 184 (1964).

63. Goodrich, *Law in the Courts of Love.*

64. "Unmasking the Boston Police Department's Gang Database."

65. Marcia Siegel suggests dance as that which perpetually exists at the vanishing point. Siegel, *At the Vanishing Point.*

66. I take here the vital and beloved work of Randy Martin, not least his book *Critical Moves: Dance Studies in Theory and Politics*, as a north star. Martin boldly brought dance studies to bear upon the concerns and debates of political theory and emboldens me

to shepherd dance studies toward another untouchable field; my indebtedness is gestured toward in the parallel title of this book. Martin, *Critical Moves*.

67. Exemplar readers on the capacious themes of dance studies include: Manning et al., *Futures of Dance Studies*; Dils and Albright, *Moving History / Dancing Cultures*.

68. Kraut, *Choreographing Copyright*; Khubchandani, *Ishtyle*; Murphy, *The People Have Never Stopped Dancing*; Siegel, "A Right to Boogie Queerly"; Whatley et al., *Dance, Disability, and Law*; Fortuna, *Moving Otherwise*; Chambers-Letson, *A Race So Different*.

69. Mulcahy, "Dances with Laws."

70. Responding to Julie Stone Peters's generative, historical research in *Law as Performance, Performing Law* (ed. Peter Goodrich, Bernadette Meyler, and Anna Jayne Kimmel) continues to suggest new entry into these synergistic disciplines. See also: Moten, "Jurisgenerative Grammar (for Alto)"; Yapp, "To Free Speech from Free Speech"; Shimakawa and Pellegrini, "Reenactibility"; Castañeda, *Disappearing Rooms*.

71. Wynter, "'No Humans Involved,'" 47.

72. I rely on the ecumenical to name this planetary orientation, in line with Katherine McKittrick, who writes, "Because [Wynter's] ongoing work still strives, as her earlier work had done, to fully realize that emancipatory legacy by putting forward an alternative, yet no less secular, version of humanness imagined outside liberal monohumanism, her overall project can be identified as that of a counterhumanism—one now ecumenically 'made to the measure of the world.'" McKittrick, *Sylvia Wynter: On Being Human as Praxis*, 11. See also 22.

73. Wynter, "'No Humans Involved,'" 59.

74. King, "Humans Involved,"162.

75. I intentionally invoke the critical projects of both Kandice Chuh and Victoria Fortuna when I write of an otherwise, here and throughout this book.

76. King, "Humans Involved," 162–85.

77. King, *The Black Shoals*, 73.

78. Wilderson, *Red, White and Black*, 207.

79. McKittrick, *Dear Science and Other Stories*, 36.

80. King, *The Black Shoals*, 15–21.

81. Exemplary voices on the critique of Man through the sciences include Katherine McKittrick, Zakiyyah Iman Jackson, and the wide oeuvre of Sylvia Wynter. McKittrick, *Dear Science and Other Stories*; Jackson, *Becoming Human*.

82. Silva, "Before Man: Sylvia Wynter's Rewriting of the Modern Episteme," in McKitterick, ed. *Sylvia Wynter: On Being Human as Praxis*, 100–103.

83. Silva, "Before Man: Sylvia Wynter's Rewriting of the Modern Episteme," in McKitterick, ed. *Sylvia Wynter: On Being Human as Praxis*, 104.

84. McKittrick, *Sylvia Wynter: On Being Human as Praxis*, 2.

85. I am reminded of the writings by Jacques Derrida and Carey Wolfe who, as Zakiyyah Iman Jackson summarizes, "foregrounded a need for a critical and accountable humanism rather than seeking ever-vigilant forms of anti-anthropocentricisms." Jackson, *Becoming Human*, 15.

86. Neferti X. M. Tadiar advances a critical point of view in *Remaindered Life*, not least the chapter "A Global Enterprise: Waste," in which she challenges the perverted economy of waste as the latest "product and productive strategy of capitalist war." Tadiar, *Remaindered Life*.

87. Jackson, *Becoming Human*, 9.

88. Scott, *Conscripts of Modernity.*

89. For an extended commentary on the relationship between performativity, materialization, and constitution, see: Butler, *Bodies That Matter.*

90. The work of André Lepecki and Randy Martin immediately come to mind as exemplifying the political within performance, but we could point to countless others who (unwittingly) uphold this disciplinary edge. Lepecki, *Exhausting Dance*; Martin, *Critical Moves*; Martin, *Performance as Political Act.*

91. Wynter, "'No Humans Involved.'"

Chapter 1

1. The first known instance of such a pension was supported by Louis XIV's financier, the son-in-law of Jean-Baptiste Lully, whose prominence extended into the ballet world, further entrenching these two histories of the court and the opéra. For more on this financial history of State pensions for Opéra artists, including its origins and evolutions, see: Thuillier, "Pour Un Tricentenaire"; Thuillier, *Pour Une Histoire de La Bureaucratie En France.*

2. In this way, I take seriously the provocation from Martha Merrill Umphrey, Austin Sarat, and Lawrence Douglas, who, writing from legal studies, suggest that "a musical score, a theatrical script, or a law is both itself and not yet itself; it is only fully realized in its performance"—what I will elaborate as its execution and its embodiment. Sarat et al., *Law and Performance*, 2.

3. Emergent dance notations existed prior to the Beauchamp-Feuillet system, such as *Orchésographie* (1589) by Thoinot Arbeau. I choose to locate the coeval production of legal codes and dance notations with Beauchamp-Feuillet, however, because prior systems were 1) comparatively less comprehensive and as such a "draft" of what was to come, 2) less popular and as a result less indicative of a wider socio-political ethos, and 3) in the case of *Orchésographie* specifically, steps were documented in relationship to a musical score rather than an attention toward spatial patterns—the colonial logic of cartographic dominance that I emphasize in this chapter.

4. While I suggest a division between dance score and dance notation later on with more detail as it relates to divergent temporalities, for now I want to clarify for the non-dance reader that a dance notation serves as written record and dance score serves as choreographic tool.

5. For one such example, see: Carbonnier, "Le Code Civil," 293.

6. André Lepecki puts forward a similar but separate comparison. See: "Masculinity, Solipsism, Choreography," in *Exhausting Dance.*

7. Scott's arguments build significantly on Talal Asad's essay, "Conscripts of Western Civilization?" Scott, *Conscripts of Modernity.*

8. Scott, *Conscripts of Modernity*, 1.

9. Although Samera Esmeir's theorization of juridical humanity centers a particular history of British colonialism in Egypt, the wider orientation toward modern positive law remains salient to my project. Esmeir, *Juridical Humanity.*

10. Needham, "Louis XIV and the Académie Royale de Danse, 1661: A Commentary and Translation," 180. The Lettres Patent continue in its personified address: "Dance helps one to ride horseback and carry arms. It renders one more skilled at serving one's Prince in battle, and pleasing him in divertissements." Trans. in Franko, *Dance as Text*, 181.

11. Foster, *Choreographing Empathy*, 18.

12. Duc Saint-Simon in *The Memoirs of Louis XIV*, ed. Widger.

13. I appreciate the temporal limits of the legal category of citizenship, which was not legitimated in France as a democratic concept until the French Revolution. Given the transhistorical nature of this chapter, however, and the pre-existence of state membership in the *ancien régime*, I choose to use "citizen" to reference the hierarchical and differentiated affordances of rights between class, race, and gendered lines. For general background, see: Tilly, "The Emergence of Citizenship in France and Elsewhere." My gratitude to those at DSA 2022 for first raising this comment.

14. Linda Tomko reminds us that the Beauchamp-Feuillet system of notation was never meant to be inclusive. Rather, "it attempted to represent only the French noble style of dancing." Tomko, "Dance Notation and Cultural Agency," 2.

15. Astier, "Louis XIV, 'Premier Danseur,'" in *Sun King: The Ascendancy of French Culture During the Reign of Louis XIV*, ed. Rubin.

16. Merrick, "The Body Politics of French Absolutism," in *From the Royal to the Republican Body: Incorporating the Political in Seventeenth- and Eighteenth-Century France*, ed. Melzer and Norberg, 14. Bodily decorum was rehearsed elsewhere too, in other sites where aesthetics and athletics become a stage for a politics of the colonial body. For example, there is an interesting parallel to be drawn to boxing as a "gentleman's sport" and colonial measure of social control. Seda, "Fighting in the Shadow of an Apartheid State."

17. Foster, *Choreographing Empathy*, 23.

18. For a detailed analysis of this system, see: Guest, *Choreo-Graphics: A Comparison of Dance Notation Systems from the Fifteenth Century to the Present*, 12–24.

19. I would be remiss not to acknowledge the presence of previous dance notation systems, not least the highly important work of Thoinot Arbeau, including *Orchésographie* (1588), and the lesser-known work of André Lorin. In 1706 John Weaver would translate Feuillet's *Chorégraphie* as *Orchésography,* and Feuillet would acknowledge Arbeau in his introduction.

20. Foster, *Choreographing Empathy*, 31.

21. Foster, *Choreographing Empathy*, 15–72.

22. I follow this date in part due to the acute event of the founding of the Royal Academy of Dance by Louis XIV in 1662. For more on the preceding period as relevant here, including under the reign of Louis XIII, see: Franko, *Dance as Text,* 3.

23. Lepecki, *Exhausting Dance*, 6.

24. Louppe, *Traces of Dance*, 32.

25. Lepecki writes that "choreopolicing, as separate and largely antithetical to choreo-politics, imposes a forced ontological fitting between pregiven movements, bodies in conformity, and pre-assigned places for circulation. In contradistinction, we can say that choreopolitics requires a redistribution and reinvention of bodies, affects, and senses through which one may learn how to move politically, how to invent, activate, seek, or experiment with a movement whose only sense (meaning and direction) is the experimental exercise of freedom." Lepecki, "Choreopolice and Choreopolitics: Or, the Task of the Dancer," 20. We might also think these terms in parallel to Michel de Certeau's distinction between strategy and tactics, respectively.

26. Indeed, it extends well past the seventeenth century, backward in times toward not only sixteenth-century geometric dance but also writings of Quintilian. For more on this trajectory, see: Franko, *Dance as Text*, 15–20.

27. Franko, *Dance as Text*, 4.

28. Franko, *Dance as Text*, 15; Franko, *Text as Dance*; Franko, "The Conduct of Contemplation and the Gestural Ethics of Interpretation in Walter Benjamin's 'Epistemo-Critical Prologue.'"

29. Franko, *Dance as Text*, 15.

30. Lepecki, *Exhausting Dance*, 25–26.

31. Merryman and Pérez-Perdomo, *The Civil Law Tradition*. For the ways in which French legal tradition has spread, see also: Bell, *French Legal Cultures*.

32. Marie Seong-Hak Kim's scholarship documents the ardent process of legal unification, a process that was itself disorganized and operated in fits and starts across a long history spanning several centuries. See: Kim, *Custom, Law, and Monarchy*; Dauchy, "French Law and Its Expansion in the Early Modern Period."

33. For more generalist histories and comprehensive overviews, see: Bell, "Sources of Law"; Franko, *Dance as Text*, 3; Steiner, "Codification," in *French Law: A Comparative Approach*, 25–43.

34. Franko, "Editor's Note: Revaluing the Score: Archival Futurity."

35. "About," Dance Notation Bureau. Web.

36. For example, Gabriele Brandstetter writes that "choreography is a form of writing along the boundary between presence and no longer being there." Considering choreography as a form of writing, that is in a sense its score, extends a boundary between presence and the not-yet-here. Brandstetter, "Choreography as a Cenotaph," 104.

37. Scott, *Conscripts of Modernity*, 9.

38. For a comparative analysis of these individuals, see: Lepecki, "Inscribing Dance," in Lepecki, ed, *Of the Presence of the Body*, 125–129.

39. For more context on the epistemic evolution of dance notation, see: Franko, "Writing for the Body;" Guest, *Dance Notation*; Tomko, "Dance Notation and Cultural Agency."

40. Laban, *Laban's Dance Notation Charts*; Guest and Anderson, *Labanotation; or, Kinetography Laban*; Sutil, "Laban's Choreosophical Model"; Louppe, "Les Notations En Danse, Gardiennes de l'invention."

41. Foster, "Simply(?) The Doing of It, Like Two Arms Going Round and Round."

42. Peters, *Law as Performance*.

43. By "futures past," I invoke the temporal polysemy of Reinhardt Koselleck, what David Scott summaries as "horizons of possible futures that are not, any longer, ours to imagine." It is a sign of foreclosure, of former futures no longer awaiting arrival. Scott, *Conscripts of Modernity*, 29. See also: Koselleck, *Futures Past*.

44. Schneider, *Performing Remains*, 90.

45. For more of this history, see: Hodson, "Searching for Nijinsky's Sacre."

46. Jordan, "Using the Humphrey Scores," 52. Emphasis added.

47. Through this phrasing, I intentionally gesture toward choreographer Bill T. Jones and his influential work, *Ghostcatching* (1999) and *After Ghostcatching* (2011).

48. Franko, "Editor's Note: Revaluing the Score: Archival Futurity."

49. Jacques Derrida, *Archive Fever*; cited in Schneider, *Performing Remains*, 108.

50. Cover, "Nomos and Narrative," 26. Emphasis added.

51. Admittedly, there is a question of tense at play here: laws are designed to discipline members of society into becoming model citizens in an ideal state rather than only for the pre-existing model citizen in the present.

52. Contributing artists include: Alice Sheppard, Ann Carlson, Aszure Barton, Brenda Way, Caleb Teicher with Isabela Dos Santos, Camille A. Brown, Deborah Hay, Eiko Otake, Elizabeth Streb, Emily Johnson, Faye Driscoll, Jawole Willa Jo Zollar with Vincent Thomas, Chanon Judson and Ausar Johnson, Kyle Abraham, Lucinda Childs, mayfield brooks, Molissa Fenley, Nora Chipaumire, Okwui Okpokwasili, Pam Tanowitz, Ralph Lemon, Ronald K. Brown, Rosie Herrera, Sarah Michelson, Shamel Pitts, Wally Cardona, and Zoe Scofield.

53. Erica Arban surveys the paradoxes of music and originalism in law, even if she stops short of articulating a method of legal studies derived from the discipline of music. Arban, "Seeing Law in Terms of Music." See also: Frank, "Words and Music"; Posner, "Bork and Beethoven"; Manderson, *Songs Without Music;* Manderson and Caudill, "Modes of Law."

54. Levinson and Balkin, "Law, Music, and Other Performing Arts."

55. Samuel Lipman cited in: Posner, "Bork and Beethoven," 1366.

56. Bentham, *Of Laws in General*, 1.

57. *Dance Notation Bureau.* "About." Web.

58. Latour, *The Making of Law*, 142 (footnote 22).

59. David Scott defines "problem-spaces" as a concept that is both discursive and symbolic, "a context of knowledge and power" with a temporal dimension. Scott, *Conscripts of Modernity*, 3–4.

60. Benjamin, "Critique of Violence," 47.

61. Benjamin, "Critique of Violence," 59.

62. Hibbitts, "Coming to Our Senses," 959.

63. Latour, *The Making of Law*, 11.

64. A founder of legal sociology, Jean Carbonnier reflects on the flexibility of law with particular attention to French civil code. His writing gives permission to much of my own thought and interpretation. Carbonnier, *Flexible Droit – Pour Une Sociologie Du Droit sans Rigueur.*

65. For Victoria Fortuna, "moving otherwise" names the potential for concert dance practices to intervene within practices of (State) violence that shape everyday movements, gestures, and comportments—or as legal scholar Robert Cover suggests, the legal alterity of "the what might be." Fortuna, *Moving Otherwise*; Cover, "Nomos and Narrative," 10.

66. Moten, "Jurisgenerative Grammar (for Alto)," 128.

67. Moten, "Preface for a Solo by Miles Davis."

68. Hartman, *Scenes of Subjection*, 113–16; Moten, "Come On, Get It!"

69. Jacobs and Child, "The Loophole of Retreat," *Incidents in the Life of a Slave Girl*, 146–150.

70. Fred Moten defines performance with debt to Hortense Spillers "as the improvisatory enactment of theoretical practice *by the putative object* of theoretical practice given in no-thingly, new-thingly resistance to already given protocols." Moten, "Performance and Preformance," in Crawford and Snorton, *The Flesh of the Matter: A Critical Forum on Hortense Spillers*, 95.

71. Danielle Goldman critiques these general principles in regard to movement improvisation. Goldman, *I Want to Be Ready*, 2.

72. Goldman, *I Want to Be Ready,* borrowing from Houston Baker, 3–7.

73. brooks, "IWB = IMPROVISING WHILE BLACK."

74. brooks, 39.

75. Promotional video for Improvising While Black (IWB): Afropessimist Musings on Black Bodies in Revolt. Presented by *Movement Research,* July 20, 2018.

76. mayfield brooks presented IWB: Dancing in the Hold as a three-part series April 2018 at Gibney. Moten, *In the Break*, 85–169; Spillers "Mama's Baby, Papa's Maybe," 74. See also Moten, *Stolen Life*, 260–61.

77. Han, "Slavery as Contract," 408.

78. *Betty's Case* refers to a "freedom suit" wherein, having crossed state lines from Tennessee to Massachusetts with her owners, Betty was declared free by Chief Justice Lemuel Shaw of the Supreme Court of Massachusetts. She surprised the justice, however, by choosing to return to Tennessee with her owners. Han, "Slavery as Contract," 408.

79. For more on blackness and nonperformance, see: Moten, "Erotics of Fugitivity," *Stolen Life*, 241–266.

80. Bibler, "Disorientation as Critical Practice."

81. As presented in Danielle Goldman's study of contact improvisation and techniques of nonviolent protest, for example. Goldman, *I Want to Be Ready*, 94–111.

82. Franko, "Figural Inversions of Louis XIV's Dancing Body," 36.

83. Cerwonka and Malkki, *Improvising Theory*, 163.

84. Cerwonka and Malkki, *Improvising Theory*, 163.

85. Latour, *The Making of Law*, 150.

86. Latour, *The Making of Law*, 147.

87. Movement performers include: (New York) Simon Courchel, Natalie Green, raja feather kelly, Cori Kresge, Christopher Ralph, Anna Schön, Saúl Ulerio, Christopher Williams; (Canada) Mocean Dance, Rhonda Baker, Sara Coffin; (Turkey) TORK Dance, Tan Temel and Sernaz Demeral; and (Poland) Agnieszka Kryst, Jan Lorys, Ramona Nagabczynska, Pawel Sakowicz.

88. "There Might Be Others," *Rebecca Lazier*, Web.

89. Lazier and Trueman, *There Might Be Others*, 6. Emphasis added.

90. *There Might Be Others* premiered in 2016 at New York Live Arts before touring internationally. In 2018, a showing was presented at Princeton University's Living at the Intersection Symposium. A student of the dance department at that time, I was invited to rehearse and to partake in a portion of the demonstration. The experience has lingered with me since.

91. Lazier and Trueman, *There Might Be Others*, 21.

92. For critical theories of relationality as I intend it here, see: Glissant, *Poetics of Relation*, 170. Benítez Rojo et al., *The Repeating Island*, 15–18.

93. McKittrick, "Yours in the Intellectional Struggle," in *Sylvia Wynter* ed. McKittrick, 7–8.

94. The possibility of community created by a dance score is not unique to Lazier's work; Hetty Blades extends this politics to a COVID-era setting. We see this also in the intended reach and coalition building named in Sarah Dahnke's multi-year project, "Dances for Solidarity." Blades, "Affective Traces in Virtual Spaces."

95. Glissant, *Poetics of Relation*, 131.

96. Lazier and Trueman, *There Might Be Others*, 7.

Chapter 2

1. *Les Épaves*, Fanny Reybaud defines the *épave* as "*un nègre ou un mulâtre qui n'appartient à personne et qui n'a pourtant aucun titre de liberté* (a Negro or a mulatto who belongs to no one and yet has no title to freedom)." Reybaud, *Quatre nouvelles antillaises*, 87.

2. Reybaud, *Quatre nouvelles antillaises*, 127.

3. Reybaud, *Quatre nouvelles antillaises*, 133.

4. For an exemplary volume reflective of this potential, see: Bissell and Haviland, *The Sentient Archive.* In particular, the introduction asks: "What would it mean to say the body is an archive?," or more specifically, "What sort of investigations or practices might facilitate the archiving of bodied acts or events, as well as their potential for retrieval and reenactment?" and "What is being stored, retrieved, or transmitted, and what or who shapes the body in storing or recovering its knowledge?" xv.

5. As dance scholar Susan Foster ruminates in *Choreographing History*: "This affiliation, based on a kind of kinesthetic empathy between living and dead but imagined bodies, enjoys no primal status outside the world of writing. It possesses no organic authority; it offers no ultimate validation for sentiment. But it is redolent with physical vitality and embraces a concern for beings that live and have lived. Once the historian's body recognizes value and meaning in kinesthesia, *it cannot disanimate the physical action of past bodies it has begun to sense.*" Foster, *Choreographing History*, 7. Emphasis added. For a separate but related genealogy of sentient flesh within a global dance studies tradition, see: Mitra, "Unmaking Contact: Choreographic Touch at the Intersections of Race, Caste, and Gender."

6. Emily Johnson, "The Stories in Our Bodies," cited in Bissell and Haviland, *The Sentient Archive*, 149–150.

7. As Rebecca Schneider asks, "If we consider performance as a process of disappearance, of an ephemerality read as vanishment (versus material remains), are we limiting ourselves to an understanding of performance predetermined by our cultural habituation to the logic of the archive?" Her groundbreaking work continues to challenge epistemologies of the archive in which, as she names, flesh slips from bone as archival blindspot. Schneider, "Performance Remains," 100–102.

8. Hartman, *Scenes of Subjection*, 127–128.

9. Lubrin, *Code Noir: Fictions.*

10. Dayan, "Legal Slaves and Civil Bodies," 53.

11. Peter Goodrich defines minor jurisprudences as "forms of legal knowledge that escape the phantom of a sovereign and unitary law. A minor jurisprudence is one which neither aspires nor pretends to be the only law or universal jurisprudence." Goodrich, *Law in the Courts of Love*, 2.

12. Alexander Weheilye's work here is a critical position from which I draw, including the generous invitation to reconsider "the object of knowledge in the service of producing new formations of humanity." Weheilye, *Habeaus Viscus*, 4.

13. "Recueils de Règlements, Édits, Déclarations et Arrêts."

14. Jean Nirot offers a concise summary of the myths and realities surrounding its circulation in contemporary France. Corporeal punishment was detailed, even as "crimes and barbarous and inhuman treatment of slaves by their masters" was duly denied. Nirot, "Le Code Noir."

15. Sala-Molins, *Le Code Noir, Ou, Le Calvaire de Canaan.*

16. Voltaire, cited in: Atwill, "Slavery in the French Colonies."

17. Giacomel, *Code noir: autopsie d'un crime contre l'humanité.*

18. For more on the historical trajectory and entanglements of these categories, see: Peabody, *There Are No Slaves in France*; Peabody, *The Color of Liberty.*

19. "Recueils de Règlements, Édits, Déclarations et Arrêts."

20. The *Code Noir* moves crudely and ambiguously between language of *nègre* and *esclave*, conflating race and status. It leans more heavily toward usage of *esclave,* however, in a definition, which I attempt mirror in this chapter without neglecting the very real

racialized characteristics of the code. Later laws in France would more explicitly engage and disenfranchise blackness on its own terms, however, pointing to the more structural slippage and racial violence. R. A. Judy offers a useful genealogy of term *nègre* as it emerged from the *Code Noir.* Judy, *Sentient Flesh,* 187–190. For a public-facing summary of this shifting linguistic practice, see: Renard, "De l'esclave à la négritude: une histoire du mot "Noir.'"

21. The iterative nature of the codes repeats framing of colonial history as a process, not an event—an ongoing, performative set of actions rather than a singular violence. This formulation intentionally parallel's Patrick Wolfe's declaration that "settler-colonialism is a structure, not an event." Wolfe, "Settler Colonialism and the Elimination of the Native," 388.

22. Generalized, the fifty-four articles of the original *Code Noir* are often summarized in four or five categories: promotion of Catholicism, including marriage, baptism, and burial (Art. 1–10); quotidian conditions such as food, shelter, and clothing (Art. 11–20); relationship to property, capital, and sale and resulting punishments (Art. 21–48); and finally conditions for manumission and emancipation (Art. 49–54).

23. Art. 2: Tous les Esclaves qui seront dans nos Isles, seront baptisés & instruits dans la Religion Catholique, Apostolique & romaine. Enjoignons aux Habitans qui achèteront des Nègres nouvellement arrives, d'en avertir les Gouverneur & Intendant desdites Isles, dans huitaine au plus tard, à peine d'amende arbitraire, lesquels donneront les ordres nécessaires pour les faire instruire & baptiser dans le tems convenable; Art. 8: Déclarons nos Sujets qui ne font pas de la Religion Catholique, Apostlique & Romaine, incapables de contracter aucun mariage valable. Déclarons bâtards les enfans qui naîtront de telles conjonctions, que nous voulons être tenues & réputées, tenons & réputons pour vrais concubinages; Art. 38: L'Esclave fugitif qui aura été en fuite pendant un mois, à compter du jour que son Maître l'aura dénoncé en Justice, aura les oreilles coupées, & fera marqué d'une fleur-de-lys sur une épaule; & s'il récidive un autre mois, à compter pareillement du jour de la dénonciation, il aura le jarret coupé, & fera marqué d'une fleur-de-lys sur l'autre épaule, & la troisième fois il fera puni de mort. "Recueils de Règlements, Édits, Déclarations et Arrêts."

24. Art. 11. Les maitres seront tenus de faire enterrer en terre sainte, dans les cimetières destines a cet effet, leurs esclaves baptises; et a l'regard de ceux qui mourront sans avoir reçu le baptême, ils seront enterres la nuit, dans quelque champ voisin du lieu ou ils seront décédés. Palmer, "The Code Noir of 1724."

25. I find a parallel in André Lepecki's interpretation of Althusser, writing: "When Althusser writes that the individual 'shall submit freely to the commandments of the Subject, i.e., in order that he shall (freely) accept his subjection, i.e., in order that he shall make the gestures and actions of his subjection "all by himself"' (1994: 136), this sounds a lot like the fundamental mechanism choreography sets in place for its representational and reproductive success." Lepecki, *Exhausting Dance*, 8.

26. Roach, "Body of Law," in *From the Royal to the Republican Body*, ed. Melzer and Norberg, 117.

27. Talal Asad theorizes "difference being managed" in response to Stanley Diamon's well-known essay, "Conscripts of Western Society." For more on this, see: David Scott, "Conscripts of Modernity," in *Conscripts of Modernity.*

28. For a rigorous account of the history of passing in the United States, see: Hobbs, *A Chosen Exile.*

29. In this framing, dance became a process of resistance, as dance circulated as ritual in Vodoun tradition and ceremony, allowing those interpellated by the *Code Noir* to resist its religious hegemony.

30. From the Stono Rebellion of 1739 to the Haitian Revolution, physical resistance was a constant refrain in securing a new future.

31. Rachel Jean-Baptiste discusses alternative futures through mixed-race identity in colonial French Africa as a performance of belonging, further inscribing law and the body. See: Jean-Baptiste, *Multi-Racial Identities in Colonial Francophone Africa*; Brooks, *Bodies in Dissent.*

32. Emery, *Black Dance from 1619 to Today.*

33. The laws referenced here refer to a different but overlapping set of codes, namely local ordinances in Martinque and not the *Code Noir* itself. But the colonial logic remains in which the raced body was deemed unruly before the law. For more on the creolization of the Caribbean and French colonial history from the 1640s–1790s, including engagement with the *Code Noir* and writings by Labat. See: Garraway, *The Libertine Colony.*

34. *Calendas* was used to denote a dance deemed as African by European settler-colonizers, or otherwise deemed non-white in its aesthetic. Its origins more precisely index a hybrid form of voodoo tradition and martial arts, but often gloss a generalist understanding of diasporic culture.

35. Labat, "Nouveau Voyage Aux Isles de l'Amérique, 1700," in *Le Code Noir Ou Recueil Des Règlements Rendus Jusqu'à Présent.*

36. Judy, *Sentient Flesh*, 216.

37. For an extended read of Juba performance tradition as a particular revolutionary history of both the enjoyment and contestation of the flesh, see: Judy, "Sentient Flesh Dancing," in *Sentient Flesh*, 215–251.

38. Melzer and Norberg, "Introduction," in *From the Royal to the Republican Body.*

39. Goubert, *L'Ancien Régime*, I: La Société, 11.

40. Foster, *Choreographing Empathy*, 31.

41. In *Les Épaves,* M. de La Rebelière cries out: "*L'esclave Donatien m'a offensé de gestes et de paroles; tous ceux qui sont ici présents pourront le témoigner. Je demande qu'ici, sur l'heure, il soit mis aux quatre piquets pour recevoir vingt-neuf coups de fouet. C'est la loi. Allons, messieurs de la maréchaussée, faites votre devoir* (The slave Donatien has offended me with gestures and words; all those present here will be able to testify to this. I demand that here, now, he be put on the four stakes to receive twenty-nine lashes. It is the law. Come, gentlemen of the constabulary, do your duty)." Reybaud, *Quatre nouvelles antillaises*, 133.

42. "Transcription of 'The Code Noir' (The Black Code)," *National Park Service.*

43. Garrigus, "The 'Code Noir' (1685)," in *Le Code Noir Ou Recueil des Règlements Rendus Jusqu'à Présent.*

44. Achille Mbembe invokes the term "manners" to draw parallels between the logics of "social grace and social control." Specifically, he turns to Norbert Elias, who defines manners as the embodiment of what is "considered socially acceptable behavior," the "precepts of conduct," and the "framework for conviviality." Mbembe, *Necropolitics*, 199, footnote 33.

45. Here I think with Susan Buck-Morss's critical reconsideration of the master-slave dialectic. Buck-Morss, "Hegel and Haiti."

46. Dance scholar Ann Cooper Albright gives space to the question, "How is one touched by history?" as a methodology of perception and recovery rooted within embodied ways of knowing. I'm especially appreciative of her invocation of Toni Morrison, in a reminder that proprioceptive alternatives might produce "not the difference between fact

and fiction, but fact and truth." "Touching History," *The Sentient Archive*. ed. Bissel et al. See also: Toni Morrison, "The Site of Memory," in *Out There: Marginalization and Contemporary Cultures*, ed. Russell Ferguson et al., 303.

47. Hartman, *Scenes of Subjection*, 39.

48. *Les Paladins* restaged this opéra in 2019, offering a contemporary interpretation to this often-forgotten score.

49. Derrida, *Specters of Marx*, 51.

50. Miller, *For Derrida*, 142.

51. Derrida maintains: "The operation that amounts to founding, inaugurating, justifying law, to making law, would consist of a coup de force, of a performative and therefore interpretative violence that in itself is neither just nor unjust and that no justice and no earlier and previously founding law, no preexisting foundation, could, by definition, guarantee or contradict or invalidate." Derrida, "The Force of Law." When R. A. Judy writes that "the rift [between body and flesh] is not a singular event or action, but it is an ongoing, processual activity through and in which individual consciousness has the actual presence," he seems to suggest a similar thesis, but his attention to semiosis routes him another way. Judy, *Sentient Flesh*, 6.

52. As Reybaud defined in the novella: "*C'est un nègre ou un mulâtre qui n'appartient à personne et qui n'a pourtant aucun titre de liberté; le gouvernement s'en saisit et le vend à son profit* (He is a negro or a mulatto who belongs to no one and yet has no title to freedom; the government seizes it and sells it for its own profit)." Scribe and Bara, "Le Code Noir: Opéra-Comique en Trois Actes," 39.

53. "What right? The right to ask him what he is, ask for his free papers, and if he cannot produce them, to declare him épave and put him up for sale. That is the law: the *Code noir* is precise." Reybaud, trans. in Sollors, *Neither Black nor White Yet Both*.

54. Werner Sollors offers a detailed comparison of the plots of these three texts, alongside Victor Sejour's "Le Mulâtre," in: Sollors, *Neither Black nor White Yet Both*.

55. Scott Sanders suggests a more implicit, indirect comparison of theatricality to the *Code Noir* in his tracing of colonial legality in Marivaux's theater from the 1700s. Sanders, "Code Noir in Marivaux's Theatre."

56. Andersen, cited in Sollors, *Neither Black nor White Yet Both*, 179–80.

57. Garrigus, "The 'Code Noir' (1685)," in *Le Code Noir Ou Recueil des Règlements Rendus Jusqu'à Présent*.

58. Reybaud, for example, writes with straightforward reminder that "Any slave who marries a white woman is free by law." Indeed, the narrator is revealed as none other than a descendent of the interracial marriage, foreshadowing the centrality of raced status to the plot. Sollors, *Neither Black nor White Yet Both*, 172.

59. For a feminist-abolitionist reading of Reybaud's work, see: Curtis, "Excluded from Paradise"; Enz, "Who Belongs to Whom?"

60. Scribe and Bara, "Le Code Noir: Opéra-Comique en Trois Actes," 112.

61. Foster, "Choreographies of Gender," 4.

62. Sollors, *Neither Black nor White Yet Both*, 184.

63. *Bulletin des salons* (12 juin 1842) in Scribe and Bara, "Le Code Noir: Opéra-Comique en Trois Actes," xxv.

64. For a recent imperial history of blackface, see: Hoxworth, *Transoceanic Blackface*.

65. Hartman, *Scenes of Subjection*, 32–36.

66. Gilroy, *The Black Atlantic*, 57.

67. I am attentive here to the formative work of Saidiya Hartman, who cautions against uncritical consumption of the subjugated, the violent, the spectacle in a reminder that

recuperative acts can be as violating, too. Terror and joy share in a complicated relationality when sensationalized and severed from the historical now. Hartman, *Scenes of Subjection.*

68. Palmer, "The Code Noir of 1724."

69. Spillers, for example, writes a line that always causes me to take an extra breath: "If we think of the "flesh" as a primary narrative, then we mean its seared, divided, ripped-apartness, riveted to the ship's hole, fallen, or 'escaped' overboard." Spillers, "Mama's Baby, Papa's Maybe: An American Grammar Book," 67.

70. Butler, *Excitable Speech*, 5.

71. Brissot, *Réflexions sur le Code Noir.*

72. Brissot, *Réflexions sur le Code Noir.*

73. Brissot, *Réflexions sur le Code Noir.*

74. Olson, "The Turn to Passion: Has Law and Literature Become Law and Affect?"

75. Brissot, *Réflexions sur le Code Noir.*

76. Brissot, *Réflexions sur le Code Noir.*

77. Foster, *Choreographing Empathy*, 2.

78. Hartman, *Scenes of Subjection*, 86–90.

79. Barthes, *Le Degré Zero*, 39. Cited in: Judy, *Sentient Flesh*, 181.

80. Barthes, "From The Neutral," 16. Cited in: Han, *Mu, 49 Marks of Abolition*, 150.

81. Han, *Mu, 49 Marks of Abolition*, 152.

82. Dorinne Kondo draws an overt line between ethnography's corporeal epistemologies and the construction of race and race-making processes, influential to my own method of research. Kondo, *Worldmaking*, 5–8.

83. Anne Cheng's contributions to *New Directions in Law and Literature* resists this claim, as does the recent *Law and Performance* anthology, yet the most notable contributions are by scholars outside of legal studies. Anker and Meyler, *New Directions in Law and Literature*; Sarat et al., *Law and Performance.*

84. Nader, *The Life of the Law: Anthropological Projects.*

85. Sala-Molins, *Le Code Noir, Ou, Le Calvaire de Canaan. Pratiques Théoriques*, 7. trans. Anna Jayne Kimmel.

86. Gbaguidi, "Code Noir."

87. "Choreography of the Sign," Pélagie Gbaguidi, 2025. Web. For reference, see: https://pelagiegbaguidi.com/works/choreography-of-sign.

88. "Code Noir," Pélagie Gbaguidi, 2006. Web. See: https://pelagiegbaguidi.com/projects/code-noir.

89. See Götl for more complete history on the evolution of the status of witnesses as related to laws of slavery in France: T. Göltl, "Trials of Enslavers in Former French Colonies in the Eighteenth and Nineteenth Centuries: Testimonies of the Enslaved Between Gratitude and Fear," Slavery & Abolition 45, no. 1 (2024): 117–34. See Orlando Patterson for more on "liminal incorporation." Patterson, *Slavery and Social Death*, 45–51.

90. The article in full reads: Art. 26: "Les Esclaves qui ne seront point nourris, vêtus & entretenues par leurs Maîtres, selon que nous l'avons ordonné par ces prétextes, pourront en donner avis à notre Procureur, & mettre leurs mémoires entre ces mains, sur lesquels & même d'office, si les avis lui en viennent d'ailleurs, les Maîtres seront poursuivis à sa Requête [. . .]." "Recueils de Réglemens, Édits, Déclarations et Arrêts."

91. It is important to recognize, as Louis Sala-Molins identifies, that "no master was ever punished for crimes committed against the bodies (can one say 'the person'?) of slaves. And I can conclude from this that the *Code Noir* articles 31 and 36 take away all the

credibility of article 26." The risk and obstacle replete in such potential to move otherwise, as more than the nonhuman status intended, saturates the archive surrounding the *Code Noir*, and many scholars are quick to dismiss the agency endowed to Art. 26 in light of the net detriment of the code (including parameters to legal personhood defined in Art. 31 and 36). This includes potential retaliation for speaking out and linguistic difference of translation required for effective testimony to be given. Peabody, "Slaves as Witnesses, Slaves as Evidence"; Sala-Molins, *Dark Side of the Light*, 35.

92. Garrigus, "The 'Code Noir' (1685)," in *Le Code Noir Ou Recueil des Règlements Rendus Jusqu'à Présent.*

93. "Pascale Marthine Tayou Code Noir Art. 5, 2018."

94. Naimou, *Salvage Work,* 9. See also: Young, "Lost Daughters and Sunken Ships: Salvaging the Archive."

95. Sharpe, "The Weather," *In the Wake.*

96. Art. 44: Déclarons les esclaves être meubles et comme tels entrer dans la communauté, n'avoir point de suite par hypothèque, se partager également entre les cohéritiers, sans préciput et droit d'aînesse, n'être sujets au douaire coutumier, au retrait féodal et lignager, aux droits féodaux et seigneuriaux, aux formalités des décrets, ni au retranchement des quatre quints, en cas de disposition à cause de mort et testamentaire. See also Art. 30 and 31 for the absence of legal personality.

97. For a broad yet forceful critique of the slave as example of legal nonperson, see: Patterson, *Slavery and Social Death*, 38–51. Or what Colin Dayan theorizes as a position of negative personhood for enslaved life. Dayan, "Legal Slaves and Civil Bodies, " 53–55. For more on the legal traditions of personhood, see: Kurki, A *Theory of Legal Personhood.*

98. Political philosophers suggest that this shift in language is a mark of an Anglo-legal conception of chattel slavery (as opposed to Roman and feudal law whereby the legalized practice of slavery equated human form with immovable property). For example, see the work of Sala-Molins, *Dark Side of the Light;* Wood, "Across Oceans and Revolutions: Law and Slavery in French Saint-Domingue and Beyond," 761.

99. Dayan, "Legal Slaves and Civil Bodies," 56.

100. Wynter, "Unsettling the Coloniality of Being/Power/Truth/Freedom."

101. Dayan, "Legal Slaves and Civil Bodies," 53.

102. Dayan, "Legal Slaves and Civil Bodies," 62.

103. Agamben, *The Open.*

Chapter 3

1. Excerpts from the section "Coding Blackness and the Idle Body" were previously published in "The Right to Stillness: Tracing Corporeal Ambiguity in Legal Interpretation." *Southern California Interdisciplinary Law Journal,* Spring 2026. My gratitude to the editorial team at *SCILJ* for permission to feature that content here.

2. Colonial humanism, as Gary Wilder theorizes, operated on a tripartite ethnologism of temporalities, racialization, and nationalism. This chapter turns on a similar focus. Wilder, *The French Imperial Nation-State.*

3. McKittrick et al., "Rhythm, or On Sylvia Wynter's Science of the Word," 870.

4. Katherine McKittrick illuminates the rhythmic underpinnings of Wynter's theory with particular finesse as she models a "rhythmic reading practice." McKittrick et al., "Rhythm, or On Sylvia Wynter's Science of the Word," 867.

5. Barthes, *How to Live Together*, 7.

6. Barthes, *How to Live Together*, 7–8.

7. The histories here are many and plural, if outside the scope of this chapter. For an illustrative example, see: Dubois, *A Colony of Citizens.*

8. Derrida, quoted in: Read, *The Fact of Blackness*, 191.

9. These patterns repeat historically beyond the space of French legal codes. Consider, for example, the fraught biopolitics of racialized life in the United States where in the one-drop rule, otherwise termed hypodescent, cast widely for black life in a violent extrapolation of workforce and racial capital whereas blood quantum politics eradicated legal recognition for indigenous life in what we might term inversely as hyperdescent.

10. Puar, "Spatial Debilities," 402.

11. McKittrick et al., "Rhythm, or On Sylvia Wynter's Science of the Word," 870.

12. Rifkin, *Beyond Settler Time,* viii.

13. Elizabeth Freeman presents a similar argument of temporalized bodies, if her commitment to Foucauldian analysis, queer hypersociality, and Anglophone literary canon diverges from the aims of *Legal Moves.* I recommend her book, *Beside You in Time,* to all as a companion work for those interested in themes of this chapter.

14. Wolfe, *Traces of History.*

15. For more on the history of legal transplants, see: Cairns, *Codification, Transplants, and History*; Gross, "Legal Transplants"; Tomlins, "Transplants and Timing"; Vetter, "Another Legal Transplant"; and Watson, *Legal Transplants.*

16. Many scholars and activists sit with these critical affiliations. A few guiding authors, include, for me: Rifkin, *Fictions of Land and Flesh*; Wolfe, *Traces of History*; King, *The Black Shoals*; King, *Otherwise Worlds.*

17. A note on terminology is in order. I find standard in Danielle Beaujon's methodology: "I use Algerian to refer to what French administrators would have called *indigènes* or Français Musulmans d'Algérie. Although Algerian flattens ethnic, linguistic, religious, and class divisions, I use it to distinguish Algerians from French and European settler populations, whom I refer to as European. Algerian Jews had also lived in Algeria for centuries, but in police parlance, *indigène* meant the nominally Muslim population, and my use of Algerian refers to this same group. I intentionally leave the word *indigène* untranslated in quotes, as the offensive colonial term has no obvious English translation." Beaujon, *Criminalizing the Casbahs*, xii.

18. McManus, "Race, Time, and the Petrified Subject in Algeria," 295.

19. By naming an "apparatus of re-capture," I intentionally return the reader to the André Lepecki's writing who transfers the more Deleuzian term to the space of the choreographic. Lepecki, "Choreography as Apparatus of Capture," 119–123.

20. Lepecki, *Exhausting Dance*, 8.

21. Cooppan, "Time-Maps," 397.

22. Isabelle Merle is careful to name the code as regime in order to emphasize its force. Merle, "Retour Sur Le Régime De L'Indigénat," 77.

23. As Isabelle Merle notes, there was no singular piece of legislation or legal document to the regime. Rather, the reference points to a piecemeal mode of legal authority, a catch-all for the numerous, overlapping, and at times competing sites of law which produced the regulatory framework for French colonialism. Merle, "Retour Sur Le Régime De L'Indigénat."

24. Doho, *Le Code de l'indigénat: Ou Le Fondement Des Etats Autocratiques En Afrique Francophone.*

25. McDougall, "Savage Wars? Codes of Violence in Algeria, 1830s–1990s."

26. Le Cour Grandmaison, "The Exception and the Rule: On French Colonial Law."

27. Barkat, *Le Corps d'exception*, 72.

28. Barkat, *Le Corps d'exception*, 72.

29. Rifkin, *Beyond Settler Time*, vii.

30. McManus, "Race, Time, and the Petrified Subject in Algeria," 292.

31. McManus, "Race, Time, and the Petrified Subject in Algeria," 292.

32. McManus, "Race, Time, and the Petrified Subject in Algeria," 294.

33. Surkis, *Sex, Law, and Sovereignty in French Algeria, 1830–1930*, 120.

34. Art. 1 of the *Code de l'indigénat* reads: "*L'indigène musulman est français; néanmoins il continuera à être régi par la loi musulmane. Il peut être admis à servir dans les armées de terre et de mer. Il peut être appelé à des fonctions et emplois civils en Algérie. Il peut, sur sa demande, être admis à jouir des droits de citoyen français; dans ce cas, il est régi par les lois civiles et politiques de la France.* (The Muslim native is French; nevertheless, he will continue to be governed by Muslim law. He may be admitted to serve in the land and sea armies. He may be called to civil functions and employment in Algeria. He may, upon his request, be admitted to enjoy the rights of a French citizen; in this case, he is governed by the civil and political laws of France.)"

35. For example, the 1870 Crémieux Decree reversed a policy and granted French citizenship to Jewish but not Muslim people, thus reversing the 1865 Sénatus-Consulte that offered pathways of naturalization to both Jewish and Muslim Algerians and inflating tensions between indigenous Algerians. For more, see: Brett, "Legislating for Inequality in Algeria: The Senatus-Consulte of 14 July 1865"; Marglin, *Across Legal Lines.*

36. Religious categories defined within French colonial policies, including the *Code de l'indigénat*, frequently operated along practices of racial discrimination rather than a person's specific religious practice. The colonial codes created a discriminatory process of exclusion as they reconfigured populations by instituting ethno-racial lines of division that did not precede the colonial project. The contemporary distinction in Algeria between Arab and Kabyle remains heavily racialized; its colonial legacy critiqued in the 2005 petition, "*Nous sommes les Indigènes de la République* (We are the Indigenous of the Republic)," among other twenty-first century residues. See also: Le Cour Grandmaison, "The Exception and the Rule: On French Colonial Law."

37. Surkis, *Sex, Law, and Sovereignty in French Algeria, 1830–1930.*

38. McManus, "Race, Time, and the Petrified Subject in Algeria," 288.

39. Edward Said is one of many critics to catalogue this trope, its widespread distribution, and its harmful legacy. Said, *Orientalism.* Mariam Helah Davis details a more specific, if no less impactful, critique of the assumptions (and impositions) of cultural difference, economic modernity, and racial capital as foundational to French colonialization of Algeria. Davis, *Markets of Civilization.*

40. Surkis, *Sex, Law, and Sovereignty in French Algeria, 1830–1930*, 7.

41. Surkis, *Sex, Law, and Sovereignty in French Algeria, 1830–1930*, 24.

42. Surkis, *Sex, Law, and Sovereignty in French Algeria, 1830–1930*, 182.

43. Judith Surkis emphasizes this tension when she reflects on the gendered politics of French legal code in Algeria: "She thus personified the French Civil Code's superiority.

This 'protective' gesture was also disciplinary." Surkis, *Sex, Law, and Sovereignty in French Algeria, 1830–1930*, 203. Gary Wilder critiques this argument of benevolent legal pluralism with nuance. Wilder, *The French Imperial Nation-State*.

44. Summary of explanatory statement of State Councilor Flandrin read on June 22, 1865, as summarized by C. R. Ageron in *Les Algériens musulmans et la France (1871–1919)*. Cited in Barkat, *Le Corps d'exception*.

45. As Barkat writes: "*La fonction essentielle du dispositif est d'interpréter la situation culturale de ces indigènes candidats à l'exercice de la politique et de déterminer qui a vocation à devenir citoyen non à partir de l'évidence de son humanité, mais selon son degré de conformité au modèle culturel français* (The essential function of the dispositif is to interpret the cultural situation of the indigenous candidates for the exercise of politics and to determine who has a vocation to become a citizen not from the evidence of his humanity, but according to his degree of conformity to the French cultural model)." Barkat, *Le Corps d'exception*, 31. Emphasis added.

46. Surkis, *Sex, Law, and Sovereignty in French Algeria, 1830–1930*, 19.

47. Surkis, *Sex, Law, and Sovereignty in French Algeria, 1830–1930*, 5.

48. Puar, "Spatial Debilities," 402.

49. Wilder, *The French Imperial Nation-State*, 115–116.

50. Puar, "Spatial Debilities," 404.

51. For a fuller history of the deep, and deeply complicated, racial logic of the French imperial project, see: McDougall, "Savage Wars? Codes of Violence in Algeria, 1830s–1990s."

52. I draw upon Jasbir Puar here, who draws upon Kyla Schuller: "If biopolitics functions in part through the 'racialization of temporality,'" writes Puar, "this process entails several modes of temporal differentiation: withholding futurity, making impossible anything but a slowed (down) life, and immobilizing the body 'within the past of civilization itself' (Schuller 2018: 58), thereby putting under duress ascriptions of the past, the present, and the future." Puar, "Spatial Debilities," 404.

53. Spillers, "Mama's Baby, Papa's Maybe," 66.

54. Barkat, *Le Corps d'exception*. Written in three parts, Samira Benhaddou's work stands as the most comprehensive analysis of these codes. Benhaddou, "La Matraque Coloniale: Le Code De L'indigénat En Algérie;" Thénault, *Violence ordinaire dans l'Algérie coloniale*.

55. Barthes, *How to Live Together*, 7–8.

56. For example, see annex of Special Offenses listed in: Loi du 21 décembre 1897 relative aux pouvoirs disciplinaires des administrateurs des communes mixtes, en Algérie.

57. Elsewhere this was phrased as the ambiguous and open-ended restriction against "Remarks made in public against France and its government." See Loi du 21 décembre 1897.

58. Loi du 21 décembre 1897, offense 18.

59. ARRÊTÉ GÉNÉRAL SUR LES INFRACTIONS DE L'INDIGÉNAT, Préfecture d'Alger, 9 février 1875

60. Loi du 21 décembre 1897, offenses 10, 12, 13, 18.

61. Jasbir Puar articulates this all too well in her forceful article on slow and debilitated life in Palestine. Puar, "Spatial Debilities."

62. Mann, "What Was the 'Indigénat'? The 'Empire of Law' in French West Africa," 233.

63. See generally: Ruskola, *Legal Orientalism*.

64. Foster, "The Ballerina's Phallic Point."

65. Thénault, *Une Drôle Justice*. Cited in: Mourouga, "The Code de l'Indigénat and Colonial Management in Algeria (1865–1944)."

66. "M. le Gouverneur, comme nous tous vous êtes au courant de la mortalité effrayante qui frappe les prestataires employés à la construction de la route de Tananarive-Tamatave [. . .]. C'est donc avec une fréquence vraiment inquiétante que se multiplient ces actes d'arbitraire dont chaque jour, colons et Malgaches ont à se plaindre. L'indigène est arrêté, emprisonné pendant des mois sans jugement, sans interrogatoire; et cela avec d'autant moins de ménagements que le détenu est toujours utilisé comme main-d'œuvre économique." Pétition de 51 colons français au gouverneur général de Madagascar, le 13 janvier 1900.

67. Rifkin offers an powerful read of post-Einsteinian notions of time in regard to Indian law and policy. I take inspiration from his frame throughout this chapter. Rifkin, *Beyond Settler Time*, ix.

68. Adeyemi, "Beyond 90°: The Angularities of Black/Queer/Women/Lean," 10.

69. Ann Cooper Albright cited in Adeyemi, "Beyond 90°: The Angularities of Black/Queer/Women/Lean," 10.

70. Reprinted in Benhaddou, *La Matrique Coloniale*, 188–92. trans. by Kimmel.

71. Saada, "The Empire of Law: Dignity, Prestige, and Domination in the 'Colonial Situation,'" 110.

72. For more, see: Betts, *Assimilation and Association in French Colonial Theory, 1890–1914*.

73. McDougall, "Savage Wars? Codes of Violence in Algeria, 1830s–1990s," 121.

74. McDougall, "Savage Wars? Codes of Violence in Algeria, 1830s–1990s," 121.

75. Benhaddou, "La Matraque Coloniale: Le Code De L'indigénat En Algérie," 141–78.

76. I acknowledge that even this reform remained controversial as it was diluted from its original, more sweeping, proposition.

77. El Atti, "Algeria Pushes Forward Draft Law to Hold France Accountable for Its Colonized Past."

78. Puar, "Spatial Debilities," 404.

79. Cooppan, "Time-Maps, 399.

80. The residue of French law in US contexts, and wider civil legal inheritance process, extends beyond the Black Codes. Gross, "Legal Transplants."

81. Cramer and Raengo, "Freeing Black Codes: Liquid Blackness Plays the Jazz Ensemble," 8.

82. For more on the postbellum history of the period of Reconstruction, see: Du Bois, *Black Reconstruction in America*.

83. Lepecki, "Choreography as an Apparatus of Capture."

84. The landmark case, *Papachristou v. City of Jacksonville* (1972), would begin to interrupt this history by declaring the Jacksonville vagrancy ordinance unconstitutionally vague. For a deeper reading of this case as it relates to vagueness and choreographic attention, see: Kimmel, "The Right to Stillness."

85. Goluboff's work is exceptional in theorizing the impact of and resistance to vagrancy that shaped American protest culture in the 1960s. Goluboff, *Vagrant Nation*.

86. Blackmon, *Slavery by Another Name*.

87. Goodell, "Fugitives from Slavery," 29.

88. Lepecki, *Exhausting Dance*, 3.

89. Cited in Richardson, "Florida Black Codes," 371–72.

90. Acts of the General Assembly of the State of Virginia, Passed in 1865–66, 91–93.

91. "Persons able to work but habitually living upon the earnings of their wives or minor children shall be deemed vagrants." Jacksonville Ordinance Code § 257.

92. The incident in question follows a petitioner who, having entered a café, was seen alone on the dance floor having been there thirty minutes. The officer, following a routine check, arrested him loitering in spite of the provided reason of waiting for a bus (with proof of a bus schedule and fare on his person) and testimony to having purchased food and drink at the establishment. *Thompson v. City of Louisville*, 362, US 199 (1960).

93. And therefore not culpable of any of the named unlawful conducts of Louisville Ordinance against loitering, which instead named "It shall be unlawful for any person . . . to sleep, lie, loaf, or trespass in or about any premises, building, or other structure in the City of Louisville, without first having obtained the consent of the owner or controller of said premises, structure, or building." § 85–12, Ordinances of the City of Louisville.

94. *Thompson v. City of Louisville*, 361–362 US 199 (1960).

95. *Thompson v. City of Louisville*, 362 US 199 (1960).

96. *Thompson v. City of Louisville*, 362 US 199 (1960).

97. For more on corporeal ambiguity in legal interpretation and its consequences, see: Kimmel, "The Right to Stillness."

98. *Garner v. Louisiana* 368 US 157 (1961).

99. *Garner v. Louisiana* 368 US at 169.

100. "No Evidence to Support a Conviction," 1139.

101. *Thompson v. City of Louisville*, 362 US 199 (1960). A similarly overt violation of corporeal ambiguity comes in *Johnson v. Florida* wherein "judgment cannot stand, since there was no evidence establishing the 'wandering or strolling' ingredient." *Johnson v. Florida*, 391 US 596 (1968). Risa Goluboff elsewhere writes of "the importance of facts." Goluboff, *Vagrant Nation: Police Power, Constitutional Change, and the Making of the 1960s*, 267–87.

102. Goluboff, *Vagrant Nation*, 4.

103. Goluboff and Schragger, "Grants Pass and the Vagrancy Revolution Revisited."

104. For more on similar themes, see: Kimmel, "'Naked Athena.'"

105. For example, see: Anderson, Patrick. "Dramaturgies of Policing: Performance Theory, Police Violence, and the Limits of Accountability." *Theatre Journal* (Washington, D.C.) 73.4 (2021): 533–549.

106. For example, "Appellant, found by officers at 4:25 a.m. sitting on a bench at a bus stop, was charged with violating a Florida vagrancy law making it a misdemeanor to be found 'wandering or strolling around from place to place without any lawful purpose or object.'" *Johnson v. Florida*, 391 US 596 (1968).

107. This is sometimes phrased as "for no apparent reason," but the subsequent logic holds.

108. Anne Cheng demonstrates this point with her critical review of the "Case of Twenty-Two Lewd Chinese Women" moved from the San Francisco District Court to the US Supreme Court. Her analysis points, unequivocally, to the interrelated perceptions of legality, aesthetics, and race, as manifest in Asian femininity and its ornamentation. "The display of extravagant Asiatic ornamentality," she writes, "generates a vertiginous drama toggling between visible and the invisible, the present and the imagined. As we will see, the moment the yellow woman materializes as a recognizable legal category is also the very moment when she becomes unassimilable and disappears into the thingness that defines

her." This leads Cheng to make the claim, "The forensic use of visual evidence started not with the introduction of modern technologies like photography, but instead with the phantasmic construction of 'illegible' and 'foreign' bodies." Cheng, *Ornamentalism*, 39–40.

109. The "Walking While Trans" ban refers to Penal Law §240.37, which criminalizes loitering for the intent of prostitution. As the NYCLU notes, however, for decades this law has been used against "innocuous behavior, like waiting for a friend or waving down a taxi." The ready shift between these gerunds—walking, loitering, waiting, waiving—is precisely the point, as law and law enforcement allow slippage and conflation across these choreographic differences. "NYCLU Statement on the Repeal and Seal of the Walking While Trans Ban."

110. *City of Grants Pass v. Johnson*, 603 US 520.

111. For more, see: Nicolazzo, *Vagrant Figures*, as well as Beier, *Masterless Men.*

112. Puar, "Spatial Debilities," 404.

113. I choose to write of refusal in lieu of resistance in alliance with Alexander Weheliye's critique of resistance as rhetoric that "tendency to blind us, whether through strenuous denials or exalted celebrations of their existence, to the manifold occurrences of freedom in zones of indistinction." Weheliye, *Habeas Viscus,* 2.

114. Lepecki, *Exhausting Dance*, 15.

115. Rao, *Stillness Manifesto.*

116. Adeyemi, "Beyond 90°: The Angularities of Black/Queer/Women/Lean."

117. Dowling, *Here Is a Figure*, 1 and jacket cover.

118. Young, *Falling, Floating, Flickering.*

119. Adeyemi, "Beyond 90°: The Angularities of Black/Queer/Women/Lean," 10.

120. Moten, "Performance and Preformance," in Crawford and Snorton, ed. *The Flesh of the Matter,* 96.

121. Sosa in McNamara, "Black Power Naps Is Addressing How Systemic Racism Impacts Sleep."

122. niv Acosta and Fanny Sosa. Cited in: Khanmalek and Rhodes, A *Decolonial Feminist Epistemology of the Bed.*

123. niv Acosta, quoted in Michael Love, "If You're Black, Rest Is Power."

124. Seymour, "MoMA Apologises to Artist Heather Agyepong."

125. Grandner et al., "Sleep Disparity, Race/Ethnicity, and Socioeconomic Position."

126. In the chapter, "A Place Where the Soul Can Rest," bell hooks laments on the absence of feminist spaces to rest in public: "The street corner turns every woman who dares lurk into a body selling herself, a body looking for drugs, a body going down. A female lurking, lingering, lounging on a street corner is seen by everyone, looked at, observed. Whether she wants to be or not she is prey for the predator, for the Man, be he pimp, police, or just passerby. In cities women have no outdoor territory to occupy. They must be endlessly moving or enclosed. They must have a destination. They cannot loiter or linger." Hooks, *Belonging* , 143–152. The front porch becomes the antithesis: "Verandas and porches were made for females to have outdoor space to occupy . . . a porch was a sign of living a life without shame. To come out on the porch was to see and be seen, to have nothing to hide . . . to reside if only for a time, in that place of leisure and rest." Ibid.

127. Hersey, *Rest is Resistance*; Hersey and McCalman, *We Will Rest!*

128. Williams, *The Necessary Art of Leisure.*

129. Hersey, *Rest Is Resistance.* Emphasis added.

130. Hersey, *Rest Is Resistance.*

131. McKinney cited in Grabenstein, "Using Our Bodies."

132. Cast members include: Bianca Cabrera, Clarissa Dyas, Laura Elaine Ellis, Sonsherée Giles, MaryStarr Hope, and Megan Lowe. Collaborating artists include: Sean Riley (Set and Rigging Design), Jack Beuttler (Lighting Design), Jamielyn Duggan (Costumes), and Pamela Z (Music). The work was first presented in the San Francisco Civic Center Area, but later restaged at Sing Sing Prison (Ossining, NY), Zidel Yards (Portland, OR), and the Contemporary Arts Center (New Orleans, LA).

133. Foster, *Choreographing Empathy*, 26.

Interlude

1. King, *The Black Shoals*, 181.

2. Shakespeare, *The Tempest*, 1.2.258, cited in King, *The Black Shoals*, 184. The final set of adjectives is King's.

3. Moten, *Stolen Life*, 251.

4. This quote reflects Leslie Fiedler's point of view, summarized by Meredith Anne Skura. Skura, "Discourse and the Individual," 50.

5. In this essay, Hortense Spillers features language of dance studies—choreographs, repertoire, movement, intimacy, flesh, stage—to amplify the construction of legal/cultural/geographic border politics in the Americas, already gesturing toward the aims of *Legal Moves*. "Who Cuts the Border? Some Readings on America" in Spillers, *Black, White, and in Color*, 325.

6. Busia, "Silencing Sycorax," 85, 99. This excerpt is repeated in Jodi Byrd's "'This Island's Mine': The Parallax Logics of Caliban's Cacophony," *The Transit of Empire*, 59.

7. Wynter, "Afterword: Beyond Miranda's Meanings," 355–370.

8. King, *The Black Shoals*, 198.

9. Lara, "Beyond Caliban's Curses," 80.

10. Aimé Césaire's postcolonial adaptation stands as hallmark of this tradition, though others proliferate. Césaire et al., *A Tempest: Based on Shakespeare's The Tempest, Adaptation for a Black Theatre*; Goldberg, *Tempest in the Caribbean*.

11. Frey, "The Tempest and the New World."

12. Wynter, "Unsettling the Coloniality of Being/Power/Truth/Freedom," 296–97.

13. Brown, "'This Thing of Darkness I Acknowledge Mine,'" 63.

14. Foster, *Knowing as Moving*, 5.

15. White, *The Legal Imagination*, 555.

16. For more, see Sylvia Wynter's engagement with Césaire's science of the Word. McKittrick, *Sylvia Wynter: On Being Human as Praxis*, 17.

17. Esmeir, *Juridical Humanity*.

18. Skura, "Discourse and the Individual," 58.

19. Lara, "Beyond Caliban's Curses," 81.

20. King, *The Black Shoals*, 181.

21. King, *The Black Shoals*, 185.

22. King, *The Black Shoals*, 175.

23. Kamau Brathwaite cited in Fécu's "Sycorax's Other Sons."

24. Anker and Meyler acknowledge the future of the law and literature movement "would conceive of law as performance, seeing law as a collection of collaborative performance processes and events." Anker and Meyler, eds., *New Directions in Law and Literature*, 24.

25. King, *The Black Shoals*, 206.

26. King, *The Black Shoals*, 183.

Chapter 4

1. Einaudi, *Octobre 1961: Un Massacre à Paris*, 11.

2. Papon later challenged that he himself was not afforded full rights in the process of his trial. In 2001, the Chamber of the European Court of Human Rights ruled admissible the application of *Papon v. France* for violations of Art. 6, Section 1 "right to a fair trial" and Protocol No. 7, Art. 2 "right to appeal in criminal matters."

3. Papon was stripped of this medal in 1999 in the aftermath of the trial's 1998 verdict.

4. This new deployment was signaled by the Special Powers Act of March 16, 1956 in which police power was transferred to the military and colonial measures deployed abroad entered France, including "arbitrary arrest, systematic violence . . . and forms of brutality that culminated in the event of 17 October." House and MacMaster, *Paris 1961: Algerians, State Terror, and Memory*, 28.

5. Lia Brozgal thoughtfully takes on this fraught entanglement in the final chapter of her book, "The Entangled Stories of October 17, Vichy, the Jews, and the Holocaust." Brozgal, *Absent the Archive.*

6. Yoneyama, *Cold War Ruins*, 4.

7. Derrida, *On Cosmopolitanism and Forgiveness.*

8. Derrida, "Force of Law: The 'Mystical Foundation of Authority,'" 250.

9. Lisa Lowe, cited in Yoneyama, *Cold War Ruins*, 9. Lowe, *The Intimacies of Four Continents.*

10. El-Tayeb, *European Others*, 38.

11. Randall Williams, cited in Yoneyama, *Cold War Ruins*, 8. Williams, *The Divided World.*

12. Arguably, the most well-cited theorist here is Immanuel Kant, whose political philosophy transitions from the external value system of honor to the intrinsic recognition of dignity. For more on the morals of human rights, see: Etinson, "What's So Special About Human Dignity?"; Habermas, "The Concept of Human Dignity and the Realistic Utopia of Human Rights."

13. For a detailed history of the two most prominent traditions of dignity in Western critical theory, namely Christian theology and Kantian philosophy, see: Rosen, *Dignity: Its History and Meaning.*

14. Beitz, "Human Dignity in the Theory of Human Rights: Nothing But a Phrase?," 260.

15. Other scholars are more forthright in their critique of the term: Pinker, "The Stupidity of Dignity"; Macklin, "Dignity Is a Useless Concept"; Joern and Eckert, "Legal Roots of Human Dignity in German Law," in *The Concept of Human Dignity in Human Rights Discourse*, ed. D. Krezmer and E. Klein; Allan and Bagaric, "The Vacuous Concept of Dignity."

16. Anker, *Fictions of Dignity*, 2. The phrase "bodily integrity" draws upon the work of Carolyn Dean. Dean, *The Frail Social Body.*

17. See Judith Butler's *Bodies That Matter* (1993) for an extended commentary on the relationship between performativity, materialization, and constitution.

18. This interview includes an acknowledgement of Wynter's time as a dancer in college during the height of her intellectual formation. This biographical detail draws attention to

the emergence of movement and corporeality within her understanding of humanisms, as movement preceded her formal entry into writing. Wynter and Scott, "The Re-Enchantment of Humanism," 120.

19. Dipesh Chakrabarty's work casts a long shadow to which I am very much in debt. I also want to acknowledge Susan Foster's leadership in organizing the series, Provincializing Dance Studies, hosted by the Dance Studies Association between 2020–2025. Chakrabarty, *Provincializing Europe.*

20. House and MacMaster, *Paris 1961: Algerians, State Terror, and Memory*, 1. House and MacMaster intentionally title their book without invocation of "massacre" to allow for multiple, conflicting histories to be included. Other scholars tend to center on "massacre," permitting that the scope and scale of the event differs across records.

21. This term was used by Papon and other State officials regardless of status of French citizenship.

22. For example, the Géronimi Report suggests 246 violent Algerian deaths in 1961, while the Mandelkin Report suggests far fewer. House and MacMaster offer a comprehensive overview of these divergent accounts. House and MacMaster, *Paris 1961: Algerians, State Terror, and Memory.*

23. This curfew restricted the movement of French Muslim Algerians from 8:30pm–5:30am. The protest, then, was planned from 8:30–9:30pm in obvious violation of this policy. It is worth noting, however, that this curfew held no official legal weight, but it was often enforced with intensity. Its exclusive application to French Muslin Algerians made it overtly racial and discriminatory. House and MacMaster, *Paris 1961: Algerians, State Terror, and Memory*, 100.

24. APP-HA111. Cadavres F.M.A. Repêches en Seine in file "Statistiques des victimes algériennes." For additional statistics, see: "Geronimi Report", 18–19.

25. APP-HA110, Statistiques des victims algériannes. October 1961; daily detail of recovered bodies.

26. APP-HA110, Au suject des manifestations organisées par le FLN le 17 octobre 1961; see also: House and MacMaster, *Paris 1961: Algerians, State Terror, and Memory*, 102, 115–17.

27. For one of many recounts of this relationality, see: Sherman, "Climax in Algeria," 134–42.

28. Agamben, *State of Exception.*

29. Rothberg, "A Tale of Three Ghettos: Race, Gender, and 'Universality' After October 17, 1961," in *Multidirectional Memory.*

30. APP-H1B34. Déclaration Sur la Répression et les Mesures policières dans la région Parisienne. Front de Libération Nationale, Fédération de France. Paris, 17 octobre 1961.

31. In 2012, then-President Hollande issued a statement acknowledging the bloody deaths of October 17; President Macron also held a memorial in 2021 to pay tribute to the 60th anniversary. Both, however, fell short of an explicit apology.

32. House and MacMaster, *Paris 1961: Algerians, State Terror, and Memory*, 101.

33. House and MacMaster, *Paris 1961: Algerians, State Terror, and Memory*, 120.

34. House and MacMaster, *Paris 1961: Algerians, State Terror, and Memory*, 120.

35. Kagan, "Massacre in the City," 80–86. Desjarlais, "Intersecting Lives," *The Visual Afterlife of Abdelkader Bennahar*, 127–178.

36. Brozgal, *Absent the Archive*, 2.

37. Waldron, *Dignity, Rank, and Rights*, 215–216; Bloch, *Natural Law and Human Dignity*, 188.

38. Derrida, "Before the Law."

39. Jasbir Puar extends this argument into the twenty-first century with her discussion of Arab, Muslim, and Sikh Americans following September 11. Puar, *Terrorist Assemblages*, 41.

40. Although Algerian revolutionary forces in general, and FLN and OAS forces in particular, are known for their use of violence in pursuit of anti-colonial futures, coordinated efforts of non-violent resistance continued alongside, not least by protestors on October 17, 1961.

41. John Lewis, cited in: Foster, "Choreographies of Protest," 399. Emphasis own.

42. For this reason, I am skeptical of the emphasis on non-violence in protest as a unidirectional demand on the protestor, often uplifted by dance scholars who tarry in tactics of comportment, civil disobedience, and techniques of the body. See: Foster, "Choreographies of Protest."

43. Kedhar, "'Hands Up! Don't Shoot!': Gesture, Choreography, and Protest in Ferguson."

44. Beaujon, "Race and Policing in France: An Imperial Legacy."

45. Adeyemi, "Beyond 90°: The Angularities of Black/Queer/Women/Lean," 12. See generally: Wynter, "Unsettling the Coloniality of Being/Power/Truth/Freedom."

46. King, "Humans Involved," 175.

47. King, "Humans Involved," 175.

48. "Humanist secular thought that emerged from the fifteenth-century conquest and enslavement of Native and Black peoples produced the geometry of the line," writes Tiffany King, extending the stakes. King, "Humans Involved," 175.

49. Fanon, *The Wretched of the Earth*, 312.

50. Dean, *The Frail Social Body*, 2.

51. Davies, "Mobility: AXIS Dancers Push the Boundaries of Access," 46.

52. UN General Assembly, Resolution 217A (III), Universal Declaration of Human Rights, A/RES/217(III).

53. Lynn Hunt charts an excellent history between these two documents in a robust history of human rights. Hunt, *Inventing Human Rights*. Dignity would not enter into French constitutional practice until 1994. Girard and Hennette-Vauchez, *La Dignité de La Personne Humaine*; Robcis, "The Biopolitics of Dignity."

54. "The Rights of Man, after all, had been defined as 'inalienable' because they were supposed to be independent of all governments; but it turned out that the moment human beings lacked their own government and had to fall back upon their minimum rights, no authority was left to protect them and no institution was willing to guarantee them." Arendt, *The Origins of Totalitarianism*, 291–92.

55. In this chapter, I feature 1948 as the founding year of human rights in international law. I value, however, the counternarratives to this hegemony that present a necessary alternative genealogy. For example, see: Madhok, *Vernacular Rights Cultures*.

56. Habermas, "The Concept of Human Dignity and the Realistic Utopia of Human Rights."

57. Fabre-Magnan in Robcis, "The Biopolitics of Dignity," 323.

58. Fabre-Magnan in Robcis, "The Biopolitics of Dignity," 323.

59. Puar, *Terrorist Assemblages*, 8.

60. Waldron, *Dignity, Rank, and Rights*, 215–16. See also: Bloch, *Natural Law and Human Dignity*, 188.

61. Whitman, "The Two Western Cultures of Privacy: Dignity versus Liberty"; Robcis, "The Biopolitics of Dignity." I also return to Mark Franko's reminder that: "Needless to say, this study of the genealogy of the vertical station of the body was and remains highly pertinent to any social history of ballet." Franko, *Dance as Text,* footnote 9.

62. Consider, for example, how Mark Franko summaries that "the symbolic content of power (verticality, aura, sublime balance) depended upon fleshly signs." Franko, *Dance as Text*, xix.

63. Gottschild contrasts this description of European dance with Africanist traditions: "Africanist dance idioms show a democratic equality of body parts. The spine is just one of many possible movement centers, and it rarely remains static. The Africanist dancing body is polycentric. One part of the body is played against another, and movements may simultaneously originate from more than one focal point: the head and pelvis, for example. It's also polyrhythmic (different body parts moving to two or more rhythms simultaneously) and [demonstrating] privileges flexible, bent-leg postures that reaffirm contact with the earth, sometimes called a 'get down pose.' The component and auxiliary parts of the torso, of course—shoulder, chest, rib cage, waist, pelvis—can be independently moved or articulated in different directions." Gottschild, *Digging the Africanist Presence in American Performance*, in "The Black Dancing Body as a Measure of Culture," 26–27.

64. Gottschild, "The Black Dancing Body as a Measure of Culture," 27.

65. Needham, "Louis XIV and the Académie Royale de Danse, 1661: A Commentary and Translation."

66. Dean, *The Frail Social Body*, 36. Footnote 1. Sumi Madhok repeats a similar refrain: "The concrete human of human rights is a binary and cisgendered, heterosexual, unencumbered, possessive, propertied, able bodied, white male abstracted from all relations and commitments, and predominantly located in the Global North." Madhok, *Vernacular Rights Cultures*, 10.

67. Kealiinohomoku, Joann. "An Anthropologist Looks at Ballet as a Form of Ethnic Dance."

68. Schiller in Beitz, "Human Dignity in the Theory of Human Rights: Nothing But a Phrase?," 272. See also: Schiller, "On Grace and Dignity."

69. Schiller, "On Grace and Dignity," 376.

70. Schiller, "On Grace and Dignity," 377. Emphasis added.

71. Schiller, "On Grace and Dignity," 376. Emphasis added.

72. For example, Orit Kamir reflects that: "In the context of our modern, liberal, humanistic worldview, human dignity entails, above all, personal autonomy, self-determination, and self-governance. This human essence establishes every individual's rights to life, nourishment, clothing, housing, basic security against suffering and cruelty, liberty, control over one's body, basic pursuit of happiness, choice of sexual and intimate fulfillment, basic freedom of thought, speech, religion, and movement." Kamir, "Honor and Dignity in the Film Unforgiven," 204.

73. Judy, "Introduction: For Dignity; Tunisia and the Poetry of Emergent Democratic Humanism."

74. Mirandola begins his oration with the following: "I once read that Abdullah the Muslim, when asked what was most worthy of awe and wonder in this theater of the world, answered, 'There is nothing to see more wonderful than man!'" Cited in Judy, "Introduction: For Dignity; Tunisia and the Poetry of Emergent Democratic Humanism," 14.

75. Judy, "Introduction: For Dignity; Tunisia and the Poetry of Emergent Democratic Humanism," 14.

76. Robcis, "The Biopolitics of Dignity."

77. Anker, *Fictions of Dignity,* 4. Emphasis own.

78. Anker, *Fictions of Dignity*, 20.

79. Emmanuelle Saada also notes a peculiar presence of "dignity" in the French colonial archive, one which reveals a self-conscious, not self-confident, anxiety for the colonizer. Saada, "The Empire of Law.'"

80. This potential redaction precedes my visit. As scholars note: "While the historian Einaudi was permitted to make a formal deposition during Papon's trial, the post-war events were completely ignored by the presiding judges in the trial, and the documents of 1961 were kept classified in the national archives. These archives are subject to the most restrictive legislation in Europe. A law in 1979 stipulated that the documents be held classified for up to 30 years, and sometimes 60 or even 100 years." Thull and Arens, "Who Benefits from the Official Silence?"

81. Byrd, *The Transit of Empire.* See also: Vimalassery, Pegues, and Goldsten, "Introduction: On Colonial Unknowing."

82. APP-HA110. Maurice PAPON. "Ordre du Jour." From Le Préfet de Police. Paris, 1 novembre 1961.

83. The few instances of humanity came from reference to *L'Humanité,* though many times the claims of articles in this communist-affiliated newspaper that highlighted potential abuses were marked as "absolument faux/absolutely false."

84. Jean-Luc Einaudi, quoted in Cohen, "Trial of Vichy Officer Lifts Veil on Killing of Algerians."

85. APP-HA110. Folder 4562: Manifestations du 17 octobre 1961. Letter from Group de l'Union des Etudiants Communistes de Sc Po and Groupe des Etudiants du Parti Socialiste Unifié de Sc Po. October 18, 1961.

86. APP-H1B21, Instructions of Zouaoui, October 14, 1961, for the organization of the demonstration. Repeated in House and MacMaster, *Paris 1961*, 114.

87. Kamir, "Honor and Dignity in the Film Unforgiven," 200.

88. Kamir, "Honor and Dignity in the Film Unforgiven," 193.

89. Mignolo, "Chapter 4: Sylvia Wynter: What Does It Mean to Be Human?" *in Sylvia Wynter: On Being Human as Practice*, 106–123.

90. APP-H1B34. Le dossier du 17 octobre, "MALLEK n'est plus un 'disparu': il a été tortué et assassiné." Liberation, Paris, 17 octobre 1961. Stamped November 1, 1961.

91. Siegel, *At the Vanishing Point.*

92. Einudi, *Octobre 1961.* trans. Anna Jayne Kimmel.

93. Hartman, *Scenes of Subjection*, 25.

94. Césaire, "L'homme de culture et ses responsabilités," 122. trans. Anna Jayne Kimmel.

95. UN General Assembly, Resolution 217A (III), Universal Declaration of Human Rights, A/RES/217(III) (December 10, 1948).

96. Rancière, "The Cause of the Other," 28. Emphasis added.

97. This critique extends across black and indigenous scholarship. Jackson, *Becoming Human*; Coulthard, *Red Skin White Masks.*

98. There is a long and robust tradition to this line of critique; for introduction into the debate, I recommend Manu Vimalassery et. al "On Colonial Unknowing" (2016) and sources from its footnote 2: Barker, "The Specters of Recognition"; Barker, *Native Acts*; Klopotek, *Recognition Odyssey*; Simpson, *Mohawk Interruptus*; Coulthard, *Red Skin,*

White Masks. See also: Ouden and O'Brien, eds., *Recognition, Sovereignty Struggles, and Indigenous Rights in the United States*.

99. Stora, "Cicatriser l'Algérie," 240. For more on the differentiated memory of Paris 1961, see: Rice, "Rehearsing October 17, 1961: The Role of Fiction in Remembering the Battle of Paris."

100. "H1B Series," in Archives de La Préfecture de Police (APP), (subject to dérogation), vol. 34–36 (Paris, n.d.).

101. No language of dignity was included in this report. Stora, *Les Questions Mémorielles Portant Sur La Colonisation et la Guerre d'Algérie*.

102. Barkat, *Le Corps D'exception*, 69.

103. Yasmina Adi features this iconography in her documentary film of the event, *Ici On Noie Les Algériens – 17 Octobre 1961* (2011).

104. Tristan, *Le Silence du Fleuve*.

105. Swan Lake was selected for this protest as it was the repertoire most recently learned, as the company had performed the work in July. Significantly, it also does not feature extensive large jumps—a safety requirement when dancing on an unsprung floor such as the impromptu stage assembled for the protest. And yet, it's all too easy to conjure images of similar scenes of protests that center a dancing swan: in October 2020, ballet dancers staged Swan Lake outside of the Houses of Parliament in London to demand increased pay for art workers during the COVID pandemic; in March 2020, Imira Bagrautinova of the Mariinsky Theatre performed Swan Lake on ice in an environmental protest against Russia's proposed development project in the Gulf of Finland; in 2018, Argentinian dancers took to the streets against government austerity measures; and in 2014, ballet dancers in Odessa performed Swan Lake in front of military tanks to protest Putin's military presence in Ukraine. Baulac, "Reflection on Paris Opera Ballet and Proposed Pension Reform Interview by Anna Kimmel."

106. Mainwaring, "In Paris, Even the Ballet Dancers Are on Strike."

107. Baulac, "Reflection on Paris Opera Ballet and Proposed Pension Reform Interview by Anna Kimmel."

108. "Isambert: Recueil Général Des Anciennes Lois Françaises, Depuis l'an 420 Jusqu'à La Révolution de 1789: Contenant La Notice Des Principaux Monumens Des Mérovingiens, Des Carlovingiens et Des Capétiens, et Le Texte Des Ordonnances, Édits, Déclarations, Lettres Patentes, Règlemens."

109. Baulac, "Reflection on Paris Opera Ballet and Proposed Pension Reform Interview by Anna Kimmel."

110. Baulac, "Reflection on Paris Opera Ballet and Proposed Pension Reform Interview by Anna Kimmel."

111. Kimmel, "'Naked Athena.'"

112. I understand that authors do not always, arguably do not often, have control over the title of their work and thus do not critique Mainwaring for this choice. Indeed, her article features nuanced French history translated for an American readership and exemplifies quality public-facing writing.

Chapter 5

1. An earlier version of this chapter was originally published in *Dance Research Journal*, Vol. 55, No. 2, 2023.

2. The Hirak movement is an effervescent phenomenon whose history and legacy exceed the scope of this chapter. While I will offer brief context throughout, I encourage

the curious reader to explore further readings in English, French, and Arabic compiled by Muriam Haleh Davis and Thomas Serres.

3. Smail, "Melissa Ziad, la ballerine de l'espoir."

4. G., Rania. "'On Ne Peut Gagner Sa Liberté Qu'en Montrant à l'ennemi Que l'on Est Prêt à Tout Pour l'obtenir.' DZ1 MARS 2019 DZ Work 2019 / ♥📷 Photography & Retouching: @ranougraphy Dancer: @melziad' Poetic Protest."

5. The reformed constitution modified the right to public assembly by stating: "The organizers of marches are required to declare to the competent services the names of those responsible for organizing the march, the times of its start and end, the route and the slogans to be raised, in accordance with the law" on the pretext that it is "contrary to public order and the laws of the Republic." Such legalized permission implies gatekeepers, and authority remains held by the central few rather than being recuperated by the assembled bodies. It echoes the arguments presented by legal scholar Tabatha Abu El-Haj in her article, "The Neglected Right of Assembly." Indeed, Abu El-Haj critiques the rise of required permits in the United States as she "cautions against collapsing the collective right of assembly into the individual right of free expression." Yet, while Amnesty International lists the United States as green with respect to the right of peaceful assembly, Algeria earns a red mark. This difference, to some extent, signals a larger trend for historically white or self-regarded Western nations to remain referents for ideal democratic behavior even in the face of infringements, and non-white nations are quickly denounced as unstable to sustain democracy, a paternalistic view if ever. "Algeria's Constitution of 2020"; Abu El-Haj.

6. Foster, "Choreographies of Protest"; Diverlus, "Black Lives Matter Toronto: Urgency as Choreographic Necessity"; Kedhar, "'Hands Up! Don't Shoot!': Gesture, Choreography, and Protest in Ferguson."

7. As the Front Line Defenders summarized, "The charges routinely levied against them include 'weakening the morale of the army' (Art.75), 'inciting an unarmed gathering' (Art. 100), 'undermining the integrity of the national territory' (Art.79), also referred to as 'undermining national unity,' 'offending public bodies' (Art. 144; 144bis and 146), and 'offense against the precepts of Islam' (Art. 144bis 2), all stemming from exercising their right to free speech or peaceful assembly and association." These discriminatory policings violate not only national pretense, but Algeria's signatory status to the 1966 International Covenant on Civil and Political Rights, the 1981 African Charter on Human and Peoples' Rights, and the 2004 Arab Charter of Human Rights, all of which recognize the right to freely assemble. "Harassment of Algerian Human Rights Defenders Must End," 2021; "Algeria: Peaceful Protesters Detained Arbitrarily Must Be Released," 2020.

8. Le Bon, *The Crowd: Study of the Popular Mind.*

9. Notably, Randy Martin writes against Le Bon by instead positing the rationality of social movements as mirroring economic rationality. While I agree, I find the legal language and misperception of crowds equally problematic and thus worthy of renewed attention.

10. John Inazu brilliantly charts this trajectory of legal transformation in the US context. Inazu, *Liberty's Refuge.*

11. Kramer, *The People Themselves*, 3.

12. Canetti, 9.

13. Khalil, *Crowds and Politics in North Africa*, 8.

14. Le Bon's psychological orientation to crowd theory has been amplified by scholars such as Sigmund Freud and Herbert Blumer, but more recently has been challenged by scholars from other disciplines. For example, Norris Johnson (1987) critiques a

monolithically violent reading of stampeding crowd, instead locating gestures of care from within the collective; Alexander Berlonghi (1995) has classified crowds by their intent, thereby differentiating crowds from a universal mob mentality and emphasizing safety; Jodi Dean (2016) emphasizes the affective dimension of political parties that crosses the individual and the multitude; and Jennifer Gosetti-Ferencei (2020) threads associations between individuality, anonymity, and conformity during an age of mass media. Andrea Khalil (2014) grounds her critique in the particular politics of the Maghreb, while Christian Borch (2012) charts these various genealogies. Together, these scholars point to the insurgent need for crowd studies, if the field still remains negligent towards more corporeal methods of dance studies.

15. Canetti, 15. When reading Canetti in such a utopic light, I want to also acknowledge the ahistorical criticism sharply leveraged against him by Susan Sontag (1982).

16. Massumi, *Parables for the Virtual*, 26.

17. Butler, *Notes Toward a Performative Theory of Assembly*.

18. An exception is Noémie Solomon's "Conducting Movement: Xavier Le Roy and the Amplification of Le Sacre du Printemps," though Solomon underscores Canetti's attention to the role of the conductor, rather than his implications on assembly. Solomon, "Conducting Movement," 2011.

19. I intentionally conflate movement as an individual gesture and movement as a social phenomenon, forcing a consideration of the similarities between the two that respects the writing of Randy Martin.

20. Royona Mitra makes a necessary intervention to discourse on contact improvisation by acknowledging its colonial residues. Mitra, "Unmaking Contact."

21. Djelloul and Mezoued, "The Spatial Underpinnings of the Revolutionary Protests in Algiers."

22. Djebar, 31.

23. The link between kinesthetic and affective knowledge has previously been established, poignantly argued by Carrie Noland against a constructivist metaphor of the body. "I must be touched to feel," she writes, an assertation that only reaffirms the need to consider the values uniquely bound up in the right to assembly. Noland, *Agency and Embodiment*, 23.

24. Merleau-Ponty, *The Visible and the Invisible: Followed by Working Notes*, 136.

25. Metzl, *The Protest Psychosis*.

26. Lepecki, *Of the Presence of the Body*, 2.

27. Norris, *Defund Fear: Safety without Policing, Prisons, and Punishment*.

28. Le Bon, *Crowds, Psychology, and Politics, 1871–1899*.

29. Martin, *Critical Moves*, 20.

30. Burt, "Avoiding Capture."

31. For a wider history, see: Gotman, *Choreomania: Dance and Disorder*.

32. *Protecting American Monuments, Memorials, and Statues and Combating Recent Criminal Violence*, 2020. *Billing Code 3295-F0-P*.

33. *Americans for Prosperity Foundation v. Bonta*, 594 US 595 (2021).

34. The landmark decision of *NAACP v. Claiborne Hardware Co.* (1982) decided that, while states can regulate economic activities, they cannot overregulate or prohibit peaceful boycotts. Inazu, *Liberty's Refuge*, 191 n. 15.

35. Inazu, *Liberty's Refuge*, 5.

36. White, "Right of Assembly." Web.

37. Butler, *Notes Toward a Performative Theory of Assembly.*

38. Speech act theory emerged in its contemporary form in the 1950s as a result of a critique of the positivist philosophy of language. At the same time, the right to association began to emerge in US legal discourse in the midcentury as conservative government fears of Communist affiliations mushroomed. For example, J. L. Austin's influential text, *How To Do Things With Words*, was published in 1955 as the rhetoric of association grew in the United States and legal addresses of assembly waned. John Inazu frames this shift in response to the National Security Era and the Equality Era. While separate intellectual trajectories, both intersect on a realization of the power of words to actualize new futures.

39. Algerian legal scholar Chafika Kahina Bouagache attributes Algeria's formulation of association as rooted in its deep-seated tradition of political organizations, including groups such as the North African Star (ENA) and the Algerian People's Party (PPA) that precipitated its decolonial war of liberation from France. These organizations would be succeeded by: the Algerian National Movement (MNA), the National Liberation Front (FLN), and later movements such as the Socialist Forces Front (FFS) and the Islamic Salvation Front (FIS). Bouagache, "The Algerian Law on Associations Within Its Historical Context." Writing of the Algerian War for Independence, Assia Djebar adds (in the fictionalized voice of a police officer): "All these pointless ceremonies; these days, they should forbid any large gatherings at all, even for their dead." Djebar, *Children of the New World*, 29.

40. Reflecting on the values of this space of appearance, Hannah Arendt writes: "It does not survive the actuality of the movement which brought it into being, but disappears not only with the dispersal of men—as in the case of great catastrophes when the body politic of a people is destroyed—but with the disappearance or arrest of the activities themselves. Wherever people gather together, it is potentially there, but only potentially, not necessarily and not forever." Arendt, *The Human Condition*, 199. Judith Butler later reframes Arendt's theory as gendered conditions of appearance: "The Arendtian presupposition form *The Human Condition* presumes that the body does not enter in to the speech act, and that the speech act is understood as a mode of thinking and judging. The public sphere in which the speech act qualifies as a paradigmatic political action is one that has already, in her view, been separated from the private sphere, the domain of women, slaves, children, and those too old or inform to work." Butler, *Notes Toward a Performative Theory of Assembly*, 45.

41. For a foundational study, see the anthology by Martin Loughlin and Neil Walker that presents multiple discourse strands within this subfield. More specifically, one epistemic branch of constitutional paradoxes—including scholars Paolo Carrozza and Emilios Christodoulidis and indicative of my own position—presents a "radical potential thesis, whereby constituent power is neither colonized by nor in symbiosis with the legal, but remains a latent revolutionary possibility which lies behind the shadows the legally constituted authority of the polity (e.g. Negri)." Loughlin and Walker, *The Paradox of Constitutionalism*, 6.

42. For more on this history, see the works of Muriam Haleh Davis and Thomas Serres, including: Davis and Serres, "Political Contestation in Algeria," 99–112.

43. "By showing how bodies make articulate choices based upon their intelligent reading of other bodies, I will endeavor to frame a new perspective on individual agency and collective action, one that casts the body in a central role as enabling human beings to

work together to create social betterment . . . showing how dance studies is itself a form of social theory." Foster, "Choreographies of Protest," 396; "When politics is treated merely as an idea or ideology, it occurs in stillness, awaiting something that will bring people to action or mobilize them. But this presumed gap between a thinking mind and an acting body makes it impossible to understand how people move from a passive to active state. The presumption of bodies already in motion, what dance takes as its normative condition, could bridge the various splits between mind and body, subject and object, and process and structure." Martin, *Critical Moves,* 3.

44. Butler, *Notes Toward a Performative Theory of Assembly*, 156; Butler, *Excitable Speech*. Inazu too reminds us of the "expressive function" of the act of gathering implicit to crowds, a function that operates in excess to verbal signification. Inazu, *Liberty's Refuge*, 2.

45. Here we can follow an intellectual history out from the interpellation theorized by Louis Althusser that includes J. L. Austin (1975), Shoshana Felman (1980), Jacques Derrida (1988), Judith Butler (1997), and Eve Sedgewick (2003). From marriage to consent, speech acts have always been entangled in the legal. Tattooing becomes a surprising encounter of the body and free speech protection, for example as ruled in *Buehrle v. City of Key West* 813 F.3d 973 (11th Cir. 2015).

46. See also Susan Foster's critique of Gene Sharp and his distinction between symbolic action and physical intervention. Foster, "Choreographies of Protest." For a historical view on the successful use of the right to peaceably assemble for meaningful change, see: Lumsden's *Rampant Women,* which accentuates the intersection between the women's suffrage movement in the United States and the constitutional right to peaceably assemble.

47. A predecessor to this law of association appeared in 1987 in the Bendjedid era. (*Code Penal* 2005)

48. This includes the most recent constitution in 2020 in which government permits are required. A more complete history has been offered by Chafika Kahina Bouagache, but stops in 2007, well before the Hirak protests of 2019–2020 that influenced my research. Bouagache, "The Algerian Law on Associations Within Its Historical Context."

49. For example, "Algerians' non-violent protest is also a challenge to a state-controlled memory and identity based on violent resistance." Mitiche, "How Algeria's Non-Violent Protests Challenge Regime Narrative of 'Armed Resistance.'"

50. Allen, "Critics Say Anti-Protest Bill in Florida Threatens Freedom of Speech."

51. Derrida, "Force of Law: The 'Mystical Foundation of Authority,'" 35.

52. Cover, "Violence and the Word."

53. Cover, "Nomos and Narrative."

54. Benjamin, "Critique of Violence," 41.

55. In response to Walter Benjamin's essay, Derrida reflects this critique of violence back toward the State: "How are we to distinguish between the force of law of a legitimate power and the supposedly originary violence that must have established this authority and that could not itself have been authorized by any anterior legitimacy, so that, in this initial moment, it is neither legal nor illegal—or, others would quickly say, neither just nor unjust?" Derrida, "Force of Law: The 'Mystical Foundation of Authority,'" 6. In a discussion of legality and illegality, George Lukács cautions that a romanization of the illegal only reinforces the aura of legal authority. Implicit, then, is the importance of gesture and action for the life of law, beyond its own text. His writing emerges from the proletarian class struggle, but it is important to continue to articulate not only the boundary between

legal and illegal, but how and why that boundary arrives in the public consciousness. Lukács, "Legality and Illegality."

56. Or at least the recognition of its limitations and violences. Abu El-Haj, Amnesty International Public Statement.

57. The pandemic response of 2020 only reinforced dichotomizing language via labels of essential and nonessential, a value judgement that universalized worth in problematic, and not always obvious, ways. French dancers, in red bonnets and sleek black silhouettes, performed this dichotomy in a screen dance, *Pas Essential*. Accessed: https://www.youtube.com/watch?v=gYmnXijsvik.

58. *Code Penal*. 2005. 4th ed. Depot Legal 3388–2004. Republique Algerienne Democratique et Populaire: Ministere de la Justice: Les Editions de l'O.N.T.E.

59. For example, Peter Gelderloo's *How Nonviolence Protects the State* presents the controversial argument that pacifism merely perpetuates the quotidian violence of the status quo.

60. Abu El-Haj, "Defining Peaceably," 962.

61. Inazu, *Liberty's Refuge*, 2.

62. Here we might also think with petition clause. McKinely, "Lobbying and the Petition Clause."

63. Rue Didouche Mourad spills into Place Maurice Audin, memorializing two of Algeria's revolutionary heroes.

64. For example, the Algerian National Ballet remains more rooted in traditional performance culture, with ballet here referencing large-scale dance broadly construed, rather than specifically the imported, classically-European form. Abroad, London Algerian Ballet's "A Journey to Algeria" also relies upon traditional dance forms. Felicia McCarren's publication, *One Dead at the Paris Opera Ballet: La Source 1866–2014*, explores Algerian representation in the colonial ballet *La Source*, but not Algerian ballet itself. Finally, Hervé Koubi's company—perhaps the most internationally known Algerian choreographer—features an all-male cast. Each of these examples speaks to the surprising performance of Ziad.

65. G. Rania, 2019.

66. Austin, *How To Do Things with Words*.

67. Martin, *Critical Moves*, 4. Emphasis added.

68. Abu El-Haj, "The Neglected Right of Assembly," 543.

69. Benjamin discusses the "spectral" presence of police who "intervene in countless cases where no clear legal" or illegal "situation exists," such that the inciting behavior or prenotion toward violence may well stem from the State. Supposed security can obscure harassment, surveillance, and violence: a prolepsis of their future enforcement. Benjamin, "Critique of Violence," 47–48.

70. As J. L. Austin defined: "I explained the performance of an act in this new and second sense as the performance of an 'illocutionary' act, i.e. performance of an act *in* saying something as opposed to performance of an act *of* saying something; and I shall refer to the doctrine of the different types of function of language here in question as the doctrine of 'illocutionary forces.'" Austin, *How To Do Things with Words*, 99.

71. Derrida, "Force of Law," 36.

72. As choreographer Bill. T Jones reflected, it "encouraged an unselfconscious, direct physical intimacy in which all differences—weight, size, psychological temperament, even gender and race—were negated in favor of cohesion-tissue to tissue, bone to bone, muscle

to muscle." Jones and Gillespie, *Last Night on Earth*, 15. See also: Foster, "Choreographies of Protest"; Goldman, *I Want to Be Ready*; Banes, *Democracy's Body*.

73. Loughlin and Walker, *The Paradox of Constitutionalism*, 2.

74. For example, Selma Kasmi reflected: "The Hirak was a blessing for the country, for its people and its history. It was a wonderful moment where a people that have been torn apart by successive tragedies—notably the civil war of the 1990s—were reunited. The feelings of pride, nationalism, of civic involvement and collective joy that we witnessed over the year could have constituted the cement for the construction of a new Algeria that seemed to want to forgive and heal from its wounds. But since the former army chief of staff, Ahmed Gaid Salah, forbade the carrying of the Amazigh [also known as Berber] flag last June and the following spate of arrests and intimidation, Algerians found themselves faced with blatant attempts to divide the population." Davis and Kasmi, "Voices from the Middle East."

75. Khalil, "Crowds and Politics in North Africa," 9.

76. Lepecki, *Of the Presence of the Body*.

77. Arabella Stranger's reading of Ruth Gilmore offers a necessary example of what such politics look like in scholarly form. Stranger, *Dancing on Violent Ground*.

78. A lacuna of assembly not yet discussed includes the realm of the virtual, as noted by scholars such as John Inazu. This extends to social media protests, especially those orchestrated throughout the Arab Spring's internet revolution and exemplified by Ziad's post that opened this chapter, accentuating the role that media has played more broadly saturates concerns of justice.

79. Martin, *Critical Moves*, 110. See also: DeFrantz, "Composite Bodies of Dance."

80. Martin, *Critical Moves*, 109.

81. National and international solidarities contributed to this multiplicity. In France, home of over 845,000 residents of Algerian diaspora (estimated to be the largest minority population in France) (*Ined* 2020), the Hirak continued until pandemic restrictions led to a separate set of questions concerning the right to assembly. In forced absence, the digital became its own repository, where borders and materialization of the composite body blurred.

82. Philosopher and historian Ibn Khaldun (1332–1406) popularized this term, *asabiyya*, in his most well-known text on the history of empires, *Al-Muqaddimah*.

83. I'm ever indebted to the generative writings of Fred Moten, who challenges new forms of being in the world and being in relation to both the past and one another.

84. "The 18 commandments of the pacifist and civilized demonstrator" by Lazhari Labter.

"I shall walk peacefully and quietly.

I shall behave as a dignified and civilized person will I behave,

I shall carry water and vinegar [to clean the face in case of tear gas (Editor's note).]

I shall answer no provocation.

I shall isolate and hand over to the police the *baltaguias* [the name given to provocateurs paid by the forces in power to create violence.]

Not a stone will I throw.

Not a window will I break.

Not a word out of place shall I speak.

I shall not touch people or property.

To the policeman and the gendarme, I shall smile.

To the woman, I will offer a rose.

With the thirsty, I will share my water.

Old people, women, and children, I will watch over.

I shall march with determination.

I shall go through wind and storms.

I shall be a worthy heir to the Novembrists [the Algerian independence activists who launched the anti-colonial insurrection on November 1, 1954.]

After the march, I will clean the streets and squares.

To the world watching me, I shall provide a lesson and a great example.

Because I know that Liberty at the end of the road will wait for me and in her open arms she will welcome me!" Labter, "Les '18 commandements' du manifestant en Algérie."

85. Djebar, *Children of the New World*, 16.

86. Norris Johnson articulates another instance of a caring crowd. Johnson, "Panic at 'The Who Concert Stampede.'"

87. Achille Mbembe defines entanglement as the interwoven "presents, pasts, and futures that retain their depths of other presents, pasts, and futures, each age bearing, altering, and maintaining the previous ones." Mbembe, *On the Postcolony*, 16.

88. Expressive association denotes the right to associate for expressive purposes, for example political purposes, as established in *NAACP v. Alabama* (1958).

89. Although the 1793 constitution was enacted by the National Convention and endorsed by a public referendum, it was suspended the same year and never formally implemented.

90. Derrida, "Force of Law," 7.

91. Writing in the aftermath of the German Revolution and the end of World War I, Benjamin begins from the premised divorce of law and justice as Kant had previously separated law from virtue (see Kant's *Doctrine of Law* and *Doctrine of Virtue*). Benjamin promotes the mythic origins of law; but as it toggles dual perspectives, its ambiguous position has been read by Butler (2012), Derrida (1992), and Arendt (1970) for its "messianic-marxism" that leaves it problematically open to fascist sympathies.

92. Murphy, "Protest or Riot?: Interpreting Collective Action in Contemporary France."

93. I refer to being-with in the Heideggerian tradition of the German *dasein,* often translated as *being there* or *presence,* a particular type of *being in the world.*

94. The reading of Frantz Fanon as condoning revolutionary violence comes as much from his writings as from Jean-Paul Sartre's preface to *The Wretched of the Earth*, which encourages the reader to jump to such a conclusion.

95. To my knowledge, Ziad experienced no legal ramifications from her protest.

Chapter 6

1. Schipper, "Artworks," in *William Forsythe Choreographic Objects. Human Writes.* Web. A full cast list is not publicly available, an archival error or harbinger of the dehumanizing impasse of human rights themselves.

2. *Human Writes* premiered in Zurich (2005) and toured to: Dresden (2006), Frankfurt (2007), Brussels (2007), Istanbul (2008), Berlin (2010), Geneva (2012), and Stockholm (2012). It has not been performed since, but was considered for São Paulo, Brazil in 2018.

3. Franko et al., "Dialogues: Genesis and Concept of Human Writes," 6.

4. Minow, "Interpretating Rights," 1879.

5. Cover, "Violence and the Word," 1601.

6. Doolittle and Flynn, "Human Rights," 277.

7. Kim, "Unbecoming Human."

8. Brandstetter, "Transcription – Materiality – Signature. Dancing and Writing Between Resistance and Excess," in *Emerging Bodies,* ed. Klein and Noeth.

9. Drawings from *Human Writes* are housed in the collections of Staatliche Kunstsammlungen Dresden (SKD) British Museum, London; Akademie der Künste, Berlin; Folkwang Museum, Essen; Kunsthaus, Zurich.

10. Glissant, *Poetics of Relation*, 162.

11. Jackson, *Becoming Human*, 19.

12. Brandstetter, "Transcription – Materiality – Signature. Dancing and Writing Between Resistance and Excess," 121.

13. Cover, "Violence and the Word," 1601.

14. Tenta, "A Conversation on Human Writes Interview by Anna Kimmel."

15. Lowe, *The Intimacies of Four Continents*, 19.

16. King, *The Black Shoals*, 225, note 16.

17. Lepecki, *Exhausting Dance,* 26. For more on the distinction between flesh and bone in performance studies temporalities, see: Schneider, *Performing Remains.*

18. Bradley and Marassa, "Awakening to the World: Relation, Totality, and Writing from Below," 113.

19. Sabsay articulates a related Foucauldian argument when she argues that we cannot locate a "neat distinction between body and discourse" in formations of biopolitical power. Sabsay, "Permeable Bodies: Vulnerability, Affective Powers, Hegemony," in *Vulnerability in Resistance*, ed. Butler et al, 283.

20. An exception to this paralysis is Alessandra Nicifero's chapter, "Questioning the Truth: *Rachid Ouramdane's Investigation of Torture in* Des Témoins Ordinaires/Ordinary Witnesses." The larger volume, too, reflects a more nascent ambition of dance studies. In parallel to my argument on the Western aesthetic bias of dignity, Nicifero writes: "Alastair Macaulay, chief dance critic of the *New York Times*, in a positive review of *Ordinary Witnesses*, still could not resist using the names of recognizable steps to label what he had difficulty otherwise describing. He wrote in parenthesis: (You want to give these turns a ballet label: a manège of chaînés renversés, perhaps.)"

21. Naomi Jackson and Toni Shapiro-Phim's *Dance, Human Rights, and Social Justice* offers a rich selection of international dance works and dancers that have engaged with the topic of human rights violations, and Eric Mullis's scholarship presents dance as a means of social remembrance of violence. But as a whole, dance scholarship on human rights neglects to turn from political representation toward legal implication. Jackson and Phim, eds., *Dance, Human Rights, and Social Justice: Dignity in Motion*; Mullis, "Dancing for Human Rights." See also: Mulcahy and Seear, "A 'Tick and Flick' Exercise."

22. Thomas, "A Conversation on Human Writes Interview by Anna Kimmel"; Hall, *Representation.*

23. Joseph Slaughter attaches this paradox to literary dominance when he writes that "the discursive victory of human rights means that ours is at once the Age of Human Rights and the Age of Human Rights Abuse." Slaughter, *Human Rights, Inc.*, 2.

24. Thomas, "A Conversation on Human Writes Interview by Anna Kimmel."

25. Thomas, "A Conversation on Human Writes Interview by Anna Kimmel."

26. Art. 27 states that "Everyone has the right freely to participate in the cultural life of the community, to enjoy the arts and to share in scientific advancement and its benefits."

27. Thomas, Keenan, and Franko. "Dialogues: Genesis and Concept of Human Writes."

28. Kafka, *In the Penal Colony.*

29. Thomas and Forsythe, "Program Notes for the Performance Installation Human Writes."

30. Thomas, "A Conversation on Human Writes Interview by Anna Kimmel."

31. Here I learn from and think with: Susan Buck-Morss, Dipesh Chakrabarty, Paul Gilroy, Saidiya Hartman, Lisa Lowe, and Cedric Robinson, amongst others in this tradition.

32. "The anticolonial movement had initiated a radical critique of the heart of European self-consciousness by demonstrating just how deeply its celebrated concept of Man depended upon the systematic degradation of non-European men and women. [. . .] The systematic objectification and violence of colonialism gave the lie to Europe's humanism." Wynter and Scott, "The Re-Enchantment of Humanism," 120.

33. The back jacket summarizes Moyn's argument: "The age of human rights has been kindest to the rich." Moyn, *Not Enough.* See also: Esmeir, *Juridical Humanity*; Madhok, *Vernacular Rights Cultures*; Gilroy, "Darker than Blue."

34. Forsythe, "Dance Geometry."

35. Wynter and Scott, "The Re-Enchantment of Humanism," 153–58.

36. Han, *Mu, 49 Marks of Abolition*, 65.

37. Han, *Mu, 49 Marks of Abolition*, 66.

38. Saidiya Hartman draws attention to the "conflation of coercion and consent" which defined a slave society and, as I argue, continues to enable anti-black politics on a global scale in the era of human rights. Hartman, *Scenes of Subjection*, 10.

39. Han, *Mu, 49 Marks of Abolition*, 66.

40. Musser, *Sensational Flesh*, 45–48.

41. Jackson, *Becoming Human*, 204.

42. Mbembe, *Necropolitics*, cited in Jackson, *Becoming Human*, 204.

43. Thomas, "Program Notes for the Performance Installation Human Writes."

44. For more theorization of the table within the context of human rights, see: "On tables, doors and listening spaces: Parliamentary human rights scrutiny processes and engagement of others." Mulcahy and Seear, "A 'Tick and Flick' Exercise."

45. Minow, "Rights Interpretation," 1867.

46. Jackson, *Becoming Human*, 2; Césaire, *Discourse on Colonialism*; Fanon, *The Wretched of the Earth*, 313.

47. Jackson, *Becoming Human*, 5.

48. UNESCO General Conference, Universal Declaration on Bioethics and Human Rights, 33rd sess., October 19, 2005.

49. The Belmont Report (1979) has been heralded as the first citation of vulnerability in normative bioethical practice. For more on this trajectory, see: Rheeder, "Respect for Vulnerability Is a Human Right."

50. While one might point to 2001 as the first instance of the vulnerability criterion, it cohered by 2007 as a more codified reference. For reference, Art. 14 of the ECHR states: "The enjoyment of the rights and freedoms set forth in this Convention shall be secured without discrimination on any ground such as sex, race, colour, language, religion, political

or other opinion, national or social origin, association with a national minority, property, birth or other status." See: Kim, "Les Vulnérables."

51. "Vulnerability: Degree of people, resources, property, environments are susceptible to be harmed, degraded, destroyed or exposed to hostile factors." *Black's Law Dictionary,* 2nd edition.

52. For foundational texts from vulnerability literature and the legal subject, see: Fineman, "Vulnerability and Social Justice"; Hoffmaster, "What Does Vulnerability Mean?"; Fineman, "The Vulnerable Subject and the Responsive State"; Fineman and Grear, *Vulnerability.*

53. Puar, *The Right to Maim,* 138.

54. In March 2025, the Trump-led United States was added to the human rights watchlist, CIVICUS Monitor.

55. Puar, *The Right to Maim.*

56. King, "Humans Involved," 175.

57. Rey Chow questions: "How would we write this space in such a way as to refuse the facile turn of sanctifying the defiled image with pieties and thus enriching ourselves precisely with what can be called the surplus value of the oppressed, a surplus value that results from exchanging the defiled image for something more noble?" Chow, *Writing Diaspora,* 30. I turn also to Judith Butler as they consider the role of vulnerability in the human, and wonders with their reader, "Who counts as human? Whose lives count as lives? And, finally, what makes for a grievable life? . . . Each of us is constituted politically in part by virtue of the social vulnerability of our bodies—as a site of desire and physical vulnerability, as a site of a publicity at once assertive and exposed." Butler, *Precarious Life,* 20.

58. Brandstetter, "Transcription – Materiality – Signature. Dancing and Writing Between Resistance and Excess," 127.

59. For a mapping of types of dignity as they relate to vulnerabilities, see: Bird, "Four Concepts of Dignity."

60. Forsythe, "Dance Geometry."

61. Forsythe, "Dance Geometry."

62. Forsythe, "Dance Geometry."

63. Forsythe, "Dance Geometry."

64. Fineman, "Vulnerability and Social Justice," 342.

65. Golomb, "Channels Through the Humane," 302.

66. The reference to bare life positions this work within the genealogy of Giorgio Agamben, including the critique that came after.

67. Golomb, "Channels Through the Humane," 304.

68. Richter, "A Conversation on Human Writes. Interview by Anna Kimmel."

69. Minow, "Interpretating Rights."

70. Butler et al., *Vulnerability in Resistance,* 12.

71. Elaine Scarry, *The Body in Pain,* cited in Cover, "Violence and the Word," 1602–03.

72. Kim writes, for example, in equal exchange: "Focusing on the vulnerability of the group or the status of the applicant, this approach demands that the respondent state afford 'special protection' to vulnerable groups." Kim, "Les Vulnérables," 618. See also 623, 631.

73. Édouard Glissant's poetics of relation— as the realization of difference—further saturates the performance as a critique of a monolithic order of human rights. *Human Writes* provides this "graphic encounter with difference" in the halls of the UN. Bradley and Marassa, 114.

74. Menon, "Desiring Children," 178.

75. Fineman, "Vulnerability and Social Justice;" Fineman, "The Vulnerable Subject and the Responsive State;" Fineman and Grear, *Vulnerability.*

76. Kim, "Les Vulnérables," 618.

77. Butler et al., eds., *Vulnerability in Resistance*, 16. Emphasis added.

78. Minow, "Interpretating Rights," 1884.

79. I participated in the Human Rights Project in 2022 when presented at the Festival de Marseille.

80. Bradley and Marassa, 113.

81. Cheng, "Chapter 3: Skin, Tattoos, and the Lure of the Surface," *Second Skin.*

82. Cheng, *Second Skin*, 28.

83. Wynter and Scott, "The Re-Enchantment of Humanism," 196–97. Emphasis added.

84. Wynter and Scott, "The Re-Enchantment of Humanism," 206. Emphasis added.

85. "This new object of knowledge is that of our genres of being human, of the governing sociogenic principles in whose symbolically coded and prescribed terms we inscript and thereby experience ourselves as an I and we. Lawlikely, yet hitherto non-consciously so. It is the making conscious of these processes for which a planetary—and in your terms, re-enchanted—humanism calls." Wynter and Scott, "The Re-Enchantment of Humanism," 207.

Epilogue

1. Dance Studies Association, "Statement on the Inviolability of Movement as a Right."

2. Dance Studies Association, "Statement on the Inviolability of Movement as a Right."

3. Wynter, "No Humans Involved," 67.

4. Sotomayor, *Noem v. Vasquez Perdomo*, 25A169. 606 US _____ (2025).

5. Johnson, "The Stories in Our Bodies," cited in Bissell and Haviland, *The Sentient Archive*, 149–150.

BIBLIOGRAPHY

Archives

Les archives de la préfecture de police (APP), subject to derogation. Accessed Pré-Saint-Gervais, France, 2022. Includes:
APP-HA Series, vol. 110
APP-HA Series, vol. 111
APP-H1B Series, vol. 21
APP-H1B Series, vol. 34

Legal Documents

Americans for Prosperity Foundation v. Bonta, 594 US 595 (2021)
City of Grants Pass v. Johnson, 603 US 520 (2024)
Garner v. Louisiana, 368 US 157 (1961)
Jacobellis v. Ohio, 378 US 184 (1964)
Johnson v. Florida, 391 US 596 (1968)
Noem v. Vasquez Perdomo, 25A169. 606 US ______ (2025).
Papachristou v. City of Jacksonville, 405 US 156 (1972)
State v. Kimberly Potter, 27-CR-21-7460 (2021)
Thompson v. City of Louisville, 362 US 199 (1960)
United States v. Koon, 833 F. Supp. 769 (C.D. Cal. 1993)
Acts of the General Assembly of the State of Virginia (1865–66)

France. "Recueils de Réglemens, Édits, Déclarations et Arrêts, Concernant Le Commerce, l'administration de La Justice, & La Police Des Colonies Françaises de l'Amerique, & Les Engagés." In *Avec Le Code Noir, et l'addition Audit Code. Nouvelle Édition. Slavery & Anti-Slavery. Part 1, Debates Over Slavery and Abolition.* Libraires Associés, 1765.

France. "Recueil général des anciennes lois françaises, depuis l'an 420 jusqu'à la révolution de 1789: contenant la notice des principaux monumens des Mérovingiens, des Carlovingiens et des Capétiens, et le texte des ordonnances, édits, déclarations, lettres patentes, règlemens." Belin-Leprieur, Paris (1821–1833).

Arrêté Général Sur Les Infractions De L'indigénat, Préfecture d'Alger (1875).

Code Penal. 2005. 4th ed. Depot Legal 3388–2004. République Algérienne Democratique et Populaire: Ministere de la Justice: Les Éditions de l'O.N.T.E.

UN General Assembly, Resolution 217A (III), Universal Declaration of Human Rights, A/RES/217(III) (1948).

UNESCO General Conference. Universal Declaration on Bioethics and Human Rights. 33rd Session, Paris, October 19, 2005.

Bibliography

"About." *Dance Notation Bureau.* Web.

"Algeria's Constitution of 2020." *Constitute Project.* With updates by International IDEA. Web.

"NYCLU Statement on the Repeal and Seal of the Walking While Trans Ban." https://www.nyclu.org/press-release/nyclu-statement-repeal-and-seal-walking-while-trans-ban

"Pascale Marthine Tayou Code Noir Art. 5, 2018." *Artsy.* Web.

"Transcription of 'The Code Noir' (The Black Code)." *National Park Service,* Ulysses S Grant National Historic Site. Web.

"Unmasking the Boston Police Department's Gang Database: How an Arbitrary System Criminalizes Innocent Conduct." *Harvard Law Review* 137, no. 5 (2024): 1.

Abu El-Haj, Tabatha. "Defining Peaceably: Policing the Line Between Constitutionally Protected Protest and Unlawful Speech." *Missouri Law Review* 80, no. 4 (2015): 961–986.

Abu El-Haj, Tabatha. "The Neglected Right of Assembly." *UCLA Law Review* 56, no. 3 (2009): 543–589.

Adeyemi, Kemi. "Beyond 90°: The Angularities of Black/Queer/Women/Lean." *Women & Performance* (Abingdon) 29, no. 1 (2019): 9–24.

Agamben, Giorgio. *State of Exception.* Translated by Kevin Attell. University of Chicago Press, 2004.

Agamben, Giorgio. *The Open: Man and Animal.* Translated by Kevin Attell. Stanford University Press, 2004.

Ahmed, Sara. *The Cultural Politics of Emotion.* Edinburgh University Press, 2004.

Allen, Greg. "Critics Say Anti-Protest Bill in Florida Threatens Freedom of Speech." Law. *NPR News.* April 9, 2021.

Amnesty International. "Algeria: Peaceful Protesters Detained Arbitrarily Must Be Released." News. March 6, 2020.

Amnesty International. "Suppressing Free Speech and Assembly: The Targeting of Hirak Activists in Algeria." February 23, 2021.

Amnesty International Public Statement. MDE 28/3707/2021. February 23, 2021.

Anker, Elizabeth S. *Fictions of Dignity: Embodying Human Rights in World Literature.* Cornell University Press, 2017.

Anker, Elizabeth S., and Bernadette Meyler, eds. *New Directions in Law and Literature.* Oxford University Press, 2017.

Arban, Erica. "Seeing Law in Terms of Music: A Short Essay on Affinities Between Music and Law." Les *Cahiers de Droit* 58, no. 1–2 (2017): 67–86.

Arbeau, Thoinot. *Orchésographie: et traicté en forme de dialogue par lequel toutes personnes peuvent facilement apprendre et pratiquer l'honneste exercice des danses / par Thoinot Arbeau.* D. Guéniot, 1589

Arendt, Hannah. *The Human Condition.* University of Chicago Press, 1958.

Arendt, Hannah. *On Violence.* Harcourt Brace Jovanovich, 1970.

Arendt, Hannah. *The Origins of Totalitarianism.* Harcourt Brace Jovanovich, 1976.

Asad, Talal, Christine W. Gailey, and Stanley Diamond, eds. "Conscripts of Western Civilization?" In *Dialectical Anthropology Volume 1: Civilization in Crisis: Anthropological Perspectives.* University Press of Florida, 1992.

Astier, Régine. "Louis XIV, 'Premier Danseur.'" In *Sun King: The Ascendancy of French Culture During the Reign of Louis XIV,* edited by David Lee Rubin. Folger Shakespeare Library, 1992.

Atwill, Nicole. "Slavery in the French Colonies: Le Code Noir (the Black Code) of 1685." *Library of Congress Blogs*, January 2011.

Austin, J. L. *How to Do Things with Words: The William James Lectures Delivered at Harvard University in 1955*. Harvard University Press. 1975.

Bagaric, Mirko, and James Allan. "The Vacuous Concept of Dignity." *Journal of Human Rights* 5, no. 2 (2006): 257–70.

Banes, Sally. *Democracy's Body: Judson Dance Theater, 1962–1964*. Duke University Press. 1993.

Barak, Aharon. *Purposive Interpretation in Law*. Translated by Sari Bashi. Princeton University Press, 2005.

Barkat, Sidi Mohammed. *Le Corps d'exception: Les Artifices Du Pouvoir Colonial et La Destruction de La Vie*. Amsterdam, 2005.

Barker, Joanne. *Native Acts: Law, Recognition, and Cultural Authenticity*. Duke University Press, 2011.

Barker, Joanne. "The Specters of Recognition." In *Formations of United States Colonialism*, edited by Alyosha Goldstein. Duke University Press, 2014.

Barthes, Roland. *How to Live Together: Novelistic Simulations of Some Everyday Spaces*. Translated by Kate Briggs. Columbia University Press, 2013.

Baulac, Léonore. "Reflection on Paris Opéra Ballet and Proposed Pension Reform." Interview by Anna Kimmel, Zoom, October 2021.

Beaujon, Danielle. *Criminalizing the Casbahs: Policing North Africans in Marseille and Algiers, 1918–1954*. Cornell University Press, 2025.

Beaujon, Danielle. "Race and Policing in France: An Imperial Legacy." *Cornell University Press Authors' Blog*. 2025.

Beier, A. L. *Masterless Men: The Vagrancy Problem in England 1560–1640*. Methuen, 1985.

Beitz, Charles. "Human Dignity in the Theory of Human Rights: Nothing But a Phrase?" *Philosophy & Public Affairs* 41, no. 3 (2013): 259–90.

Bell, John. "Sources of Law." *The Cambridge Law Journal* 77, no. 1 (2018): 40–71.

Bell, John. *French Legal Cultures*. Cambridge University Press, 2001.

Benhaddou, Samira. "La matraque coloniale: le code de l'indigénat en Algérie." *Je veux comprendre* (Paris), no. 7 (2020).

Benítez Rojo, Antonio. *The Repeating Island: The Caribbean and the Postmodern Perspective*. Translated by James E. Maraniss. Duke University Press, 1997.

Benjamin, Walter, Peter D. Fenves, and Julia Ng. *Toward the Critique of Violence: A Critical Edition*. Stanford University Press, 2021.

Bentham, Jeremy, and H. L. A. Hart. *Of Laws in General*. The Collected Works. University of London, Athlone Press, 1970.

Berlonghi, Alexander E. "Understanding and Planning for Different Spectator Crowds." Safety Science 18, no. 4 (1995): 239–247.

Betts, Raymond F. *Assimilation and Association in French Colonial Theory, 1890–1914*. University of Nebraska Press, 2005.

Bibler, Zena. "Disorientation as Critical Practice: Confronting Anti-Black Perceptual Regimes and Activating the Otherwise in Mayfield Brooks's Improvising While Black Pedagogy." *Dance Research Journal* 54, no. 1 (2022): 30–49.

Binder, Guyora, and Robert Weisberg. *Literary Criticisms of Law*. Princeton University Press, 2000.

Bird, Colin. "Four Concepts of Dignity." In *Human Dignity and Political Criticism*. Cambridge University Press, 2021.

Bissell, Bill, and Linda Caruso Haviland, eds. *The Sentient Archive: Bodies, Performance, and Memory*. Wesleyan University Press, 2018.

Black, Henry Campbell. *Black's Law Dictionary,* 2nd edition. West Publishing Company, 1891.

Blackmon, Douglas A. *Slavery by Another Name : The Re-Enslavement of Black Americans from the Civil War to World War II*. Anchor Books, 2010.

Blades, Hetty. "Affective Traces in Virtual Spaces: Annotation and Emerging Dance Scores." *Performance Research* 20, no. 6 (2015): 26–34.

Bloch, Ernst. *Natural Law and Human Dignity*. Translated by Dennis J. Schmidt. MIT Press, 1986.

Borch, Christian. *The Politics of Crowds: An Alternative History of Sociology*. Cambridge University Press, 2012.

Bouagache, Chafika Kahina. "The Algerian Law on Associations Within Its Historical Context." *The International Journal of Not-for-Profit Law* 9, no. 2 (2007).

Bourdieu, Pierre. *Outline of a Theory of Practice*. Translated by Richard Nice. Cambridge University Press, 1977.

Bradley, Rizvana, and Damien-Adia Marassa. "Awakening to the World: Relation, Totality, and Writing from Below." *Discourse* 36, no. 1 (2014): 112–31.

Brandstetter, Gabriele. "Choreography as a Cenotaph: The Memory of Movement." In *ReMembering the Body: [On the Occasion of the Exhibition "STRESS" at the MAK, Vienna]. Imprint Ostfildern-Ruit: Hatje Cantz*. 2000.

Brandstetter, Gabriele. "Transcription – Materiality – Signature. Dancing and Writing Between Resistance and Excess." In *Emerging Bodies: The Performance of Worldmaking in Dance and Choreography [Dance Congress, Hambourg]*, edited by Gabriele Klein and Sandra Noeth. Transcript, 2011.

Brett, Michael. "Legislating for Inequality in Algeria: The Senatus-Consulte of 14 July 1865." *Bulletin of the School of Oriental and African Studies, University of London* 51, no. 3 (1988): 440–61.

Brissot, J. P., and Société des amis des noirs. *Réflexions Sur Le Code Noir, et Dénonciation d'un Crime Affreux Commis à Saint-Domingue*. Translated by *A Colony in Crisis: The Saint-Domingue Grain Shortage of 1789*. A Paris: De l'imprimerie du Patriote François, place du Théâtre Italien, 1790.

Brooks, Daphne. *Bodies in Dissent: Spectacular Performances of Race and Freedom, 1850–1910*. Duke University Press, 2006.

brooks, mayfield. "IWB = IMPROVISING WHILE BLACK: Writings, INterventions, Interruptions, Questions with Interview by Karen Nelson." *Contact Quarterly* 41, no. 1 (2016): 33–39.

Brown, Paul. "'This thing of darkness I acknowledge mine': The Tempest and the discourse of colonialism" in *Political Shakespeare: New essays in cultural materialism*, ed. Jonathan Dollimore and Alan Sinfield, Cornell University Press, 1985, 48–71.

Buck-Morss, Susan. "Hegel and Haiti." *Critical Inquiry* 26, no. 4 (2000): 821–65.

Burke, Siobhan. "'There Might Be Others,' a Work of Spontaneous Sound and Movement." *The New York Times*, March 16, 2016.

Burt, Ramsay. "Avoiding Capture." *Dance Research Journal* 50, no. 3 (2018): 99–119.

Busia, Abena P. A. "Silencing Sycorax: On African Colonial Discourse and the Unvoiced Female." *Cultural Critique*, no. 14 (1989): 81–104.

Butler, Judith. *Bodies That Matter: On the Discursive Limits of Sex*. Routledge, 1993.

Butler, Judith. *Excitable Speech: A Politics of the Performative*. Routledge, 1997.

Butler, Judith. *Notes Toward a Performative Theory of Assembly.* Harvard University Press. 2015.

Butler, Judith. *Precarious Life: The Powers of Mourning and Violence.* Verso, 2020.

Butler, Judith. "Walter Benjamin and the Critique of Violence." In *Parting Ways: Jewishness and the Critique of Zionism.* Columbia University Press, 2012.

Butler, Judith, Zeynep Gambetti, and Leticia Sabsay, eds. *Vulnerability in Resistance.* Duke University Press, 2016.

Brozgal, Lia Nicole. *Absent the Archive: Cultural Traces of a Massacre in Paris, 17 October 1961.* Liverpool University Press, 2020.

Byrd, Jodi A. *The Transit of Empire: Indigenous Critiques of Colonialism.* University of Minnesota Press, 2011.

Cairns, John W. *Codification, Transplants and History: Law Reform in Louisiana (1808) and Quebec (1866).* Talbot Publishing, an imprint of The Lawbook Exchange, Ltd., 2015.

Canetti, Elias. *Crowds and Power.* Translated by Carol Stewart. Farrar, Straus and Giroux, 1984.

Canetti, Elias. "Elias Canetti: Discussion with Theodor W. Adorno." *Thesis Eleven* 45, no. 1 (1996): 1–15.

Carbonnier, Jean. "Le Code Civil." In *Les Lieux De Mémoire: II. La Nation: Le Territoire, L'état, Le Patrimoine,* edited by Pierre Nora. Gallimard, 1986.

Carbonnier, Jean. *Flexible Droit – Pour Une Sociologie Du Droit sans Rigueur.* 10th ed. L.G.D.J., 2011.

Castañeda, Michelle. *Disappearing Rooms: The Hidden Theaters of Immigration Law.* Duke University Press, 2023.

Cerwonka, Allaine, and Liisa H. Malkki. *Improvising Theory: Process and Temporality in Ethnographic Fieldwork.* University of Chicago Press, 2007.

Césaire, Aimé. *Discourse on Colonialism.* Translated by Joan Pankham, 2000.

Césaire, Aimé. "L'homme de Culture et Ses Responsabilités." *Présence Africaine* 24, no. 25 (1959): 116–22.

Césaire, Aimé. "Poetry and Knowledge." In *Refusal of the Shadow: Surrealism and the Caribbean,* edited by Michael Richardson. Verso, 1996.

Césaire, Aimé, Richard Miller, and William Shakespeare. "A Tempest: Based on Shakespeare's The Tempest, Adaptation for a Black Theatre." In *A Tempest: Based on Shakespeare's The Tempest, Adaptation for a Black Theatre,* 1st TCG ed. TCG Translations, 2002.

Chakrabarty, Dipesh. *Provincializing Europe: Postcolonial Thought and Historical Difference.* Princeton University Press, 2007.

Chambers-Letson, Joshua Takano. *A Race So Different: Performance and Law in Asian America.* New York University Press, 2013.

Cheng, Anne Anlin. *Ornamentalism.* Oxford University Press, 2019.

Cheng, Anne. *Second Skin: Josephine Baker and the Modern Surface.* Oxford University Press, 2011.

Chow, Rey. *Writing Diaspora: Tactics of Intervention in Contemporary Cultural Studies.* Indiana University Press, 1993.

Christ, Birte, and Wibke Schniedermann. "Towards Legality and Affect." *Law, Culture and the Humanities* 20, no. 2 (2023): 248–56.

Chuh, Kandice. *The Difference Aesthetics Makes: On the Humanities "After Man."* Duke University Press, 2019.

Cohen, Rodger. "Trial of Vichy Official Lifts Veil on Killing of Algerians: Two of France's Most Painful Memories Are Linked by a Single Thread." *The New York Times,* 1997.

Constable, Marianne, Leti Volpp, and Bryan Wagner, eds. *Looking for Law in All the Wrong Places: Justice Beyond and Between*. Townsend Center for the Humanities, University of California Press, 2019.

Cooper, Frederick. *Citizenship Between Empire and Nation: Remaking France and French Africa, 1945–1960*. Princeton University Press, 2014.

Cooppan, Vilashini. "Time-Maps." *Critical Times* 2, no. 3 (2019): 396–415.

Coulthard, Glen Sean. *Red Skin, White Masks: Rejecting the Colonial Politics of Recognition*. University of Minnesota Press, 2014.

Cover, Robert. "Nomos and Narrative." *Harvard Law Review* 97, no. 1 (1983): 4–65.

Cover, Robert. "Violence and the Word." *The Yale Law Journal* 95 (1986): 1600–1629.

Cramer, Lauren McLeod, and Alessandra Raengo. "Freeing Black Codes: Liquid Blackness Plays the Jazz Ensemble." *The Black Scholar* 47, no. 3 (2017).

Crawford, Margo Natalie, and C. Riley Snorton, eds. *The Flesh of the Matter: A Critical Forum on Hortense Spillers*. 1st ed. Vanderbilt University Press, 2024.

Curtis, Lesley. "Excluded from Paradise: Race, Romance, and Haiti in the Colonial Novels of Fanny Reybaud." *Lingua Romana* 11, no. 1 (2012): 49–63.

Dance Studies Association. "Statement on the Inviolability of Movement as a Right." January 24, 2020.

Dauchy, Serge. "French Law and Its Expansion in the Early Modern Period." In *The Oxford Handbook of European Legal History*, edited by Heikki Pihlajamäki, Markus Dirk Dubber, and Andrew Mark Godfrey. Oxford Handbooks. Oxford University Press, 2018.

Davies, Telory. "Mobility: AXIS Dancers Push the Boundaries of Access." *Text and Performance Quarterly* 28, no. 1–2 (2008): 43–63.

Davis, Muriam Haleh. *Markets of Civilization: Islam and Racial Capitalism in Algeria*. Duke University Press, 2022.

Davis, Muriam Haleh, and Selma Kasmi. "Voices from the Middle East: The Future of the Hirak Movement in Algeria." Middle East Report. 2020.

Davis, Muriam Haleh, and Thomas Serres. "Political Contestation in Algeria: Between Postcolonial Legacies and the Arab Spring." *Middle East Critique* 22, no. 2 (2013): 99–112.

Davis, Muriam Helah, Thomas Serres, and the Middle East Pedagogy Initiative (MESPI). "Essential Readings: The Hirak (Algerian Uprisings of 2019)." Jadaliyya. Middle East Studies Pedagogy Initiative (MESPI). December 16, 2020.

Dayan, Colin. "Legal Slaves and Civil Bodies." In *Materializing Democracy: Toward a Revitalized Cultural Politics*, edited by Russ Castronovo and Dana D. Nelson. Duke University Press, 2002.

Dean, Carolyn J. *The Frail Social Body: Pornography, Homosexuality, and Other Fantasies in Interwar France*. University of California Press, 2000.

Dean, Jodi. *Crowds and Party*. Verso, 2016.

DeFrantz, Thomas. 2005."Composite Bodies of Dance: The Repertory of the Alvin Ailey American Dance Theater." *Theatre Journal* 57, no. 4 (2005): 659–678.

Den Ouden, Amy E., and Jean M. O'Brien, eds. *Recognition, Sovereignty Struggles, & Indigenous Rights in the United States: A Sourcebook*. The University of North Carolina Press, 2013.

Derrida, Jacques. *Archive Fever: A Freudian Impression*. University of Chicago Press, 1995.

Derrida, Jacques. *Before the Law: The Complete Text of 'Préjugés'*. Translated by Sandra Van Reenen and Jacques de Ville. University of Minnesota Press, 2018.

Derrida, Jacques. "Force of Law: The 'Mystical Foundation of Authority.'" In *Deconstruction and the Possibility of Justice*, edited by Drucilla Cornell, Michel Rosenfeld, and David Gray Carlson. Routledge, Chapman and Hall, Inc, 1992.

Derrida, Jacques. *Limited Inc.* Northwestern University Press, 1988.

Derrida, Jacques. *On Cosmopolitanism and Forgiveness.* Translated by Mark Dooley and Michael Hughes. With Simon Critchley and Richard Kearney. Thinking in Action. Routledge, 2001.

Derrida, Jacques. *Specters of Marx: The State of the Debt, the Work of Mourning, and the New International.* Routledge, 1994.

Desjarlais, Robert. "Intersecting Lives." In *The Visual Afterlife of Abdelkader Bennahar*, Duke University Press, 2025.

Desmond, Jane, ed. *Dancing Desires: Choreographing Sexualities On and Off the Stage.* University of Wisconsin Press, 2001.

Dils, Ann, and Ann Cooper Albright, eds. *Moving History / Dancing Cultures: A Dance History Reader.* Wesleyan University Press, 2001.

Djebar, Assia. *Children of the New World: A Novel of the Algerian War.* Translated by Marjolijn De Jager. Feminist Press at the City University of New York, 2005.

Djelloul, Ghaliya N., and Aniss M. Mezoued. "The Spatial Underpinnings of the Revolutionary Protests in Algiers." Point de vue. Forum Vies Mobiles. January 7, 2019.

Doho, Gilbert. *Le Code De L'indigénat: Ou Le Fondement Des Etats Autocratiques En Afrique Francophone.* L'Harmattan, 2017.

Doolittle, Lisa, and Anne Flynn. 2005. "Human Rights: Not Like a Document, Like a Dance." In *Right to Dance: Dancing for Rights*, edited by Naomi Jackson, Banff Centre Press. 269–291.

Dowling, Sarah. *Here Is a Figure: Grounding Literary Form.* Northwestern University Press, 2025.

Du Bois, W. E. B. *Black Reconstruction in America, 1860–1880.* The Free Press, 1998.

Dubois, Laurent. *A Colony of Citizens: Revolution and Slave Emancipation in the French Caribbean, 1787–1804.* The University of North Carolina Press, 2004.

Eckert, Joern. "Legal Roots of Human Dignity in German Law." In *The Concept of Human Dignity in Human Rights Discourse*, edited by D. Kretzmer and E. Klein. Kluwer Law International, 2002.

Einaudi, Jean-Luc. *Octobre 1961: Un Massacre à Paris.* Fayard, 2001.

El Atti, Basma. "Algeria Pushes Forward Draft Law to Hold France Accountable for Its Colonized Past." *The New Arab.* March 25, 2025.

El-Tayeb, Fatima. *European Others Queering Ethnicity in Postnational Europe.* University of Minnesota Press, 2011.

Emery, Lynne F. *Black Dance from 1619 to Today.* Princeton Book, 1988.

Enz, Molley Krueger. "Who Belongs to Whom?: Codes, Property, and Ownership in Madame Charles Reybaud's 'Les Épaves.'" *Nineteenth-Century French Studies* 39, no. 3/4 (2011): 229–39.

Esmeir, Samera. *Juridical Humanity: A Colonial History.* Stanford University Press, 2012.

Etinson, Adam. "What's So Special About Human Dignity?" *Philosophy & Public Affairs* 48, no. 4 (2020): 353–81.

Fanon, Frantz. *The Wretched of the Earth.* Translated by Constance Farrington. Grove Press, 1963.

Fécu, Yanie. "Sycorax's Other Son." *Cabinet*, no. 67 (2019).

Felman, Shoshana. *The Scandal of the Speaking Body: Don Juan with J. L. Austin, or Seduction in Two Languages.* Stanford University Press, 2002.

Ferguson, Russell, and The New Museum of Contemporary Art, eds. *Out There: Marginalization and Contemporary Cultures.* Documentary sources in contemporary art. MIT Press, 1992.

Fineman, Martha A. "Vulnerability and Social Justice." *Valparaiso University Law Review* 53, no. 2 (2019): 341–370.

Fineman, Martha A. "The Vulnerable Subject and the Responsive State." *Emory Law Journal* 60, no. 2 (2010).

Fineman, Martha A., and Anna Grear. *Vulnerability: Reflections on a New Ethical Foundation for Law and Politics.* Ashgate, 2013.

Fleetwood, Nicole. "Excess Flesh: Black Women Performing Hypervisibility." In *Troubling Vision: Performance, Visuality, and Blackness.* University of Chicago Press, 2011.

Fortuna, Victoria. *Moving Otherwise: Dance, Violence, and Memory in Buenos Aires.* Oxford University Press, 2019.

Foster, Susan Leigh. "Choreographies of Gender." *Signs: Journal of Women in Culture and Society* 24, no. 1 (1998): 1–33.

Foster, Susan Leigh. "Choreographies of Protest." *Theatre Journal* 55, no. 3 (2003): 395–412.

Foster, Susan Leigh. *Choreographing Empathy: Kinesthesia in Performance.* Routledge, 2011.

Foster, Susan Leigh, ed. *Choreographing History.* Indiana University Press, 1995.

Foster, Susan Leigh. *Knowing as Moving: Perception, Memory, and Place.* Duke University Press, 2025.

Foster, Susan. "Simply(?) The Doing of It, Like Two Arms Going Round and Round." In *Moving History / Dancing Cultures: A Dance History Reader,* edited by Ann Dils and Ann Cooper Albright. Wesleyan University Press, 2001.

Foster, Susan, and Linda Caruso Haviland. "The Ballerina's Phallic Point." *Three Performed Lectures. The Pew Center for Arts and Heritage.* March 21, 2011.

Foucault, Michel. *The Order of Things: An Archaeology of Human Sciences.* Knopf Doubleday Publishing Group, 1994.

Frank, Jerome. "Words and Music: Some Remarks on Statutory Interpretation." *Columbia Law Review* 47, no. 8 (1947): 1259–78.

Franko, Mark. "The Conduct of Contemplation and the Gestural Ethics of Interpretation in Walter Benjamin's 'Epistemo-Critical Prologue.'" *Performance Philosophy* 3, no. 1 (2017).

Franko, Mark. *Dance as Text: Ideologies of the Baroque Body.* Oxford University Press, 2015.

Franko, Mark. "Editor's Note: Revaluing the Score: Archival Futurity." *Dance Research Journal* 44, no. 2 (2012): 1–2.

Franko, Mark. "Figural Inversions of Louis XIV's Dancing Body." In *Acting on the Past: Historical Performance Across the Disciplines,* edited by Mark Franko and Annette Richards. Wesleyan University Press, 2000.

Franko, Mark. *Text as Dance: Walter Benjamin, Louis Marin and Choreographies of the Baroque.* Methuen Drama, 2025.

Franko, Mark. "Writing for the Body: Notation, Reconstruction, and Reinvention in Dance." *Common Knowledge* 17, no. 2 (2011): 321–34.

Franko, Mark, Kendall Thomas, and Thomas Keenan. "Dialogues: Genesis and Concept of *Human Writes.*" *Dance Research Journal* 42, no. 2 (2010): 1–10.

Freeman, Elizabeth. *Beside You in Time: Sense Methods & Queer Sociabilities in the American 19th Century*. Duke University Press, 2019.

Frey, Charles. "The Tempest and the New World." *Shakespeare Quarterly* 30, no. 1 (1979): 29–41.

Front Line Defenders. "Harassment of Algerian Human Rights Defenders Must End." April 2, 2021.

Fuente, Alejandro de la, and Ariela Gross. "The Precarious Status of Free People of Color on the Move in Antebellum Virginia." In *The Experience of Mobility*, edited by Claudia Moatti, Emmanuelle Chevreau, and Ariela Gross. Éditions Ausonius, 2021.

G., J. E. "No Evidence to Support a Conviction. The Supreme Court's Decisions in Thompson v. City of Louisville and Garner v. Louisiana." *University of Pennsylvania Law Review* 110, no. 8 (1962): 1137–46.

G., Rania. "'On Ne Peut Gagner Sa Liberté Qu'en Montrant à L'ennemi Que L'on Est Prêt à Tout Pour L'obtenir.' DZ1 MARS 2019 DZ Work 2O19 / Photography & Retouching: @ranougraphy Dancer: @melziad'Poetic Protest.'" Instagram, 2019.

Garraway, Doris Lorraine. *The Libertine Colony: Creolization in the Early French Caribbean*. Duke University Press, 2005.

Gbaguidi, Pélagie. "Code Noir." *Pélagie Gbaguidi*, Web.

Gelderloos, Peter. *How Nonviolence Protects the State*. South End Press, 2007.

Giacomel, Robert. *Le Code Noir: Autopsie D'un Crime Contre L'humanité*. Lacour, 2003.

Gilroy, Paul. *The Black Atlantic: Modernity and Double Consciousness*. Harvard University Press, 1995.

Gilroy, Paul. "Darker than Blue: On the Moral Economies of Black Atlantic Culture." In *W.E.B. Du Bois Lectures*. Harvard University Press, 2010.

Girard, Charlotte, and Stéphanie Hennette-Vauchez. *La Dignité de La Personne Humaine: Recherche Sur Le Processus de Juridicisation*. Presses Universitaires de France, 2005.

Glissant, Édouard. *Poetics of Relation*. Translated by Betsy Wing. University of Michigan Press, 2009.

Goldberg, Jonathan. *Tempest in the Caribbean*. University of Minnesota Press, 2004.

Goldman, Danielle. *I Want to Be Ready: Improvised Dance as a Practice of Freedom*. University of Michigan Press, 2010.

Golomb, Sariel. "Channels Through the Humane The Exiled Body in Crystal Pite's Flight Pattern." *Theatre Journal* 75, no. 3 (2023): 301–20.

Göltl, Teresa. "Trials of Enslavers in Former French Colonies in the Eighteenth and Nineteenth Centuries: Testimonies of the Enslaved Between Gratitude and Fear." *Slavery & Abolition* 45, no. 1 (2024): 117–34.

Goluboff, Risa Lauren. *Vagrant Nation: Police Power, Constitutional Change, and the Making of the 1960s*. Oxford University Press, 2016.

Goluboff, Risa, and Richard Schragger. "Grants Pass and the Vagrancy Revolution Revisited." *The Supreme Court Review* 2024 (2025): 191–233.

Goodell, William. "Fugitives from Slavery." In *American Slave Code, in Theory and Practice: Its Distinctive Features Shown By Its Statutes, Judicial Decisions, & Illustrative Facts*. Clarke, Beeton, and Co. Foreign Booksellers, 1853.

Goodrich, Peter, Bernadette Meyler, and Anna Jayne Kimmel, eds. *Performing Law: Actors, Affects, Spaces*. Cambridge University Press, 2026.

Goodrich, Peter. *Law in the Courts of Love: Literature and Other Minor Jurisprudences*. Routledge, 1996.

Goodrich, Peter. "Specula Laws: Image, Aesthetic and Common Law." *Law and Critique* 2, no. 2 (1991): 233–54.

Gosetti-Ferencei, Jennifer Anna. "Being In the Crowd: Anonymity, Conformity, and Individuality in Modern Life." Oxford University Press, 2020.

Gotman, Kélina. *Choreomania: Dance and Disorder.* Oxford University Press, 2018.

Gottschild, Brenda Dixon. "The Black Dancing Body as a Measure of Culture." *Choros International Dance Journal* 7 (2018): 41–51.

Goubert, Pierre. *L'Ancien Régime I: La Société.* Armand Colins, 1969.

Grabenstein, Darcy. "Using Our Bodies as Sites of Restful Resistance." thINKing DANCE. December 21, 2022, Web.

Grandner, Michael A., Natasha J. Williams, Kristen L. Knutson, Dorothy Roberts, and Girardin Jean-Louis. "Sleep Disparity, Race/Ethnicity, and Socioeconomic Position." *Sleep Medicine* 18 (2016): 7–18.

Grey, Thomas C. "Do We Have an Unwritten Constitution?" In *Formalism and Pragmatism in American Law.* Brill, 2014.

Gross, Ariela Julie. "Legal Transplants: Slavery and the Civil Law in Louisiana." USC Law Legal Studies Paper No. 09–16. May 12, 2009.

Guest, Ann Hutchinson. *Choreo-Graphics: A Comparison of Dance Notation Systems from the Fifteenth Century to the Present.* Gordon and Breach, 1989.

Guest, Ann Hutchinson. *Dance Notation: The Process of Recording Movement on Paper.* Dance Horizons, 1984.

Guest, Ann Hutchinson., and Doug Anderson. *Labanotation; or, Kinetography Laban; the System of Analyzing and Recording Movement.* Rev. and Expanded ed. TAB Paperbook; No. 27. Theatre Arts Books, 1970.

Habermas, Jürgen. "The Concept of Human Dignity and the Realistic Utopia of Human Rights." *Metaphilosophy* 41, no. 4 (2010).

Hall, Stuart, ed. *Representation: Cultural Representations and Signifying Practices. Culture, Media, and Identities.* Sage in association with the Open University, 1997.

Han, Sora Y. *Mu, 49 Marks of Abolition.* Duke University Press, 2024.

Han, Sora. "Slavery as Contract: Betty's Case and the Question of Freedom." *Law and Literature* 27, no. 3 (2015): 395–416.

Harney, Stefano, and Fred Moten. "Michael Brown." *Boundary 2* 42, no. 4 (2015): 81–87.

Hartman, Saidiya V. *Scenes of Subjection: Terror, Slavery, and Self-Making in Nineteenth-Century America.* W. W. Norton & Company, Incorporated, 2022.

Hersey, Tricia. *Rest Is Resistance: A Manifesto.* Little, Brown Spark, 2022.

Hersey, Tricia, and George McCalman. *We Will Rest!: The Art of Escape.* Little, Brown Spark, 2024.

Hibbitts, Bernard. "Coming to Our Senses: Communication and Legal Expression in Performance Cultures." *Emory Law Journal* 41 (1992): 873–960.

Hobbs, Allyson Vanessa. *A Chosen Exile: A History of Racial Passing in American Life.* Harvard University Press, 2014.

Hodson, Millicent. "Searching for Nijinsky's Sacre." In *Moving History / Dancing Cultures: A Dance History Reader,* edited by Ann Dils and Ann Cooper Albright. Wesleyan University Press, 2001.

Hoffmaster, Barry. "What Does Vulnerability Mean?" *Hastings Center Report* 36, no. 2 (2006): 38–45.

Hooks, Bell. *Belonging: A Culture of Place.* Routledge, 2009.

House, Jim, and Neil MacMaster. *Paris 1961: Algerians, State Terror, and Memory.* Oxford University Press, 2006.

Hoxworth, Kellen. *Transoceanic Blackface: Empire, Race, Performance.* Northwestern University Press, 2024.

Hunt, Lynn. *Inventing Human Rights: A History.* W. W. Norton & Company, Inc., 2008.

Hyde, Alan. *Bodies of Law.* Princeton University Press, 1997.

Ife, Fahima. *Maroon Choreography.* Duke University Press, 2021.

Inazu, John D. *Liberty's Refuge: The Forgotten Freedom of Assembly.* Yale University Press, 2012.

Inazu, John. Interviewed by Anna Jayne Kimmel on Zoom, July 5, 2021.

INED: Institut National D'Études Démographiques. "Combien y A-t-Il d'immigrés En France?" Tout savoir sur la population. Updated April 6, 2020.

International Center for Not-For-Profit Law (ICNL). "Law 91–19 Amending and Supplementing Law 89–28 of 1989 on Public Meetings and Demonstrations." Digital Legal Library.

Jackson, Naomi M., and Toni Samantha Phim, eds. *Dance, Human Rights, and Social Justice: Dignity in Motion.* Scarecrow Press, 2008.

Jackson, Zakiyyah Iman. *Becoming Human: Matter and Meaning in an Antiblack World.* New York University Press, 2020.

Jacobs, Harriet A. *Incidents in the Life of a Slave Girl.* Edited by Lydia Maria Child and Jean Fagan Yellin. Harvard University Press, 2009.

Jean-Baptiste, Rachel. *Multiracial Identities in Colonial French Africa: Race, Childhood, and Citizenship.* Cambridge University Press, 2023.

Johnson, Norris. 1987. "Panic at 'The Who Concert Stampede': An Empirical Assessment." *Social Problems* 34, no. 4 (1987): 362–373.

Jones, Bill T., Peggy Gillespie, and Gerald Arpino. *Last Night on Earth.* Pantheon Books, 1995.

Jordan, Stephanie. "Using the Humphrey Scores." *Dance Research Journal* 14, no. 1/2 (1981–82): 51–53.

Judy, R. A. "Introduction: For Dignity; Tunisia and the Poetry of Emergent Democratic Humanism." *Boundary 2* 39, no. 1 (2012): 1–16.

Judy, R. A. *Sentient Flesh: Thinking in Disorder, Poiēsis in Black.* Black Outdoors: Innovations in the Poetics of Study. Duke University Press, 2020.

Kafka, Franz. trans. Ian Johnston. "In the Penal Colony." *Kafka Online.*

Kaiser, Paul. "Dance Geometry: William Forsythe in Dialogue with Paul Kaiser." *Performance Research* 4, no. 2 (1999): 64–71.

Kamir, Orit. *Applying Dignity, Respect, Honor and Human Rights to a Pluralistic, Multicultural Universe.* EUI Working Papers. Robert Schuman Centre for Advanced Studies Global Governance Programme-178, 2015.

Kamir, Orit. "Honor and Dignity in the Film 'Unforgiven': Implications for Sociolegal Theory." *Law & Society Review* 40, no. 1 (2006): 193–233.

Kealiinohomoku, Joann. "An Anthropologist Looks at Ballet as a Form of Ethnic Dance." in *Moving History / Dancing Cultures : A Dance History Reader.* eds. Albright, Ann Cooper, and Ann Dils. Wesleyan University Press, 2001, 73–90.

Kedhar, Anusha. "'Hands Up! Don't Shoot!': Gesture, Choreography, and Protest in Ferguson." *The Feminist Wire*, 2014.

Khalil, Andrea Flores. *Crowds and Politics in North Africa: Tunisia, Algeria and Libya.* Routledge, 2014.

Khanmalek, Tala, and Heidi Andrea Restrepo Rhodes. "A Decolonial Feminist Epistemology of the Bed: A Compendium Incomplete of Sick and Disabled Queer Brown Femme Bodies of Knowledge." *Frontiers: A Journal of Women Studies* 41, no. 1 (2020): 35–58.

Khubchandani, Kareem. *Ishtyle: Accenting Gay Indian Nightlife.* University of Michigan Press, 2020.

Kim, Eunjung. "Unbecoming Human: An Ethics of Objects." *A Journal of Lesbian and Gay Studies* 21, no. 2–3 (2015): 295–320.

Kim, Marie Seong-Hak. *Custom, Law, and Monarchy: A Legal History of Early Modern France.* Oxford University Press, 2021.

Kim, So Yeon. "Les Vulnérables: Evaluating the Vulnerability Criterion in Article 14 Cases by the European Court of Human Rights." *Legal Studies* 41, no. 4 (2021): 617–32.

Kimmel, Anna Jayne. "Exposing Forms 'Naked Athena' and Classical Lines." In *Performing Law: Actors, Affects, Spaces,* edited by Anna Jayne Kimmel, Peter Goodrich, and Bernadette Meyler. Cambridge University Press, 2026.

Kimmel, Anna Jayne. "The Right to Stillness: Tracing Corporeal Ambiguity Across Legal Interpretations." *Southern California Interdisciplinary Law Journal,* Forthcoming v. 35, no. 1 (2026).

King, Tiffany Lethabo. *The Black Shoals: Offshore Formations of Black and Native Studies.* Duke University Press, 2019.

King, Tiffany Lethabo. "Humans Involved: Lurking in the Lines of Posthumanist Flight." *Critical Ethnic Studies* 3, no. 1 (2017): 162–85.

King, Tiffany Lethabo, Jenell Navarro, and Andrea Smith. *Otherwise Worlds: Against Settler Colonialism and Anti-Blackness.* Duke University Press, 2020.

Klopotek, Brian. *Recognition Odysseys: Indigeneity, Race, and Federal Tribal Recognition Policy in Three Louisiana Indian Communities.* Duke University Press, 2011.

Kondo, Dorinne K. *Worldmaking: Race, Performance, and the Work of Creativity.* Duke University Press, 2018.

Koselleck, Reinhart. *Futures Past: On the Semantics of Historical Time.* Translated by Keith Tribe. MIT Press, 1990.

Kramer, Larry. *The People Themselves: Popular Constitutionalism and Judicial Review.* Oxford University Press, 2004.

Kraut, Anthea. *Choreographing Copyright: Race, Gender, and Intellectual Property Rights in American Dance.* Oxford University Press, 2016.

Kurki, Visa. *A Theory of Legal Personhood.* Oxford Legal Philosophy. Oxford Academic, 2019.

Laban, Rudolf von. *Laban's Dance Notation Charts: Basic Symbols Taken from Dance Script / by Rud. v. Laban.* Associated music publishers, inc., [c1928], 1928.

Labat, Jean-Baptiste. "Nouveau Voyage Aux Isles de l'Amérique, 1700." In *Le Code Noir Ou Recueil Des Reglements Rendus Jusqu'a Present,* reprint by Societé d'Histoire de la Guadeloupe, translated by John Garrigus. Prault, 1767.

Labter, Lazhari. "Les '18 commandements' du manifestant en Algérie." Monde. L'Obs. March 8, 2019.

Lara, Irene. "Beyond Caliban's Curses: The Decolonial Feminist Literacy of Sycorax." *Journal of International Women's Studies* 9, no. 1 (2007): 80–98.

Latour, Bruno. *The Making of Law: An Ethnography of the Conseil d'Etat*. Polity, 2010.

Lazier, Rebecca, and Dan Trueman. *There Might Be Others*. Operating System Press, 2016.

Le Bon, Gustave. *The Crowd: Study of the Popular Mind*. Classic Books International, (1896) 2009.

Le Cour Grandmaison, Olivier. "The Exception and the Rule: On French Colonial Law." *Diogenes* 53, no. 4 (2006): 34–53.

Lepecki, André. "Choreography as Apparatus of Capture." *TDR: The Drama Review* 51, no. 2 (2007): 119–23.

Lepecki, André. "Choreopolice and Choreopolitics: Or, the Task of the Dancer." *TDR: The Drama Review* 57, no. 4 (2013): 13–27.

Lepecki, André. *Exhausting Dance: Performance and the Politics of Movement*. Routledge, 2006.

Lepecki, André, ed. *Of the Presence of the Body: Essays on Dance and Performance Theory*. Wesleyan University Press, 2004.

Levinson, Sanford, and J. M. Balkin. "Law, Music, and Other Performing Arts." *University of Pennsylvania Law Review* 139, no. 6 (1991): 1597–658.

Loughlin, Martin, and Neil Walker, eds. *The Paradox of Constitutionalism: Constituent Power and Constitutional Form*. Oxford University Press, 2008.

Louppe, Laurence. "Les Notations En Danse, Gardiennes de l'invention." *Résonance*, no. 7 (October 1994): Ircam-Centre Georges-Pompidou.

Louppe, Laurence. *Traces of Dance: Drawings and Notations of Choreographers*. Dis Voir, 1994.

Love Michael, Michael. "If You're Black, Rest Is Power." *Paper Magazine*. Web. January 25, 2019.

Lowe, Lisa. *The Intimacies of Four Continents*. Duke University Press, 2015.

Lubrin, Canisia. *Code Noir: Fictions*. Soft Skull, 2025.

Lukács, Georg. "Legality and Illegality." In *History and Class Consciousness: Studies in Marxist Dialectics*. Translated by Rodney Livingstone. The MIT Press, 1968.

Lumsden, Linda J. *Rampant Women: Suffragists and the Right of Assembly*. University of Tennessee Press, 1997.

Macklin, Ruth. "Dignity Is a Useless Concept." *BMJ* 327, no. 7429 (2003): 1419–1420.

Madhok, Sumi. *Vernacular Rights Cultures: The Politics of Origins, Human Rights, and Gendered Struggles for Justice*. Cambridge University Press, 2021.

Mainwaring, Madison. "In Paris, Even the Ballet Dancers Are on Strike." *The New York Times*, January 13, 2020.

Mainwaring, Madison. "Vogue Dancers Subvert a Baroque Spectacle at Paris Opera." *The New York Times*, September 25, 2019.

Manderson, Desmond. *Songs Without Music: Aesthetic Dimensions of Law and Justice. Philosophy, Social Theory, and the Rule of Law*. University of California Press, 2000.

Manderson, Desmond, and David Caudill. "Modes of Law: Music and Legal Theory – An Interdisciplinary Workshop Introduction." *Cardozo Law Review* 20, nos. 5–6 (1999): 1225–330.

Mann, Gregory. "What Was the 'Indigénat'? The 'Empire of Law' in French West Africa." *The Journal of African History* 50, no. 3 (2009).

Manning, Susan, Janice Ross, and Rebecca Schneider, eds. *Futures of Dance Studies.* The University of Wisconsin Press, 2020.

Marglin, Jessica M. *Across Legal Lines: Jews and Muslims in Modern Morocco.* Yale University Press, 2016.

Martin, Randy. *Critical Moves: Dance Studies in Theory and Politics.* Duke University Press, 1998.

Massumi, Brian. *Parables for the Virtual: Movement, Affect, Sensation.* Duke University Press, 2021.

Mbembe, Achille. *Necropolitics.* Translated by Steven Corcoran. Duke University Press, 2019.

Mbembe, Achille. *On the Postcolony.* University of California Press, 2001.

McCarren, Felicia M. *One Dead at the Paris Opera Ballet: La Source 1866–2014.* Oxford University Press, 2020.

McDougall, James. "Savage Wars? Codes of Violence in Algeria, 1830s–1990s." *Third World Quarterly* 26, no. 1 (2005): 117–31.

McKinley, Maggie. 2016."Lobbying and the Petition Clause." *Stanford Law Review* 68 (5): 1131–1206.

McKittrick, Katherine. *Dear Science and Other Stories.* Duke University Press, 2021.

McKittrick, Katherine, ed. *Sylvia Wynter: On Being Human as Praxis.* Duke University Press, 2015.

McKittrick, Katherine, Frances H. O'Shaughnessy, and Kendall Witaszek. "Rhythm, or On Sylvia Wynter's Science of the Word." *American Quarterly* 70, no. 4 (2018): 867–74.

McManus, Anne-Marie. "Race, Time, and the Petrified Subject in Algeria: Reading Frantz Fanon's Algerian Writings and Kateb Yacine's *Nedjma*." *Comparative Studies of South Asia, Africa, and the Middle East* 44, no. 2 (2024): 287–302.

McNamara, Brittney. "Black Power Naps Is Addressing How Systemic Racism Impacts Sleep." *British Vogue,* July 13, 2020.

Melzer, Sara E., and Kathryn Norberg, eds. *From the Royal to the Republican Body: Incorporating the Political in Seventeenth- and Eighteenth-Century France.* University of California Press, 1998.

Menon, Jisha. "Desiring Children: Vulnerability and the Sex Offender." In *Performing Law: Actors, Affects, Spaces,* edited by Peter Goodrich, Anna Jayne Kimmel, and Bernadette Meyler. Cambridge University Press, 2026.

Merle, Isabelle. "Retour Sur Le Régime De L'Indigénat: Genèse Et Contradictions Des Principes Répressifs Dans L'Empire Français." *French Politics, Culture and Society* 20, no. 2 (2002): 77–97.

Merleau-Ponty, Maurice. *The Visible and the Invisible: Followed by Working Notes.* Studies in Phenomenology and Existential Philosophy, edited by Claude Lefort. Northwestern University Press, 1968.

Merrick, Jeffrey. "The Body Politics of French Absolutism." In *From the Royal to the Republican Body: Incorporating the Political in Seventeenth- and Eighteenth-Century France,* edited by Sara E. Melzer and Kathryn Norberg. University of California Press, 1998.

Merryman, John Henry, and Rogelio Pérez-Perdomo. *The Civil Law Tradition: An Introduction to the Legal Systems of Europe and Latin America.* Stanford University Press, 2019.

Metzl, Jonathan. *The Protest Psychosis: How Schizophrenia Became a Black Disease.* Beacon Press, 2009.

Meyler, Bernadette. *Theaters of Pardoning.* Cornell University Press, 2019.

Miller, Joseph Hillis. *For Derrida*. Fordham University Press, 2009.

Minow, Martha. "Interpreting Rights: An Essay for Robert Cover." *The Yale Law Journal* 96, no. 8 (1987): 1860–1915.

Mitiche, Ahmed. "How Algeria's Non-Violent Protests Challenge Regime Narrative of 'Armed Resistance.'" Perspectives. *The New Arab*. April 24, 2019.

Mitra, Royona. "Unmaking Contact: Choreographic Touch at the Intersections of Race, Caste, and Gender." *Dance Research Journal* 53, no. 3 (2021): 6–24.

Morris, Gay, and Jens Richard Giersdorf, eds. *Choreographies of 21st Century Wars*. Oxford University Press, 2016.

Moten, Fred. "Come On, Get It!" *The New Inquiry*, February 19, 2018.

Moten, Fred. *In the Break: The Aesthetics of the Black Radical Tradition*. University of Minnesota Press, 2003.

Moten, Fred. "Jurisgenerative Grammar (for Alto)." In *The Oxford Handbook of Critical Improvisation Studies*, edited by Benjamin Piekut and George E. Lewis, Volume 1. Oxford University Press, 2016.

Moten, Fred. "Preface for a Solo by Miles Davis." *Women & Performance: A Journal of Feminist Theory* 17, no. 2 (2007): 217–46.

Moten, Fred. *Stolen Life*. Consent Not to Be a Single Being, v. 2. Duke University Press, 2018.

Mourouga, Erell. *The Code de l'Indigénat and Colonial Management in Algeria (1865–1944): Hierarchy, Ethnic Division, and Politicisation of Identity*. The Beacon Journal, 2023 Edition, 29–38.

Moyn, Samuel. *Not Enough: Human Rights in an Unequal World*. The Belknap Press of Harvard University Press, 2018.

Mulcahy, Sean. "Dances with Laws: From Metaphor to Methodology." *Law and Humanities* 15, no. 1 (2021): 106–33.

Mulcahy, Sean, and Kate Seear. "A 'Tick and Flick' Exercise: Movement and Form in Australian Parliamentary Human Rights Scrutiny." *Dance Research Journal* 55, no. 3 (2023): 47–64.

Mullis, Eric. "Dancing for Human Rights: Engaging Labor Rights and Social Remembrance in 'Poor Mouth.'" *Dance Research: The Journal of the Society for Dance Research* 34, no. 2 (2016): 220–42.

Murphy, Jacqueline Shea. *The People Have Never Stopped Dancing: Native American Modern Dance Histories*. University of Minnesota Press, 2007.

Murphy, John. "Protest or Riot? Interpreting Collective Action in Contemporary France." *Anthropological Quarterly* 84, no. 4 (2011): 977–1009.

Musser, Amber Jamilla. *Sensational Flesh: Race, Power, and Masochism*. New York University, 2014.

Nader, Laura. *The Life of the Law: Anthropological Projects*. University of California Press, 2002.

Naimou, Angela. *Salvage Work: U.S. and Caribbean Literatures amid the Debris of Legal Personhood*. Fordham University Press, 2015.

Needham, Maureen. "Louis XIV and the Académie Royale de Danse, 1661: A Commentary and Translation." *Dance Chronicle* 20, no. 2 (1997): 173–90.

Nicolazzo, Sal. *Vagrant Figures: Law, Literature, and the Origins of the Police*. The Lewis Walpole Series in Eighteenth-Century Culture and History. Yale University Press, 2021.

Nirot, Jean-François. "Le Code Noir: [Idées Reçues Sur Un Texte Symbolique]." In *Idées Reçues. Histoire & Civilisations.* Cavalier bleu, 2015.

Nirot, Jean-François, and Jérémy Richard. "L'Édit Royal de Mars 1685 Touchant La Police Des Îles de l'Amérique Française Dit « Code Noir »: Comparaison Des Éditions Anciennes à Partir de La Version « Guadeloupe »." *Bulletin de La Société d'Histoire de La Guadeloupe* 156 (210 AD).

Noland, Carrie. *Agency and Embodiment: Performing Gestures/Producing Culture.* Harvard University Press, 2009.

Norris, Zach. *Defund Fear: Safety Without Policing, Prisons, and Punishment.* Beacon Press, 2021.

Nye, Robert A. "Two Paths to a Psychology of Social Action: Gustave Le Bon and Georges Sorel." *The Journal of Modern History* 45, no. 3 (1973): 411–38.

Olson, Greta. "The Turn to Passion: Has Law and Literature Become Law and Affect?" *Law & Literature* 28, no. 3 (2015): 335–53.

Olson, Greta. *From Law and Literature to Legality and Affect.* Oxford University Press, 2022.

Palmer, Vernon Valentine. "The Code Noir of 1724." *The Tulane European and Civil Law Forum* 34, no. 103 (2019).

Patterson, Orlando. *Slavery and Social Death: A Comparative Study.* Harvard University Press, 2018.

Peabody, Sue, ed. *The Color of Liberty: Histories of Race in France.* Duke University Press, 2003.

Peabody, Sue. "Slaves as Witnesses, Slaves as Evidence: French and British Prosecution of Slave Trade in the Indian Ocean." In *Voices in the Legal Archives in the French Colonial World: The King Is Word*, edited by Nancy Christie, Michael Gauvreau, and Matthew Gerber. Routledge, 2020.

Peabody, Sue. *"There Are No Slaves in France": The Political Culture of Race and Slavery in the Ancien Régime.* Oxford University Press, 1996.

Peters, Julie Stone. "Law, Literature, and the Vanishing Real: On the Future of an Interdisciplinary Illusion." *PMLA* 120, no. 2 (2005): 442–53.

Peters, Julie Stone. *Law as Performance: Theatricality, Spectatorship, and the Making of Law in Ancient, Medieval, and Early Modern Europe.* Oxford University Press, 2022.

Pinker, Steven. "The Stupidity of Dignity." *The New Republic* 28, no. 5 (2008).

Posner, Richard A. "Bork and Beethoven." *Stanford Law Review* 42 (1990): 1365.

Puar, Jasbir K. *The Right to Maim: Debility, Capacity, Disability.* Duke University Press, 2017.

Puar, Jasbir K. "Spatial Debilities: Slow Life and Carceral Capitalism in Palestine." *The South Atlantic Quarterly* 120, no. 2 (2021): 393–414.

Puar, Jasbir K. *Terrorist Assemblages: Homonationalism in Queer Times.* Duke University Press, 2007.

Rachidi, Ilhem. "Algeria's Hirak: Defenders of Freedom of Expression." Carnegie Endowment for International Peace. January 19, 2021.

Ramshaw, Sara. *Justice as Improvisation: The Law of the Extempore.* Routledge, 2013.

Rancière, Jacques. "The Cause of the Other." *Parallax* 4, no. 2 (1998): 25–33.

Rankine, Claudia. *Citizen: An American Lyric.* Graywolf Press, 2014.

Rao, Shabari. *Stillness Manifesto.* Web.

Read, Alan, ed. *The Fact of Blackness: Frantz Fanon and Visual Representation*. Institute of Contemporary Arts, 1996.

Read, Alan. *Theatre & Law*. Palgrave, 2016.

Renard, Camille. "De l'esclave à La Négritude: Une Histoire Du Mot 'Noir.'" *Radiofrance*, May 10, 2018.

Reybaud, Henriette-Étiennette-Fanny. *Quatre Nouvelles Antillaises: Marie d'Énambuc, Les Épaves, Sydonie, Madame de Rieux*. Translated by Lesley C. Curtis. Autrement mêmes. L'Harmattan, 2014.

Rheeder, Riaan. "Respect for Vulnerability Is a Human Right: Article 8 of the UNESCO Declaration on Bioethics and Human Rights and Senior Citizens in South Africa." *South African Journal of Bioethics and Law* 9, no. 1 (2016).

Rice, Alison. "Rehearsing October 17, 1961: The Role of Fiction in Remembering the Battle of Paris." In *L'Esprit Créateur 54 (4): The Algerian War of Independence and Its Legacy in Algeria, France, and Beyond*, 2014.

Richardson, Joe M. "Florida Black Codes." *The Florida Historical Quarterly* 47, no. 4 (1969): 365–79.

Richter, Julian. A Conversation on Human Writes. Interview by Anna Kimmel. Zoom. 2022.

Rifkin, Mark. *Beyond Settler Time: Temporal Sovereignty and Indigenous Self-Determination*. Duke University Press, 2017.

Rifkin, Mark. *Fictions of Land and Flesh: Blackness, Indigeneity, Speculation*. Duke University Press, 2019.

Robcis, Camille. "The Biopolitics of Dignity." *The South Atlantic Quarterly* 115, no. 2 (2016): 313–30.

Rosen, Michael. *Dignity: Its History and Meaning*. Harvard University Press, 2018.

Rothberg, Michael. "A Tale of Three Ghettos: Race, Gender, and 'Universality' After October 17, 1961." In *Multidirectional Memory: Remembering the Holocaust in the Age of Decolonization*. Stanford University Press, 2009, 227–66.

Ruskola, Teemu. *Legal Orientalism: China, the United States, and Modern Law*. Harvard University Press, 2013.

Saada, Emmanuelle. "The Empire of Law: Dignity, Prestige, and Domination in the 'Colonial Situation.'" *French Politics, Culture & Society* 20, no. 2 (2002): 98–120.

Saada, Emmanuelle, and Gérard Noiriel. "Les enfants de la colonie: les métis de l'Empire français, entre sujétion et citoyenneté." L'espace de l'histoire. Éd. la Découverte, 2007.

Said, Edward W. *Orientalism*. In *Orientalism*, Reprinted with a new afterword. Penguin, 1995.

Saint-Simon, Duc de Louis de Rouvroy. *The Memoirs of Louis XIV, His Court and of The Regency, Complete*. Edited by David Widger. Vol. 12. Project Gutenberg eBook, 2006.

Sala-Molins, Louis. *Le Code Noir Ou Le Calvaire de Canaan. Pratiques Théoriques*. Presses Universitaires de France, 1987.

Sala-Molins, Louis. *Dark Side of the Light: Slavery and the French Enlightenment*. University of Minnesota Press, 2006.

Sanchez, Rosa, Morgan Winsor, Kiara Alfonseca, and Ivan Pereira. "Officer Who Fatally Shot Daunte Wright During Traffic Stop Meant to Use Taser, Police Chief Says." *ABC News*, 2021.

Sanders, Scott. "Code Noir in Marivaux's Theatre." *Eighteenth-Century Fiction* 32, no. 2 (2020): 271–96.

Sarat, Austin, Lawrence Douglas, and Martha Merrill Umphrey, eds. *Law and Performance.* University of Massachusetts Press, 2018.

Schiller, Friedrich. "On Grace and Dignity." In *Friedrich Schiller: Poet of Freedom, II.* Schiller Institute, 1988, 361–428.

Schipper, Imanuel. "Artworks." In *William Forsythe Choreographic Objects. Human Writes.* Web.

Schneider, Rebecca. "Performance Remains." *Performance Research* 6, no. 2 (2001): 100–108.

Schneider, Rebecca. *Performing Remains: Art and War in Times of Theatrical Reenactment.* Routledge, 2011.

Scott, David. *Conscripts of Modernity: The Tragedy of Colonial Enlightenment.* Duke University Press, 2004.

Scribe, Eugène, and Olivier Bara. "Le Code Noir: Opéra-Comique en Trois Actes." *Autrement mêmes* (Paris) 136 (2018).

Seda, Abraham. "Fighting in the Shadow of an Apartheid State: Boxing and Colonialism in Zimbabwe." *Kronos* 48, no. 1 (2022): 53–68.

Sedgwick, Eve Kosofsky. *Touching Feeling: Affect, Pedagogy, Performativity.* Duke University Press, 2003.

Seymour, Tom. "MoMA Apologises to Artist Heather Agyepong, Who was Ejected from Exhibit Intended as Safe Space for Black Visitors." *The Art Newspaper,* March 28, 2023.

Shakespeare, William. *The Tempest.* With Barbara A. Mowat and Paul Werstine. Folger Shakespeare Library. Simon & Schuster, 2004.

Sharp, Gene. *Non-Violent Action: An Introductory Outline for Study Groups.* Friends Peace Committee, 1963.

Sharpe, Christina. *In the Wake: On Blackness and Being.* Duke University Press, 2016.

Sherman, Alfred. "Climax in Algeria: The O. A. S. and the Pieds Noirs." *The World Today* 18, no. 4 (1962): 134–42.

Shimakawa, Karen, and Ann Pellegrini. "Reenactibility." In *Law and Performance,* edited by Austin Sarat, Lawrence Douglas, and Martha Merrill Umphrey. University of Massachusetts Press, 2018.

Siegel, Marcia B. *At the Vanishing Point: A Critic Looks at Dance.* Saturday Review Press, 1972.

Siegel, Paul. "A Right to Boogie Queerly: The First Amendment on the Dance Floor." In *Dancing Desires: Choreographing Sexualities On and Off the Stage. Studies in Dance History,* edited by Jane Desmond. University of Wisconsin Press, 2001.

Silva, Denise Ferreira da. "Before Man: Sylvia Wynter's Rewriting of the Modern Episteme." In *Sylvia Wynter: On Being Human as Praxis,* edited by Katherine McKittrick. Duke University Press, 2015.

Silva, Denise Ferreira da. "No-Bodies: Law, Raciality and Violence." *Griffith Law Review,* 18, no. 2 (2009): 212–36.

Silva, Denise Ferreira da, and Hortense Spillers. "Sending Language into Battle: Interview with Hortense J. Spillers." *Boundary2* 51, no. 1 (2024): 3–37.

Simpson, Audra. *Mohawk Interruptus: Political Life Across the Borders of Settler States.* Duke University Press, 2014.

Skura, Meredith Anne. "Discourse and the Individual: The Case of Colonialism in 'The Tempest.'" *Shakespeare Quarterly* 40, no. 1 (1989): 42–69.

Slaughter, Joseph R. *Human Rights, Inc: The World Novel, Narrative Form, and International Law.* Fordham University Press, 2007.

Smail, K. 2019. "Melissa Ziad, la ballerine de l'espoir." *El Watan.* March 9, 2019.

Sollors, Werner. *Neither Black nor White Yet Both: Thematic Explorations of Interracial Literature.* Harvard University Press, 1999.

Solomon, Noémie. 2011."Conducting Movement: Xavier Le Roy and the Amplification of 'Le Sacre Du Printemps.'" *Dance Research Journal* 43 (1): 65–80.

Sontag, Susan. "Elias Canetti." *Essays and Memoir.* Granta. March 1, 1982.

Spillers, Hortense J. "Mama's Baby, Papa's Maybe: An American Grammar Book." *Diacritics* 17, no. 2 (1987): 64–81.

Spillers, Hortense J. "Who Cuts the Border? Some Readings on America." In *Black, White, and in Color: Essays on American Literature and Culture.* The University of Chicago Press, 2003.

Steiner, Eva. "Codification." In *French Law: A Comparative Approach,* edited by Eva Steiner. Oxford University Press, 2018.

Stern, Simon, Maksymilian Del Mar, and Bernadette Meyler, eds. *The Oxford Handbook of Law and Humanities.* Oxford University Press, 2020.

Stora, Benjamin. "Cicatriser l'Algérie." In *Oublier Nos Crimes: L'amnésie Nationale, Une Spé- Cificité Française?* Autrement, 1994.

Stora, Benjamin. *Les Questions Mémorielles Portant Sur La Colonisation Et La Guerre D'algérie.* Elysee, 2021.

Stranger, Arabella. *Dancing on Violent Ground: Utopia as Dispossession in Euro-American Theater Dance.* Northwestern University Press, 2021.

Surkis, Judith. *Sex, Law, and Sovereignty in French Algeria, 1830–1930.* Cornell University Press, 2019.

Sutil, Nicolas Salazar. "Laban's Choreosophical Model: Movement Visualisation Analysis and the Graphic Media Approach to Dance Studies." *Dance Research: The Journal of the Society for Dance Research* 30, no. 2 (2012): 147–68.

Tadiar, Neferti Xina M. *Remaindered Life.* Duke University Press, 2022.

Tagliavia, Francesca Martinez. 2013."The Imagination of Crowds: The Efficacy of a False Hypothesis." Re-Visiones, no. 3 (2013): 1–12.

Tenta, Anna. A Conversation on Human Writes. Interview by Anna Jayne Kimmel, Zoom, July 22, 2022.

Thénault, Sylvie. *Violence ordinaire dans l'Algérie coloniale: Camps, internements, assignations à résidence.* Histoire. Odile Jacob, 2012.

Thomas, Kendall. A Conversation on Human Writes. Interview by Anna Jayne Kimmel, Zoom, July 6, 2022.

Thuillier, Guy. "Pour Un Tricentenaire: Les Pensions de Retraite Des Artistes de l'Opera de 1698 à 1914." *La Revue Adminstrative, Presses Universitaires de France,* no. 299 (1997): 509–17.

Thuillier, Guy. *Pour Une Histoire de La Bureaucratie En France. Histoire Économique et Financière de La France.* Comité, 1999.

Thull, Françoise, and Marianne Arens. "Who Benefits from the Official Silence?: Maurice Papon and the October 1961 Massacre of Paris." In *World Socialist Web Site (WSWS),* October 2021.

Tilly, Charles. "The Emergence of Citizenship in France and Elsewhere." *International Review of Social History* 40 (1995).

Tomko, Linda. "Dance Notation and Cultural Agency: A Meditation Spurred by Choreo-Graphics." *Dance Research Journal* 31, no. 1 (1999): 1–4.

Tomlins, Christopher. "Transplants and Timing: Passages in the Creation of an Anglo-American Law of Slavery." *Theoretical Inquiries in Law* 10, no. 2 (2009): 389–421.

Tristan, Anne, and Association Au Nom Mémoire. *Le silence du fleuve*. Syros, 1991.

Van der Kolk, Bessel A. *The Body Keeps the Score: Brain, Mind, and Body in the Healing of Trauma*. Penguin Books, 2015.

van Ginneken, Jaap. *Crowds, Psychology, and Politics*, 1871–1899. Cambridge University Press, 1992.

Vetter, Bernard Keith. "Another Legal Transplant: The Application of the Roman Law of Slavery in the United States – the Unique Case of the State of Louisiana." *Fundamina: A Journal of Legal History* 2005, no. 1 (2005): 375–84.

Vimalassery, Manu, Juliana Hu Pegues, and Alyosha Goldstein. "Introduction: On Colonial Unknowing." *Theory & Event* 19, no. 4 (2016).

Waldron, Jeremy. "Dignity, Rank, and Rights." In *The Tanner Lectures on Human Values*. University of California Berkeley, 2009.

Waldron, Jeremy. "Is Dignity the Foundation of Human Rights?" In *Philosophical Foundations of Human Rights*, edited by S. Matthew Liao, Rowan Cruft, and Massimo Renzo. Oxford University Press, 2015.

Watson, Alan. *Legal Transplants: An Approach to Comparative Law*. University of Georgia Press, 1993.

Weheliye, Alexander G. *Habeas Viscus: Racializing Assemblages, Biopolitics, and Black Feminist Theories of the Human*. Duke University Press, 2014.

Whatley, Sarah, Charlotte Waelde, Shawn Harmon, Abbe Brown, Karen Wood, and Hetty Blades, eds. *Dance, Disability, and Law: InVisible Labor*. Intellect, 2018.

White, James Boyd. *The Legal Imagination: Studies in the Nature of Legal Thought and Expression*. Little, Brown and Company, 1973.

White, Hayden. "Right of Assembly." Arcade: Literature, the Humanities, & the World. 2012.

Whitman, James. "The Two Western Cultures of Privacy: Dignity versus Liberty." *The Yale Law Journal* 113, no. 6 (2004): 1151–221.

Wilder, Gary. *The French Imperial Nation-State: Negritude & Colonial Humanism Between the Two World Wars*. The University of Chicago Press, 2005.

Wilderson, Frank B. *Red, White and Black: Cinema and the Structure of U. S. Antagonisms*. Duke University Press, 2010.

Williams, Luke. "The Necessary Art of Leisure." *Hyperallergic*, January 4, 2022. Web.

Williams, Randall. *The Divided World: Human Rights and Its Violence*. University of Minnesota Press, 2010.

Wilson, Theodore Branter. *The Black Codes of the South*. University of Alabama Press, 1965.

Wolfe, Patrick. "Settler Colonialism and the Elimination of the Native." *Journal of Genocide Research* 8, no. 4 (2006): 387–409.

Wolfe, Patrick. *Traces of History: Elementary Structures of Race*. Verso, 2016.

Wood, Laurie. "Across Oceans and Revolutions: Law and Slavery in French Saint-Domingue and Beyond." *Reviewed Work: The Old Regime and the Haitian Revolution by Malick W. Ghachem, Law & Social Inquiry* 39, no. 3 (2014): 758–82.

Wynter, Sylvia. "Afterword: Beyond Miranda's Meanings: Un/Silencing the 'Demonic Ground' of Caliban's 'Woman.'" In *Out of the Kumbla: Caribbean Women and Literature*, edited by Carole Boyce Davies and Elaine Savory. Africa World Press, 1990.

Wynter, Sylvia. "'No Humans Involved': An Open Letter to My Colleagues." In *Forum N.H.I: Knowledge for the 21st Century*. 1994.

Wynter, Sylvia. "Unsettling the Coloniality of Being/Power/Truth/Freedom: Towards the Human, After Man, Its Overrepresentation--An Argument." *CR: The New Centennial Review* 3, no. 3 (2003): 257–337.

Wynter, Sylvia, and David Scott. "The Re-Enchantment of Humanism: An Interview with Sylvia Wynter." *Small Axe* 8, no. September (2000): 119–207.

Yapp, Hentyle. "To Free Speech from Free Speech: Marxism, Mediation, and Disability Aesthetics in Hou Hsiao-Hsien's *A City of Sadness*." *Journal of Literary & Cultural Disability Studies* 15, no. 2 (2021): 169–85.

Yoneyama, Lisa. *Cold War Ruins: Transpacific Critique of American Justice and Japanese War Crimes*. Duke University Press, 2016.

Young, Hershini Bhana. *Falling, Floating, Flickering: Disability and Differential Movement in African Diasporic Performance*. New York University Press, 2023.

Young, Hershini Bhana. "Lost Daughters and Sunken Ships: Salvaging the Archive." *Social Text* 41, no. 4 (2023): 37–60.

Zackin, Emily J. "Looking for Rights in All the Wrong Places: Why State Constitutions Contain America's Positive Rights." In *Princeton Studies in American Politics: Historical, International, and Comparative Perspectives*. Princeton University Press, 2013.

Ziad, Melissa. 2019."L'art Subversif Est La Forme d'art Connue Par Les Sociétés Lors de Périodes Révolutionnaires et Destinée à Modi er Le Système En Place Par l'illustration de Ses Défauts Ou Par La Promotion de Valeurs Différentes Voire Antagonistes. Une Alternative Au Système Dominant Peut s'exprimer Par La Créativité Artistique, Amorçant Ainsi Une Révolution Des Modes de Pensée. 01MARS2019/ DZ By: @ranougraphy #5ememandat #danse #algerie #algerienneDZ #revolution #manifestation #alger #2019." Instagram. @melziad.

INDEX

Figures are designated with italicized page numbers.

FSC
www.fsc.org
MIX
Papier | Fördert gute Waldnutzung
FSC® C083411

Kolibri 360 GmbH
Ferdinand-Jühlke-Straße 7
99095 Erfurt, Deutschland
produktsicherheit@kolibri360.de